THE CHINESE

Portrait of a People

JOHN FRASER

Collins
TORONTO • LONDON

First published 1980
by Collins Publishers
100 Lesmill Road, Don Mills, Ontario
© 1980 by John Fraser

Canadian Cataloguing in Publication Data
Fraser, John, 1944–
The Chinese: portrait of a people

ISBN 0-00-216817-0

1. China—Social conditions—1976–
2. China—Description and travel—1976–
I. Title: The Chinese: portrait of a people.

DS712.F72   951.05′7   C80-094809-2
Originally published in the United States of America in 1980 by Summit Books,
New York, New York
Printed in the United States of America

_____ Acknowledgments _____

I am grateful for the consistent support and generous encouragement of Richard J. Doyle, Editor-in-Chief of the Toronto _Globe and Mail._

The advice and direction of Jonathan Segal, Senior Editor of Summit Books, were invaluable throughout the writing of this book, as was the boundless enthusiasm of my literary agent, Nancy Colbert.

During the two years I lived in the People's Republic of China, I benefited from the services and assistance of the Information Department of the Ministry of Foreign Affairs.

Three colleagues in Peking—Georges Biannic and Francis Deron of Agence France-Presse and Nigel Wade of the London _Daily Telegraph_—went far beyond ordinary friendship and professional courtesy as we all sought to understand unusual and dramatic events in China. They are journalists in the truest sense, who, at the time of testing, were willing to witness and eager to report without fear or favor.

Finally, to those Chinese friends and associates who dared to reach out and welcome the stranger in their midst, I owe a new understanding of courage, honesty and fidelity.

A Note on Style

For the most part, this book follows the romanization system of the Chinese written language developed by the government of the People's Republic of China and known as Pinyin. In this system, certain sounds ascribed to letters do not bear any obvious relationship to English; in such cases, a simple phonetic approximation for the pronunciation of the word will follow the first reference in parentheses. Where the English pronunciation and the sounds suggested by the Pinyin spelling are similar, no parenthetical assistance will be needed. For example, the street near Peking's Democracy Wall is first identified as Xidan (pronounced "she-dan") Avenue, while the capital of Sichuan province, Chengdu, sounds as spelled.

In common with recent North American newspaper and newsmagazine practice, certain well-established Chinese place names (such as Peking, Canton or Tibet), as well as the names of historical figures (Mao Tsetung, Chou Enlai or Chiang Kaishek), will be left in the more familiar spellings, although the hyphen which traditionally separated the two given names has been dropped in accordance with contemporary Chinese usage.

Although Pinyin is now being widely used throughout the world, there are three letters it employs that will always bedevil English-speaking readers. For future reference, they are provided below, along with approximate phonetic equivalents:

X—"sh" (example: Xidan)
Q—"ch" (example: Jiang Qing, Chairman Mao's widow)
C—"ts" (example: Cao Yu, the famous playwright)

For my parents

Contents

PROLOGUE   *15*

I
Songs of Innocence

1 THE FIRST STEPS   *23*
2 STRANGERS   *36*

II
Outside Looking In

3 THE STATE OF AN UNPREDICTABLE NATION   *51*
4 THE FOREIGN GHETTO   *66*
5 OFFICIALS AND BUREAUCRATS   *86*
6 MODEL HEROES, MODEL LIVES   *99*
7 NATIONAL MINORITIES   *110*
8 THE PRICE OF A SONG   *124*
9 FOREIGN GAMES   *145*
10 THE OTHER CHINA   *165*
11 THE FOREIGN "EXPERTS"   *176*

III
Xidan

PROLOGUE   *199*

12 THE "TINY DEMOCRACY MOVEMENT"   *203*

IV
Inside Looking Out

13 NEW FRIENDS   *275*

14 THE ACTIVISTS   *297*

15 THE POLICE   *318*

16 THE CITY VERSUS THE COUNTRY   *334*

17 THE PLEASURES OF THE PEOPLE   *353*

18 THE BURDEN OF THE MASSES   *381*

19 THE FOUR SEASONS   *415*

20 THE CHINESE WAY   *433*

EPILOGUE—VOICES IN THE MULTITUDE   *451*

The Chinese

Prologue

In the fall of 1976, I was called into my editor's office at the Toronto *Globe and Mail* and asked if I would like to become the newspaper's resident correspondent in Peking. It was a journalist's dream come true, of course, and even had I been a more traditional newspaperman, rather than the *Globe*'s current theater critic and former dance critic, I could not have been more elated and excited.

To begin with, China is not just China at the *Globe and Mail.* The only national daily in Canada, it operates the oldest-established Western newspaper bureau in the Communist capital, and the experiences and ordeals of previous correspondents have become part of the legend of the newsroom. When the *Globe* opened an office in Peking in 1959, for example, the first correspondent and the paper itself were viciously attacked for being "soft on Communism" in the columns of *Time* magazine. Later, *Time* wrote that the *Globe* was "a sycophantic admirer" of Mao Tsetung's "red hordes." On the subject of China the rhetoric was particularly virulent because Editor-in-Chief Henry Luce, who was born in China of missionary parents, had made a personal commitment to defend the cause of the defeated Guomindang Government of Generalissimo Chiang Kaishek. In those days, Chiang was still convinced he could retake the Communist-controlled Mainland from his island redoubt of Taiwan, and Henry Luce sounded many of the battle clarions in the propaganda war. That was *Time* style two decades ago.

In the ensuing years, *Globe* correspondents covered the major events inside China under exceedingly difficult conditions, and there was considerable pride in their accomplishments at the home office. For most of that period, the newspaper was also the only North American news agency operating in China, and its Peking dispatches have been regularly carried by other newspapers around the world. On its own merits alone, the posting was a plum for any journalist; added to this was its unique position, which gave that same journalist an amazing opportunity for international readership. After the initial euphoria inevitably faded, however, trepidation set in with a vengeance. I had no more than the average knowledge of China, and the fact that I was an arts critic being transformed into a foreign correspondent summoned up visions in some people's minds of Evelyn Waugh's satirical novel *Scoop,* in which a gardening columnist was sent by mistake to cover an East African war. The precedent, three decades before, of Brooks Atkinson, who was also a theater critic sent to cover China, didn't diminish any of the initial mirth.

I was blessed, fortunately, with plenty of time to prepare myself for the adventure. I enrolled in an immersion language course to learn as much as I could of the national, or Peking, dialect; as well, I read everything I could put my hands on and talked to anyone who had had previous Chinese experience or was a specialist in the history, politics or culture of the place. From the outset, the passage to China and the Chinese was a shared venture with my wife, Elizabeth MacCallum, who took a leave of absence as a writer and director of science programs with the Canadian Broadcasting Corporation: together we supported and consoled each other through the miseries of learning a new language and adjusting to the realities of what we came to consider the most extraordinary country on earth.

Good luck descends upon some of the unlikeliest souls. It is a simple, bald fact of fortune that the time Elizabeth and I spent in China coincided with some of the most extraordinary developments in its recent history. For me, the most amazing and wonderful event was the chance to get beyond the hitherto impassable barriers of fear, ideology and mutual distrust and make real Chinese friends and contacts. Seven correspondents from the *Globe and Mail* had labored under inordinate hardships in Peking during the two decades prior to my posting, and yet I was the very first, in all that time, to be able to invite a Chinese friend of my own choice to my home, the very first to go into Chinese homes for a meal and a relaxed evening of conversation. I was able to do that because I had the unbelievable good fortune to be in China at a remarkable, unprecedented time in its history—when the movement at the Xidan Wall flourished and the Chinese people were for the first time under Communist rule given the opportunity, and were in fact indirectly encouraged, to make contact with Western foreigners. The phenomenon didn't last very long—only four months—before the authorities sought to control this unexpected and unbridled interchange between foreigners and Chinese. But during that period and forever afterward I was forcibly made aware of a world quite different from the generally accepted one presented by the Chinese Communist Party and reinforced by the majority of Western observers who have sought to explain inexplicable things to outsiders thirsty for knowledge and insight into an amazing people.

Along the way, I found myself something of a participant in the unfolding drama of renewal and change in China. I say this not to brag, but to point out the unusualness of the times and, perhaps, to reinforce the fact that I did not take an orthodox approach to journalism in China. By instinct and training, I had a predisposition to push beyond observable facts: to me, as a theater and dance critic, the creative wellspring of any action seemed as important to understand and report on as the manifestation of the action itself. Coupled with this was my own impulsive nature, which turned out to be an asset (for once) at a time when unthinkable things were being done and impulsive thoughts found open expression. Singular events occurred during my time in China, and I was drawn to them not only out of professional curiosity, but also through a growing affection for Chinese people, an affection that eventually turned into an expansive love affair.

Love makes one incautious: as a Chinese friend once told me, I had enough mastery of the Chinese language to get into trouble, but not nearly enough to get out of it. The observation came toward the end of my stay in China, when I was far wiser than when I had come. By that time, I had been involved in events that still make me shake my head in wonder: addressing a mass gathering of over ten thousand Chinese, being chased through the streets of Peking at midnight by members of the Public Security Bureau, and trying to maintain new but emotionally potent friendships in an atmosphere of danger and tangible repression.

This book, then, is written out of a desire not only to show the China that I saw, but also to set down a record of events and people that are far more complicated than they seem from the outside, thanks to the pervasiveness of official propaganda and the difficulty foreigners have traditionally experienced in making genuine contacts with the Chinese inside China. It is not a definitive account; in fact, I don't believe any one person can provide such a thing. Yet I learned enough from the Chinese to become a student again, and this book is a product of the lessons I was taught by the people themselves. I also suffer under a kind of mandate, and I use the word "suffer" advisedly. I was asked by people in China whom I greatly admired to write about their hopes and aspirations, their frustrations and bitterness, their pride and their shame. I interpreted this request as a plea to depict the Chinese as I came to see them, in their presiding humanity—not as a race or breed apart. When one accepts this view, it becomes increasingly difficult to talk about "us" and "them," while the uniqueness of Chinese culture and tradition becomes an embellishment to the human condition rather than an exception or a curiosity.

I have tried to set these matters down in something of the sequence in which they occurred. We arrived in China in the bleak midwinter, a few days before my predecessor, Ross Munro, was being forced to leave the country because of official displeasure at his reports. Elizabeth and I had taken an extensive trip throughout Asia before arriving, but the demands of the posting, the strangeness of the place and the nature of Munro's hasty and unceremonious departure filled us with foreboding. We stumbled through the first weeks in a daze as I began to take stock of the China traditionally seen by resident foreigners since the Communists took over in 1949. This was China from the outside looking in—the world of officialdom, of the Party line, of foreign policy, of model citizens and model communes: in sum, the China that the authorities wished to present to the outside world, the China that foreign observers like me tried to peer beyond.

And then there was a remarkable event, or rather a series of events. Thousands of Peking citizens gathered at a rather nondescript corner of their city and spoke from the depth of their souls.

In one amazing week, three decades of externally observed silence and acquiescence were obliterated. The events of those days still seem to me to have been so miraculous that I have tried to set them down as they occurred, without benefit of hindsight or the wisdom of historical perspective. It was an unfolding drama that I was myself hopelessly caught up in, and to present it in any other context would be facile and dishonest. During the ensuing period, when I was able to get beyond the official China, there was plenty of time to sort things out and analyze the new world I had entered, and this period forms the last section of the book. Reaching such a world was not as difficult as it may seem. It required only an open heart and a willingness to learn, albeit allied with good luck and the tricks and twists of history.

Yet there is always a beginning. The pungent philosophy of ancient China is universal: setting off to the land of Kublai Khan and Mao Tsetung, I was struck by that well-worn saw which holds that a journey of ten thousand miles commences with the first step.

I
Songs of Innocence

1

The First Steps

Thousands of tourists are now pouring into China. The once-forbidden land of the Middle Kingdom is no farther away than the nearest travel agency. This new accessibility, however, does not seem to have diminished the sense of awe and achievement each voyager feels upon first setting foot in the People's Republic: the enormous colorful billboards and ubiquitous propaganda slogans which festoon the exterior of airport and railway terminals, the martial arrival music blaring out of loudspeakers, the masses, first perceived in their blue or green proletarian garb—it's all there, just as you've read, and it's happening now as you disembark from your train or airplane. These images became so trite within two years of the "opening" of China as to warrant mockery in the cartoons of *The New Yorker*.

I suppose I was no different, although I arrived with Elizabeth in December 1977, several months before the initial wave of professional Western tourists descended on China. What I mostly remember from that first day is panic. I worried about Ross Munro's imminent eviction notice and how it might affect our living and working conditions. We were at the end of a long journey that had included an extended stay in India, where I had picked up an absurd intestinal affliction which left me spending a woeful amount of time scouting out Asian washrooms. A four-day stay in Hong Kong had been disastrous. Having successfully acclimatized myself to India, I went through quite severe culture shock in the famous Crown Colony from the very moment I arrived at the airport and was picked up by one of the plush Rolls-Royce limousines of the equally plush Peninsula Hotel. In Calcutta, our departure point, I had been a witness to the unavoidable but strangely heroic confrontation with harsh reality in which the struggle for daily survival is an act of faith and courage. In Hong Kong, I felt as if I were trapped inside the world's largest duty-free shop; there didn't seem to be anything but glossy jewelry, camera, tape and clothing stores. For the first time in my life, I was struck by the truly monstrous inequality of fate. There seemed no rational explanation why someone should be born into the relentless struggle of Calcutta and someone else should be plunked into the midst of the opulent, materialistic excess of Hong Kong. This was a purely emotional reaction, unsupported by any experience. In time I would discover that the struggle for survival in Hong Kong, away from the golden tourist quarter, has its own special drama, but at the time I was choice material for the rankest sort of Maoist ideology aimed at "foreign friends" who were heartsick at their own good fortune in life.

We took the old way up to Peking: by train from Hong Kong to Canton and from there by airplane. The formalities at the small and pleasingly quaint border-station village of Shumchun were effortless. I was treated, as most foreigners are, to painstaking kindness and civility, while my small Chinese vocabulary was accorded excessive praise by every customs and security official I encountered. It was the first time I had ever set foot inside a Communist country, and I was disarmed at how unthreatening and genial everything seemed. While I was waiting in one of the Shumchun reception rooms, I strolled out to a balcony and observed a cluster of workers returning home for lunch. They were laughing and talking animatedly as they walked along, and if the terrible weight of state oppression bore down heavily upon them, I couldn't tell it. In fact, the whole scene was positively bucolic, and I became bemused by the pervading peacefulness. The crass hustle of Hong Kong was far away, and like many Westerners who come to China for the first time, I felt transported nostalgically to a simpler, less complicated past I had never known but happily imagined—a past from my own land, curiously, not China's.

Superimposing Western fantasies on China is a historic fallacy that dates back a long time. When the first Jesuits came to China during the seventeenth century, they saw a land of almost complete perfection, marred only by the absence of Christianity. Today, latter-day, secular Jesuits also see a land of almost complete perfection, marred only by the absence of certain human rights or certain academic standards or certain sociological insights or whatever their field of expertise or special interest happens to be. I don't mock them because I was among their number until I had my eyes opened by Chinese people themselves.

Even then, though, my journalistic good angel was with me. I had been in such a state going through customs that I had inadvertently forgotten to get some money changed into Chinese currency. I didn't realize this until a young waitress came to ask us about lunch and request payment in advance. The special banking desk for foreigners had closed at noon, and there was a discussion among several officials about how the problem could be rectified. Finally, a young man said there was one banking counter still open, and he volunteered to take me there. He was cheerful and I liked him instantly. His excessive solicitude for me—"Please watch this step," "You must be very tired," "I will help you at the bank"—was slightly ludicrous, but since I had expected to be treated severely as the successor to a journalist soon to be expelled, I was happily relieved and even beguiled by the courtesies.

I descended a stairway and went through a series of dark passageways, emerging in the midst of a scene I can describe only as a vision straight from Dante's *Inferno.* This, I learned, was the clearing room for Hong Kong Chinese who were either returning home or on their way to visit Mainland relatives. There were hundreds of them, jammed like cattle into pens. Because we had traveled first class on the train from Hong Kong, I hadn't realized how many had come up with us. After the ease with which we had passed through customs, I could scarcely believe what I was witnessing. Suitcases and bundles of clothes attached to shoulder poles were being brusquely opened up by customs officials. Clothes were flying up in the air in all directions. The officials were barking arrogant taunts in the faces of old women and young children alike, while a couple of officials lounging on the sidelines were doubled over in the mirth of the sideshow. The stoic, resigned look on the faces of the Hong Kong Chinese told me that they had been through all this before, that it wasn't anything strange but simply normal procedure.

As we made our way through the dense throngs to the banking desk, my charming guide started shoving people left and right while barking at them as if they were unruly children. As people tried to make way for us, a small girl—she couldn't have been more than six—got caught up in the jumble of legs and fell down. I saw it happen out of the corner of my eye and tried to reach down to pull her up. My guide immediately motioned me away and started shouting something to the child and her mother. I didn't know what was happening. It was my first experience at being treated as a foreign Pooh-Bah, and I didn't like it.

Things got worse at the banking counter, where only two windows were open for about three hundred Hong Kong Chinese. Some of them had been waiting there already for over an hour, but my guide walked up authoritatively to the front, pushed a middle-aged man out of the way and had a short discussion with the teller. After this, he turned to me with his consistently courteous smile, which now seemed like an ugly, leering grin, and said, "Please. Now you change money." I did as bidden. After all, I had been repeatedly warned by experts in the West not to judge China by our standards, and if I was being really honest with myself, I was certainly grateful that I wasn't waiting at the end of that chaotic lineup.

These people were being treated as the scum of the earth, and the contrast with the treatment accorded to the rich foreigners upstairs was so marked as to be unbelievable. I think the only feeling I had at the time was a hope that the customs guards treated their own citizens better than these ironically named "compatriots." I didn't realize, of course, that in 1977 their own people didn't take trips outside the country unless they were important high officials, so the thought was irrelevant.*

The train ride to Canton and the short wait at the airport terminal were uneventful, if tiring, so that by the time we arrived in Peking, where the Munros came to pick us up, all I wanted to do was go to bed. Munro had booked us a room in the Peking Hotel for the three nights he and his wife would still be living in the bureau

*I was to visit Shumchun many times more, and I always took a look at the Overseas Chinese reception center. To me, it became a kind of acid test to check whether things were really improving in China, as the government propaganda kept saying. Happily, it can be reported that the situation got markedly better, and once I even saw a customs officer help an old woman with her shoulder pole.

apartment. His carefully laid plans for a smooth transition between correspondents had been destroyed by the necessity of the hasty exit. On the way into town, he reeled off the things he had to do the next day and then proceeded to tell me what I had to do. I was not well disposed toward him at this time, and the peremptory way he seemed to assume my total ignorance of everything only added to the irritation. Two years later I was to hear myself being precisely as peremptory with my successor, by which time I had learned to have a lot more respect and liking for Munro.

Finally, Elizabeth and I were left alone in the dour confines of our hotel room, and after about two minutes of emotional stocktaking, I decided I was utterly miserable and thoroughly depressed. The little bit I had already seen of Peking was hideous. Miles of blank, uniform Stalinist buildings; huge broad avenues which that evening had seemed totally deserted as I looked out the back window of a Volkswagen floating alone over a vast sea of concrete. The lobby of the Peking Hotel was grotesque and forbidding, and I wasn't in the least cheered by the propaganda sign, in English and Chinese, that faced me as soon as I was inside: "We have friends all over the world."

The lighting in our room was harsh, and the one novelty among the otherwise spartan embellishments was an electrical contraption that operated the curtains. I pressed the switch and with a great clanking and whirring the heavy gray curtains slowly parted to reveal Chang An Avenue and the Ministry of Foreign Trade on the other side; it was like opening the stage curtain on the ultimate play by Samuel Beckett—no dialogue, no action, no actors, nothing save the inchoate fears of the audience, who projected onto the vacuum any foreboding that was rattling around in their minds.

How Elizabeth and I clung to each other that night! That is, until the door, which I thought I had locked, was opened with a loud bang, pouring corridor light into the room. It was the floor boy, come to change the ubiquitous thermos of hot water, and he was so used to walking in on hotel guests in this manner that he went straight to the table, left the thermos and said good night to us before I even had a chance to start spluttering. Thus are the revels of the night punctuated in New China.

The business of privacy in hotel rooms became a sore point the following summer when thousands of tourists engulfed the country. The Chinese were unprepared for all the ramifications of this invasion, and many of the practices of quieter days—like barging in unannounced—caused so much annoyance that the authorities began to take notice and do something about it. Before I left China, most floor boys had learned to knock at doors, and some hotels even offered "Do Not Disturb" signs to patrons.

Although our experience was dramatic enough, it wasn't a patch on what happened to a poor French traveler in Shanghai a few months later. Her tale became symbolic of the problem and was widely reported. She was in a state of high excitement on her trip, and China had her in its thrall. After a day's sight-seeing, she returned gratefully to her room in the Peace Hotel along the old Bund, took off her clothes and had a long, luxurious soak in the old-fashioned, comfortable bathroom tub. Restored and relaxed, she dried herself off and went into the adjoining room to put on her clothes before going down to dinner. Inevitably, the floor boy barged in unannounced with the thermos bottle and caught her naked. They were both a bit shocked, and he quickly retreated. She said later that she even smiled at their mutual embarrassment as she speculated about what might have happened in a Western hotel.

Before she had finished dressing, however, there was a very stern knock on the door—the first she had encountered on her trip to China. She opened it and faced two older men and a severe-looking woman.

"There has been an incident," said one of the men in careful English. "Would you come downstairs and discuss it."

Clearly the situation was getting out of hand, so the woman composed herself and tried to think of the best way to handle the situation as she headed toward a small conference room where five or six other staff members had assembled, including the errant floor boy.

"There has been an incident," said the oldest official again. "You were naked when this comrade came into the room."

"That's true," she said, "but it was not a serious incident. No one has trained him to knock before entering. He didn't say or do anything wrong. You shouldn't make such a fuss. I didn't mind and it wasn't his fault."

"Of course it wasn't *his* fault," exploded the official. "You are to blame. It is not permitted to be naked in the hotel room. It is only permitted to be naked in the bathroom. You have made him very upset, and he will have to go home to rest."

There were a number of reactions to this story, which were all rather curious. One acknowledged expert on China, visiting Peking on an important academic tour, pompously pronounced that if one looked at Chinese history one could see that Western concepts of privacy were alien to the Chinese experience. Other people, less concerned with being able to justify and explain every absurd thing that happens in China, just shook their heads and laughed. Underlying their mirth is a condescending attitude which holds that "they" are simply different from "us."

The uncomplicated truth of the matter, however, is that those who can afford or command privacy in China have it, and those who can't don't. If you think for one moment that senior state leaders or persons with any level of authority don't seek and get the kind of privacy any normal person wants from time to time, you're wrong. The curtains around all the passenger windows of the huge Red Flag limousines which avert the gaze of the masses from the passengers inside should at least provide a hint of the reality. China is a very crowded country, and of necessity, privacy is at a premium. It is also a totalitarian state in which the government has turned that necessity to its own advantage, institutionalizing every neighborhood snoop in the country. The floor boy in Shanghai has, either consciously or otherwise, been encouraged to keep an eye on everything, but he would certainly have thought twice before walking into the hotel room of a visiting high Party official. Even if he were naive enough to assume he could do so, a host of flunkies would have prevented him before he even got near the door—flunkies whose job it is, among other things, to ensure privacy. When a citizen in the West decides to enter public life, he gives up a great deal of his privacy and knows that this is part of the price he must pay; when an official reaches high office in China, he is given the kind of privacy a Trappist monk would envy and knows that this is part of his reward.

One of the most poignant sights I ever saw in China occurs nightly beneath the walls of the Forbidden City in the center of Peking. Between these walls and the romantic moat, there is a narrow roadway and a tall hedge. If you stroll along the road between dusk and 10 P.M. of any day, you may notice the peculiar formation of the parked bicycles. They are not all uniformly lined up in the usual fashion. Instead, a number of them are in pairs, with their front wheels carefully positioned together and the back wheels facing out in opposite directions. That is a sign. Between the hedge and the wall are a couple who have come here for a bit of privacy. Some of the couples may be indulging in a bit of necking or other erotic games. Mostly, though, they are simply talking quietly to each other or watching the passing scene through the hedge. All they want is to be left alone for a little while, and this is one of the few places where such things are possible. In their unavoidably crowded homes or dormitories, there is no privacy; in their places of work, there is even less. Such is the common understanding of the need for privacy among the people—even most police—that these couples are left alone when the bikes are in that special position. From this we learned that the lack of privacy does not indicate an equivalent lack of desire for it.

I saw my first Red Flag limousine, with its heavy curtains, on our first morning when we went to the hotel entrance to find a taxi. Munro had arranged for us to go to the Capital Hospital for medical tests, an essential precondition to getting a driver's license, as well as permission to swim in public pools. The cars are quite remarkable for a country that was never supposed to forget the class struggle—a favorite slogan of Chairman Mao, who himself rode about in these veritable mastodons of the road. Like most newcomers, I gaped and gawked a bit and thought this was rather a bad image for a proletarian official to have. Not being able to fit it into the popular image of China, I dismissed it. Only later was I to discover its origins and its hated symbolism.

At the time, I was far more concerned with convincing a tough, uncompromising witch of a doctor that I wasn't color-blind. Actually, I am a tiny bit color-blind and have a problem distinguishing between dark brown and dark green. It was something of a secret, since part of my job as an arts critic was commenting on set designs and costumes, so I usually avoided references to these colors. But I had no problem with any other colors and zipped through all but four color tests the doctor showed me. The tests are Western in origin. You have to identify the Arabic numeral in the middle of a whole bunch of colored dots. Each test is created to find a specific color-blindness problem: sometimes you can't see any number at all, and sometimes you see a number you shouldn't. Four wrong out of twelve attracted the curiosity of this inveterate sleuth, who was about sixty years old and somewhat nicer than I am making her out to be. She reached up into her library of visual tattletales and pulled down a whole book of little dots that concentrated on green/brown problems. It was hopeless. I couldn't see any numbers. As she flipped through the pages, clucking her tongue in disinterested concern, I started guessing wildly at any number that came into my head.

"Seven," I said desperately. "No, no—eight. Yes, I think I see an eight."

More tsk-tsk-tsking and a few more pages. "What do you see?"

"Three," I blurted out. Elizabeth had joined me by this point and was looking on with the smug satisfaction of a spouse who has told her husband a hundred times he's color-blind, and he has denied it to the hilt. The doctor looked at me with real pain in her eyes.

"It's not a number," she said, "it's an animal."

Elizabeth roared the kind of laugh that reminds you that marriage has its vicissitudes.

The doctor turned a few more pages. "Now what do you see?"

Triumph! Standing out boldly on the page was a pink chicken. It was so real I could practically see it laying orange eggs. "A chicken, a chicken," I said excitedly as I traced the shape with my fingers. The doctor pulled the book away and gravely shook her head. I looked up at Elizabeth. "It was a chicken—didn't you see it? It was a pink chicken."

The head-shaking appeared to be infectious, because my wife was doing it now.

"Are you kidding?" she said. "It was a green cow."

The result was that I failed the test and was refused permission to apply for a driver's license. This had immediate consequences, as it meant Elizabeth, who passed the color test, was going to have to do a lot of off-hours driving for me. The *Globe and Mail* employs a full-time driver for the correspondent in Peking, but he is there mostly to do errands and generally doesn't work nights, which was when I had to file stories at the faraway cable office. The doctor had a streak of decency, however. She said that since I was a bit nervous and had passed most of the test, I could try it again later when I was more rested. There was hope.

Five days later I returned to the hospital to try the test once more. I hung around the waiting room until I ascertained that the old lady wasn't on duty and was soon trying my best to charm a much younger colleague. After I had gone through the first book again, this time with eight hits, two misses and two lucky guesses, she turned to me and said, "You have a small problem, don't you?"

It was just a very, very small problem, I said. I could see colors perfectly well—certainly well enough to drive. "Look," I said, pointing to the table, "I can tell this is brown, and your pants are blue and the cover of that book is red."

"Yes, yes, I can see," she said, as she fingered the piece of paper that held the results of my last test. I had had to bring it back to get the original verdict changed.

"Who was it who examined you the last time?" she asked.

"It was another woman, older than you and heavier."

"Did she have gray hair and wear glasses?"

"Yes," I said, not sure what this was all about.

The doctor folded the piece of paper and handed it back to me without making any changes. "That was my supervisor. Sorry."

"Sorry about what?" I demanded. "What's the problem?"

"Sorry. Can't change it. You must come back and get her to change it. She is my superior."

Four weeks later, I came back again—this time on the warpath. I had done some checking and found out that a lot of people with little disabilities had cheated on their tests and were successfully driving around town. A French diplomat with a slight hearing problem had faked the tuning-fork test; an English journalist's wife with slightly high blood pressure drank gallons of coffee just before she was checked; a Palestinian representative who had an artificial foot thanks to an earlier skirmish with Israeli commando troops (which did not, I hasten to add, take place in China) simply lied about his handicap.

I did not feel I had to stand apart from accepted international practice, so I made my preparations. Elizabeth, by this time, was bored with the game of staying up till 1 and 2 A.M. to wait for me to finish writing and drive me to the cable office. I had her full cooperation. Since she would be allowed in the room during the test, we practiced a scheme whereby she stood behind me and traced the figures from the book on my back. We rehearsed this several times and I became quite confident.

"I hope they don't bring the animal book out," she said. "I don't think I can cough like a cow."

Another friend was enlisted in the enterprise. His job was to keep up a barrage of chatter to distract the doctor's attention while Elizabeth was tracing the figures on my back. Incredible as it may seem, the whole plan came off perfectly, and I got every number right. The old doctor didn't even reach for her animal book. Then she took my piece of paper, checked it against my expanding medical file and noticed that I had tried to get the verdict changed between my first and present visits with her. The pen was in her hand, only inches away from making a little mark that would give me a driver's license and restore peace and calm to my domestic life.

"Very strange," she said, pushing her glasses from the bridge of her nose to her forehead. "You failed twice, but on the third attempt you got a perfect score."

Even a Chinese barber's blade could have cut the tension in the air at that moment. Elizabeth's commitment to my passing the test was greater than my own.

"I was nervous," I said, remembering her earlier explanation on my behalf. "I always get nervous before tests."

I think she suspected something was fishy, but bless her, she signed it, and off we went.

By that time, I had become suspicious of Chinese hospitals, despite all the amazing and positive things I had heard about Chinese medical care. The little I had seen on the streets and in the countryside convinced me that public health care must be fairly good. Patently healthy and robust children are a sign that something is being done right. But the Western-style hospitals (as opposed to the traditional Chinese medical hospitals, of which we knew nothing for some time) had old-fashioned and often primitive facilities. In itself, this isn't particularly bothersome. China is a very poor country, and you don't demand or expect something like a privately endowed teaching hospital in Texas. But I wasn't convinced that either basic methodology or sanitation was being observed.

After we had completed the eye test that first day, we went to have chest X-rays farther down the hall. The hospital was still using the antiquated fluoroscope machines that one has to stand behind while the doctor makes an examination on the screen in front. When she was a child, Elizabeth had been a victim of scoliosis and had had to have several operations to straighten the curvature of her spine. The procedure had left two steel bars in her back. The attending doctor had never seen anything like it and got so excited she went running out of the room to call some of her colleagues, leaving the machine on and Elizabeth still behind it. Unlike the doctor, my wife knew enough about X-ray dangers to register a loud complaint.

The few excursions we took alone on the streets of Peking showed us clearly how poor and backward China was—and how crowded. And this was the capital city, which presumably had about the best standards in the country. The judgment was premature and unfair, of course, but we were newcomers and had to make the adjustment from our own understanding of the optimistic and romantic propaganda we had read prior to our arrival. Thirty years of socialist construction didn't seem very impressive at first glance. Elizabeth and I also had to cope with vague, inchoate fears which were also the product of inexperience. Once, during this period, we were out on a crowded street and got separated. It was only for a matter of minutes, but we panicked a little and Elizabeth got her first strong sensation of being terribly alone and a very long way from home. The Chinese in the streets seemed to stare at us as though we were animals from a zoo, and I felt self-conscious in my Western clothing and with my white, Caucasian face. Was this what it was like for strange-looking outsiders who first came to my own country? It was a novel experience for me, and not pleasant at all.

"Ah, Pékin, Pékin," as some of our French colleagues would say with a mixture of derision and affection. How strange it all seemed at the beginning and how familiar and even beloved it was when we had to depart. Those first few days are scrambled in my brain as a kaleidoscope of confusing images, faces without names, inexplicable behavior among both the foreign residents and the Chinese officials with whom we had to deal.

The Munros gave us whirlwind driving tours around town, and Ross had an annoying habit of grilling me on my sense of direction, which was nonexistent at that moment. "That's the Peking Hotel ahead, John. So which direction are we heading?"

"South?"

"Come on! It's west. The best way to figure out Peking is landmarks and compass points: the hotels, the cable office, the Workers' Stadium. After a while you'll get to know some of the street names, but you have to get the building landmarks firmly fixed in your mind."

"Right, Ross."

There seemed to be endless application forms to fill out: residency permits, journalist's visas, insurance transfers, bank accounts.

I was forever writing out my humble *curriculum vitae* in blank spaces and never quite sure what on earth I was doing it for. Munro took me to a few diplomatic receptions, each of exactly one hour's duration, at which a variety of people were introduced to me, whom I promptly forgot. And then, suddenly, it was time for him to go.

The Munros' departure was brisk and efficient. Although the Chinese Government had made no secret of its displeasure and dislike of Munro, no untoward obstacles were put in his way. Things had changed from the terrible days of the Cultural Revolution, when one *Globe and Mail* correspondent had spent a harrowing day with a nasty customs official who went through all his property *after* it had been carefully packed and stored in sealed wooden crates. I had wanted much more time with Munro, although he and his wife had done a good job of explaining bureau procedure and day-to-day problems in so short a time. Still, as we waved good-bye to them at Peking Airport with a small group of his friends, Elizabeth and I were relieved that we could move out of a hotel and into what would be our new home. Two months of constant travel had taken its toll, and we longed to settle down in a place we could call our own.

2

Strangers

The Peking we came to love was not the city we first arrived in. For anyone who has even the vaguest conception of the unique cultural legacy of China, modern Peking, transformed by thirty years of Communist rule, is devastated territory, a dead place seemingly animated only by the circumspect blobs that move about on foot or by bike. Had we arrived in summer, or especially during the triumphant Peking autumn, this view would have been ameliorated by the abundance of trees whose foliage softens the stark outlines of conformist, Soviet-inspired architecture. But we arrived in the dead of winter, when the city is at its bleakest and the air is often so weighed down by pollution and muck that you can scarcely see a half block ahead.

Even in summer, much of the vitality of Peking is hidden behind walls or down narrow lanes, so that if you keep to the main streets, cocooned in a car, the place will seem forever alien. Chang An Avenue, the main thoroughfare, and Tienanmen Square itself are dismal disappointments. The vast acres of pavement bordered by huge, ugly Stalinist buildings seem designed to reduce human beings to minuscule proportions. The architecture, planning and subsequent development of all capital cities define a nation's vision. It's no good arguing that the Communists were handed a bankrupt nation and had to do the best they could. The amount of toil they demanded of their people to tear down the unique and irreplaceable city walls and build such monsters as the Great Hall of the People belies a government merely coping with necessity. There was an iconoclastic vehemence behind the act. The Communists wanted a symbol of the kind of changes they planned to bring about in this ancient land, and the vast desert of Tienanmen Square is the result.

I found all this depressing but, fortunately, not dispiriting. It was a challenge, and I didn't intend to be defeated. A few years earlier a Canadian diplomat freshly posted to Peking had been taken on his first tour of the city. He and his wife were driven past all the high points, and with a sense of increasing despair, they realized that this was a city like no other. There was no downtown that the diplomat could recognize as such—no sense of the vitality and mystique that marks an exciting city. As his tour came to its harsh conclusion in Tienanmen Square, he hunched lower and lower in the seat of the car. Finally, he looked around him and surveyed the interminable panorama. "This city sucks," he said. Others like him have asked for immediate transfers within a week of arrival.

Grimy and depressing as it seemed to be, Peking was our new home, and we set about discovering it methodically. We were aided, I suppose, by our own natures, as well as by the daily presence of four remarkable Chinese who worked for the *Globe and Mail* bureau. Lazy unless goaded into action, I would have been content to hibernate in the bureau apartment, waiting for official trips to materialize so I could fill out the cable forms I sent back to Toronto. Elizabeth, however, detests being housebound, and she had us out on bicycles before I even had a chance to devise stratagems to stay inside. My wife was born with a fierce determination, which was often at odds with her shyness and easily aroused fear of being rebuffed or defeated. My own forte is people, all shapes, sizes and colors. I am fascinated by the complexities of human beings and the reasons they do things the way they do. Like Mutt and Jeff, we took our foibles and fancies to an unsuspecting audience, which often responded with affection and curiosity. My gregariousness and indiscriminate snooping were balanced by Elizabeth's prudence and immaculate eye for detail.

I discovered the back lanes of Peking in this manner day after day. It was mostly a view of walls, punctuated by brief glimpses through courtyard doors. When we got off the bikes and walked around, we were invariably surrounded by hordes of giggling kids and curious adults; there would be occasional conversations of an exceedingly superficial sort, which nevertheless left us elated and excited. Sometimes there would be sullen glares too, and these I tried to ignore. It is not possible to walk anonymously through a street in China; you are forced to react in some way. Some foreigners resent being stared at and can get quite snarky and irritable after they have settled down in Peking and are no longer frightened by the setting. For ourselves, we always smiled and often said *"Ni hao?"* ("How are you?") to nearly every passing face, because to ignore the effect you are having on people or to be annoyed at it is to admit that there is no possibility of contact, no common ground, no shared humanity.

Right from the beginning, albeit unconsciously, that was something I would never admit. Usually when Elizabeth and I were depressed with life in the foreign ghetto, we would go out on our bikes and come back renewed and refreshed. Nothing extraordinary ever happened, but we had forced ourselves, however insignificantly, on the city and its people, and that act alone made me feel that we actually existed in Peking. Even when these outings were disasters, either because we got no response or because our own moods made us indifferent to the passing scenes, we never gave up our manic compulsion to push out beyond the ghetto. To admit defeat also meant that I had to accept life in China exclusively on terms dictated by the Chinese Government, and those terms struck me as being perilously close to the ones I had lived under at private boarding schools in Canada. The Grade Nines rarely mixed with the Grade Tens and never had anything to do with the privileged crowd in the most senior grade. Prefects and teachers, however intelligent or kind, ordered our lives from dawn to dusk. Above all, there was the final authority of the Headmaster. In respecting the various restraints all societies are forced to impose upon themselves, whether it is the governing of a nation or a school, those prohibitions which are arbitrary or fundamentally unfair naturally arouse opposition. I was not an international spy, whatever the Chinese Government thought of all foreign journalists; I was a former dance and theater critic who was now living and working in China, and I was damned if the Headmaster and all his staff were going to prevent me from trying to meet the Grade Nines or the Grade Twelves—or the staff members, for that matter.

With such chips on our shoulders, Elizabeth and I gradually expanded our daily excursions. Unlike the diplomats or even the foreign students attending classes at several Peking institutions, I had no fixed schedule that defined the hours I could go out. This gave us flexibility and freedom. One day shortly after arriving, we were cycling through the back lanes in the Drum Tower neighborhood of northwest Peking when we saw some Chinese youths walking ahead of us carrying ice skates. Rounding the next corner, we came to a beautiful little lake completely frozen over, where hundreds of people were whizzing around on the ice. Skating! We were not Canadians for nothing, and the possibility of ice skating dazzled us. For some reason, it was among a number of things I had not thought about before coming, but this was soon rectified with the purchase of Chinese racing skates, which cost only about $9 (absurdly cheap to us, but a sizable dent in a Chinese wallet).

Within two days we were out on the ice, and it was a glorious, giddy experience. We were bundled up in Chinese duffel coats, which toned down our strangeness, and I discovered for the first time that when the Chinese are at play, they are at their most relaxed with foreigners. We bumped and crashed into each other, laughed all the time, shook hands, waved in the distance; none of the encounters, save one, led to anything but brief pleasantries, but the whole business was a considerable step up from bike rides down the lanes.

The other great diversion in those days was hunting for old, broken-down Chinese furniture in Peking's "commission," or secondhand, stores. In our naiveté back in Canada, we had supposed that China would give us a chance to shuck our relentless materialism. Our folly was to have imagined that the Chinese people were not like other mortals, that if they had a bit more purchasing power —as some are beginning to have now—they would not waste it on things which had only ephemeral value, that they cared not a whit about the cut or color of the cloth on their backs.

We also didn't know that the degree to which Chinese society was cut off from foreigners would force us to spend an inordinate amount of time hunting through shops because there was little else to do during leisure time, particularly in the winter. It was also fun. Thus it was that the five or six commission shops around Peking became favorite haunts for hundreds of foreigners, especially the ruthless wives of French diplomats, who learned the game sooner and fought harder than anyone else.

The furniture to be found in these places—scroll tables, money chests, ornate chairs, leather trunks, small side tables—was usually in a completely dilapidated state, and anyone who didn't know how well it could be redone at the local furniture-repair shop would have avoided most of it. Some was very ugly, but it was all Chinese, and the very act of discovery enhanced the appeal. You could easily spend a happy morning scooting about the various shops to see what was in. Inevitably you learned a bit about Chinese crafts, and following the business through to the repair shop was a small but undeniably diverting pleasure. Most of all, it was another one of the exercises that got us out of the foreigners' ghetto.

The best time to go was first thing in the morning, especially in the weeks preceding a major Chinese holiday or festival, when ordinary Chinese sold their few remaining old pieces of furniture to get a bit of extra money for a festive meal or to buy a special gift. No group of foreigners surpassed the French at nabbing the most unusual finds. They reigned as supreme in this area as the Japanese wives did in the Chinese antique stores, although for different reasons—the Japanese came with such large wads of Chinese currency that no one could beat them to anything they really wanted, particularly porcelains.

Right from the beginning, we were helped in our desire to meet and treat Chinese people as equals and friends by the four staff members employed by the *Globe.* The linchpin was the interpreter, Mr. Hao, who guided us through the intricacies of Chinese bureaucracy and was practically our nursemaid during the first confusing days. Then there were the driver, Mr. Wang; the cook, Mr. Chen; and the housekeeper, Mrs. Liu. It was surely an anomaly of remarkable proportions that only in Communist China could two hopelessly Western bourgeois live in a style more suitable to nineteenth-century capitalist compradors. I remember vividly having a conversation with a very rich woman several years before in which she bemoaned the fact that no one seemed to understand the problems of "keeping a good household staff busy and satisfied." I roared my disdain to Elizabeth later. Imagine someone in this day and age talking like that. I vaguely remembered my grandfather's large house in Toronto, which had a household staff, and throughout my youth my parents had always employed a live-in housekeeper and cook. But those days were gone for most of my generation, and had I ever paused to analyze the situation, I would have concluded that they were happily gone, for reasons of romantic egalitarianism as well as the nature of today's mobility and leisure time in the affluent world. Even if you had the money, who would want to be tied down to the kind of daily ritual and ordered existence that a household staff would inevitably bring?

Not I, anyway, and initially the prospect of ordering the lives of four total strangers—three of whom spoke no English—filled us with trepidation. I shouldn't have worried. It was *they* who set about ordering our lives, once they had learned our particular interests and idiosyncrasies. Mercifully, they didn't live in—no Chinese staff live with foreigners, although they do with important Chinese officials' families—so we had the evenings and weekends to ourselves. We got along famously right from the beginning, and it was from these four that our affection for the Chinese people first grew.

Instinctively, we never regarded them as "our staff." Their lives and our lives had come together through a fluke, and since they were already established in the bureau, we turned to them as colleagues for help and understanding. In addition, the system whereby their services were made available to the *Globe* reinforced the idea that they were not beholden to us for their livelihood.

The staff worked for an organization called the Diplomatic Service Bureau, and it was to this outfit that all foreigners posted to Peking had to apply if they wanted Chinese workers. I never paid their salaries; instead I sent a sum of money for their services to the bureau, which in turn gave them a salary predetermined by the state. With the interpreter, for example, I sent off 350 yuan (about $275) a month to the bureau, but I'm sure he never received more than 70 or 80 yuan, if not less. At the time this struck me as inherently unfair—not the price I paid the bureau, which was a very small sum for the services of an educated, perceptive person, but the discrepancy between what he got and what the *Globe* had to put out. If it annoyed any of the Chinese staff working for diplomats or journalists in Peking, I never heard about it. One time I broached the subject to an exceedingly bright interpreter at a European embassy who, after I had got to know him well, never hesitated to make a criticism of his government or "feudal" Chinese habits if he felt so inclined. But he wouldn't hear of my arguments: "I accept this," he said very matter-of-factly, without the least trace of rhetorical grandstanding. "Most people are so poor in this country, I wouldn't feel right taking any more money than I do already. I'm lucky. I live in the city and have an interesting job. It would be wrong to demand more when so many others have so much less." I believed and respected him, even though I knew there were other Chinese who resented the arbitrary way wages were kept so low.

In fact, I remained predisposed to believe the Chinese who talked this way, not because I wanted to believe that people could see beyond self-interest (I knew I could myself, so I didn't need Maoism to persuade me that Chinese people were also capable of it), but because I had the daily example of our own, benevolent Gang of Four—as opposed to the real Gang of Four, the name ascribed to a quartet of state leaders who were purged shortly after Mao Tsetung died—back in the bureau. We discussed most things openly with the *Globe*'s Chinese staff and worked out understandings that were models of diplomacy, tact and compromise. When Mr. Wang, the driver, first realized that I wouldn't be able to drive, he volunteered to work after hours. In two years, Elizabeth and I never heard a serious gripe or complaint from them and they never heard one from us. There were misunderstandings and cultural mix-ups, but they were always resolved with laughter and a mutual concern for the other person's feelings.

With the exception of the interpreter, who called us by our given names, the staff used our Chinese names, which had been given to us by language teachers in Toronto—mine was Fu Ruizhe, which means "lucky philosopher," and Elizabeth's was Mai Kailan, which means "generous orchid" (the pronunciation was a Chinese approximation of our family names). By this time we had been accorded one of those signal honors which used to make me swell with pride. We were encouraged by the staff to use the familiar and affectionate prefixes of *lao* or *xiao* (pronounced "shao") with their family names. Thus Mr. Chen, the cook, became Lao Chen, or Old Chen—except that the English doesn't give you the spirit of the term, which is rough and warm at the same time. Mr. Hao, the interpreter, was younger than anyone else, so he became Xiao Hao, or Little Hao; while the housekeeper, Mrs. Liu, let us call her Liu Ayi, or Auntie Liu. If this all sounds a trifle cute and cloying, I don't care: we had a relationship based on respect and fondness, which grew steadily, and I began thinking of us all as a Unit, the basic work and social grouping of all Chinese people under Communism. It was a nice feeling.

No one engaged my admiration more than Lao Chen, the cook, who was a Shandong peasant and a man of quiet, unassuming but inestimable wisdom. As time went by, I was to blow hot and cold about the vagaries of Communism in China, but even when I was feeling angriest at the mindless, stupid dogmatism that could dispatch people to prison or even death for their thoughts, I was also forced to remember Lao Chen and what he represented. Shandong people are supposed to produce the best cooks in China. This is a myth, as it turns out: Sichuan or Guangdong people make just as admirable—or bad—cooks. But the myth may well have given Lao Chen his only lucky break in prerevolutionary China: he got a job as a kitchen scullery that eventually led him from his native province to Peking.

Until he learned to read in his forties during one of the Communist literacy campaigns, he had had no formal education. He was initially a product of his native wit and his own determination, but the revolution gave him his pride. He had had a miserable job in the old Soviet Embassy in Peking, which as far as I could figure out didn't improve appreciably during the alliance between China and the Soviet Union throughout the 1950s. A visit to Vietnam much later confirmed my view that Soviet comrades with a bit of power and position can be the most pompous, arrogant and abusive masters the world has ever seen, and that their style lacks even the formal etiquette ascribed to the British Raj in colonial India.

In any event, Lao Chen had been sacked along with all the other Chinese staff at the Soviet Embassy in 1966 and had come straight to the *Globe and Mail,* where he impressed six correspondents with his hard work, his uncomplicated devotion to Chinese socialism and his uproarious love of life. During the worst madness of the Cultural Revolution, Lao Chen showed through his actions and demeanor that there was at least one Chinese who had integrity and decency, and because he existed, one knew there were more. He did not consider the Communist Party an oppressive menace; for him the Party represented a better life for both him and his children.

I could not exclude him from my understanding of China because he was "not typical" in that he was sufficiently trusted to work with foreigners. If I had excluded him, then I couldn't include the host of young people who had so many grievances against the same Party. They too are not supposed to be typical. For me, Lao Chen represented something that was fine and good in China, and because he ascribed his lot to the Communist Party I had to accept that there was something fine and good in it too. He was a product of that prerevolutionary faith and determination for a better life which helped bring Mao Tsetung to power and defined the new integrity and courage of modern China. He was also a participant in the first few years of postrevolutionary reconstruction, when the government had broad popular support and the future, for the first time in over a century, seemed bright.

As I was not to see the truly dark side of Chinese Communism for nearly a year, at least as it affected us directly, I succumbed to Sinophilia quite quickly. I confused love of the people with love of the system, accepting all the frustrations imposed to divide foreigners and Chinese people with equilibrium, while studiously ignoring certain troubling little details that emerged every now and then. The country was clearly changing radically for the better from its immediate past, and the pace of events was so fast it was almost impossible to stop and reflect on what everything meant.

My earliest encounter with a Chinese citizen, free of official circumspection, however, is something I look back on with feelings of personal bitterness and deep regret—although the incident served to remind me to keep my eyes and ears open at all times and push beyond the directly observable routine of Chinese life that foreigners could see. Less than a week after we had arrived, Elizabeth and I joined two Canadian acquaintances at a carpet exhibition assembled for the benefit of "foreign friends." It was a pleasant Sunday-afternoon diversion, and the carpets were of good quality at a fair price. The display room was at the back of a large exhibition hall. There were several rooms you had to pass through first, one of which contained a selection of Chinese-made musical instruments, including an upright piano. As an amateur pianist I was curious about the quality of the local product, and after a half hour of fighting three hundred other foreigners knee-deep in silk carpets, I excused myself for a few minutes and went to look over the instruments.

I believe I was playing one of Bach's two-part inventions, or something equally pretentious considering the setting, when a young man of about twenty-five came up to me with a broad, encouraging grin stretched across his handsome face.

"*Ni hao?*" I said.

To my surprise, he began speaking in slow but carefully correct English. "You play the piano very well," he said.

All Chinese conversations with foreigners seem to begin with a compliment of some sort, and I learned very quickly how to play the game I called "Opening a Conversation."

"No. I play very badly," I said. "But you speak English very well."

"No, not at all. I speak it only a little and very poorly. I must study much harder. But I think you really do play very well."

It was the first time I had played the game, and despite the beginner's luck of the first gambit, I was raw and ignorant. For one thing, I didn't even know that it was supposed to be impossible to have conversations like the one I was about to have.

"Are you a diplomat?" he asked me.

"No. I'm a journalist."

His eyes lit up. "A journalist! I think that must be the most wonderful job in the world. You have the opportunity to travel and make the acquaintance of many people. I think you have to be very intelligent to be a journalist."

"It's a good job, all right," I agreed, "but you don't always have to be intelligent."

"Oh, I think so. Very intelligent. What country are you from?"

"Canada."

He stopped for a moment. I was so naive at the time, I was actually being paternalistic to him and hadn't even asked him where he was from and what he did. The remembrance of this ignorance is painful for me to recall now—ignorance of what to ask him, of course, but most of all ignorance of his own courage in even speaking to me in this forthright manner.

"Canada? Didn't I hear something about a Canadian journalist who got into trouble with our government?"

I was surprised he knew about Munro and his troubles. It was my initial understanding that Chinese people were unaware of the affairs of foreigners. "That was the last correspondent," I said. "He wrote some articles about life in China that the government didn't like, so he had to leave fast and I had to get here faster."

"I think that is very wrong, don't you? I think people should be allowed to think and write what they see and feel. I believe our government was wrong to make trouble for him."

So help me God, I then indirectly *defended* the Chinese Government by telling him—nay, lecturing—about injustices in Canada and the United States as well as the good things in his country, all based on six days' experience.

"But still," he said (and kindly, too, for he must have known I was a fool at that moment), "I think my country is very backward in many ways."

I asked him whether he could come and visit me in my apartment, and he smiled. "No. I don't think so. You would get into serious trouble."

Dimly, I perceived I was talking to a remarkable person who knew that my trouble would be minuscule compared with the trouble to which he would be subjected. I asked him how long it would be before Chinese people and foreigners could meet naturally in Peking, without either side's feeling any fear.

"Maybe fifteen years. Maybe longer. I think my country is very backward in this matter."

That was it. We shook hands, and I went to join Elizabeth and the others. I told them I had had an interesting conversation, and the Canadian couple, who had already been in Peking for several months, was flabbergasted—although nothing had struck me as strange.

"Are you sure he said those things?" asked one of our friends. "I've never heard of anything like that."

The incredulity made me ask several experienced foreigners in Peking about the business, and they all expressed surprise. One United States diplomat was convinced it was a setup and told me I had better watch myself before I fell into a trap. Instinct forced me to write a veiled account of the conversation for my newspaper, being careful to omit any references that might have identified the person. I was grateful for the opportunity because, while I wanted to distance myself from my predecessor's approach to China reporting, I also wanted to show the Chinese authorities that I was not frightened to write what I saw and heard. In this way I established a link between Ross Munro's years and my own, and it is the only thing I look back on without regret in the whole incident.

Within a few months I had forgotten all about it. It seemed a strange thing, almost unreal, and since I never ran across anyone else who spoke like that, I dismissed it. He wouldn't come back to my mind again until the following November, when I would meet thousands of his brothers- and sisters-in-arms at the Xidan (pronounced "she-dan") Democracy Wall and I was able to shed the conceit that I had ever understood Chinese people properly. It was not that I lived unobservant in China until that time. With eyes and ears and a willingness to witness, a professional journalist can pick up a lot, and I set about the business of being just such a professional journalist with enthusiasm.

This was objective journalism with a vengeance, the kind that had regularly poured out of Peking for years. It wasn't false, as such, and my work certainly reflected accurately what I could see. I learned a great deal about how official China operates and the games the senior leadership in the Party's Politburo plays. For the first time in ages, journalists were being allowed to travel all over the country, even to the once-forbidden province of Sichuan, where one hundred million people had gone through a tumultuous two decades which outsiders scarcely knew the first thing about. Increasingly frequent visits by foreign businessmen and government leaders brought far greater access to the thinking and actions of official China, while foreigners and Chinese alike were invited to try their hand at the intricate and complex game of figuring out which faction was winning the day within the power structure of the country. Never in my life had I witnessed the degree to which people picked over and speculated on the significance of government statements and official editorials, trying to winnow the chaff of propaganda from the hard kernels of political action; this wretched metaphor is apt because it was grueling, tedious work.

In between the traveling and the winnowing, there was the foreigner's life in Peking to be enjoyed or hated. Elizabeth hated it terribly at first, causing some morose scenes, but she is not a quitter, and by the end of spring we had become regulars. I had also started falling in love with Peking. Images haunted me with their beauty and poignancy. Driving to the cable office late at night, I would pass solitary workers heading off for late-shift work on their bikes. As often as not, they would be singing some complicated Peking Opera aria, or perhaps a lusty peasant song, which filled the still night air with as vibrant and human a sound as I have ever heard. By day, Chinese children were an endless source of hilarity and affection, especially when they played by their grandparents' side. On the face of it, there was a cohesion to everyday life and society that I had never seen in the West, although this was primarily because I was a participant in my own society, while in China I was only an observer.

After the late-night drives to the cable office, I would come back to the apartment and tiptoe into the bedroom, trying not to wake my sleeping wife. In the few minutes it took me to doze off, the sweet sounds of a Peking night continued and came into the room through the balcony window. Another singer, perhaps, cycling by. If he was in full voice, one of the guards from the People's Liberation Army outside might shout a sarcastic comment, and there would be a chorus of giggles all along the road. At other times, the wagonloads of produce from the nearby communes would pass through our quarter, and the clip-clop of the mules and horses that pulled them was wildly nostalgic, reminding me of the horse-drawn milk and ice wagons that I heard in my boyhood, during the fifties in Toronto. I had learned that the drovers who brought these wagons into Peking were among the most independent souls in China, thanks to their late-night work and the fact that they were on the road most of the time. How I loved their raucous bark as they urged the animals on. I had survived the initial period of stark terror as a foreign correspondent. Life was becoming more pleasant with every passing day, and I was running my own show halfway around the world. Sleep came very easily.

II
Outside
Looking In

3

The State of an Unpredictable Nation

C hina in 1977 was a country poised on a precipice. The chaos and destruction that Chairman Mao Tsetung had unleashed with the Cultural Revolution eleven years before had been succeeded by one of the worst totalitarian regimes the ancient land had ever seen. By the time the doddering old Father of New China died in 1976, even brutally guarded secrecy couldn't disguise the calamitous state of the economy, and part of the country was actually seething in revolt. If they weren't involved in internecine rebellion or intrigue, most other Chinese people had become resigned to an arbitrarily imposed fate and lived out their lives in as docile a manner as possible, hoping to avoid any sort of serious confrontation with the police or political watchdogs. If the Party Central Committee announced that Defense Minister Lin Biao, "Chairman Mao's chosen successor and closest comrade-in-arms," was now a traitor and running dog of the imperialists, with a history of proven deceit that went back to the early days when his brilliant guerrilla tactics helped put Mao into power, so be it. If Communist ideology suddenly decreed that China's ancient and wisest sage, Confucius, was evil and poisoning the nation's lifeblood, so be it. If the procedures used at a model farming commune were proclaimed as universally applicable to all farming communes, no matter how criminally inappropriate or counterproductive, so be it.

Those who saw through this thick veil of hypocrisy and deceit mostly bided their time, waiting for changes at the top of one of the world's most rigid power structures.

The change came swiftly and ruthlessly the year before I arrived. The new premier of the state council, Hua Guofeng, acting with the approval, if not the insistence, of most of his colleagues on the political bureau of the Chinese Communist Party as well as the army and the police, purged those leaders and their followers who were most closely allied to the terminal ideology of the recently deceased Mao.

Because Chinese people have had no say about who their leaders will be, changes at the top are usually conducted in this fashion. Each change, however, requires a massive rewriting of history and a nationwide political campaign to carry the purge down to the grass roots so that everyone gets the new line straight. Many people who have vaguely studied China from afar have been amused by the seeming childishness and absurdity of the propaganda that floated such campaigns, knowing little of the emotional and physical price paid by the Chinese people. Who could possibly believe the ridiculous account of the demise of Lin Biao, for example? The propaganda said he had tried to assassinate Mao and when the attempt failed had staged a getaway to his secret sponsors in the Soviet Union, but the plane he stole had crashed, killing all aboard. Even the leader of China's then closest ideological ally, Albania's Enver Hoxha, snorted when he heard this wild tale, pronouncing it "more frivolous than a James Bond thriller."

But Mr. Hoxha and others of different political persuasions who scorned the nonsense did not have the propaganda forced down their gullets day and night, week after week, in films and on radio, at political meetings and sports rallies, at their schools and their factories, on the trains and in the parks. The enormity of such lies, indeed their very obviousness, conspires with the frightening completeness of their dissemination to convince most people that they must be accepted. For Mao's brand of Communism, acceptance was the truth; or perhaps better than the truth, because acceptance indicated that the masses were following "the correct line," which was infinitely preferable to a slavish subservience to truth. But the business still had to be conceived, organized and propagated: a lie without a good backup could be more dangerous than the honest recital of real facts. Thus was born the Gang of Four, and there has been no more delicate propaganda battle in the history of New China, with so much at stake. The Chinese people have an affection for rough pungency, and it finds an outlet in every aspect of their lives, whether it is street talk, education, store purchases or philosophical debate. It is entirely appropriate that Communist propagandists would naturally incorporate such pungency in their work. It has, after all, the ring of authenticity, and so it was not surprising that the Gang of Four took on a vaguely vaudevillian aspect which found its most perfect expression not in government explanations and ideological editorials, but in the popular banter between professional stage comedians, which is known in China as "cross talk."

It was not just a faction that Chairman Hua had purged. The most prominent member of the Gang of Four was the late chairman's own wife, and a mountain range of propaganda was needed to float the idea that Mao had taken to his own bed a viper who deceived him almost up to the time of his death. Madame Mao—or Jiang Qing (pronounced "ching"), as she is correctly called (although she changed her name several times before she first met Mao in the 1930s)—was chosen along with three other principal allies of Mao to be the sacrificial victims in the latest ideological-line change within the Party. A political campaign needs a focus, and the Gang of Four served this end admirably. There were, of course, many other strict adherents of Chairman Mao's final radical philosophy, which had caused so much tragedy in China. They too were purged or neutralized in the days to come, but without any fanfare because the Gang of Four campaign required a single symbol for total effectiveness.

At the root of the dilemma facing the new leadership was the role of Mao himself. When Nikita Khrushchev succeeded Stalin, he denounced the old Soviet tyrant for the personality cult he had erected around himself and for the millions of people he had ruthlessly executed or sentenced to concentration camps. The dismay and disillusionment this remarkable attack aroused throughout the entire Communist world was felt particularly keenly in China. Ironically, China had no reason whatsoever to love Stalin, who had persistently misunderstood the reality of the Chinese Communist Revolution and undercut Mao and his movement right from the beginning. Sometimes it seemed as if the Communists came to power in Peking despite Stalin, a fact never perceived by the Cold

War warriors in the United States, who saw the Communist bloc as a monolithic entity thirty years ago. But within many ruling Communist parties, Stalin was a symbol of unity; moreover, the totality of Khrushchev's denunciation of the Stalin myth called into question the legitimacy of all Communist governments, and no one was more incensed at this than Mao.

Villainy is as relative as goodness, and while the full account of Mao's record in China is far from complete, he was clearly not an ogre of the proportions of Stalin. As the leader of the Chinese Communist Revolution and the architect of his country's phenomenal recovery and reconstruction during the first decade of power, he earned one of the most indelible and honorable positions in Chinese history. The problem was that he chose not to retire when he had already achieved this position; instead he spent the last two decades of his life undoing just about everything he had helped create. It was only through Mao's consent that the radical faction, now isolated under the grab-bag title of the Gang of Four, ascended to and retained power. They had no other authority save his, and through Mao they forced most of the population of China to pay lip service to ideas few people really understood and fewer cared for. Mao's wife, Jiang Qing, was a particularly spiteful creature who won the enmity of most Chinese, as far as it is possible to determine. She was indeed a kind of monster, as her record amply shows, but it is very important to remember that she represented her husband, and in a terrifyingly real sense, she was the physical embodiment of Mao Tsetung Thought during the chairman's later years.

The Party stalwarts who had managed to withstand Mao's numerous purges throughout the years moved swiftly at his demise to end any further drift in the direction the chairman had decreed. But they did not intend to make Khrushchev's mistake, and a way had to be found to somehow preserve Mao's reputation while at the same time dismantling much of what he stood for—especially what he stood for during the 1960s and 1970s.

Clearly, most Chinese people were disgusted with what the Cultural Revolution had brought them: chaos, repression, a nearly bankrupt economy, a tenuous agricultural development, an experimental education system that was a terrible failure, the denial of a unique cultural legacy, a backward national security and defense program quite ill equipped for the modern age. Despite all the show tours and brave rhetoric that so impressed foreign visitors,

Mao nearly succeeded in returning China—at least spiritually—to the way he found it, thereby negating his own contributions. Certainly there had been no significant changes in the material well-being of most ordinary Chinese since the late fifties—a glaringly obvious fact rarely noted by ecstatic visitors from the West.

This was not the sort of thing to encourage the confidence of the masses in the Communist Party; yet the same Party dared not destroy the myth of Mao because it was so bound up in its own legitimacy and survival.

Accordingly, following a well-used format, the propaganda department conceived a tale of sinister plots in which close colleagues of Mao were supposed to have formulated knavish tricks to frustrate his plans. In this way, Lin Biao wreaked havoc from 1966 to 1971, and the Gang of Four carried forward his perfidy, even while sneakily attacking Lin, from 1972 until the "glorious day when the wise leader Chairman Hua Guofeng and the Party Central Committee smashed the anti-Party, anti-socialist, anti-Mao faction in one decisive blow." The rogues' list neatly covers the years of the Cultural Revolution, without naming the principal culprit; this was the first of many devices used to extricate Mao from his own mess for the benefit of the present leadership.

When I arrived at the end of 1977, the campaign could not have been described as a roaring success. Although Chinese people seemed genuinely relieved that the latest batch of monsters and devils had been removed from office, life had not changed very much. There had been too many political campaigns, too many lies in the past twenty years for the people to respond with anything but weary cynicism. They were resigned, not stupid. Early on, we heard from foreign students at Peking University that some adventurous souls had a sarcastic joke whenever the Gang of Four came up for discussion in the privacy of their rooms. "Oh, yes, the Gang of Four," they would say, simultaneously holding up an outstretched hand to indicate that there were five members of the Gang. The biggest one, Mao himself, could not be named.

Unable or unwilling to conceive of a China fundamentally different from the one they had taken over, Hua and his colleagues flustered and floundered through the first post-Mao months, united only in their distaste for the people they had purged. The stage was set, however, for the return to power of the feistiest politician of our age. In a broadly popular move, Deng Xiaoping (pronounced "shao-ping"), the diminutive septuagenarian from Sichuan province, was appointed senior vice-premier. Extraordinarily durable, Deng had been a principal victim of the Cultural Revolution when he fell from grace along with his first patron, former head of state Liu Shaoqi (pronounced "shao-chee"). Six years later, Premier Chou Enlai brought him back to power, but Deng fell again in 1976 shortly after Chou died. With his Third Coming ("two more than Christ himself has been able to manage," said one caustic foreign observer), many people predicted a battle royal in the leadership because Hua's chairmanship of the Communist Party and his appointment as premier of the state council had been made possible, in part, by Deng's downfall.

A wall poster that went up in Peking much later made several criticisms of Deng's subsequent actions, but praised the vice-premier for his ability "to keep the total picture of the nation in front of him." That is as good an estimation of the man's genius as there is. Although he certainly has a vindictive streak and a personal enemies list, he never evens the score for past grievances unless such an action fits into a broader plan. And unlike any of his colleagues in the Politburo, he had a plan and a vision—although it is not nearly as novel or radical as many people, inside and outside China, have supposed. Deng was hard at work on this same plan and vision in 1966 when Mao first purged him. Many of the changes in China that have dazzled the world in the past few years were simply a reversion to pre–Cultural Revolution policies. The truly curious thing about the Deng Xiaoping phenomenon is that he, like Jiang Qing, is also a manifestation of Mao's own thinking.

It is not for frivolous reasons or paper shortages that the complete works of Mao Tsetung are not available to the Chinese people. As he brooded about the future of his country, the Great Helmsman's mind wandered. If you trace most of the so-called line struggles between factions inside the Communist Party, you get back to the common denominator—Mao. Unfortunately for China, when Mao changed his mind about a particular course or direction, the rest of the country was required to follow suit and officially forget what had been said and done before.

Every serious China-watcher has a handy list of Mao quotes, and for each controversial move that his successors took—whether it was the new school examination system, salary increases for factory workers, private plots for peasants or the importation of foreign technology—there was a quote from Mao (usually from the Cultural Revolution period) showing him in the opposite camp, sometimes violently so. But the quotes of Mao, like the books of the Bible, cover many contingencies.

After nearly two decades in Peking, the *Globe and Mail* bureau had become a staggering repository of the man's sheer verbiage. There were little red books and big red books, bulky selected works and thin monographs of poetry, long interviews and endless speeches, learned studies and propagandistic potboilers. He talked a lot and wrote a lot. The utterances range from the blunt to the mystical, from the contradictory and inexplicable to plain and ordinary common sense. His political heirs, therefore, were left with a problem similar to that of the early Christian Church: what to do with all the Holy Writ.

Mao was a thinker often at odds with himself. One day he could argue that sweet reason and patience were the only weapons to be used against ideological enemies, and another day he could issue the order to "bombard the headquarters" he himself had erected with his closest allies and colleagues. He could evoke God and the never-ending warfare of class struggle in almost the same breath. Here was a leader who fancied himself as both Mystic and Everyman; what one side created, the other side was compelled to destroy. In the twilight of his life, he reestablished his dwindling political power with a vision of perpetual revolution that will always have the power to excite and inspire romantics everywhere. In rejecting this vision, which for China had turned into a nightmare, Deng had only to dip into those works of Chairman Mao which coincided with his own initial political ascendancy: there was an ample enough store of quotation to back up every move.

In fact, Mao had predicted that this would come to pass after his death, when he warned his followers that enemies might use his own words against him. The joke in this was that Mao himself had had to suppress much of his own previous writing for exactly the same reason. The library in the *Globe and Mail* bureau can be neatly divided between those works which became prohibited and those which have been rehabilitated. Various correspondents just kept shuffling them in the shelves to suit the order of the day. The most pathetic volume is a previous interpreter's copy of the little red book of Chairman Mao's Thought, selected and edited by Lin Biao in 1967. After Lin's fall, the nervous interpreter had ripped out the picture of the "closest comrade-in-arms" as well as his introduction. Even where Marshal Lin's name was isolated in otherwise allowable prose, it had been scratched out so thoroughly that the paper was cut.

The campaign to defuse radical Maoism, still going on, is one of the world's current wonders. The first and most important undertaking was to isolate all the pent-up frustration and justifiable anger of the Chinese people and direct it away from the Communist Party by focusing on that all-purpose monster of the propaganda department: the Gang of Four. The best ally in the campaign was Chairman Mao himself, especially since his corpse was safely tucked away in a crystal sarcophagus at Tienanmen Square. To give you something of the flavor of the campaign, it is necessary only to quote a small section of Chairman Hua's political report to the Eleventh National Congress of the Communist Party of China in August 1977. It is not important here to understand the obscure political and literary references. Instead consider the style and purpose. If you become confused by the specifics, then you have a strong bond with the broad masses of the Chinese people, who often woke up in the morning to discover that black was white and night was day:

> On May 3, 1975, at a meeting of the Political Bureau of the Central Committee, Chairman Mao once again criticized the Gang of Four for their sectarian activities against the Party. He gave them a strong warning: "Practice Marxism-Leninism, and not revisionism; unite, and don't split; be open and aboveboard, and don't intrigue and conspire. Don't function as a gang of four. Stop doing that anymore. Why do you keep on doing so? Why don't you unite with the more than two hundred Members of the Central Committee of the Party? A few banding together is no good, never any good." As revisionism, splittism and conspiracy were the quintessence of the Gang of Four, Chairman Mao repeatedly stressed the principles of the "three do's and three don'ts." He excoriated them, saying that they "don't believe in the three principles, nor do they listen to me. They have forgotten the three principles which were stressed at the Ninth and Tenth Congresses. I suggest all present discuss these principles again." Chairman Mao explicitly instructed the Politburo to discuss this matter and emphasized that the question of the Gang of Four "should be settled in the second half of the year, if not in the first. If not this year, then next. Or if not next year, the year after." This clearly indicates that Chairman Mao was determined to settle the question of the Gang of Four.

In accordance with Chairman Mao's instructions, the Politburo, with Comrade Deng Xiaoping in charge, severely criticized the Gang of Four. Both earlier and later, the Politburo issued a number of documents with Chairman Mao's approval to counter interference and sabotage by the Gang of Four, strengthen the Party's leadership in all branches of work and implement Chairman Mao's revolutionary line.

In July 1975, Chairman Mao made two significant statements about the Party's policy on literature and art. On the 25th he wrote an important comment on *Pioneers,* a good film depicting the revolutionary spirit of the Daqing [pronounced "da-ching"] oil workers. As the Gang of Four were against the slogan "In industry, learn from Daqing," they cooked up ten charges and tried to kill *Pioneers* with one blow. Chairman Mao wrote on a letter from the screenwriter of *Pioneers,* "There is nothing seriously wrong with this film. I suggest that it be approved for release. We shouldn't demand perfection. And to bring as many as ten charges against it is really going too far. This hampers the readjustment of the Party's policy on literature and art." Chairman Mao's instruction was a sharp denunciation of the Gang of Four for undermining this policy.

After having been severely criticized by Chairman Mao on many occasions, the Gang of Four kept constantly on the lookout for new openings, biding their time for a counterattack. In August 1975 Chairman Mao commented penetratingly on the novel *Water Margin.* Thinking this gave them an opportunity, the Gang of Four maliciously distorted his comments and launched a vicious propaganda drive to smear the Chairman and split the Central Committee. At the First National Conference on Learning from Dazhai in Agriculture, convened in September, the agenda approved by Chairman Mao was about the whole nation learning from Dazhai and about the need to build Dazhai-type counties across the country. However, right there in Dazhai itself, Jiang Qing ranted and raved at length that in *Water Margin* "the crucial point is that Song Jiang makes Zhao Kai a figurehead," attacking Premier Chou and Comrade Deng Xiaoping by innuendo. What was more, she came out with a preposterous demand that her taped talk be relayed and the text printed and distributed at the conference. When informed of this, Chairman Mao was infuriated, dismissing her talk as "Shit. Wide of the mark." His unequivocal instructions were: "Don't distribute the text, don't play the recording, don't print the text." Thus was the arrogance of the reactionary Gang of Four deflated.

In the original Chinese printed version of this speech by Chairman Hua, as well as in all the subsequent official translations, the state publishing house followed the common practice of putting any direct quotation attributed to Mao in boldface type, in exactly the same manner that some editions of the Bible use red ink to print the words of Christ. In both cases, this is done to venerate the speaker and stimulate a sense of awe for the words. Undeniably, on the printed page, this device enhances and elevates such timeless utterances as "Shit. Wide of the mark." Characteristically, the quote is pungent, thus bearing that extra measure of authenticity.

Picking through speeches like this was the lot of Sinologists and Communist Party cadres alike. Where the Sinologist would have a good chuckle at the reference to "Comrade Deng Xiaoping" doing Mao's purported bidding scarcely a year before Mao stripped him of all his posts and exiled him to the provinces, the cadre would have to consume the lie whole as he struggled to get "the correct line" firmly fixed in his head. But not too firmly fixed, because ideology and policy, to give them their due in China, are far from static. Those references to "Dazhai-type counties across the country" are a good example.

Dazhai was a small, poor stretch of land in China's bleak northeast. Its history is now so lost in tons of propaganda that it is impossible to separate fact from fantasy. The kindest interpretation, which is not necessarily the correct one, has it that by dint of their own resources and sweat, the peasants of Dazhai turned an arid and unlikely county into a productive, fertile proposition. When this fact became known to the Party propagandists, the county was cited as a model commune whose style of work and overall example should be emulated by the whole country.

Initially, as far as I was ever able to determine, Dazhai was simply a symbol of self-reliance and hard work. In the mania that developed around the place, particularly as a result of the Cultural Revolution, symbolic emulation had been abandoned in favor of exact duplication. Here was a classic theological confrontation worthy of the Christian Church at the time of the Reformation: was Communion bread the real body of Christ or did it merely represent His spiritual presence? Should China copy Dazhai exactly, or simply emulate its spirit?

Throughout China, the slogan "In Agriculture, Learn from Dazhai" was painted on every conceivable wall, bridge or building. It was carved into the sides of mountains. Even parks sported floral arrangements in the shape of the slogan. Songs and poems were commissioned to celebrate the county, and the traffic between Peking and Dazhai was dense as a steady stream of Chinese and foreign visitors came reverentially to see this place which outdrew Lourdes in its appeal. State leaders loved to be photographed doing "hard labor" there—an act similar in intent to the Pope's annual foot-washing of young priests in Rome or Queen Elizabeth's distribution of Maundy Money.

Not surprisingly, as it eventually turned out, the actual production figures at Dazhai soon seemed too scanty to support the miracle and were adjusted upward in conformity with "socialist reality," which held that the aim or goal, rather than the actual facts, should be presented to the masses to inspire them to greater efforts.

With the carnival-type atmosphere that descended on Dazhai, there wasn't much time for real work, and so the discrepancy between what was actually done and what was reported for national emulation widened. In addition, a whole bureaucracy within the bureaucracy was created which dispatched Dazhai Inspectors across the length and breadth of China to discipline any commune that was not measuring up to the model in both practice and (alleged) results. I later learned from one of those inspectors that local Party chiefs and commune leaders fixed their books and staged phony demonstrations of Dazhai emulation for these inspections—which, you have to grant, was completely in line with what was being done at the Model Pacesetter.

The tragedy in all this was the havoc it unleashed on Chinese agriculture. Inevitably, many communes took the business seriously, and against all common sense transformed profitable farming operations appropriate, say, for the fertile south into cumbersome replicas of methods used in the infertile, hilly north. One of the major grievances the Chinese authorities had against my predecessor, Ross Munro, was that he had had the temerity to go to Dazhai and sniff out some of the fraud. He found it curious that the hardworking, salt-of-the-earth peasants of Dazhai could be picking fruit in the orchard all day with shiny new leather shoes on their feet. At the time, he had no conception of the depth of the duplicity going on in the place, but this tiny little fact he discovered—part of his theory about the "theater" of such tours for foreigners—unleashed some vicious rhetoric from officials at the Chinese Foreign Ministry. "What's the point of taking him around the country if he thinks it's all theater?" asked one outraged official of another journalist. And the next time Munro requested a trip to a certain place, the same bureaucrat said he didn't think the local officials would really want to see him ("for obvious reasons," to quote Munro's subsequent eviction notice from the country).

Chairman Hua made his adoring references to Dazhai in August 1977. In less than two years, Dazhai became something of a national embarrassment and its leaders were forced to make self-criticisms. The whole concept of such models' being religiously copied, regardless of local conditions, was dismissed as claptrap, and Chairman Hua himself would never again utter the name of the place. Just as the Gang of Four became Nonpersons, Dazhai became a Nonplace for a period. In August 1979, two Swedish friends decided they wanted to see Dazhai because they had read so much about it in the past. It was only because they were experienced diplomats that they managed the feat, since the China Travel Service did everything within its power to discourage them. Luck was on their side, and they visited Dazhai before it had been totally obliterated from the political map, but the ecstatic guided tours of yore were gone. All those at Dazhai were deep into self-criticism; as well, they were doing something that had been alien to the place for a decade: work. Now that the secret state subsidies which financed the myth had been withdrawn, the residents of Dazhai were abruptly catapulted back into the real and grueling world of the Chinese peasantry. The whole saga would make a superb satire on the stage, the kind that Chinese people adore. It is unlikely to appear in theaters for some time, however. If ever. Toward the end of 1979, a reformed Dazhai was cautiously and quietly revealed by the authorities. Shorn of its socialist miracles, Dazhai was returned to the onerous reality of Chinese agriculture.

Despite these presiding hypocrisies and deceits, the changes in China continued apace. For young people who did not know life before the Cultural Revolution, the changes were dazzling and held out the prospect of things they had never dreamed possible. It was a dizzy time, and even older people, who knew the strict limits any totalitarian power had to maintain in order to hold on to its presiding authority, got caught up in the euphoria.

Besides, most of the changes *were* for the better, and with the well-remembered contrast of the Cultural Revolution (officially declared over by Chairman Hua in 1977), there was every reason to rejoice. Peking Opera and other beloved regional art forms returned to the stages, replacing the handful of "revolutionary" offerings foisted on audiences by Jiang Qing. Teachers regained respectable status, and with advancement hitched once more to a comprehensive examination system, rebellious students quickly buckled down to work. An outraged peasantry—still accounting for eighty percent of the population—had its tiny private plots and cooperative markets restored, and food production took an immediate turn for the better. The Communist Party undertook the dangerous and embarrassing task of rehabilitating millions of innocent people—dead and alive—who had been made victims of countless Maoist purges and political campaigns. It became permissible for women to get their hair curled and for young couples to dance. A quotation from guess who was dredged up to "make foreign things serve China," and Western businessmen with technology and services for sale scrambled to get into the newly emerging China market. Factory workers got pay increases as well as a genuine say about who their immediate superiors should be, and experiments began to widen a little the franchise of citizens voting for state leaders. Long-closed churches and temples reopened. Tourism was encouraged, and the Chinese people were told that the long dark night was over at last and they could "emancipate their minds" and "search truth from facts."

Deng Xiaoping presided over this dramatic sequence of changes with a personally restrained presence. He knew, and has obviously forced his nominal superior, Hua Guofeng, to recognize, that massive political campaigns, which Mao so adored, could only bring more ruin to the country. Stability and Unity were the twin objectives as the backward nation set about to realize the Four Modernizations in agriculture, industry, national defense and science and technology. The goal was set for the year 2000, by which time China was to catch up to "advanced world levels" and surpass them if possible. Internal conflicts in the leadership were worked out behind closed doors. Some measure of the degree of struggle going on at the top—all of it unobserved by outsiders and most Chinese alike—can be taken from the singular fact that in September 1980, Chairman Hua was forced to announce his own resignation from the premiership and formal control of day-to-day government. Deng also resigned one of his numerous positions, but his "retirement" was different: In less than four years after his return, his own political troops had control of virtually all the country, while Hua's retreat was punctuated by often abject denials of previous positions. These events, however, lay ahead.

Much of what I saw in China occurred in the initial period of breathtaking change. In setting things down now, one is inevitably forced to see certain patterns and developments, but this was not primarily the case at the time, particularly for a journalist who must report on the events of the day. In this light, the arrival in China of Bob Hope, Pierre Cardin and Coca-Cola often took on the same importance, if not more as far as newspaper and newsmagazine editors were concerned, as the more fundamental and dramatic fissures in Chinese society, exposed for the first time to the often uncomprehending eyes of outsiders. Anyone who had any liking for the Chinese people found himself rejoicing at the new possibilities, while at the same time standing wide-eyed before revelations of reality that few foreign observers in the past had had the wisdom to see or the courage to write about.

However daring, the new leadership of the Communist Party was old and retained a vivid memory of prerevolutionary China. These men operate on an understanding that whatever they do, it is better than what went before. Deng Xiaoping and his allies had conceived of a comprehensive plan for both material and ideological development that was thwarted by the Cultural Revolution. When they returned to power, they simply turned the clocks back to 1966, when they had last been at work, and began to pick up the pieces to put them in the old puzzle.

But something wasn't quite right. It was not simply that there was a huge new generation who knew nothing of the evil of old China, who listened to tales of reactionary landlords and marauding foreign powers with the same amount of detachment as my generation in the West listens to tales of the Great Depression and World War II. It was also a generation whose formative years were molded by the cataclysmic events of the Cultural Revolution. This was a crucial element which hadn't been worked out in the reversion to all the pre-1966 planning. Mao, the old fox, clearly used the Cultural Revolution to regain the personal power he had lost to an ascendant Communist Party, thanks to his own mistakes. But given to metaphysical thinking as well, he also argued—and no doubt believed—that he was bringing the experience of revolution to a generation that had no direct knowledge of it. This was part of his campaign to make "class struggle" unending. It was the most supreme of ironies to discover that Mao's new generation of revolutionaries not only rejected Maoism, but were busy planting some seeds of revolt against totalitarian Communism itself. If Mao had intended to leave a time bomb behind for his successors, he succeeded amazingly well.

Such revelations were not easily discerned at first, however. For the majority of Chinese and foreign residents, the most obvious reality was that great changes were now possible. A predictable future of continuity is reassuring only to those in a state of bliss and peace; for a nation worn down by repression, predictions became impossible—and happily so. It was a moment for hope and great expectations, the best of times since the heroic decade of the fifties, when the population had been widely united with the common purpose of rebuilding its shattered and humiliated land. The awesome patience and endurance of the Chinese people had initially been rewarded by Mao and then betrayed. Now it seemed time for at least a modest dividend.

4

The Foreign Ghetto

O nly an Agatha Christie could do true justice to the foreigners' ghetto in Peking. That no one has written a superb thriller using this unlikely background for a setting can be attributed only to the fact that the right person has not been able to gain sufficient access to soak up its unique ambience. Far too mundane and bland for the exploits of James Bond, the three foreign residents' compounds in the northeast quarter of the Communist capital also lack the shadow of menace that heightens the intrigue of John le Carré's spy capers. But Miss Marple or Hercule Poirot would be in *terra cognita* and have a field day.

Consider first the living conditions. After the Communists came to power in 1949 and moved the seat of government from the Guomindang capital of Nanking to Peking, they were content for the first few years to let diplomats live in the old embassy quarter, near Tienanmen Square in the center of town. The quarter is famous throughout the world because of the role foreigners living there played in resisting the Boxer Rebellion siege at the beginning of this century. Even today, when there are no diplomats there, a stroll through the former legation quarter is a romantic, exciting experience because some of the old buildings and walls still stand. As it consolidated its rule, however, and with the advice of Soviet experts, the Chinese Government began moving embassies and diplomatic residents to a new section of town. The official explanation for this was not unreasonable, but as it turned out, there were other considerations as well. The government was required to provide both protection and services to foreign envoys and their retinues. Because of the limitations of space in the legation quarter, diplomats began spreading out in various parts of the city and lived contentedly beside Chinese neighbors. Even the few accredited Western journalists had relative freedom of choice to find a place and set up a bureau. Reuters, the English news agency, had a wonderful traditional Chinese house near the center of town, whose rear courtyard backed onto the moat of the Forbidden City.

Inevitably, this situation allowed both diplomats and journalists to observe the daily life of Peking's citizens at close quarters. The curiosity about life-styles was equally reciprocated by the citizens. With the start of the divisive nationwide political campaigns in 1957, however, such access to Chinese society became intolerable to the Communist Party, which was seeking to isolate Chinese people not only from their own past, but from any foreign influences not specifically approved by officials. Within a few years, the diplomats and journalists found themselves in the unwanted isolation of the new foreigners' ghettoes, where the government said it was better able to consolidate services and security.

By the time Elizabeth and I arrived, there were three specific districts: Jian Guo Men Wai and Qi (pronounced "chee") Jia Yuan, which were side by side, with the foreigners-only Friendship Store and International Club as the connecting bridge, and San Li Tun, which was a couple of kilometers north and where we lived. Each district contained embassies and diplomatic apartments. Whether in separate compounds or in clusters of buildings, foreigners lived and worked behind high fences or walls guarded twenty-four hours by specially trained troops of the People's Liberation Army. The soldiers' job, we quickly learned, was not primarily to protect foreigners, but to keep unauthorized Chinese out.

Had it applied to embassies alone, this security system could be justified to some extent, but since it was also applied to ordinary apartment buildings housing nondiplomatic personnel, such as journalists and resident businessmen, it was easy to see the true intent behind it all. Historically, Chinese governments have gone to no end of trouble to keep foreigners and Chinese citizens apart, so the Communists cannot be accused of inventing the practice. They do, however, have a genius for co-opting historical precedents like this and transforming them into rigid institutions.

The traditional role foreigners have played in Chinese history is also of some importance. By forcing successive imperial Chinese governments to grant extraterritorial rights to foreign nationals, rapacious and marauding imperialist powers left behind a legacy of haughty aloofness and evil deeds that are an indelible part of Chinese revolutionary lore. A turn-of-the-century sign in a Shanghai foreigners' park about "no dogs or Chinese" endures as a symbol of fundamental injustice which Mao's minions in the propaganda department found useful to their own purposes.

But 1977 was not 1909 or even 1949. The extraterritorial rights of foreigners had been done away with before the Communists came to power, yet Mao never trusted his people sufficiently to allow a truly free exchange of ideas between them and foreigners. In this, as in so many other things, he was in perfect communion with the Guomindang Government of Chiang Kaishek and the court of the horrible old Dowager Empress in the nineteenth century.

During our entire stay in China, I never personally experienced any evidence of natural hostility toward foreigners, except for the actions of some police thugs, who were under orders, and a few officials, who were more concerned with their own precarious positions than with anything else. The only notable exceptions were disturbances between some foreign students, mostly African, and their Chinese colleagues.

This was not a case of xenophobia, however, but of racism, pure and simple. Certainly there were cultural aggravations on both sides, but the undertow was undeniably racist, also on both sides —a fact the Chinese Government, for ideological reasons, hates like the devil to admit, although racism is a phenomenon common to all countries and all races. The most notorious incident took place in Shanghai in July 1978, when a three-day melee closed down the Shanghai Textile Institute. There are two versions of the cause of the disturbances: one from the foreign students involved who spoke to foreign correspondents and the other, official version from the New China News Agency, Xinhua (pronounced "shin-hua"). Neither came close to the roots of the problem.

The official Chinese explanation holds that the affair began when

Chinese students asked a foreign student who was playing music on his tape deck to turn down the volume. The authorities noted that all students were preparing for crucial final examinations and study time was at a premium. The foreign student, for reasons unexplained by Xinhua, chose to be provocative and turned the volume up. This aroused the indignation of several Chinese students, who expressed themselves by throwing stones. The matter got out of hand very quickly, and a pitched battle soon began which did not end until the Public Security Bureau sent in a sufficient number of police to quell the riot. Xinhua did not explain why it had taken three days to send in "sufficient" reinforcements, and although the government admitted there were faults on both sides, the explanation clearly held that the Chinese students were the lesser offenders.

The foreign students, however, maintain that the original request "to turn down the volume" was expressed as "Turn off your machine, black devil." Not surprisingly, this didn't go down well with the foreign students, who were all from Third World countries. In the days following the melee, it became clear that long-standing and simmering discontent focused on this isolated aggravation and exploded.

The foreign students were disgruntled at the restrictions placed on their lives, both inside the institute and around Shanghai. On June 30, a Mauritanian had been arrested by the Public Security Bureau on charges of raping a Chinese girl and was subsequently expelled from the country. His colleagues maintained that this was a frame-up and that any relations between foreigners, especially black ones, and Chinese girls so horrified the authorities (and many ordinary Chinese citizens) that the Mauritanian was served up as a sacrificial victim. The students themselves pointed out that there was considerable resentment among their Chinese colleagues of the government grants to foreign students. "If we bought a small present for a Chinese girlfriend from the Friendship Store, no matter how trivial, the Chinese boys would get jealous," said one student from Mali. "They said that blacks lived in trees in their own countries, but that when they came to China they were given better living conditions than Chinese. We are laughed and stared at in the streets and the resentment built up with every little incident. Not one of us will ever forget that during the three days that our dormitory was surrounded, the Chinese police stood idly by as rocks and insults were hurled at us. The police made no effort to control the Chinese, even when they started bringing in other students as reinforcements."

The toll at the end was seven Chinese and sixteen foreigners hospitalized (one had an eye gouged out). The government removed all foreign students from the institute for a few days and postponed examinations for a week. The Soviet Union had a field day in international propaganda while the Chinese Government tried to do everything within its system to make sure there would be no repetition.

The trouble was that the system itself encourages the problem. In restricting normal exchanges between outsiders and Chinese citizens, and then isolating all foreigners with special perquisites and privileges, it provides the basic ingredients of animosity from the start. Students from affluent Western countries who have come to soak up the mystique of the Middle Kingdom can assimilate these restrictions far more easily than students from poor, backward countries who have come to China to learn a trade.

Sometimes African students can arrive in China without knowing that all the courses will be taught in Chinese. This may seem absurd, but it does happen. The Africans have been sent by their own governments because the Chinese have offered to provide the education free of charge—a laudable international exchange. But for the unfortunate students, life quickly becomes hell. Unlike many Western students who have had extensive training in Chinese, they must often spend up to two years at an isolated suburban language institute to assimilate enough Chinese to enable them to take the technical course they had thought they would begin right away. If the students come from a particularly poor country, the small stipends they receive from the Chinese Government will not be sufficient to buy much more than basic necessities. When the holidays come, all their more affluent colleagues will be setting off on exciting trips inside or outside China, while they rot for weeks on end at the institute. Nearly all of the Third World students who come to China are male, which complicates the situation grievously, since the authorities go to fanatical lengths to separate not only foreigners from Chinese but the sexes as well. Their own embassies, if they are lucky enough to be studying in Peking—which at least has a larger foreign community—are often unwilling or unable to alleviate the problem. It is not surprising, therefore, that their attitude very quickly becomes bloody-minded—which only serves further to compound their misery. There are exceptions, and I have talked to well-adjusted, if somewhat cynical, African students who survive the system handily. But serious or small incidents in Peking, Nanking and Shanghai occur with sufficient consistency to confirm the general mood of ill feeling and resentment.

All this only serves to dramatize one segment of the foreign residents' lot in China, as well as giving it a sociological sheen that was not easily apparent in day-to-day life. What would have particularly appealed to Agatha Christie's quirky sleuths was the reality of life behind the guarded walls of the compounds.

The single most startling fact is that there is no system of law and order. For all the guards at the gates and restrictions on Chinese comings and goings, the government had apparently forgotten that diplomatic and other foreign personnel are quite capable of committing their own acts of violence. They are also capable of stealing and, conceivably, of murdering. Fights and thefts recur with sufficient consistency to become part of the folklore of the foreign community. From time to time, delinquency-prone offspring of some diplomats form gangs inside the compound complexes. These kids have beaten up smaller children—sometimes with extreme viciousness—and staged impressive robberies in the homes of vacationing diplomats. The most common occurrences were acts of vandalism, particularly with automobiles.

When such things happen for the first time, the foreigner naturally thinks of turning to the Public Security Bureau for assistance, and that's when his first surprise comes. Occasionally, the police will deign to visit the scene of a crime inside the compound, but generally they are loath to do so. The attitude is that what goes on inside these places is not their concern so long as Chinese citizens are not involved. If foreigners like to bash and rob one another, so be it. The foreign community, by its very nature, is not much help either. The turnover of diplomats is so rapid that an internally conceived program of security would collapse as soon as the most active members moved on to a new posting. The truly surprising thing is that there is not more violence and vandalism than there already is.

I did a story on this problem that got me labeled "the bigot of Peking" because much of the trouble is associated with the Africans. Certainly, the cultural adjustments for an African in China appear to be more extreme, but the problem here was not essentially racial, but economic. Like African students, African diplomats often have very little money, even though the Chinese Government has a policy of subsidizing their embassy costs as well as certain other services and commodities. Most Western diplomats come to Peking on relatively short postings without their offspring, who are sent to boarding schools in their own countries. Most African diplomats come with their children on unbearably long postings. The children are sent either to small embassy schools or to special Chinese institutions. Consequently, the teen-aged population of the foreign compounds has a racial preponderance of blacks, and the normal frustrations of such an age group become compounded and exaggerated in the isolation. Delinquency, a problem every society has to face, becomes known inside the Peking foreigners' ghetto as "the black problem." The Chinese Government, as host, was the worst offender and never even made arrangements for organized sports between diplomatic children and Chinese youngsters.

For affluent whites, like Elizabeth and me, this situation was something to be wary about, but it did not intrude upon our lives unduly. Apart from what I could observe with my own eyes, I was able to get ample information on the subject from blacks themselves, as well as from a foreign doctor who often had to patch up the results of violence. Our immediate neighbors were from Mali, and the plight of the wife was not untypical.

Several years before, there had been an incident outside the compounds in which a Chinese male had attacked a foreign woman with a knife. She wasn't seriously wounded, and it was one of only two or three incidents of this kind with foreigners that ever occurred in Peking. The attacker, who was caught and executed within hours by the Chinese authorities, had entered into the realm of dark humor by our time and was usually referred to as "Wang the Ripper." The story, though, fed on our neighbor's imagination, along with the heavy isolation which seemed so unnatural to her. As a result, she never went outside the compound walls except to buy food at the nearby Friendship Store or to attend formal state functions, to which she traveled with her husband in an embassy car. For nearly eight years she lived like this, with no home leave and no trips outside Peking. Her nine-year-old daughter knew no life save the compound and the French Embassy school, and nothing we or anyone else said could persuade the woman to widen her horizons a little. When they were finally recalled home in 1979, it seemed to her like the end of a prison sentence.

Western diplomats and journalists did not have it this hard, although the isolation took its toll. It is a generally consistent social law in Peking that personal problems can become exaggerated within a very short time. We had heard this before we came and now discovered it to be true, both for ourselves and for our friends. The reputation of one of my predecessors in the bureau as a carefree and careless womanizer still makes the rounds in Peking, although he and his notoriously tempestuous marriage had long ago decamped. In effect, the foreign community was a little village, and while this could and did make for some strong bonds of loyalty, the vagaries of little villages—like gossip, scandal and social intrigue—were also rampant.

The smallness also enhanced the absurdity of some aspects of diplomatic life. In London or Paris or Washington, an ambassador in his imposing embassy is really rather splendid to behold, even though his powers over the years have been whittled away by governments loath to leave any aspect of foreign policy to lone individuals in the field. Today, most embassies are tied to their foreign ministries by the umbilical cord of telex machines which pronounce what shall and what shall not be done. In Peking, there are few props for an ambassador to help him forget this situation, and if he tries to carry on in the old style, he cuts an absurd, farcical figure. The most successful ambassadors are those who adapt and find means to do what they feel must be done within the restraints of the system. The Canadian Ambassador, Arthur Menzies, was an outstanding example of this sort, and so was Leonard Woodcock, the head of the United States Liaison Office, who in 1979 became the first American Ambassador to China since the Communists took over.

Woodcock, of necessity, had to keep a fairly low profile as he went about the business of trying to help in the normalization process, which had bedeviled successive United States administrations. The former labor organizer and union chief would occasionally step beyond the bounds someone in his office was supposed to maintain, but it was never without a larger purpose and usually to good effect. When the final negotiations were held toward the end of 1978, Woodcock had established himself as a strong and authoritative presence who was able to act well beyond the role of his office.

Menzies, on the other hand, had a far more typical existence in Peking. Canada, apart from wheat purchases, was not of great importance to China. Menzies saw his chore as one of reminding the Chinese that there were links worth preserving and useful connections to make, even if the government couldn't perceive them itself. The son of a Protestant missionary and himself born in China, he had a real affection for the place and an ability to crack through protocol and stuffiness if he decided that that was the order of the day.

On the other side, I never had to look any further than the French Embassy and its unbelievably pompous and protocol-ridden ambassador, Claude Arnaud. France's recognition of China in 1964 was a breakthrough in Western relations with the East and part of the erratic, but undeniably global, vision of Charles de Gaulle. The French deluded themselves, however, by assuming that this singular act assured them perpetual special status with the Chinese. Arnaud comported himself in a style that would have been more appropriate for Count Talleyrand, except that in Peking he didn't have eighteenth-century Europe as a backdrop. He detested journalists as scum and treated them as such. Not surprisingly, this feeling was reciprocated by the journalists. He also rarely disguised his contempt for anyone below the rank of ambassador, and for this he became widely known in Peking as *le petit Louis* or *le petit crétin*.

Arnaud took it as a point of personal humiliation if he ever heard any political information on China from news reports before his own officers had told him about it. He bullied and badgered them ruthlessly, and I couldn't begin to count the number of evenings I spent with disgruntled and nearly mutinous French diplomats who fulminated about his arrogance and stupidity. The poor officers had no choice but to come begging to the journalists to find out what dispatches were being sent so they could run back and inform Arnaud ahead of time. But even this was often counterproductive, because journalists' opinions were considered, by definition, to be inferior and as a result were routinely discounted. Consequently, there was considerable satisfaction among the resident correspondents when Arnaud's practice and style left him exposed. This occurred rather dramatically during the official visit to Peking of the mayor of Paris, Jacques Chirac, who was briefed on the Chinese political situation by Arnaud and his officers. Since Chirac had come as the guest of the mayor of Peking, Wu De, he was particularly interested in the political status of his host.

For some weeks, journalists had been speculating that Wu De was about to fall from grace. He had been too closely associated with the Gang of Four, and veiled criticisms appeared regularly in the official press, while direct attacks were going up on poster walls. Our speculation was based on logic and the manifestations of attack that were all around Peking for any fool to see. Instead, Chirac was informed that Wu De was in complete control of things and a respected member of the Central Committee. When Chirac got back to Paris, he was asked about the speculation over Wu De. Repeating the wisdom he had learned from Arnaud and his team, he told *Paris-Match* magazine that Wu De was unassailable and speculation about his political demise was journalistic fantasy. The magazine hit the stands the day the Central Committee removed Wu De as mayor of Peking and criticized him for mismanagement.

Pompous ambassadors, however, added color and texture to the passing scene, and an Arnaud would make a fabulous peripheral character in any thriller set in Peking. I adored watching him at the endless round of diplomatic receptions and cocktail parties. Though he aped the style of General de Gaulle, God had not been kind enough to raise him physically to the same lofty heights of grandeur. He had a comical aspect when he came into a crowded room as his keen eye surveyed the assembled throng in search of someone of his own rank worthy to talk with. I once went up to him in the midst of this preparatory process to see how he could cope with scum. With all the disingenuous charm of a boy next door, I held out my hand and said, "Hello, Mr. Ambassador. My name is Fraser. I'm a Canadian journalist." My hand was left waving in the breeze, and in a beautiful touch, he looked vaguely in my direction and mumbled in French the word *journaliste.* Summoning up my ample store of North American gaucherie, I pushed on relentlessly. "How are things? I hear the Chinese Education Ministry has dropped French as a possible second-language course for Chinese students. That's not so good, is it?" He emitted a sort of low growl that sounded like "aahhh," and his wildly roving eyes finally fixed on the six-foot-four-inch form of the Swedish Ambassador, to whom he abruptly repaired. A few minutes later, I was talking to Arthur Menzies, the Canadian Ambassador, when one of Arnaud's junior political officers came toward us, nervously looking over his shoulder. Without pausing to notice Menzies' presence, he broke into our conversation and said, "Is Arnaud here? I did not know if he comes to this reception." I told him Arnaud was indeed here and talking to the Swedish Ambassador. "Then I go," said the young Frenchman. "I thought maybe he would not come. It is not to be endured when he is around. I leave, I leave."

Just as he was about to stage his getaway, the Canadian Ambassador stuck out his hand. "Hello," he said. "My name is Menzies. I work for the *Globe and Mail.*" The diplomat looked bewildered, briefly grabbed the hand, saying *"Bonjour, bonjour"* and then let it go with a brief "Good-bye." He went off to a side wall behind a row of pillars and made his way discreetly out of the reception room.

One of the most superb places to observe the antics of high envoys, as well as the ornately formal style of Chinese Communist potentates, was the Great Hall of the People. In the days when China had been successfully isolated by the United States and had few diplomatic ties, the government conceived a program of lavish dinners and flag-waving entertainments for the few visiting heads of state who actually turned up in Peking. Originally these were held in the Grand Ballroom of the old Peking Hotel. The *Globe*'s first correspondent in Peking, Frederick Nossal, described these affairs beautifully, contrasting the fifteen courses and the entertainment extravaganzas with the lot of the ordinary citizen. Normally such comparisons would be unfair, but they were made inevitable by the hypocrisy surrounding the propaganda about the state leaders and their alleged love of the simple, proletarian life. It was also a time when millions of Chinese were facing real starvation owing to the gross planning errors Mao and his government had made during the Great Leap Forward. Nossal had no idea at the time of the magnitude of the tragedy—indeed, the whole terrible truth has only recently emerged—but he had some intimation of it. This made his accounts of the state banquets compelling reading.

When these functions were moved to the Great Hall of the People, the government toned down the proceedings somewhat and the number of courses fell to eight. The whole process was run like clockwork, and the program was invariable. Diplomats from all accredited embassies would gather at the Great Hall by 7 P.M., assembling at one side of an antechamber attached to the main banqueting room. On the other side, invited Chinese guests stood in little clusters around tables holding drinks, hors d'oeuvre and cigarettes. Never the twain did meet. Outside, at the head of the interminable main staircase, the visiting head of state and his party would group themselves underneath a large traditional Chinese painting with the host of the evening (either Premier Chou Enlai, in the old days, or one of his senior vice-premiers) and his party. A picture would be taken, and then the whole throng would move into the antechamber to shake hands with the resident envoys and their spouses. The band of the People's Liberation Army would play the same tunes each time.

After the introductions were made, each guest went to a preordained table. Sometimes three thousand people came to these affairs, and members of the Foreign Ministry's protocol department would be there to tell each person as he came in at which table he would be sitting. The protocol people rarely looked at a list; it was all done by memory and face recognition—a truly amazing feat. Journalists were given "working invitations," which meant that spouses were not welcome. We were assigned tables at the very back of the hall beside the band, all of which suited us just fine. Our tables were the only places anyone had fun during these banquets, and since each one was presided over by at least one Chinese official, it was a rare opportunity to gather some pittance of official information. Typically, the dinner was punctuated by the speeches of the visiting head of state and the Chinese host. Toasts were made, and then it was all over. A few days later, the visiting head of state would go through the process of giving a return banquet and the same procedure at the same place would be followed exactly, except that the order of speeches was reversed.

These banquets were pompous and needlessly grandiose, but they sprang from a time when China had few friends in the world. The government obviously felt it had to put on a good show to assert its own legitimacy and make a pitch for its rightful acceptance among the community of nations. Within a year of my arrival, the decision was taken to abandon them. Smaller dinners were given for visitors, and it was not felt necessary to drag out the representatives of the entire foreign community. This change was announced as an economy measure, but in fact it was a sign that China had fully entered into the world community and had no need—or time—to put on the same old show. Only the journalists regretted the end of these affairs. They had been among the few chances to catch a glimpse of the Chinese leadership close up, no matter how peripheral the business was. At least you got to see in the flesh the people you were always writing about, which meant the leadership didn't seem quite as mythological a monolith as it usually appears. For most of the diplomats, the affairs were deadly dull. The first occasion was always interesting, but by the tenth time the dinners were a guaranteed prescription for tedium, relieved only by the antics of the Soviet Bloc diplomats, who would scan the texts of the Chinese speeches—handed out to everyone just as the leader got up to speak —to see if the comments attacking Soviet "revisionism" or "hegemonism" were nasty enough to warrant a walkout. The walkouts were charming little displays, handled with *finesse* and *politesse* by both the Soviet and the Chinese sides. The dean of the Soviet-aligned diplomatic corps would peruse the offending document quickly. Usually the speeches were harmless enough, given the heated and overblown propaganda each country regularly issues about the other. About ten times a year, however, the dean would decide the Chinese had gone over the edge. Usually this was when the particular Chinese leader at the banquet expanded for a few sentences on the menace of a certain "social-imperialist superpower practicing big-nation chauvinism and hegemony in Africa, in Asia, in the Middle East and in Indochina." Moscow was never named as such, but the rules of the game were well known by all sides.

Once he had found the offending section, the Soviet Bloc dean —usually the man from Moscow, but sometimes the representative of Fidel Castro, who was Number Two in tenure among those aligned with Moscow—would look discreetly around the room. About twenty or thirty people were waiting for this look, and it was a tip-off that it would soon be time to stage the walkout. As soon as the Chinese leader was one sentence into the pertinent paragraph, the dean would quietly get up from his seat, smile at his table companions and slowly walk off toward the main double doors leading out of the banquet hall. The rest would follow like little ducklings after their mother, while the doors would miraculously swing open from behind, pulled by two Chinese porters who always seemed to know exactly when the walkout would occur. I witnessed one amusing snafu in this business. The Cuban Ambassador was dean for the day, and after we had all raced through the transcript of the speech, he became the subject of our usual curiosity to see what sort of sign he would make. We didn't expect any, because the speech was not unduly pugnacious. The Cuban Ambassador, however, adjusted his tie clip with unusual and unnecessary hand gestures. "Aha," said the Bulgarian journalist sitting next to me, "it looks as if they shall go." And so it seemed to all the others. At one point during the speech the ambassador found himself too close to his table, and half standing up, he pushed his chair back a little. Simultaneously the ducklings all stood up, and the ambassador, who had no intention of departing, had to make manic hand gestures to get everyone seated again.

The Soviet journalists sitting at the press tables were not required to join in on this game, and we had many good laughs about how the rules were read. The big state dinners ended before the hostilities between China and Vietnam broke into open warfare, so the Vietnamese diplomats were never truly tested by the process. One of the ways they tried to impress the foreign community with their independence was never to join a walkout, even when Vietnam itself was indirectly attacked in the speech.

Socializing was one of the great pastimes of Peking evenings, as diplomats and journalists entertained one another with surpassing *esprit*. Status and hierarchy were strictly maintained on most occasions, and it was a very rare diplomat who would think of inviting a secretary or a junior administrative officer to a dinner party that included senior political officers or counselors. Although living in Peking was a bit like being at a summer camp, the business of status divided many people more than the hierarchy separating tent leader and camper. One of our good friends at the Canadian Embassy was the resident mechanic, on temporary leave from the Canadian Army for this foreign posting. Watching one or two embassy officials, who were themselves only in relatively junior postings, make sure our friend knew his lowly position was quite instructive. The mechanic was one of the most observant and questioning persons in Peking and could have told his nominal superiors a few riveting things he had picked up from here and there, but they would never have listened except, perhaps, for the ambassador himself, who always kept his eyes and ears open too.

There was a far more dramatic example at the French Embassy, which employed a young administrative officer who had a natural empathy for Chinese people and who, moreover, had learned the language well enough to understand street conversation and read wall posters. Before he went on to another posting, he was probably the best-informed foreigner in Peking on what ordinary citizens were thinking—and this was *before* Chinese people tried to establish links to the foreign community. He was under the illusion that most diplomats thought of the Chinese as real people, so he never made a secret of his genial curiosity or his fund of knowledge. He loved Chinese people, and he loved sharing the things he learned on his regular jaunts about the city in his spare time. He was always the first to know of food shortages or of some little controversy in a faraway quarter of Peking that gave substance and humanity to the soulless entity known as "the masses." Yet such was the hidebound state of the French Embassy that this man was never asked for his opinions or information. It would have been beneath contempt to ask such a lowly minion for help in trying to understand the complexity of China. This contempt was reflected in the quality of intelligence the French had to offer.

Diplomats and journalists are often accused of being spies in countries that are habitually secretive or unduly sensitive about their image. Undoubtedly, a certain measure of espionage is carried out in some places by some governments, but as far as I could ever determine, among Western nations represented in Peking, spying was the furthest from anyone's intentions. Of course, this all depends upon one's definition of spying. Most political officers and journalists were simply trying to figure out how China worked in order to report back to their governments or newspapers. If such things as food rations and living standards and political speculation are deemed state secrets, then I suppose in Peking we were all spies. Certainly, I got the distinct impression at regular junctures that this was the way the Chinese Government and police regarded us, and me in particular. But I never felt like a spy, and just about every bit of information I ever gleaned made it into my dispatches for everyone to see. The problem will take a long time to resolve because it is traditional for Chinese governments to dislike foreigners.

Journalists, for example, are divided into friendly and unfriendly groups. To give the officials at the Foreign Ministry their due, once they have deemed a journalist essentially friendly, they are prepared to put up with quite a lot—at least in their terms. But apart from a few Chinese officials who understand the Western press well, there is a woeful lack of discernment about journalistic independence. The Foreign Ministry never hesitates to get in touch with a Western ambassador when it feels one of "his" journalists is going too far. They also never believe the ambassador when he says he can't do anything about it.

But let me not portray a scene of unrelieved confrontation. If one is from an affluent Western country, as either a journalist or a diplomat, life in Peking can be remarkably pleasant—unless you are predisposed to be weighed down by life's difficulties. During my time in China, the diversions in town increased as dramatically as the possibilities of doing a more professional job. The changes ushered in by the new government had direct and immediate benefits for foreigners. The most notable were the vastly improved opportunities for travel.

Before we left China toward the end of 1979, it was possible to visit most places in the country. Even the few notable exceptions, such as certain strategically sensitive coastal provinces, were open to Overseas Chinese visiting relatives, and it appeared likely that these places too would be within an ordinary foreigner's reach before long. In the *Globe and Mail* bureau files, there is a stack of paper representing nearly two decades of formal requests for travel by various correspondents. Each correspondent had made a carbon copy of the request, directed to the Information Department of the Foreign Ministry, and some had noted the results at the bottom of the page. Requests to go to Tibet, Sichuan, Mongolia or even Shanghai were never even acknowledged. During part of the Cultural Revolution, it was not possible merely to drive the few miles to the Ming tombs or the Great Wall, on the outskirts of the city.

In my time, I got to all the places I wanted to see. I was able to climb some of the fabulous holy mountains of China, sail down the Yangtze River, snoop around the Potala Palace in Lhasa, cavort with Chinese vacationers on the beaches of Qingdao (pronounced "ching-dao") and drive all the way to the port city of Tianjin. It became possible to see China and its diversity in a way none of my predecessors would have ever dreamed. And in this unparalleled situation, I came to see that journalists were the luckiest foreigners in Peking. We were free agents—not allied to governments, as were the diplomats, or Chinese institutions, as were the students and the small group of "foreign experts" who worked in China under contract to the government, usually as translators or teachers. We were not bound by rigid protocol or the restraints of being official guests, and a whole remarkable country was beginning to open up before us.

In Peking itself, one learned to live, without too much difficulty, with the unspoken barriers that prevented meaningful contact with Chinese people. The daily workload, which wasn't onerous for the first year, and the pattern of travel and ghetto social life filled out the day amiably enough. When the spring air was still crisp, we would drive out to the old Summer Palace—not the famous Summer Palace built by the Dowager Empress, complete with a marble boat, but its predecessor, which had been sacked by invading foreign troops in the nineteenth century—and take brisk walks amid fabulous ruins and carefully tilled fields. When the sun bore down with all the ferocity of a Peking summer, we partook of lavish picnics in the cool shadows of an unrestored Ming tomb where few tourists ventured and only the local crickets kept us company. In winter, the skating at the new Summer Palace provided the kind of wild and wonderful locale that a fantasist like Coleridge might have conjured up. On the streets and in the parks the natives were not only friendly, but getting friendlier. Official guides no longer felt duty-bound to screech propaganda at you. They could even be very funny. When my mother arrived to stay with us for a while, I arranged a morning's outing for her to a well-known farming commune that most foreigners visit. She went off on her own with the China Travel Service guide, who was the soul of genuine courtesy and assistance. After the commune leader had made his standard introduction about the work and life of the peasants under his charge, my mother turned to the guide and said, "He did that very well, don't you think?"

The guide smiled. "He should," he said, "he's been doing exactly the same thing for thirty years."

In fact, my mother had a better perspective on the rapidly changing atmosphere at the time than I did, bogged down as I was by the specifics of day-to-day life and the undeniable evidence I was collecting about bureaucratic intransigence and ideological constraints. Although she had never before been near Asia, my mother set out at sixty-seven with the enthusiasm of an eighteen-year-old. It took her about two minutes to get her bearings, and before long she insisted that she wanted to go about the city on her own, although the only Chinese she seemed to retain with real fluency was *"Ni hao?"*—the simplest of greetings.

She got tremendous mileage out of that *"Ni hao?"* and once managed to persuade some youths to take her out on a rowboat in Bei Hai Park. On another occasion, she stood still in her tracks, transfixed in horror at the sight of some older women whose feet were still bound, a vivid reminder that some of the worst aspects of feudal China were less than a lifetime away. (Although the hideous practice of keeping women's feet unnaturally small had been outlawed a half century before, my mother hadn't realized that victims of the ancient practice can still be seen hobbling around the country.) Chinese people responded to her unbridled enthusiasm with humor and affection, as well as an openness I had not seen before. Shortly before she left us, I drove her out to the nearby countryside at dusk as hundreds of people of both sexes and all ages were slowly cycling their way home after work. Her head darted in all directions as she tried to take in the faces as they passed by, and suddenly there were tears pouring down her face. She and I are given to somewhat extravagant emotions anyway, but I knew what had overtaken her: the vastness of the country and the endurance of the people. Something that had only been imagined abstractly was now a reality streaming past her. The guilelessness and kindness with which she had been treated, together with the special courtesies generally accorded to older people throughout China, overwhelmed her at this darkening moment. Her visit confirmed in me something I had been slow to learn. I had been warned by all the experts to assimilate the enormous differences and cultural contrasts between ourselves and the Chinese people before attempting to find any common ground. I now knew this was exactly wrong, and the reverse was the correct order: the ties that bind us all together mean more than any barriers. Even though contact was difficult, I became more and more obsessed with trying to reach out wherever I could. I found myself devouring, rather than merely studying, every book I could get on China from the libraries at the various embassies or the bookstores in Hong Kong.

In those days before I had real Chinese friends, my closest allies and companions were unknown authors in unknown places. I had only their books, but they fired both my imagination and my anticipation. I rediscovered Simon Leys, whose *Chinese Shadows* had seemed so corrosive and bitter before I arrived. It was as if I had never read it at all. The book was utterly transformed, and I saw his passion for the Chinese condition in all the righteous anger with which he flailed away at the totalitarian regime that humiliated a great people. By this time, the government itself was acknowledging many of the iniquities Simon Leys had castigated seven years before, and part of the pleasure of the rereading was to check off those things which had already changed for the better. In another book, *Broken Images,* he had examined a celebrated work by China's most famous writer of the century: *The True Story of Ah Q* by Lu Xun (pronounced "lu-shun"). In his conclusion, Leys spoke right to the heart of a still-confused journalist in the foreigners' ghetto:

> In getting to know Ah Q, those Western readers for whom China is most alien will discover a valuable fact that remains obdurately hidden from the Yellow Peril theorists and from the apostles of Red China: this fact is that the Chinese too are human, or to put it another way, we are all Chinese.

The Death of Woman Wang by the Anglo-American historian Jonathan Spence was another revelation. On the basis of scholarly research into peasant conditions during an early reign of the Qing (pronounced "ching") Dynasty, Spence had done something radical and controversial. He had entered the mind of an eighteenth-century Chinese peasant woman who actually existed and dared to speak directly for her and through her. It got him a bit of abuse from his academic colleagues, but I understood *exactly* what he was about. At that time I knew that only a conspicuous act of imagination would ever get me over all those damned walls down the back lanes of Peking or the barriers in the people's minds. Of course, I couldn't write about this in dispatches to my newspaper, but I had been forced by circumstances to consider the contrast between life in China as presented by the New China News Agency, Xinhua, and the hints and glimpses of something quite different that I kept stumbling across. Official Chinese history read a bit like Xinhua news releases, and too many respectable historians kept referring me to the written record of the emperor's courtiers to prove the "inalienable difference between the Chinese and ourselves." Like Spence, I longed to get beyond both official and conventional accounts.

I was a sucker for two old potboilers—Edgar Snow's *Red Star Over China* and Pearl Buck's *The Good Earth.* Both of these are classics, but at the time they convinced me that it was not only possible for a foreigner to find a kind of union with the Chinese experience; it was probably imperative to do so if one was ever to come to any real understanding. Snow's reportage held out the hope that there was a hard core of decency and integrity at the roots of the Chinese Communist movement which could mitigate its evils, while *The Good Earth* glows with a love of things Chinese that transcends the novel's most sentimental moments. These books served me better in China than all the government studies and learned academic analyses I forced myself to plow through. From these latter, I discerned possible ways of analyzing political intrigues in China, and the means by which the masses are divided into workers and peasants, with further subdivision by class origin, food rations and overall "quality of life." But from Pearl Buck I learned of the old Chinese saying "Under heaven, all are one." This wisdom seemed to me inestimably more valuable.

5

Officials
and Bureaucrats

Tourists and foreign residents who have visited or lived in China during the past thirty years may not have been able to probe very deeply beneath the surface of life there, but they did get a good opportunity to study one of the abiding realities of the country—the world of bureaucrats and officials. The Chinese invented the bureaucracy over two thousand years ago, and from time to time you almost get the impression that it is the perfect manifestation of the national will. Life for Chinese and foreigners alike is hedged in by visas, permits, requests and any number of other official embell-ishments the government can dream up. The vastness of a bureauc-racy that orders the lives of a billion people can scarcely be imag-ined. In the West, where advanced technology has given governments the data bank and other impersonal systems to keep tab on citizens, the intrusion of bureaucracy is streamlined and sophisticated. In China, where the Communists have inherited his-torical bureaucratic conditions, officials are omnipresent, while the backwardness of communications simply reinforces the system.

One becomes aware of this intricate process from the first day of arrival. Let's say, as a foreign resident, you want to make a trip to Shanghai. If you are a journalist, you must first apply for permission to the Information Department of the Foreign Ministry. You do this in a formal letter, which is hand-delivered to the Ministry, and then you wait to see what the answer will be. If you have made certain special requests, such as a visit to a hospital or a factory, officials at the Foreign Ministry must phone down to Shanghai to check things out. China was the first Communist country I had ever visited, and in my naiveté I had supposed that when the central authorities snapped their fingers, the whole country instantly saluted and did as it was bidden—or else. Nothing could be further from the truth; one of the reasons Mao felt compelled to have massive nationwide political campaigns was that his desires and orders were often swallowed up by the bureaucracy and never saw the light of day.

The primitive communication system plus the size of the bureaucracy enables local officials to carry on much as they want to, provided they observe certain guidelines, such as formal loyalty to the Communist Party. A network of allegiances and other ties within the bureaucracy, which ultimately works itself right up to the various state leaders, provides protection on most occasions from undue intrusion from the central government, thus permitting a considerable degree of local autonomy. This does not necessarily work for the benefit of the people, however, and the official press often tells stories of corrupt local officials who act in a fashion similar to that of the hated old warlords, those self-elevated Pooh-Bahs who bedeviled Chinese politics for decades during the first half of this century.

Once the Foreign Ministry man had secured the necessary assistance of his Shanghai counterpart, I would be told that I could proceed to Shanghai. That sounds simple enough, but the process required the following steps: filling out an application to the Peking Public Security Bureau requesting permission to leave the city and specifying precisely the number of days I would be away and the places I was visiting; surrendering my Peking resident's passport for the duration of the trip; a PSB check with the Foreign Ministry to see if I did indeed have its permission; collecting my PSB travel pass. With this new pass in my possession, I could then apply to the China Travel Service to get a train ticket and make a reservation at a Shanghai hotel; with my travel pass, my ticket and my Shanghai reservation chit, I was then actually able to go to the train station, where my travel pass would again be inspected and stamped by the police; upon arriving in Shanghai, I would have to surrender the travel pass to get it stamped by the Shanghai police, as well as handing over my reservation chit to the local China Travel Service agent, who had to square it with the hotel's records; in Shanghai, I would have to make formal application for a return ticket (which it was not possible to reserve or buy in Peking); before leaving Shanghai, I would have to submit the travel pass again for another stamp; upon arriving home in Peking, I had to surrender the pass to the police at the railway station, and the next day I, or the *Globe's* driver, would have to go down to the local police station and retrieve my resident's passport. After a year, one step in this process was dropped, and it represented a real breakthrough: upon arriving at the train station, I was no longer required to show the travel pass at the foreigners' police depot there. The bureaucracy had figured out that since it was impossible to purchase a ticket without the pass, this step was possibly redundant, and it took the extraordinarily innovative step of eliminating it. In typical fashion, there was no announcement. I discovered the new reality by presenting myself, as I had always done, at the police depot of the train station. A young official looked up at me with a quizzical look on his face.

"Would you stamp my pass?" I asked.

"Not necessary," he said matter-of-factly.

Silly ass, I thought. He doesn't know his own business. "Of course it's not necessary, but it's required." I was a little bit abrupt because the train was due to depart in two minutes.

"Not required. Not necessary."

He talked with all the authority and assurance of one who knew the regulations perfectly, but I discovered a few minutes later that the change had come only the day before.

A number of other little barriers were dropped during my stay in China, and I learned of each one in a similar fashion. If I had argued about the unnecessary stupidity of a certain regulation the day before it changed, I would have been met with uncomprehending looks—Who is this stupid foreigner who doesn't know what a regulation is? If I argued about the business the day after the regulation was dropped, I would be met with the same look—Who is this stupid foreigner who can't understand that the regulation doesn't exist anymore? The *sang-froid* of petty officials in China, oblivious to any reason or logic beyond regulations, is incredible. It took me a while to discover that there was, in fact, a great deal of sane method in their manner.

Much of Communist China's history has been taken up with political struggle. Bureaucrats, as the custodians of government regulations and the instruments of political power, are in the front lines of these ideological wrangles. The action of today could be transformed into the noose of tomorrow, and it is a brave bureaucrat indeed who would care to buck such an all-encompassing rule of social law. Following regulations right down to the least detail offered the only conceivable protection, and even this wasn't good enough sometimes, when a new ideological faction in power announced that certain regulations were part of a sinister black line created to oppose Mao Tsetung Thought.

This sure knowledge that political fortunes change, ingrained into the bureaucracy as the single unchangeable reality, is a source of major concern for the government that succeeded Mao. It is a reality that works its way throughout Chinese society and lies behind all the official assurances that the days of national political struggles and campaigns are over. It will take many years of "Unity and Stability," however, before most Chinese people will believe it. Since the Chinese Government is convinced it does not have many years to effect major changes that will improve China and repair the damage left by the Cultural Revolution and its aftermath, there is a tone of almost hysterical urgency behind the exhortations to abandon caution and work "full out" toward modernizing the country.

Mao discovered to his chagrin that when the dust had settled after two years of Cultural Revolution anarchy, the lower and middle ranks of the bureaucracy not only had accommodated themselves to the new situation, but were as firmly entrenched as they had ever been. Because Mao had reasserted his own power, which had been dwindling, the bureaucracy was nominally more loyal to him than it had been before, but this could hardly have given him much confidence. With his death and the purge of the Gang of Four, the same bureaucracy made its necessary adjustments of loyalty and surface support and quickly returned once again to its familiar and favorite occupation—obduracy.

Within this framework, though, people are still people, and I was always impressed by the variety of types I kept meeting in the official bureaucracy. In Shanghai, with the China Travel Service, I met extreme examples at either end of the bureaucratic spectrum. The Service itself is an interesting institution and is a continuation of a system conceived by the old Guomindang Government of Chiang Kaishek, which the Communists appropriated.

The Guomindang felt that no important foreigner should travel in China unescorted. This was partly from genuine concern for foreigners who couldn't speak the language and would be at a total loss as to what to do. More importantly, it was a way of keeping tabs on foreigners, wherever they were, as well as making sure they didn't have any contact with ordinary Chinese citizens, who might give a different picture of life from the officially prescribed version.

This struck the Communists as eminently sensible, and they incorporated the China Travel Service whole, expanding its role to include all foreigners. Until the first massive tourist invasion in 1978, the Service was easily able to cope with the relatively few foreigners who were given permission to come to China. The government's official attitude was that anyone who had received permission to come to China was a "foreign friend" and had to be treated as a "guest" rather than an itinerant tourist. Such visits were also an occasion to sell the concepts of New China; consequently, the Service guides and officials were specially chosen and trained with this end in mind. They are an important, if indirect, arm of the propaganda department and have had a great deal to do with the image China has abroad.

The first official guide I had in Shanghai had had his brain transformed into chick-peas. He was a classic example of an official whose life had been so traumatized by political indoctrination that he could hardly take a breath without considering its ideological implications. He carried a little plastic-mesh bag with him at all times which contained two books—both of them editions of *Quotations from Chairman Mao Tsetung,* an English version and the original Chinese edition. Every inquiry I made, no matter how inconsequential, left him agonized as he considered what the correct response should be. At any spare or quiet moment, he would pull out the *Quotations* and mumble incantations to himself. I was new in China still and found this both comical and annoying in equal proportions: comical because it was so unreal, and annoying because I couldn't get any straight answers. The officials at the Information Department in Peking were quite straightforward as far as I could tell, and it was possible to have sensible, if formal, conversations with them. But this clown was sweating and stuttering to such an extent that I eventually realized he was on the verge of a nervous breakdown. And no wonder! He had obviously bought every ideo-logical trinket of the Mao cult, from perpetual class struggle to the infallibility of Mao's *Quotations.* Now things had changed abruptly again, and all his props were being pulled away. Events were occur-ring in the country that only a few months before had been unthink-able, and people like him who wrapped themselves in Maoist or-thodoxy were under attack.

Also, it was his job to escort members of the foreign media around Shanghai, and this had proved in the past to be a very dangerous business. When an Italian filmmaker came to China in the early seventies to make a major documentary, he too had had official escorts. When the government saw the final result, it was horrified: here was a vision of China as it really was, uncluttered by socialist reality, which is supposed to show what should be rather than what is. All the poor lower minions who had accompanied the director's tour came in for sharp criticism and were reassigned to menial jobs. So while my guide's tremulous nature was not typical, it was understandable.

Most guides are not nearly so caught out at emotional extremi-ties. Some of them can be remarkably dictatorial and abrupt, partic-ularly with inexperienced tourists, but others can be the soul of kindness and courtesy. As the number of tourists increased during my stay and as repercussions of all sorts diminished, some of them blossomed into real human beings who felt no need to push propa-ganda and could do something that had been quite unthinkable only a short time before: ask questions.

Knowledgeable travelers in China are usually outfitted with the old *Nagel's Guide Book,* which, while it has not been revised since 1966, still contains the best compendium of facts on China and Chinese culture to be found in one book. One of the most excruciat-ing experiences you could have was to be saddled with a guide who was not only ignorant about the site you were visiting, but also disinclined to make any effort to gain the accurate information. He knew what he had been told and that was all he was going to say. In time, though, some guides became genuinely appalled by their own ignorance and began asking foreigners who seemed to know what they were doing—or who had a copy of *Nagel's*—for different accounts. When my mother visited Datung, site of some splendid archeological wonders, she had just such a guide, a young woman who had not closed off her mind and was willing to learn. My mother asked her about some religious shrine they had seen and got an interesting answer.

"I just don't know," said the guide. "We know very little about such things. My grandmother knows a great deal about Buddhism and tried to tell us when we were young. But we scoffed at her, and during the Cultural Revolution we repeatedly lectured her about her superstitions and her concern about such silly thoughts. And now I would like to know about these things which are a part of my country's history, but my grandmother won't speak of them. She told me that since we were so smart and knew everything, we could find out for ourselves. I feel very badly about this, and not only because we used to be so cruel to our grandmother. I think it is very worng not to know about religion and history in your own country."

It was in Shanghai, nearly a year after the first trip, that I noticed the change most dramatically. I was steeled against another chick-pea guide, but instead got a real person, who impressed me with his confidence and open mind. There had been recent demonstrations in Shanghai, where tens of thousands of young people had protested their living conditions. During the Cultural Revolution, they had been shipped out to the countryside with the promise that eventually they could return. The government had reneged on the promise, and young people had begun sneaking back into the cities. Getting home wasn't so difficult, but surviving was another matter. Because every citizen in China belongs to some sort of controlling Unit, these returned youths found themselves in Shanghai and other cities without the right to work or to receive food rations. Such privileges were obtainable only from their Units back in the countryside. If they had families in the city, they could rely on handouts, but it was with the knowledge that they were bringing tremendous hardship on their parents and relatives. Protesting against this situation, they had taken to writing wall posters, as well as marching on municipal-authority offices. In Shanghai, according to the official press, these marches had got out to hand.

The first chance I had, I tried to get down to Shanghai to investigate the matter with the help of a few contacts I had managed to make on the previous trip. I had a little plan conceived for ditching the government guide, but to my inordinate surprise, almost the first thing he said was "I suppose you've heard about the problems here?"

After that for an opening, he proceeded to offer a realistic account of the situation, explaining that Shanghai had dispatched more than a million young people to the countryside during the late sixties alone. One of those so dispatched was his sister, and she had returned eight months before and was living with their parents. "Fortunately," he said, "her case was recently resolved and she has been assigned a job here. We are all terribly relieved, although the overall problem is still immense. You have no idea of the numbers involved, and neither does the municipal government, which is just beginning to try to work things out. They are trying one plan I've heard of. If a father or mother at a factory is prepared to retire, his or her old position at work can be filled by a son or daughter. I don't think this is a very good idea for the long term, though. It doesn't really solve the problem, and it could have a terrible effect on production, because the young people don't know how to do the jobs their parents did. But I think the government is trying."

The guide also revealed where the wall-poster wall was and told me that if I walked along the famous Bund by the waterfront for long enough, I would be sure to meet some young people who could tell me more about the situation. I already knew about the potential of the Bund, but I was flabbergasted to be told. Such a conversation would have been completely unthinkable six months before. As far as I was concerned, the result of such candor made me much more sympathetic to the problems faced by the government than I had ever intended to be. I had come to Shanghai to scratch around for a few clues, and because I thought the information would be hard to get, I could be sure the government didn't want me to find out. Inevitably this affects both the style and the tone of one's reports: if you are constantly forced to be a detective, then you are equally forced to come up with suspicions and accusations. Candor and honesty are always disarming, and I was able to write an account of the unemployed-youth crisis in Shanghai that gave some genuine dimension to the problem and showed a government struggling to come up with a solution.

This second Shanghai guide was also not typical, but one could see that the attitude of the China Travel Service was improving noticeably in certain areas. It also worsened in others. I had my gripes with the Service, but the one thing I counted on was that it stuck by foreign travelers once it had agreed to let them travel. I didn't regard the Service as saintly, but like many foreign residents,

I had no qualms whatsoever in telling our private guests that they could travel reliably around the country with the assistance of the Service guides: officious or courteous, they were all responsible. I was disabused of this comfortable theory shortly before departing China. Two guests we had invited to Peking wanted to take the famous boat trip down the Yangtze River from Sichuan province's interior to the city of Wuhan. I couldn't accompany them, because I was about to set off for Tibet, but I assured them they would be in reliable hands. It was with some horror that I later discovered what happened to them.

In Chongqing (pronounced "chong-ching") they fell into the clutches of two very chummy but unhelpful guides. Inexperienced and alone, my two women friends made their booking for the Yangtze River boat trip and were given a short trip around the town. Later in the evening, however, the guides came by and asked them to pay for all the expenses. The elder of the two, who was nearly sixty, realized that she was short of cash and offered a traveler's check. This caused a great deal of commotion, despite the fact that traveler's checks are commonly used now and easily changed by tourists at Chinese hotels. The guides convinced the older woman that she would have to come with them a considerable distance and change the check at a special bank, which would be opened in her honor.

With my assurance that no trouble would befall her in the hands of the China Travel Service, off she went on a wild taxi ride that lasted half an hour. She was led into a dark compound and had no idea on earth where she was. Down a corridor and up two flights of stairs, she walked into a room where several men were milling about. She sat down and had started signing a couple of traveler's checks when one of the guides said, "You want some nightlife?"

My friend wasn't quite sure what had been said. "What?" she asked.

"Nightlife. You want some nightlife?"

Now, no city in China has been known for its hot spots since the Communists took over, and certainly not Chongqing, the former wartime capital of Chiang Kaishek. My friend couldn't figure out what the guide was getting at and asked that the word be written down. Sure enough, "nightlife" was laboriously spelled out. At that point, a tall, thickset man came out of the background and approached my confused friend. He looked at the woman and said, in English, "Sex." The money she had exchanged was in her hand, and the man kept looking at it and then at her, and she became terribly frightened.

"No, not at all. We must go home. Now. Let's go."

She picked up her bag and raced down the stairs and through the corridor. Outside, the taxi had gone. The guides returned, and my friend paced nervously up and down. Ten minutes later the car came, and she made it home.

The next morning, the two travelers were deposited at the boat dock and the guides fled, which was strictly against the regulations, because all China Travel Service guides are required to remain with travelers until the moment when the train or airplane or boat actually departs. My friends soon found out the reason for the hasty exit: their passage had been incorrectly booked and they were billeted in steerage bunk rooms, not the tourist-class section. Curiously, this was an experience I personally would have given a lot to have, because it is extremely difficult to travel in the company of ordinary Chinese. But my friends weren't journalists or accustomed to China, and their fear and sense of betrayal increased. Because of this and a few other incidents, I do not recommend the China Travel Service to people with quite the same amount of trust as I did before.

We were to find the same variety and complexity of officials in all areas of China and all aspects of work. The ones I saw the most, though, worked at the Information Department. I never got to know much about their personal lives, but like all journalists in Peking, past and present, I had ample experience with their working style. Because we dealt with them so regularly and they constituted our principal channel into the government, journalists have always subconsciously elevated the Information Department to quite a high level. In fact it is a relatively lowly office within the Foreign Ministry, and much plagued by exasperated foreigners who don't really understand official China, as well as equally exasperated Chinese officials who haven't the least conception of how the Western press works.

For me, and for a number of my predecessors, the symbol of the Information Department was Chi Ming-tsung. (I still can't bring myself to use the new Pinyin spelling for his name—Qi Mingcong —because I wrote to him so often, with so many official requests, that the old spelling is implanted in my brain as securely as Mao

Tsetung, which should be spelled Mao Zedong.) Mr. Chi was not even the head of the department and never would be, but he had been around a long time. His career can be traced, in part, through the experiences of other journalists based in Peking. For example, he makes a cold and forbidding appearance in Colin McCullough's book *Stranger in China.* McCullough was the *Globe*'s fourth correspondent in Peking, and the Mr. Chi he knew was as sinister and unrevealing as the most inscrutable official in a Manchu court. Far more dramatically, he appears as a central figure in Anthony Grey's book *Hostage in Peking.* Grey was the Reuters China correspondent during the opening blast of the Cultural Revolution. Through no fault or sin of his own, he was placed under house arrest for two brutal and humiliating years as the Chinese and the British rattled sabers over problems in Hong Kong. Since the British had imprisoned several Communist journalists in the Crown Colony, the Chinese retaliated by attacking Grey, the only British journalist working in the country.

Thanks to Grey's hair-raising account of his ordeal in Peking, a whole body of myth has arisen about Mr. Chi. Grey's little cat, called Ming-ming, was strangled by wire in front of him one terrible night in 1967, and the correspondent was physically abused and surrounded by jeering Red Guards in a notorious "circle of hate." The perpetrators were Red Guards; this is clearly stated in the book. But because Mr. Chi was the official handling the case and was prominent in all dealings with foreign journalists—then as in my time—it is popularly believed that it was he who personally did little Ming-ming in. Hence his nickname to this day: the Strangler. (It amused me to discover later on that the Information Department officials had funny nicknames for all the correspondents, although I never discovered what they were, much to my annoyance.)

Mr. Chi, a vegetarian, was once a student in Britain and later worked at the Chinese Embassy in London, where he picked up a West End accent that would have put Bertie Wooster to shame. He dresses simply but impeccably in the standard cadre's, or official's, suit with the closed-neck collar, and his style with journalists during my stay in China could be described as forced affability. He was, of course, much more than the sum of such trivia, but it took me a while to discover this. When I first came to Peking and began dealing extensively with Mr. Chi, he gave me the shivers. Grey's account, together with Mr. Chi's own initial perfunctory and off-putting mannerisms, which made some of us feel we were being treated as naughty children, were distressing in the extreme. I used to have to work up my courage just to dial him at the office. By the end, however, I had quite a bit of sympathy for him.

A Canadian broadcast journalist, Betty Kennedy, visited China in 1973 and told me she had had a curious conversation with Mr. Chi in which she asked him what he would have wanted to be had he not become an official. Mrs. Kennedy said Mr. Chi looked at her very carefully for a moment and then answered abruptly, "A scholar." Delighted at this crack in an otherwise impervious countenance, she pushed on and asked him if he had had any choice in his career. "Oh, Mrs. Kennedy," he said, "there is never any question of choice. It doesn't exist."

Something must have happened to Mr. Chi between Grey's house arrest and the time Mrs. Kennedy saw him, but I was never able to find out what it was. A British diplomat who knew Mr. Chi in the mid-sixties and returned to Peking for a second posting in my time said he had never seen such a change in a human being in the short space of ten years. The Chi of 1967 was confident, cultured and supremely self-assured; the Chi of 1977 had developed an idiosyncratic nervousness, along with a bit of a stutter, that made many people around him nervous as well. Somehow, these things made him seem a little bit more human.

Over the years, Mr. Chi has been for journalists the embodiment of the official government line of the day. In this, he may well be the perfect official. If the government was being nasty and uncommunicative, Mr. Chi was nasty and uncommunicative. If the government was being sly and devious, Mr. Chi was sly and devious. And when I was in Peking, as ideological pressures lessened, there were few people more amenable to progressive suggestions and good talk than Chi Ming-tsung. He has done the Party's bidding faithfully for decades, and while this has never brought him high promotion, his indispensability in dealing with us meant that a great deal of trust had been placed on his shoulders. In 1980 the Foreign Ministry assigned him to its Dublin Embassy, an incongruous reward for his services.

This picture may seem condescending, but it is not really intended to be. There are many officials of the middle rank like Mr. Chi who are not as amenable to change as he is. Like the cadres in

George Orwell's *1984,* Communist Party officials in China are subject to a special set of regulations that is above what ordinary citizens have to worry about. These regulations are incorporated under the general heading of "Party Discipline"—the device used to purge and incarcerate the Gang of Four—so that officials' lives can be more effectively and rigidly controlled than those of the masses. No matter how much the Party argues that the days of serious ideological wrangles are over, the implicit threat of "Party Discipline" will remain; this is in the very nature of any totalitarian bureaucracy. Officials, no less than ordinary citizens, bide their time to see if the Party is really serious about bringing more "democracy" to all levels of national life. It will take more than just a few years of relative calm to prove the case.

6

Model Heroes, Model Lives

In 1975, a young American named Orville Schell managed to spend several months working alongside Chinese at the Shanghai Electrical Machinery Factory. The experience, as you might expect, was a major event in Schell's life, and afterward he tried to set down the things he had learned. He was particularly keen to establish the reasons why the Chinese were different from us, and in one of his essays ("Private Life in a Public Culture"), he examined the role of heroes in American and Chinese culture:

> Singular heroes hold a deep fascination for [Americans]. There is an attraction to the maverick, even the misfit, that I think is perplexing for the Chinese. Even in China, Americans insistently probe for information about these elements of society, elements that the Chinese clearly view as aberrant.
>
> Repeated and fervent questions by Americans to their Chinese hosts about homosexuality, the mentally ill, slow learners, juvenile delinquents, criminals, premarital sex, and artistic renegades attest to our abiding fascination with deviance; with individuals who spurn the pre-cut patterns. These are our heroes. But they are not the Chinese heroes, who tend to be cast in the mold of the youth hero Lei Feng.
>
> Born a poor peasant in 1939, enduring a life of oppression, but

ultimately joining the army and being admitted to what one Chinese account refers to as the "Glorious Communist Party," Lei Feng became a model of revolutionary commitment in the fifties and sixties. It would be safe to say that there is almost no one in China unfamiliar with the story of Lei Feng's model life. His rectitude and squareness would surely make him a laughing stock of most American teenagers. No sex, drugs, rebellion, or treason for Lei Feng, who spent his years earnestly "serving the people" until he was felled by a telephone pole in an untimely accident. Lei Feng was youth dedicated to the people, not his own self-expression or welfare.

This account has rather a nice ring to it and neatly exemplifies the fundamental gulf Americans and Chinese are supposed to acknowledge before they can have any understanding of each other. Nor is it as gauche as similar perceptions by such people as the film actress Shirley MacLaine. Miss MacLaine met a former nuclear physicist on a farming commune who told her that growing tomatoes and cabbages was just as important as the work he used to do in a laboratory. How we want to believe these things! Schell and MacLaine were both in China at the end of an evil epoch; the Chinese whom they had spoken to, though not evil themselves, had been forced to accommodate themselves to and reflect the prevailing ideology, especially when foreigners were around.

The question of heroes and model citizens, which Schell raises, is indicative of the kind of thinking that has bedeviled an understanding of China for thirty years. Until very recently, it had seemed that the Communist Party had encouraged all the inaccuracy for its own purposes. Schell could not have known it at the time, but Lei Feng—the blameless youth who died "serving the people"—is also a laughingstock among many Chinese youths, for the simplest of reasons: he never existed, at least not in the form served up by the Party.

Lei Feng is an invention of the propaganda department. Perhaps there was someone once, even with the same name, who actually existed and did good deeds. There's no reason on earth why he couldn't have existed: goodness and selflessness may be rare, but they are nevertheless universal traits. But the Lei Feng all Chinese people know stretches credulity to special dimensions. To present a national model hero in a country with primitive communications, it was necessary to mount propaganda campaigns that left rather messy details unexplained. How was it that several separate exhibitions of Lei Feng artifacts, which were touring the country simultaneously, all managed to have the original, handwritten copy of his simple, eloquent diary on display? We are told this blameless youth lived a life of perfect anonymity until his "untimely accident," when his friends took stock of his selflessness and made him a Communist saint. Despite this obscurity, someone had fortunately managed to take a set of twelve photographs, of quite exceptional professional quality, showing him at his everyday anonymous work: sewing on the button of a friend's jacket; standing on lonely guard duty in the bitter cold; making dinner for all his chums; teaching a young recruit how to study Mao Tsetung Thought; dutifully writing letters to his family. The photographs were plastered all over China and can be purchased in a handy postcard packet.

Lei Feng was as pure an example of "socialist realism" as one could find in China. That he didn't exist is irrelevant. The important thing is that the Party decided he should have existed, and in China that was sufficient to produce a contemporary miracle analogous to the Immaculate Conception. Lei Feng was the Party's ideal of what young people should be like and, perhaps, also an indication of what they are not like.

Any Chinese I ever spoke to outside of official occasions always snorted about Lei Feng. During our time in China, the Communist Party mounted a massive, if inconsistent, campaign to "Search Truth from Facts" and "Emancipate the Mind." Although strict boundaries were imposed on "the emancipation" (it was not permissible to question the leading role of the Communist Party, for example), the campaign did help a lot of Chinese abandon some of the more errant and perverse nonsense that had been served up with such conspicuous stupidity by the propaganda department. The Lei Feng Campaign had first been trotted out in the early sixties. During the opening years of the Cultural Revolution, when young people were being urged to rebel, the propagandists simply dropped him by the wayside, and no one thought it a terrible shame. With the need for order, and particularly following the purge of the Gang of Four, Lei Feng was resurrected. However, a generation of Chinese who had seen through this hollow hero ignored the latest efforts, and Lei Feng was one of the first casualties of the efforts to search for truth among facts.

Life everywhere is perverse, sadly, and early in 1980 the government felt the need to give Lei Feng another go. After all, there was a new and younger generation coming up who had not been poisoned by the insight gleaned from thirty years of political intrigue. In the intervening period, when Lei Feng was temporarily dead, a Chinese acquaintance described in quite amusing terms an apocryphal story of how the progaganda department was striving "night and day" to create a new Lei Feng who would do battle for the current ideological line. His diary would have to be rewritten, of course. This time, though, his deepest inner thoughts would reveal someone with grave doubts about the direction being taken by a certain political cadre in his Unit who kept spouting the words of Chairman Mao without looking at their context. Lei Feng II had also conceived of a system to speed up the cleaning of dishes in the army mess hall, but was thwarted from introducing this simple improvement by the opposition of that same sinister cadre.

The diary, as reconstructed by my friend, would have such lines as "Only when the great masses of the Chinese people learn to work wholeheartedly to increase production will their lot improve. The masses must seriously examine those comrades who try to divert their revolutionary commitment to progress with half-baked political thoughts and dubious ideology. These matters are plain facts and lead to inescapable truth which cannot be altered."

Lei Feng II would be photographed at his Unit's poster wall, and it would be carefully pointed out that his criticisms were kept for "internal discussion." Other photographs would show him helping a smiling old peasant on the way to a free market, or possibly receiving an extra two yuan on payday as his bonus for working full out at his job.

Shortly after I heard this scenario, the propaganda department did one better and came up with a model hero for the times who was not dissimilar to Lei Feng II. This is not a matter entirely for jest. The Communist Party knows that if it doesn't produce model heroes, the people might well do the unthinkable and come up with their own.

Schell's thesis that the Chinese do not identify with loners and misfits is quite amazing when you consider that the country was mobilized to revolt and then ruled by one of the greatest loners and misfits the world has ever seen. Mao Tsetung was the ultimate antithesis to Lei Feng: someone who went his own way regardless of what the majority felt, who resisted orderly compromise if it ran counter to his own ultimate purposes, and yet who would deal with the devil—whether it was Chiang Kaishek in the forties or Richard Nixon in the seventies—if it served those same purposes. When he issued the order to "bombard the headquarters" in 1966 and thereby launched the Cultural Revolution, he knew from the depths of his soul that he was appealing to a common aspiration among young people to rebel. That such things could also come from a tyrant who sought to impose his own will on everyone and everything is not contradictory; it is in the nature of human complexity.

Accepting this reality, the propaganda department sought very hard to come up with a contemporary model hero. There are certain constant ground rules in this game, of which the most important is that the hero be dead, for obvious reasons. And thus was born, or rather born again, a woman named Zhang Zhixin (pronounced "zher-shin"). Zhang came straight from the propaganda department's own bureau in Liaoning province, where she worked before her troubles commenced during the reign of Lin Biao and the Gang of Four. Her story began appearing in national newspapers in the first half of 1979 and was tied to the campaign to discredit the Gang of Four. In addition, she is to serve as a model of questioning intelligence who is nevertheless utterly devoted to the cause of the Communist Party.

Zhang probably existed, and the propaganda department was proud to be able to display photographs of her husband and children, who are still living. Her sin was to question the personality cult surrounding Mao during the Cultural Revolution, which the propagandists carefully point out was forced on the reluctant chairman by the nefarious Lin Biao. Because her work included cultural considerations, she is also supposed to have questioned the usefulness of the horrid model operas Jiang Qing supported. Zhang expressed her reservations and criticisms in private sessions between fellow Party members—the correct way—but sinister forces were on the loose, and she was arrested as a counterrevolutionary and traitor in 1969. Successive attempts to make her recant proved fruitless, and she was executed in the mid-seventies.

That is the official line, and the story was told with such pungency in the press that it struck home to many Chinese with considerable force. Somebody or some institution backed up the official version by spreading little details about her execution that had enormous appeal among young people, with their strong affection for martyrs who come to a bloody end. The details probably originated from the propaganda department, because very few officials would have had access to the original account. According to this street talk, Zhang would not stop shouting "Long Live Chairman Mao! Long Live the Communist Party!" on the execution ground, and so her throat was cut before she was shot in order that the traitor would not die saying such things.

As a model of constancy, loyalty and rational thinking, Zhang is a considerable improvement over the unbelievable Lei Feng. The basic outline of her life may well be true, but the important thing here is that in contrast to their reception of the Lei Feng Campaign, people believed it was true. At the beginning of the campaign, it seemed so real it nearly backfired. Just as most foreigners were ignorant of the widespread corruption and tyranny that settled in on China, many Chinese citizens who distanced themselves from the political fray as far as they could were also ignorant, or chose to be ignorant. Indeed, a lot of good people earnestly tried to live up to the precepts of the presiding ideology. Zhang's tale was a confirmation of the worst things they had heard or imagined. The details of her prison life were so graphic that they reminded readers of fictional heroines who had withstood the tortures of Guomindang prisons in prerevolutionary days, and they could detect no differences in the method or the purpose of the business. Among some Chinese, the saga of Zhang Zhixin did more to shake their confidence in the Communist Party than all the "counterrevolutionary" posters that ever went up on Xidan Democracy Wall. Generally, though, the campaign can be described as a success because it was the first open admission by the Party as to how bad things had been. Acknowledging the known is tremendously cathartic.

In a society that ordains model heroes, it is not very surprising to discover that ordinary citizens are expected to measure up to the models. The thrust of political meetings that most Chinese people have to attend (with a regularity that excites the envy of Western Christian clerics) is emulation. And the best way to see how this emulation is worked out is to go on official tours of China in which all Chinese participants know—or are supposed to know—their roles. When Shirley MacLaine talked to the former nuclear physicist, he knew what to say; it wasn't what he believed, but he knew what he had to do. That is an extreme example, of course, and there were many people who believed and tried to practice the gospel of the day as it was preached to them. For the most part, the Chinese people whom foreign tourists and journalists got to meet before 1978 were model citizens. This does not make them subhumans or automatons, or even necessarily insincere, but it is very important when traveling in China to examine whatever political line is being currently pushed and then make an evaluation of the things you are told.

In reading innumerable accounts written by foreign visitors to China over the past thirty years, it is positively amazing to discover that the particular insights they offer into the Chinese mentality coincide almost exactly with the particular political campaigns that were being waged. This does not mean that all the insights were wrong. Much of my journalistic output was a reflection of a period in China's history when the propagandists were calling for reexamination and frank admission of past errors. But as any intelligent Chinese does, usually in private, it is necessary to bring in a measure of critical objectivity. In Canton a few years ago, three young men examined the campaign to discredit Lin Biao. They agreed heartily with the broad consensus that Lin was an ogre, but they went one step further and questioned the nature of the system that had allowed Lin Biao to become a "chosen successor" to Mao without any reference to the wishes of the masses. That got them labeled counterrevolutionary and landed them in prison. Although they were freed after the Gang of Four fell, it wasn't for some time, despite the fact that they had called for everything the new government was trying to bring about.

The group—known by the collective name of Li Yizhe—made two mistakes: they had gone public with their criticism by pasting up a wall poster on a main street in Canton, and they didn't become total martyrs by dying. Their actions come as close to living up to the model of Zhang Zhixin as you can find, but they will never be national heroes because they might go on questioning, and you can never tell what that might produce. For lesser mortals, it is simply necessary to get through life with as little political trouble as possible, so when foreign visitors come to a model factory or commune, you find an eagerness to display the qualities expected of them. On the other hand, it is not unheard of for someone to proffer some of his or her own opinions, especially these days when the state is not bearing down on people in the same heavy-handed way as in the past. In all my time in China, I never begrudged the visits to model places and the talks with model citizens. Not only could you find out a great deal by indirection; sometimes you even got the plain truth. At the very least, such visits provided a concrete conception of what the Communist Party hoped the country would be like one day, and this could be compared with other insights and information.

I have long since lost track of the number of factories, hospitals, schools and communes I visited in China. Most journalists resented going to all of them because of the way the visits were officially arranged, but when the government started opening the country and allowed me to travel to poorer areas, like Sichuan province or the Guangxi (pronounced "guang-she") Autonomous Region, it became possible to compare the models with more ordinary existence. This took a lot of the natural paranoia out of the official visits: if you had fixed in your mind a reasonably accurate picture of the poverty and backwardness still to be surmounted, model conditions gave you a clearer idea of the possible in China. You could even rejoice a little at the life of a farming commune outside Shanghai where a family of five had three large rooms, ample food and good services. Medical care was near at hand and free; local stores had a reasonable variety of goods; quite a number of young people— much higher than the national average—had made it through high school and into technical institutions and even university; wages, commune produce distribution and the earnings from small private plots left the peasants with relative affluence. No doubt there were frustrations, disagreements and other complexities to life that it was not possible to observe, but one knew this model was an attainable material goal which struggling peasants in much poorer parts of the country might reasonably expect to reach one day.

When a Westerner first arrives in Peking, the multitude of horse-drawn carts seems quaint and backward. After a visit to Sichuan, where so much cartage is done by human beings as beasts of labor, horses and mules seem like a breakthrough, and a small tractor is a positive miracle. The introductory talks from the commune leaders and the usually inconsequential little interviews with the carefully selected peasants never produce very much telling information, although some journalists were positively manic in carefully noting down such things as grain allotments and oil rations in each area they visited. In this way, they could compare the relative standards of living throughout the country.

This is undoubtedly important journalistic work, but I was far more interested in how people coped with what they had and how they related to life around them. In model communes and model factories around the country, conditions never varied very wildly. Thanks to heavy state subsidies, the peasants at the model commune I visited outside Lhasa in Tibet—which has very poor arable land —lived as well as those in the prosperous commune near Shanghai. Of course, they didn't have access to the same quantity of manufactured goods, but I couldn't see a genuine qualitative difference in the material standard of living. Most people don't get to work at a model factory or live on a model commune, however, and it would be nearly a year before I really started understanding some of the genuine contrasts in Chinese living standards.

The one thing that did impress me during all the formally arranged visits, despite the endless digressions on the Gang of Four, who were held responsible for every conceivable evil, was the pride ordinary Chinese took in the original Revolution Mao had ushered in. Of course, they were relatively privileged compared with many of their fellow citizens, and they knew it, but their pride was not feigned, nor their hopes for the future. For all of Mao's subsequent sins, he had defined a bottom line of material poverty below which no Chinese was to fall (unless he had committed some political heresy along the way, in which case the only bottom line was death).

From time to time, we heard of villages or sections of the country where conditions were supposed to be much the same as in the bad old days, but I never saw concentrated and utter destitution in China, except on one notable occasion. At the beginning of 1979, thousands of extremely poor people poured into Peking from all over the country and staged rallies and marches protesting political discrimination and starvation. These people were called "petitioners" by the government. At some point during Mao's rule they had been labeled "bad elements." These innocent people might be capitalist-roaders, rightists, counterrevolutionaries, former petty Guomindang officials, or whatever. Some survived without too much trouble; most lived under cruel hardships.

Somewhere along the line a political campaign had needed victims, and these petitioners had been served up. Since that moment their lives had been a constant misery, and if they weren't imprisoned, they were dispatched to the countryside to forage for their livelihood under inhuman conditions. None of the benefits of the Revolution were to be theirs, and when any new political campaign came around, they could be served up as victims again and again.

They came to Peking seeking justice because they had heard a new and good government had been installed. It was an action as old as China itself: in bad times, lie low; in good times, seek redress. They were as poor as any people I had ever seen, with the numbed, glazed look in their eyes that comes from malnutrition. I had seen their like only in the worst slums of Calcutta and the countryside of North Vietnam. How many others they represented I do not know, nor does anyone else. Mao, however, often said that 95 percent of the Chinese people were essentially good and only 5 percent irredeemably bad.

Statistics are a wretched game in China, for in a country of a billion people, Mao's arithmetic means that fifty million souls are automatically damned. If you subtract a prison and work-camp population, variously estimated at from three to fifteen million souls, one might reach an approximation of the population of outcasts roaming around the country. To its credit, the government is now trying to rectify the injustices, but the process is painfully slow.

These sinister shadings are not apparent on the model communes. A few years ago, tourists were occasionally told there were certain bad elements, which commune members were attempting to reform, but this information would be presented in a context of model rehabilitation, however many decades the process was supposed to take. No doubt a model former landlord could be trotted out to talk about his past sins and how he had reformed, thanks to the generosity and kindness of the local Communist Party committee. The Chinese are no better or worse than other people. A commune population—especially a model one under the intensive eyes of government cadres—can condone hypocrisies and injustices just as readily as a neighborhood in Montreal or Boston or Wolverhampton. Foreign tourists used to marvel at the lack of self-interest apparent at such places. What they were really marveling at was the lack of self-interest as they understood it. Self-preservation can be a fairly unscrupulous business too, and of necessity it is rife in China.

And yet the central mythologies of the Revolution are a sturdy point of reference for most, just as the Christian moral ethic used to be in the West. Prelates and monarchs, landlords and lawyers might all abuse the word of Christ and the teachings of the Church, but they were referrable to as a known goal or ideal. If one changes the cast, time and locale, it is much the same thing in China today, and most people feel that the Revolution, if it is to have any meaning, must aspire to its original ideal of emancipating the masses. Disputes over the direction this emancipation should take have caused unbelievable misery to the Chinese people, but the goal has nevertheless survived.

If we mock this in the West and fail to differentiate between the power of the ideal and the sometimes hideous practice of reality in China, then we will not only fail to come to terms with a billion people; we will also never understand the forces that bind our own society together. In this light, it is not surprising that some of the most avid supporters of Maoism in the West turned out to be bedrock conservatives and activist Christian clergy. They perceived that their own societies were disintegrating and envied the social cohesion they saw on their official trips to China. What they failed to do was go a step further and try to understand the potency and satanic power of mass commitment and unbridled nationalism; that was a dangerous ignorance many Chinese themselves have come to recognize through bitter experience.

The ideal is still very much alive. I was to meet many Chinese who were in a high rage over the iniquities of state leaders, the inequalities of life and the repression of unorthodox political thinking, but I rarely met anyone who didn't have a concrete conception of an ultimate goal based on Mao's original Revolution. Socialism of some sort is a given fact in China that few would dream of changing, even those who say that China is still a long way from reaching genuine socialism. One of the real frustrations and problems the Chinese Government faces today as it tries to improve the standards of the poorest parts of the country and bring them closer to the better life in the model communes and in the cities is that its better-off citizens are not content to stand still. An ideal cuts across all sections of society and cannot be manipulated or postponed at will. An ideal can also be ruthlessly suppressed, as any Western democracy with a history of colonial power can attest. In this, as in so many areas, the Chinese are no different. A trip to Tibet is a startling reminder and puts the whole business into a shocking context.

7

National Minorities

By 3 P.M. the harsh Tibetan sun was at its hottest and Elizabeth and I walked down the main street of Lhasa, trying to see if we could discover any significant traces of traditional Tibet in this once proud and exotic capital. The route was typical of any new street built in China since 1949, and for all I knew, I could have been on the outskirts of Peking (or Shanghai, or Canton, or Nanking, or Chengdu, or Sian): there was the broad, ample roadway to accommodate the occasional truck or cadre's car that passed by; one and two-story buildings of numbing, if functional, banality lined the route; the whole prospect appeared neat and clean and soulless. Even the carefully planted trees in neat rows had been uniformly pruned, so that they had the air of a platoon of fresh recruits from the People's Liberation Army. A lone traffic light was controlled from a circular booth by a uniformed member of the Public Security Bureau while two of his colleagues stood idly by outside. Whether there was traffic or not, the PSB officer changed the lights.

Along the wide sidewalks, Chinese workers and a few families ambled by. Some looked in the store windows, while others gawked sideways at the strange spectacle of a foreign couple. Most of them sported huge metallic Mao Tsetung buttons, which have been thrown or stored away in the rest of the country. In contrast with our experience in the interior of China, a smile and a hello to these Chinese doesn't elicit much of a response at all, except for a sullen, suspicious silence.

Suddenly the street's numerous loudspeakers were turned on, and for the third time that day "The East Is Red" came blaring out. Except for the chimes of Chinese clock towers—at the railway station or cable office in Peking, for example—you rarely hear this fervent anthem of the Cultural Revolution anymore. Not so in Tibet and other so-called "national minority" areas. The only thing out of place on this street is a bunch of weird-looking people who have appreciably darker skins than the Chinese and sometimes wear clothing so wildly different from the standard proletarian garb that they look like clowns from a traveling circus. These are the Tibetans, and this used to be their city. How they came to look so strange on their own main street is a story that accrues very little credit to the Communists and underscores some of the hypocrisy behind the officially benign National Minorities Policy of the People's Republic.

That day we eventually made it to the old town of Lhasa, a section of the city that was forbidden to the few foreigners who were allowed into Tibet after the 1959 uprising was put down by Chinese troops. Here was the antithesis of the scene we had just passed. The buildings were colorful and imaginative, and the streets, which ran in all sorts of crazy directions, were alive and animated as dozens of Tibetans—looking completely natural in the national clothing—hawked everything from antique jewelry to clay pots. Like the Chinese, who themselves seemed like Martians in this part of town, the Tibetans had not set eyes on many foreigners, but here the reaction was entirely different: the clucking and smiling was infectious, and we were treated not as alien beings to be feared and resented, but as strange members of the same human race who might well be harbingers of good things.

Tibet is, without doubt, the worst example of a national-minority area in China. The oppression visited on the Tibetans, particularly during the Cultural Revolution and its aftermath, was at least the equal of—and probably far worse than—the melodramatic and mostly unbelievable crimes and persecution of the "feudal Dalai Lama clique," to quote Communist Party propaganda. To this day, the Chinese insist that the Party's policy toward national minorities is "correct," and they will only admit that "serious errors" arose under Lin Biao and the Gang of Four—which have since been rectified. But Tibet puts the lie to all that, and before one can even begin to acknowledge some of the material benefit the Communists have brought to the minority areas, there has to be a realistic appraisal of the chaos and misery that went along with it. Only in mid-1980 did the government admit that terrible abuses had preceded and followed the Cultural Revolution.

China identifies any segment of its population whose racial origin is not Chinese (or Han, the preferred racial designation) as a national minority. There are fifty-five officially designated minorities, representing just under sixty million souls, or 6 percent of the population. In addition to the misfortune of being so few in number compared with the overall figures, they live in vast tracts of land that are nearly all strategically located next to traditional Chinese enemies: Tibet is beside India; Guangxi is beside Vietnam; Xinjiang (pronounced "shin-jiang") is beside the Soviet Union; and Chinese Mongolia is beside Soviet Mongolia. The national-minority regions are often flashpoints of trouble and are thus all under strong and stern military control, no matter what you hear about local autonomy. At the very least, they are buffer zones between the enemy and the Han interior; a simple glance at a map can tell you a great deal about conditions in the minority areas before you even get there.

With this simple and stark reality foremost, one can begin to examine the National Minorities Policy more realistically. On paper it looks very good, and in a number of model areas it was carried out sufficiently well in the past to allow visitors from other countries to take a look. As far as I have been able to discover, the consensus of opinion among foreign observers who made these carefully controlled visits was predominantly positive. Here, we were told, was a policy for coping with racial differences and tensions that was superior to the melting pot in the United States and the ineffectual multiculturalism of countries like Canada or even the Soviet Union.

As in many other areas of official Chinese policy, there is a lethal dose of unctuousness in national-minority work. From reading the propaganda, one would think that it is only the goodness and essential decency of the Communist Party which allows these strange peoples to wear their quaint clothes and pray to their obsolete gods and speak their obscure languages. If one were to believe all this, one would have to conclude that China is the only country in the world that has a national-minorities policy because it is the "correct" thing to do and not because it has a national-minorities problem that requires a policy. The Tibetans, the Mongolians, the Zhiangs, the Huis, the Uighurs and all the other minorities resist Chinese cultural absorption. They always have resisted it, and history has shown that whenever they were sufficiently powerful to throw off the yoke of Chinese suzerainty, they never hesitated to do so. There are none of them powerful enough to do so now, and the Chinese are certainly not going to give them the kind of autonomy that would allow them to maintain relations with enemies who might threaten national security.

Since they won't adopt Chinese culture, they will always—however subliminally—represent a threat to the Chinese Government and therefore have to be controlled. Hence the policy. Anyone with an open mind and honest eyes learns quickly that it is a policy of containment first, ultimately leading to absorption. If you say this to an official, even a conscientious and honest one, you will be accused of slander: "How could this be so?" said a young cadre from the Foreign Ministry. "They have freedom to live their own style of life, to speak their own language, to believe what they want, to wear their distinctive national clothes, to be educated in their own schools. The new criminal code has severe punishments for any Chinese official who seriously violates any of these freedoms, and what's more, every member of a national minority has a chance now to broaden his horizons in the larger national life of China. I think your criticisms are exactly wrong!"

He believed this, too, and we were talking in Tibet, where, for the most part, he and I had seen exactly the same things and arrived at exactly the opposite conclusions. When he walked down that new main street of Lhasa, he saw a graphic picture of the progress the Communists had brought a backward people—a backwardness epitomized by the filthy back streets in the old town and the ignorant peasants, who still got down on their knees to pray to their God. When I expressed amazement at the tenacity of people's faith, he expressed chagrin at lingering "feudal, superstitious habits." He assured me that things were changing for the better, however slowly. "Eventually, they will free their minds of feudalism," he said in all sincerity, and it was then I knew for sure that the minority policy was a sham.

The only essential philosophical difference between the seemingly benign policy of the present government and the "catastrophic havoc wreaked by the Gang of Four" was the time plan and the degree of control. The "correct policy" enunciated today allows the national minorities the "freedom to maintain or *transform* [my italics] their customs and habits," and everywhere we went in Tibet we saw evidence that the weight of Party and government assistance to Tibet is on the side of transformation. Had this been the will of the Tibetan people—had they been allowed to do it for themselves—there would have been no one to say them nay. But the Chinese make sure that any aspect of Tibetan culture which might encourage "regional" nationalism is thoroughly eradicated (during the Cultural Revolution "liquidated" would have been the more correct word), so that what remains is a hollow shell, tricked out in traditional garb if necessary—and no longer than necessary —but filled up with Chinese values, Chinese culture and Communist orthodoxy.

The "catastrophic errors" of Lin Biao and the Gang of Four simply constituted the same policy as today, but administered with bludgeon and sledgehammer. The radicals were merely impatient with the slowness of the revolutionary transformation and tried to speed things up. It didn't work very well. If the Eurasian writer Han Suyin's and other pro-Chinese observers' accounts are even remotely reliable, the former Chinese Government at least gave Lhasa the look of a fully assimilated city, while the delegated model natives could spout the correct line of the day (since repudiated, with the new line being espoused by newer models). We now know that religion and Tibetan racial identity were driven underground during this period, where they thrived in persecution to such a degree that the authorities have found it not only expedient, but necessary to reopen a number of monasteries and temples to channel religious feeling into observable and controllable areas.

It is important to understand the Communist account of recent Tibetan history; otherwise it is impossible to fathom the ferocious opposition to Chinese rule on the part of Tibetan nationalists. In a paraphrase of recent government propaganda from Peking, it runs like this:

Tibet has always been an inalienable part of China. This has been confirmed by history, and the current Dalai Lama himself has admitted that this is an unalterable fact. Some people abroad are shouting for so-called Tibetan independence. This is sheer nonsense, and it is hoped that the Dalai Lama and other officials have come to understand that the peaceful liberation of Tibet and the putting down of the armed rebellion in 1959 were aimed at freeing the laboring people from feudal serfdom. Today, the million emancipated serfs, under the leadership of the Party Central Committee headed by Chairman Hua Guofeng, are working for a beautiful and prosperous Tibet and the modernization of the country. Great progress has been made in Tibet's construction, and the living standard of the Tibetans is improving.

It takes a lot of work to sort all this out. Tibetan nationalists will immediately tell you that Tibet was never an inalienable part of China, any more than it was an inalienable part of India or Great Britain—other countries whose powerful presence has required Tibetan leaders to come up with political agreements to protect its status quo. The nationalists say that the theocratic government of the fourteenth Dalai Lama accepted the presence of Chinese troops and officials after 1949, partly because there was no choice and partly because the new Chinese Government promised not to intrude in internal affairs. Instead, they point out, the Chinese Communists consistently and systematically tried to undermine the rule of the Dalai Lama to such a point that the people rose up to throw off the Chinese yoke in 1959. The uprising was doomed to failure because of the vastly superior forces of the Chinese, and also because the free world refused to come to Tibet's aid. As his predecessors had been forced to do several times in Tibet's history, the Dalai Lama left his seat in Lhasa to take up exile in another country—in this case India—but he waits with his followers until the moment he can return to his rightful place.

Very few outsiders knew what the old Tibet was like, and the reports of the few who did are conflicting, ranging from visions of Shangri-La to a veritable hell on earth. I have read a number of accounts of Tibetan life prior to the arrival of Chinese troops, including the memorable one by the current Dalai Lama's brother. In it is painted a picture of a country of serene bliss, not without its tensions and inequalities, but one that was essentially at peace with itself and in harmony with its splendid natural setting. One is instinctively suspicious of this account, and the author ends up sounding like a Buddhist version of Lei Feng; but on the other hand, every utterance of the Dalai Lama—both before and since his exile—gives evidence of a leader with a genuine interest in his people and someone completely open to reform, even with the help of the Chinese. But he wanted Tibetan reform, not Communist, and so his presence became increasingly intolerable.

Lamaism, the Tibetan form of Buddhism, seems exotic to us, but it didn't to Tibetans: it was a way of life. It was not they who rebelled against Lamaism; it was the Chinese who eradicated it and destroyed or closed down all but ten of the nearly 1,600 monasteries in the country that operated up to 1959. (This is a Chinese Government statistic, supplied to all foreign correspondents who made the trip to Lhasa in the summer of 1979.) The onus is therefore on the Chinese to prove that the Tibetans prefer the new direction taken by the Communists. On this point there is also conflicting evidence, but the strong impression I got on a very strictly orchestrated trip there was that religion is still very strong, despite the frightful bashing it received, while the longing for the return of the Dalai Lama among many ordinary people is intense.

Our government hosts trotted out numerous "former living Buddhas" and government figures from the old government, who told us how much better life was under the Chinese Communists and how the Tibetan people all rejoiced when the troops marched in. Many of these spokesmen had just recently been released from Chinese prisons after twenty years of incarceration, and their testimony had all the naturalness and spontaneity of talking dolls'. In each case they were unwilling or unable to discuss anything—even Tibetan eating habits—without reference to the good work of the Party Central Committee and the correct policies of the National Minorities Commission.

I was forced to pit this wooden and transparently doctored testimony against everything I learned from ordinary people out on the streets of Lhasa—when government men weren't around. I watched people of all ages pour into the recently reopened Jocund Monastery, at the entrance to the old town, to pray to a God who was patently real to them. (Despite the reopening, the monastery was available to the faithful only for a few inconvenient hours on three mornings of the week, when the vast majority of the Tibetans have to work. The reality of freedom of religion in China is best manifested in Tibet, where the people are genuinely religious and their fervor is more carefully monitored by the government than any quality-control section of a factory.) On two successive evenings I walked around the perimeter of the Potala Palace, the former seat and home of the Dalai Lama, and saw people quietly saying their prayers. Some spoke a bit of broken Chinese, and after they ascertained I was friendly and that no one was watching, they asked the same question: *"Dalai shenma shihou huilai?"* ("When is the Dalai Lama coming home?").

These were fragments and snippets gleaned from furtive meetings. What was far more telling and far easier to observe was the dimension of classic colonial rule forced on Tibet. Here was a very strange way to run an area whose population was supposed to be totally at ease with Chinese rule and Chinese fraternalism. As a regional center of Chinese military control, the city of Lhasa has been utterly transformed from its previous role as a Tibetan religious, cultural and political capital. The population figures tell the story, and once again these figures are supplied by Communist officials. Before the Chinese came, it was a city of 60,000 Tibetans; now the Tibetan population has decreased by 10,000—extraordinary in itself—while the imported Chinese population is around 70,000. This figure does not include members of the People's Liberation Army, which has variously been estimated at 7,000 to 25,000 (the actual figure is a state secret).

The army and Chinese civilians have done a great deal of capital construction in Tibet. Roads, new schools, a few factories and numerous administrative buildings have changed the face of Lhasa, and these things are touted as signal improvements in the lives of Tibetans.

Undoubtedly many of them are. Any government that had control of a country for thirty years and exercised absolute rule for twenty had better have something to show for itself. When you consider, however, that much of the capital construction was necessitated by the huge influx of Chinese troops and civilians—who still enjoy a measurably superior standard of living to that of the Tibetans in everything from education, medical care and pay to travel opportunities and housing—you begin to understand the nature of socialist colonialism. Only those Tibetans who have learned to abandon their Tibetanness or will spout the current Party line and work toward the assimilation of their own people into the Chinese mainstream have equivalent standards.

The notable exceptions to this general rule can be found on the few model communes foreign visitors are taken to see. Chinese subsidies and technical assistance have made an appreciable and laudable difference in a few peasant lives and skills, but even here this kind of assistance is not given without charge. Affluent Western countries assist poor Third World countries in much the same way, partly to gain influence and partly because prosperity encourages stability. In Tibet, the Communists never give anything away free: the price of such reforms is the same kind of blind obedience to the Communist Government that theocratic Lamaism demanded up to the early part of this century, but which was on the wane by the time the Communists entered the scene.

Most Chinese who are sent by the central government to Tibet resent the posting and have to be bribed with extra pay and perquisites. As soon as they can return to the interior, they do so. If they are required for long periods, they make sure their children get a proper Chinese education back in Sichuan province or one of the coastal cities. The Tibetan diet, which rests on the sturdy foundation of yak's milk and its by-products, strikes the Chinese settlers as revolting, and at great expense the government imports more tolerable fare from the interior. Of course there are also exceptions to this, but the one exception I found only reinforced the rule.

In a teahouse within the shadow of the Potala, I spoke to a Chinese cadre who had lived in Tibet for nearly twenty years. His home had been Chengdu, and when he first came, he resented the posting and hated the people. He was only nineteen at the time, but as fate had it he fell in love with a Tibetan women, and though there was considerable opposition from his family and fellow Chinese, they eventually married. He has learned the language, and he said his wife still believes in God and tells their three children many stories from Tibetan religious folklore. He himself, he indicated, doesn't believe; but he respects his wife, who works in a clothing factory, and he has learned to respect Tibetan people. He knows only two other Chinese who have ever tried to learn the language (not including special cadres who are taught minority languages in order to wield more effective political control).

The myth of Chinese respect for Tibetan history and culture was so easy to dissolve as to be laughable. Literally, every historic site or religious building to which we were taken had been chosen by our Chinese hosts not to give us more insight into Tibet but to point out "the inalienable right" of China to rule Tibet. Any historical exchange of visits between Tibetan and Chinese officials was cited as proof that Tibet is part of China. Even the wretched old Guomindang Government was trotted out to buttress the case (as sure a sign as any of how weak the argument is). At the Dalai Lama's summer palace in Norbulingka Park, his bedroom is carefully maintained the way it was the morning he fled before advancing Chinese troops in 1959. This is to support the notion that he deserted his people, although the Chinese-made quilt and thermos he used are pointed out—I'm not joking—as a proof that China has a natural right to rule.

The Chinese guides at these sites are as ignorant as any I ever came across. They know nothing but what they are told. In the whole of the vast, brooding Potala Palace, there are hundreds of square yards of painted murals, but there are only two small sections the guides can tell you anything about—the visit of a Dalai Lama to Peking centuries ago and the arrival of a Chinese princess before her marriage to a Tibetan leader: yes, absolute proof of China's inalienable right to rule. This silly business reached a perversely logical conclusion in one of the Dalai Lama's own reception halls, where the guide unctuously informs you that a former Chinese foreign minister, Vice-Premier Chen Yi, "graciously *received* the Dalai Lama" in 1956. This same guide moved smartly on to a special display case which showed how a Qing Dynasty emperor, Chien Lung, helped arbitrate the choice of a certain Dalai Lama. The guide could recite details of Chien Lung, nonstop, for fifteen minutes: the Emperor's concern for Tibet and the Tibetans, his respect for their curious tribal customs in choosing a leader, the names of his envoys in Lhasa, and so on. But when I asked her which Dalai Lama she was referring to, she didn't know. No one had told her, and in any event, it didn't seem essential to the tale. The condescending way she sniggered at the system Tibetans used to choose the Dalai Lama indicated that it was the approach she always employed, and it received equivalent sniggers from several Chinese officials who had accompanied us from Peking.

I was in a foul mood that day—visitors are told that the high altitude of Tibet often puts people in a bad temper, although I suspect it was more to do with the high hypocrisy of the Chinese Government—and I turned to Nigel Wade of the London *Daily Telegraph* and said, within easy hearing distance of the senior official, "The system doesn't seem any worse than a senile old man holding the hand of his security chief and saying, 'With you in charge, I am at ease.' " The point, I am sure, was not lost on the official. Chairman Hua's main claim to legitimacy as the leader of one billion people was based on this reported utterance of Mao Tsetung shortly before he died. The picture of the two men holding hands at this pivotal point in history has entered the iconography of Communist China and could be seen on billboards throughout the country or purchased in needlepoint at handicraft stores.

Whenever anything happened on this weeklong trip to Tibet that was spontaneous or apart from the official program, it usually highlighted the unpleasant face of colonialism in Tibet. The one incident that stands out particularly in my mind was ludicrous, especially because it took place before the outraged eyes of at least twenty Western journalists.

The day's program was devoted to a visit to a yak farm, which took five hours by bus to reach. Many of us were looking forward to the trip with keen anticipation because it offered the only chance to get out of Lhasa and see at least a small aspect of the life in the countryside, where the majority of Tibet's six million people live. We knew, of course, that we would be going to a model establishment, but quite a lot can be achieved on even the most restricted of tours. Good preparation, inquisitiveness and a willingness to snoop into places or subject matter that officials try to close off can bring surprising results. I never griped at what was formally arranged for me to see in China because perseverance and bureaucratic stupidity often conspired to bring about the truth.

We suffered a punishing bus trip to the Qinghai (pronounced "ching-hai") Plateau, at fourteen thousand feet above sea level— the highest flatland in the world. On decrepit buses we headed northeast and crossed into the Chamdo and Napchu districts of Tibet, in which rise the sources of two great rivers in Asia—the Yangtze and the Mekong. Fortunately, the calamitous state of both road and bus required numerous stops. Sometimes the radiator boiled over, and at other times we had to pile out so the bus could navigate a mud ditch with a lighter load. These unscheduled stops were glorious adventures. To the vocal exasperation of the Chinese officials accompanying us, each time we came to an unscheduled stop, twenty journalists eager for a colorful story different from the others' ran off in all directions: some toward a group of yak-wool tents of nomadic herdsmen, others to small earthen and brick cottages. On one of these occasions, with the bus seething and gasping in the distance, I stuck my head into a tent to find an ancient fellow brewing himself some yak-milk tea. He had one tooth left in his mouth, and at some time his left eye had been gouged out. Certainly I was the first foreigner from the West he had ever seen.

Amazingly, he showed not the slightest shock or surprise, but motioned me in to sit down on one of the beautiful and numerous small carpets that covered the earthen floor. The interior of the tent was jammed with pots and other vessels, as well as a variety of implements I had never seen before. I assumed that a whole family lived in the tent, of whom my host was the oldest and therefore had been left behind to look after the place while the others tended herds. He smiled and smiled at me as he poked away at a small stove in the center, fueled by dung patties, its precarious tin chimney poking through a small opening in the tent roof.

After he had presented me with a bowl of tea, he continued smiling as he inspected every part of my clothing. I was doing much the same thing to him. He spoke no Chinese or English, of course, so there were a lot of hand gestures, and at one point he reached out to feel the texture of my skin on the back of my hand. He also wanted to feel the texture of my corduroy pants. This gave me the chance to start fingering the carpets and clothing in the tent. It was a tactile encounter! How instinctively we both understood the intensity of mutual curiosity. It was at this point that Philip Short, the British Broadcasting Corporation correspondent in Peking, stuck his head into the tent to tell me that the Chinese officials were trying to round up everyone and we had better get back.

It's silly to make too many assumptions on the basis of such a fragmentary experience, but for the first time I felt a bit more benevolent toward Chinese rule in Tibet. Unlike the model citizens who had been forced to spout Party propaganda in Lhasa, this old fellow was still following his traditional life. His geniality, warmth and curiosity—his humanity—shone through immediately and spontaneously, and I felt that the almighty Party Central Committee and the "dictatorship of the proletariat" had not made too much of a dent in his life, for better or worse. For all I knew, life might even have been better now than he had ever known before—certainly better than it had been for twenty years. After all, since 1956, when the Khampa tribes to the north had started resisting Chinese rule, right through the uprising, the Sino-Indian war that affected Tibet directly, the Cultural Revolution and the fascist rule of the Gang of Four, Tibet had been through one upheaval after another. At least now there was relative peace in the land.

In this benign mood, I headed back to the bus. Short and a couple of other colleagues were ahead of me, and I later discovered that they had had similar experiences in other tents and cottages. Short and the others, I saw, had encountered a burly herdsman with his two young sons up on the road near the bus. They were in the midst of an animated conversation—or rather, there were a lot of hand and arm signals flashing about—and it soon became clear that they were heading in our same direction, so we urged them to accept a lift on the bus. The herdsman thought it was a great idea, and we were rather overcome at this opportunity not only to do a good deed, but, inevitably, to do a little interview on the side. Back on the bus we had a government translator who spoke Tibetan and English, and there was a chance of getting some practical information from a chance encounter. We were hardly trying to find out state secrets—just what his daily life was like and how he viewed the world.

We ushered the three with some ceremony into the bus, and although the two children were shy, they followed their father's lead and were clearly fascinated by the sight of so many strange faces. Two seconds into the bus, the Chinese aboard went berserk, particularly the officials posted in Lhasa (the Foreign Ministry officials accompanying us from Peking rarely intruded directly on local arrangements). With faces contorted with rage, they started screaming at the helpless herdsman and his children. I guess the officials were genuinely shocked. They'd never seen such a thing. The Tibetans were peremptorily and arrogantly ordered off the bus, but since they didn't speak Chinese, the anger had to subside a bit so that the translator could get the message across to them. This process was too slow for one official, however, so he simply began shoving the children out the door and then very belligerently pushed the father. Everything happened so quickly, it took us a few moments to react, but when we did, our reaction was explosive. The bus was filled with a cacophony of multilingual abuses.

After the Tibetans were pushed off the bus, we collected our sanity a bit, and through one of the Peking officials, we announced that we did not wish to continue on the trip unless the family were allowed onto the bus. We had invited them to join us, and now the officials had shamed us and our invitation. We peered out ahead of us and saw the three trudging along the road, occasionally looking back at what must have seemed to them a busload of madmen.

Chinese officials, faced with a tricky dispute with foreign guests, often resort to lies to wriggle out of a bad situation—but there are lies and lies. As twenty journalists watched the Tibetans walking in exactly the same direction we intended to take, the chief local official, who had never talked to the family and only bellowed at them, said, "They were confused. They thought this was the bus to Lhasa. They are not going in our direction."

The transparency of this lie started the howling in the bus again, and it wasn't until we received a promise that we could pick up the family that we quieted down. By this time, the three were some distance ahead, and it took about two minutes to catch up to them. As we approached, I noticed the same nasty official signal the driver to speed up. There was never any intention to stop for them. Thus the hollering was revived. It was in this atmosphere that we drove the final few miles to the model commune to meet the model peasants.

The grotesque sequel to this entire business came a few hours later. After what I can only assume was a serious discussion with the model yak-farm leadership, a model Tibetan, dressed in his most elaborate holiday clothes, was ceremoniously brought onto our bus for a three-minute ride. He was kept at the back with a Chinese official on either side of him, and at a time when our assigned Tibetan translator had somehow disappeared.

Tibet, as I said, is certainly the worst example of a national-minority area with which to hit the Chinese. But it exists and is a shocking indictment of a country that professes antipathy toward both colonialism and racism. The situation is far more settled and stable in other national-minority areas, but the differences are of degree, not kind. There is no doubt whatsoever that the desired final result, however long it takes, is total assimilation of all minority races into the Chinese mainstream. There are many people who will argue, and cogently, that this is not only inevitable, but essential: that this is the way of the future and of greater prosperity and opportunity for backward people. Because the Chinese Government and the Communist Party—no matter what particular faction has been in power—officially endorses separate development and separate cultures for minority populations, it is not necessary to rebut this argument. Because the policy is so often at odds with the practice, however, it is necessary to pinpoint the hypocrisy precisely.

8

The Price of a Song

On April 28, 1978, the Information Department of the Foreign Ministry, which controls all access foreign correspondents have to official life in China, granted me an extensive interview with one of China's most important literary and political figures—the novelist Shen Yanbing, better known by the pen name Mao Dun. That would mean nothing to my editors, because apart from a handful of Sinologists and Chinese-culture buffs, who had ever heard of Mao Dun in the West? I was excited, however, not only about this chance to talk to such an eminent man of Chinese culture, but because of what it represented in terms of access to Chinese leaders by foreign correspondents based in Peking.

The government had long ago adopted a policy of never permitting interviews of senior officials by local foreign journalists. Sometimes we might be included in interviews with leaders if our bosses were in town; several *Globe* correspondents in the past tried to get the publisher over on a visit just for the chance to speak to Chou Enlai for an hour. Also, distinguished and well-known journalists who were on short visits to China were sometimes accorded interviews, although until very recently all questions had to be submitted in advance. So the chance to interview Mao Dun was a real breakthrough, and it came at a time when all sorts of changes were happening every day, all of which would have been unthinkable before 1978. Consequently, I made my way to Mao Dun's office in the Chinese People's Political Consultative Conference Hall with considerable expectation that this interview might well lead to others. The whole nature of reporting on Communist China was being transformed: where once we were forced to scrounge in the journalistic equivalent of piles of chicken bones for portentous signs of direction and meaning, the prospect was now looming of more orthodox, open and rational approaches.

There was another reason for the excitement, too. In preparing to come to China, I had naturally begun to read as much Chinese literature as I could. I never made more than a cursory examination of the products of the Cultural Revolution—they induced nausea too quickly—but the novels, poems and essays that came spilling from the pens of Chinese writers between the twenties and forties were utterly compelling. China was then going through a period of intense ferment. New ideas from both the democratic West and the Soviet Union, mixed with reactions against traditional Chinese culture and the impatience of a rising generation, conspired to produce a potent atmosphere of questioning and heroic resolve. China may have been a humbled nation in the eyes of the world and an easy prey to Japanese military adventures, but it also produced some of the world's finest and most passionate writers, who ranged across the whole political and social spectrum.

It was during this volatile and creatively fertile period that Mao Dun first rose to fame in China. I had read his finest work, a novel about life in Shanghai, called *Midnight,* with a sense of awe and wonder. The French Sinologist and literary critic Jean-Pierre Dieny once described *Midnight* as "a masterpiece" and added that it presented "a fresco of life whose breadth of scope is unprecedented in China." I didn't have the Chinese literary experience to make such a sweeping judgment, but I knew a first-rate book when I was confronted by it. Mao Dun takes you into the Shanghai of the thirties not as a detached master guide, but as a committed provocateur who may not yet have decided what all the solutions are, but who certainly knows what he doesn't like. Because he tackles Shanghai with a sense of conviction, he is able to isolate the numerous characters with considerable force. His feeling for irony is impeccable, and this gives shading and substance to his merciless observations; and while there is evidence of considerable intolerance in his attitude, the conditions he depicts are repugnant and fundamentally intolerable. This all adds up to a novel of somber and turbulent passion. If this sounds contradictory, it may be in character with the man himself, who chose as a pen name a classic Chinese expression that means "contradiction." Literally, *mao dun* means "a spear and a shield," and you can get the rich, colorful meaning of the phrase as it is understood by Chinese if you think of a spear that can pierce any barrier confronting a shield that can withstand any blow.

As I drove to the meeting with Mao Dun, I remembered most vividly his depiction in *Midnight* of the capitalists of Shanghai. It was not a flat portrait of evil, so favored by the ideologues of the Cultural Revolution. Rather they were full-blown people who could encompass contradictions of their own: vague sympathy, a desire for reform, guilt over the poverty in the countryside, a cynical acceptance of their own material superiority. Mao Dun was a Marxist even then, but he could fathom and describe the complexity of the human condition on all levels. Rather than automatically dismissing all capitalists, he could see some of them as victims of the system they themselves maintained. He had the wisdom to observe that some of the world's most committed revolutionaries come not from the oppressed segment of society, but from the privileged classes, who can look out on life unencumbered by material and intellectual privation.

Mao Dun's career since he wrote *Midnight* has been fascinating. He made the difficult adjustment from observer to participant and joined Mao Tsetung's cause in the firm conviction that this was the only way China would find salvation. He was rewarded for his efforts with high office, and for a time during the fifties he was Minister of Culture. Together with the *éminence grise* of Chinese culture, the high bureaucrat Zhou Yang, he formulated theories for a new generation of intellectuals and tried to reconcile the artist's desire for uninhibited exploration with the demands of a totalitarian state which decreed that all art must first serve political ends. If that seems the essence of contradiction, then who better to struggle with it than a living symbol of contradiction itself—Mao Dun?

He was already in his late sixties when the Cultural Revolution crashed around his head. He was toppled from his minister's post, and throughout the next twelve years, Mao Dun was subjected to the endless and degrading pressures that afflicted all intellectuals, writers and artists who had displeased the radical faction clustered about Mao Tsetung in his final dotage. With the fall of the Gang of Four and the return to pre–Cultural Revolution policies in most fields, Mao Dun, at eighty-two, was elevated once again to importance, and by the time I got a chance to speak with him he was president of the All China Union of Writers, vice-president of the National Association of Writers and vice-chairman of the Chinese People's Political Consultative Conference (a nonelected, nongoverning institution comprised of appointed "patriotic" Chinese, whose importance depends exclusively on the Communist Party's arbitrary whim: during the Cultural Revolution it ceased to exist; today it is a crucial part of the propaganda campaign to encourage "National Unity and Stability"). As I was soon to discover, Mao Dun was now busy formulating new plans that would accommodate much of the official policy on culture in China today. I had prepared myself to meet a literary hero, freed from the shackles of Gang of Four oppression and eager to get the intellectual life of the country moving again. Such expectations only served to show how ignorant I was of the Communist Party's history of dealing with culture and how foolish it is to translate Western cultural values into contemporary practice—which usually has little to do with the aspirations of Chinese artists and writers.

Mao Dun turned out to be an aging mockery of what I had built him up to be. I caught him in the midst of what was clearly a difficult assignment for his somewhat confused state of mind: the assimilation of the new Party line on literature. He droned on and on about "the Party's correct policies" and the "havoc wreaked by the Gang of Four." Every question on contradictions facing Chinese writers was either ignored out of hand or sidestepped. I was presented with a sad old man who had survived a horrible disgrace to rise again another day. He was certainly not going to be disposed of again if he could help it. Except for a few moments, when I actually managed to get him to digress on his beloved daughter who died during the civil war, he declined to show his human face. Instead, he lectured me on how Chinese writers now had the freedom to explore and speak out on any issue whatsoever—"except if they oppose socialism or seek to spread bourgeois ideas." He delineated again the old Communist theories of "revolutionary romanticism and revolutionary realism" to prove that under Communism there really was true freedom of expression.

As I listened to him, noting his air of loyal confidence in the regime that had once relegated him to the dust heap of "revisionist irrelevancy," he seemed transformed into a Chinese version of Vicar Thwackum in Henry Fielding's novel *Tom Jones:* "When I speak of religion, Sir, I mean the Christian religion, and not just the Christian religion but the Church of England." Mao Dun says much the same thing when he defines how a young Chinese writer should use the freedom of expression the Party has allowed him: "He [the writer] should be an optimist and put that optimism into his writing. In describing events and developing his characters, it would be natural to look for this quality. With this optimism a writer should be able to see into the future, and by the future, of course, we mean Communism. . . ."

I felt toward Mao Dun the same sense of betrayal anyone feels when someone he admires turns out to be a bit of a fraud. For me, this fraud was symbolized by his departure. As I went out to my car, he was escorted with suitable fanfare to his waiting Red Flag limousine. The vast and sinister automobiles the Communist state makes available for its leaders are far larger than any equivalent vehicle a "feudal comprador capitalist exploiter" could have had in Shanghai during the thirties. Mao Dun got in and closed the door of the roomy back-seat passenger section. His chauffeur wheeled out of the entranceway with a blast of the car horn. The driver, as is usual in Peking, never stopped to see if there was any oncoming bicycle traffic: the horn blast was sufficient to alert the masses that greatness was descending upon them. Mao Dun sat bolt upright in the back seat, holding his cane in front of him. One could just make out his image when a shaft of sun shone through the heavily curtained windows. As I followed him along the street for about a half a mile, the limousine belched out loud honks while humble cyclists and pedestrians hurried to get out of the way. The scene could have been lifted straight out of *Midnight.*

Over the ensuing months, the newly revised line on literature was to be polished and perfected, so that by September 1979 it would be a very smooth and reasonable-sounding business. In essence, though, it hadn't changed, and if one wants to understand what is at the core of the dilemma facing all thinking people in China today, an understanding of that constant line is crucial. From it, you can work your way back through the entire history of the Communist Party's approach to culture and intellectual activity.

Suppose you are a young writer in Shanghai or Peking today, all fired up with enthusiasm to depict life around you, with the assimilated experience of a cruel decade to give that writing a real edge. You want to hold a mirror up to yourself as well as to your compatriots. Since you are of China and of the Chinese, you will be very much aware of all official policies, and if you want your work published, you will be scanning the Party's newspapers and quizzing local officials on attitudes. Along comes the following article in the leading intellectual newspaper of the country, the *Guangming Daily*. Take a look at it, and try to see some of the time bombs no Chinese would miss (the translation is official and was supplied by the New China News Agency):

> Writers should open their eyes, face life and show how people search for the truth, the good and the beautiful, says a commentator's article in *Guangming Daily* today.
>
> They should watch sharply, scout around, dare to face reality whether reality conforms to their subjective views or not, it says. Besides seeing success, brightness, festive flowers and children's laughing faces, they should also see the dregs of the past, the dark clouds and tears and sorrows of the ordinary people. They should bring to their readers the real contradictions in life, sufferings and happiness, the dialectics of life, experience and wisdom of the people's quest.
>
> However, the article says, in the early fifties and sixties, some of the writings painted a golden picture of life to please certain "superiors" and turned their backs on what undermines the socialist edifice and on the contradictions of life. These writers fed their readers with nothing but sweets, leaving the readers poorly served. The situation greatly worsened during the time of the Gang of Four, when literature distorted the truth and even deliberately forged facts so that careerists could anesthetize the people and oppress them at will.
>
> Now, the article notes, though the Gang of Four has been smashed and literature and art have been emancipated, there are still some specious notions going around that still bind the writers' minds and pens.
>
> Sometimes when a writer criticizes certain kinds of people and things, he is accused of not reflecting the essential and principal aspect of life. Life consists of thousands and tens of thousands of events. There is no situation which does not reflect the essence in one way or another, nor is there an essence devoid of the concrete. A writer should open his eyes and try to grasp the essence and the essential. However, one should not cut situations and minor aspects from the essence and de-

mand that the writer portray the so-called essentials different from what he himself saw, felt and believed.

People cannot live without an ideal and it is the duty of literature to publicize the great ideal of communism. It should give its readers some food for thought. Therefore, it is not enough just to portray things that really happened. Portraying the demands of real life does not contradict portraying the ideal and artistic imagination.

On the question of inspiring or fooling readers, the article notes that since contradictions always exist between the subjective and objective, between mankind and nature among the people, so even when communism is attained it will not be a world that is a paradise free of all unhappiness. Sometimes a writer is blamed for not inspiring and encouraging the people when he writes about some contradictions and tensions in life. How can a writer encourage and inspire his readers? By cajoling them with sweets like dealing with a child in kindergarten? The writer can inspire the readers with the truth of life, no matter how harsh and bitter, with a correct evaluation of the contradictions and difficulties in life. He should build up their confidence in the future in spite of difficulties and should also warn them of all eventualities. Would this not be considered an inspiration to the people?

Of course those who refuse to see the people's heroic exploits and achievements in building socialism and keep railing and predicting disaster for their motherland are also going against the truth of life and can write nothing but lies and fakes. It is true that after the painting of golden pictures, there could be an unacceptable tendency towards a new stereotype of wailing literature. However, the tree of life is ever green. Only by opening their eyes to life, going deep into it and portraying things as they really are can these new contradictions and imbalances be solved and more and better works produced. Chinese literature should advance along the path of profoundly and truthfully portraying life, thus gaining the confidence of the people and becoming the readers' friends and advisors and witnesses and memorial tablets to history.

Although this line is a stupendous improvement on the philosophy of literature espoused during the Cultural Revolution, when, as one observer noted, "Chinese culture was nailed to the ground and forced to grin," it is completely consistent with traditional Maoist theories on the role of culture in the state.

I couldn't resist the temptation to contrast Mao Dun's current life-style with his written legacy. I suspect that this was why I was never again formally allowed to interview an important state leader. I was not told this, of course, but as I watched reporters who took less judgmental approaches to their work get more access to officialdom, I drew what seemed to be obvious conclusions. In the end, it didn't really bother me for several reasons. First, such interviews were rarely revealing of anything other than the official line parroted daily in the official media. Secondly, it forced me (and the other journalists who declined to censor themselves for future favors) to do some real legwork to get stories. In the past, legwork never got one very far in China because society was so restricted, but as things eased up, a pair of observant eyes and strong legs could produce a great deal that was new and interesting.

Institutional reporting is the bane of journalists everywhere; in China, the problem was complicated because the major sources of information were the official press and any gleanings journalists could pick up from diplomats and members of visiting delegations who had more direct access to official life. In time, a comfortable pattern developed with which you could produce sufficient copy to satisfy editors without ever having to really work for it: far from being a hardship posting, Peking was too often a comfortable sinecure in which many journalists were unprepared not only for new challenges, but for the most basic and important function of the business—to be a witness.

In the cultural field, I was perhaps luckier than most of my colleagues because of my background in the arts. Having studied the role of culture in the West, I was fascinated to snoop around at the differences in China. Since Elizabeth and I enjoyed going to concerts, theater and films regularly, we were constantly scouring the city to see what was up. It was our luck that we came to China when the radical stranglehold on the arts was being loosened, and I paid as much attention to this field as to anything else. Professionally, this paid huge dividends, as I often got advance notice via the stages of Peking of the sorts of things that were in store for the Chinese people. It also got me out of the foreigners' ghetto and into another aspect of life around me.

One of the fundamental changes in the arts during my time in China was the distribution of tickets. From 1966 to 1978, admission to all forms of public entertainment—including movies—was through a worker's individual Unit. Tickets were usually handed out on a piecemeal basis and in strict rotation, whether someone wanted to go or not. When Mao's wife Jiang Qing controlled the arts, there was little choice in either the fare or attendance. If you were bidden, you went. Since there were only eight revolutionary model operas, three revolutionary model orchestral works, six revolutionary model ballets and precious few new movies (as late as 1977, there were only five full-length features approved during the year for general release), people were often forced to see the same thing over and over again. With very few exceptions, it was all wretched and much hated, as we learned. Unrealistic in the extreme, ballets such as *The Red Detachment of Women* stretched credulity to unprecedented extremes. The creative process of invention and imagination was turned over to political committees, and the journey from invention to production was so tortuous and laid with so many ideological traps that invention simply vanished.

A few months after we arrived, the government changed the ticket-allocation policy and permitted citizens the right to buy tickets directly from the theaters of their choice. The model operas and ballets, which had been such centerpieces of the Cultural Revolution period, vanished overnight. Apart from the fact that no one would pay the price of admission to see such awful fare, the presiding role of culture in Chinese national life ensured that the new government would seek to present a new image. In the West, we don't think too much about philosophical questions concerning culture. We know what movies we like, we know whether we would rather go to a sports event or an evening of ballet, and many of us tend to be suspicious of anyone who talks about culture with a capital "C." In the Chinese Communist Party, it is just the opposite. Anything that holds a mirror of China up to Chinese society or to the outside world is caught in cultural complexities, and the Party wouldn't dream of leaving anything so crucial as the image of China to individual artists and entrepreneurs, whether in television, stage performances, literature, painting, sports, journalism or even mountain climbing. If any endeavor reflects on the imaginative soul of the Chinese people, the Party wants its imprimatur on it. It was a "cultural" revolution that Mao launched in the sixties, not an industrial revolution. In addition to his attempt to place himself back on top of the political leadership, Mao was also trying to define the spiritual goals of China. He was content to trace out the general path and left his minions to color in the details. It was in this way that his wife, one of the most spiteful creatures of our time, was allowed to gain such ascendancy. A person of vaunting ambition who had been a second-rate and mostly failed film actress in Shanghai, Jiang Qing used her new powers first to destroy a host of real and imagined enemies, who she felt had slighted or ignored her in the past, and secondly to impose one of the most ignorant and trite artistic sensibilities—her own—on nearly a billion people.

It's one thing to say this; it is another thing entirely to witness its effects on such a vast population and on a country with such a rich and unique cultural heritage. I saw only the tail end of it all on the stages (although we got firsthand accounts of all the tragedy and human cost), but it was more than enough for a lifetime. I used to shudder thinking of those who had to put up with it for over a decade. A number of people, far better qualified than I, have itemized the damage done to traditional Chinese culture by the madness Mao permitted during the Cultural Revolution. What I witnessed was the cost in human terms, and it affected me profoundly—not just emotionally, but in my whole attitude toward the state's meddling in cultural policy. At the top, there were victims, like Mao Dun, for whom it is possible to have only a limited sympathy. You learn very quickly that when people like him are given equivalent powers, they simply seek another set of rigid strictures on creativity, however benign by comparison.

To see Mao Dun with some objectivity, you have to compare his career with that of a really supreme hack like Guo Moro, who died, at the age of eighty-seven, the year after I arrived in Peking. Poet, playwright and cultural arbiter, Guo Moro not only threw in his lot with Mao Tsetung early on—which was no sin, considering the alternatives in China—but also dwindled into the most egregious sycophant and toady. In the end, the preservation of his position was the only important thing to him, and he would have dispatched his own mother to perdition had it been necessary. He certainly never hesitated to rat on his closest friends and allies when the need arose. Until the Cultural Revolution, he was acknowledged as the supreme authority under Mao on all philosophical matters dealing with art, literature and education. His knowledge of Chinese history and cultural traditions gave him honorable title to this role. His genuinely creative work was finished before the Communists took power in 1949, and the rest of his days were spent in a Faustian feat of survival. In order to keep his nose above water during the opening blasts of the Cultural Revolution, he mounted a public stage to make a grotesque and nauseating self-criticism in which he repudiated everything he had written in the past and said it should be relegated to the garbage heap. He knew only too well who had succeeded him as cultural arbiter of the land, and he penned new-style poetry in her name:

> Dear Comrade Jiang Qing,
> You are a fine example for us all to follow.
> You are brilliant at creatively studying the overall picture . . .
> Fearlessly, you charge forward on the literary and art front.
> Thus do heroic images of
> Our workers,
> Peasants
> And soldiers
> Dominate the Chinese stage.
> We must do the same for the stage the world over!

Nine years after this immortal ode was served up to the masses, Jiang Qing fell from grace. The poet laureate of Communist China, breathing his last few gasps of life, managed to put down some new *pensées.* In the following poem, Guo Moro is more colorful than he allowed himself to be during the politically insecure days of the Cultural Revolution. He makes a reference to "the White-Boned Demon," who comes from the classic Chinese story of the Monkey King, the most beloved fictitious character in Chinese literature. The White-Boned Demon, who could change herself into anything she wanted, was a popular image for Jiang Qing, even before she fell. Guo Moro's symbolism comes from the masses; his spinelessness was his own invention. According to the New China News Agency, he wrote the following testimonial from his hospital bed, where we are told the vicissitudes of life under the Gang of Four had chased him:

> What heartening news!
> Ferreting out the Gang of Four.
> The literary rogue—
> The political rascal—
> The sinister adviser—
> The White-Boned Demon—
> All swept away by the iron broom.

At the other end of the spectrum during the Cultural Revolution were the tens of thousands of ordinary artists and intellectuals whom God had cursed with creative imaginations and whom Mao plagued with distrust and ideology. Millions of people suffered during the Cultural Revolution, but artists were the particular focal point of persecution. A great pianist had his arm broken to be taught a salient lesson; young composers were sent down to the countryside to pick cabbages; a veteran author like Ba Jin, whose novel *Family* raised the revolutionary consciousness of an entire generation of Chinese, was forced to kneel down on shards of broken glass in a huge stadium in Shanghai. Others were driven to suicide, including Lao She, who was best known in the West for his fine novel *Rickshaw Boy*. The traditional Peking Opera was decreed decadent and banished from the stage. All contact with outside culture was prohibited to the masses, although Jiang Qing set the style of the leadership by privately screening her favorite Greta Garbo films: the masses were deemed too ignorant to be able to watch such fare objectively.

Throughout China, people were told that all cultural wisdom resided with them. However, they were never allowed any discretionary power to exercise this wisdom. In fact, so-called cultural wisdom was imposed upon them by their "natural" leader, the Communist Party, whose every action was supposed to be a manifestation of the mass will. How galling this fact was to Party officials with an ounce of decency and intelligence; they knew better than anyone that the Party, in effect, had ceased to exist, having been replaced by a classic fascist regime that made the previous system seem positively liberal by contrast.

It was the degree of contrast that fooled many observers into concluding that the new government of Hua Guofeng and Deng Xiaoping was embarked on a radical scheme of liberalization in the arts, whereas it was simply reverting to the status quo before the Cultural Revolution. It also fooled many Chinese people, especially the generation that had grown up during the Cultural Revolution and knew little of the past. History is one of the best-kept secrets in China for very good reasons: the record of inconsistency is too embarrassing and might undermine the people's faith in the Party's right to govern. And to be fair, too, the contrast was exhilarating in the early days. I spent extraordinary hours in Chinese theaters, sharing with Chinese people the excitement of a rejuvenated stage. In Sichuan province, I witnessed the return of the local traditional opera with an audience that hadn't seen it for twelve years, and who cheered as actors and actresses reappeared from a nightmare limbo.

I heard young people gasp when they saw their first *tutu* on a ballet dancer, and I saw the patient but eager lineups for the first foreign films from the West to be allowed in Chinese movie houses since the fifties.

After more than a year of this, certain problems emerged to replace the presiding euphoria. For one thing, a generation of trained artists had been lost. For another, successive and convulsive waves of political campaigns had left established Chinese artists in a state of shellshock: many declined to return to their former work for fear of a future backlash. In this they showed more wisdom than younger people, who thought they had been completely liberated and had failed to comprehend the strict limitations imposed by "the dictatorship of the proletariat."

The roots of official cultural policy under the Communists can be traced back to 1942, when Mao was still in the hills of Yenan, waging one war against the Japanese invaders and another, more covert war against the Guomindang. In such a situation, one would not normally expect cultural problems to figure prominently in anything, and it is precisely because of that perception that we have such a difficult time in understanding the true nature of institutional Communism. Tourists pouring into China today who take in an evening of Peking Opera as part of their Chinese experience are usually oblivious to the fact that what they are seeing has been carefully selected to conform to strictures laid down by Mao during the height of a bloody, protracted guerrilla war.

The Yenan stronghold that Mao and his forces had occupied by 1942 was not only a military redoubt; it was also hugely symbolic of the patriotic aspirations of many Chinese people. The old Red Army was successfully fighting the Japanese, while the Guomindang Government of Generalissimo Chiang Kaishek seemed to spend most of its energies and resources in either corruption or fighting fellow Chinese who were Communists. Guomindang censorship was not well thought out, but it was systematically brutal, and it alienated most intellectuals and artists, who longed to make contributions to a war effort that would dislodge the Japanese invaders. More than this, the Communists seemed to offer hope of a truly independent, self-reliant China. Not very surprisingly, some of the brightest minds in China flocked to Yenan out of patriotic or ideological idealism.

Mao's particular genius had been to harness the Chinese peasantry to his cause. Much was made during the Cultural Revolution of his alleged peasant origins, but they were not impeccable, and he had grown up under material conditions most Chinese would have envied. His father's homestead was ample by local standards, and it was never less than amazing that millions of Chinese toured it without ever publicly expressing their surprise at how superior Mao's prerevolutionary setup was to many postrevolutionary conditions. In any event, he identified strongly with the peasantry, and because he was a stern moralist and disciplinarian, he imposed a kind of miracle on his troops that transformed them from the traditional rapacious Chinese military force to a symbol of decency, resoluteness and fairness.

All things considered, it wasn't an unfair or untrue image; but to independently inclined thinkers it seemed brighter from afar than closer up. The exigencies of warfare, of course, necessitated good discipline, but the artists and intellectuals who came to Yenan quickly realized that there was a difference between the demands of emergencies and what the Party was trying to establish on a permanent basis. Like innumerable foreign tourists who have come to China since 1949, these people had thought they were coming to a place that was attempting genuine egalitarianism.

The American journalist Theodore White visited Yenan in 1944 and discovered a tiny aspect of the truth. Sickened by the corruption and deceit of Guomindang-ruled China, he found in Yenan a kind of purity that profoundly influenced his thinking. Years later he wrote about these experiences in his autobiography, *A Personal Adventure.* Like many visitors to China today, when White stumbled onto something that didn't fit neatly into a particular vision, he dropped it:

> The Communists, in those days, believed that soldiers, officials and students should all be fed—fed enough so they could work and stride with the vigorous step that differentiated them from the sluggish officials and soldiers of the Nationalists (Guomindang).
>
> All were healthy; but I noted that complete equality fell short of luxuries: milk, for example, went to the sick or wounded in hospitals. But after that, the milk went to the families and children of high officials. I pressed the question: whose children got the milk?
>
> It embarrassed them. So I did not press further, for they were my hosts . . .

It was this kind of official hypocrisy, which Chinese people at Yenan could see on many more levels than milk supplies, which led to a confrontation. Some of the artists, especially the writers, openly voiced criticism of privilege and senseless censorship of cultural matters. They committed the unpardonable sin of contrasting ideology and practice, and they did not hesitate to find fault with Mao himself, whose attitude set the tone and style of Yenan. Mao responded in a fashion that has served the Communist Party as a model right up to the eighties.

Now sanctified as *The Yenan Talks on Literature and Art,* Mao's strictures informed all critics that any writing or creative work of art, whether it was polemical or simple entertainment, was to serve political ends first. The artist or writer was not the final arbiter of style or content: the Party was. In the context of Communist theory, in which the Party is the natural representative and protector of all the people, this line has a kind of logic. In Communist practice, however, as all Communist-controlled countries have shown, it means that the Party often defines policy with little—if any—reference to the people: the only real criterion for policy making is the retention of absolute power.

In a way, the cultural policy during the Cultural Revolution was a more honest and less confusing implementation of Mao's theories than the more humane—and covert—system employed now. The government today allows a certain latitude for error, but it remains the final arbiter. If pushed, it is just as capable as the government of Jiang Qing's day of suppressing truly questioning voices. When it urges people "to search truth from facts," the facts referred to are ultimately defined by the unquestionable authority of the Party. I saw in China indisputable proof that even an inch of latitude can produce some artistic work of merit, and I learned that many bright Chinese people are bursting with a desire to create something, somewhere. So it has been whenever the Party has released its grip.

I confess, though, that I always found it difficult to assimilate the semantics and ideology of the cultural battlefront and am much more at ease contemplating the careers of the generals and soldiers conducting the battle. To this end, the story of the most famous Communist Party cultural warrior, Zhou Yang, provides illuminating and cautionary insight. Zhou is a party ideologue first and foremost. His creative talents, as far as the record shows, were confined to translations of foreign works and a series of fairly turgid political essays churned out under the auspices of the League of Left-Wing Writers (a Shanghai-based collection of revolutionary literary figures who banded together during the thirties). But he was clearly a brilliant man, with natural critical instincts. In the West, his talents might have turned him into a superb commentator on the arts or a superlative magazine editor, the kind every writer dreams of—someone who will help provide direction to chaotic thoughts and bring order and precision to erratic writing. In China, he became a propagandist and, ultimately, an important watchdog on intellectual and cultural activities. Now he is another of the old men who rule China, but a short news item that was carried by the New China News Agency during the summer of 1979 echoed back over his extraordinary career. As usual with such articles, it meant nothing if you didn't know the background, and it left volumes unsaid if you did:

> An important task on the cultural front is to re-evaluate Lu Xun [pronounced "lu-shun"] and learn from him, said Zhou Yang, vice-president of the Chinese Academy of Social Sciences and vice-chairman of the All-China Federation of Literary and Art Circles.
>
> Zhou Yang termed Lu Xun a great man of letters and a great philosopher and revolutionary who had made very great contributions to the development of China's and to the Chinese people's liberation cause and said that he left an extremely rich cultural heritage.
>
> However, during an earlier time, Zhou Yang said, the League of Left-Wing Writers, due to their sectarianism and dogmatism, had erred in their relations to Lu Xun. But even so, they have remained comrades-in-arms with Lu Xun in the common revolutionary aim of changing the old society and creating a new one.

Such comrades! Such arms! The simple truth is that Lu Xun, the greatest political essayist and story writer China has produced in this century, was a bitter foe of Zhou Yang. To consider them comrades-in-arms opens new vistas for retrospective collaboration: the Pope and Luther, for example, working together to bring Christianity to the world; or Tito and Stalin spreading the good news about international Communism; or Hitler and Churchill fighting to protect capitalism. Lu Xun, who never became a Communist, was a highly principled man who spoke directly to the heart of Chinese dilemmas and the soul of the Chinese people. Like all great men of ideas, he was a loner. He had more cause than most to join ranks openly with the Party, but he always resisted the ultimate blandishments of membership. He understood the future too well, and perhaps his most resourceful act was to die before Mao gained absolute rule. Inevitably he would have been purged; indeed, nearly all his closest friends and associates who survived him were purged in one way or another after the Communists came to power. In each case, the man delivering the *coup de grâce* was none other than Zhou Yang, one of the greatest loyalists the Party can lay claim to.

The true story of Zhou Yang and Lu Xun is not available inside China. Even for outside journalists, it is difficult to fit the various facts together. Fortunately, two Western scholars—Simon Leys, in *Broken Images,* and Merle Goldman, in *Literary Dissent in Communist China*—have made exhaustive investigations into the background, and their various observations and findings were confirmed by every Chinese I was ever able to engage on the subject. By one Chinese friend's reckoning, Zhou Yang had taken part in thirty-seven political campaigns, line struggles or inner-Party controversies. Only once did he come a cropper, and that was during the Cultural Revolution, when Party loyalty didn't stand for anything in the wrathful wake of Jiang Qing's witch-hunt: Zhou Yang fell before a more horrible monster.

He first joined the Communist cause in the early thirties and quickly became involved in the Party's cultural policy and approach to intellectuals. Because he always followed the prevailing line with unswerving devotion, he won the patronage of Mao and the enmity of people like Lu Xun, who tried to evaluate life objectively. Lu Xun's own revolutionary instincts did not encompass sycophants, mind manipulation, censorship or the suppression of basic rights. In writing about the overall necessity of the Chinese nation to survive, Lu Xun made this ironic observation:

> When I said that the first imperative for China was to survive, I do not mean just getting along by shameful expedients. . . . In this latter field, there is one formula which doesn't seem to have occurred to anybody yet—namely the model provided by Prison Number One in Peking. The occupants are spared the worry of seeing their neighbor's house on fire, their two daily meals are guaranteed, they are hunger- and weather-proof. Their lodging is snug, and it is a robust construction unlikely ever to collapse on their heads. Well looked after by their

jailers, there is no danger of their being exposed to further brushes
with the law, and they are superbly protected from burglars there—in
short, when it comes to security you couldn't ask for more. There is
only one thing lacking: freedom.

In his strictures to writers and artists laid down in Yenan, Mao
made a special point of forbidding the withering sarcasm Lu Xun
employed so successfully. Mao said it was no longer appropriate for
use by writers under Communist rule, because there was no justification for attacking the true representative of the masses in this way:
to attack the Party was the same as attacking the people. Lu Xun
was dead by this time, and confined to a historical period; by control
of access to all but his most useful writings, he could be made to
say anything the Party wanted, just as the successors of Mao are now
utilizing the writings of the Great Helmsman.

In helping Mao to formulate his theories on culture, Zhou Yang
pushed the idea of "revolutionary romanticism" and "revolutionary realism," which generally meant that artists and writers had to
depict all socialist endeavors in an ultimately positive light. In the
Cultural Revolution, this was worked out explicitly. In films, for
example, villains always had to be depicted in lurking, sinister
positions, while heroes had to be filmed full face under highlights.
There were specific instructions to directors on the kinds of camera
angles that could be employed.

Again, this was the logical conclusion to be taken from Mao's
strictures, but Zhou Yang was far too sophisticated for such mind-
numbing and silly specifics. His task was to remold intellectual
thinking. He didn't want just a show of loyalty to Communist ethics
and principles; he wanted to direct the hearts and minds of creative
people in a way that would make such loyalty spring from the soul.
His shadowy presence could be felt behind all the ideological campaigns of the forties, fifties and early sixties.

Zhou's personality was complex, and this gave him particularly
useful insight into the equally complex minds of his charges. It was
relatively easy for him to win the confidence and trust of young
idealists coming up in literary circles. Perversely, he was also successful in retaining the trust of his victims, even while he was
orchestrating their downfall and vilification. Part of the reason is in
the very nature of Chinese Communism, with its emphasis on serious self-criticism and examination. Zhou could act the part of father

confessor perfectly, and one gets the impression some intellectuals actually felt relieved after "coming clean" with Zhou, who helped them to see their past errors.

His greatest usefulness came during the original Hundred Flowers Campaign in 1956 and its direct aftermath, the Anti-Rightist Campaign of 1957. Here Zhou excelled in first encouraging intellectuals and artists to "speak out boldly" in response to Chairman Mao's invitation to free speech and open criticism. It was a simple matter after that to zero in on all the malcontents foolish enough to expose themselves.

One of the celebrated victims of that monstrous deceit was the writer Ding Ling, a woman of firm convictions and proved creative talent, who had been a thorn in Mao's flesh since the Yenan days. Although she wasn't unduly abrasive during the Hundred Flowers Campaign, her resistance to Party strictures during the Yenan period came back to victimize her, and she was promptly dispatched to the limbo status of Nonperson, from which she did not emerge until 1979. She claimed after her most recent rehabilitation that despite all her travails, she was still a loyalist, but she scoffed at accounts of previous struggles that cited "revisionist" or other political excuses for the various terrors that were unleashed. They had very little to do with Marxism or socialism, she told a friend of mine in 1979, and everything to do with personal grudges and vendettas. The Anti-Rightist Campaign, during which literally millions of people—mostly in the cities—were demoted or lost their livelihood entirely, was the supreme example of totalitarian duplicity. In helping Mao to get over his hurt pride and sense of betrayal, Zhou cemented his record as a willing tool.

And yet there was an ambivalence in the man which was put to work by forces that had a different approach to China's future from Mao's. The Great Helmsman's economic experiments during the Great Leap Forward at the end of the fifties were an utter disaster, and the country was forced to fritter away the precious advances it had made during the period of national reconstruction after 1949. As a result of these failures, Mao's power was diminished, and the Party structure he helped to create assumed a superior position of power. Zhou Yang was not a fool, and he made his choices accordingly. In any event he was a Party man, so the shift in power from Mao's person to the Party apparatus and bureaucracy suited both his survival instincts and his philosophical imperatives. Because of the failure of the Great Leap Forward, the Party once again had need of the country's creative forces to work together and help get people's minds working toward the future. Whenever this happens, there is a lessening of the authoritarian grip of the Party over creativity.

In the dusty files of the *Globe and Mail* bureau, an edition of the *People's Daily* from August 16, 1966, contains an extraordinary statement attributed to Zhou Yang in 1961. The statement was used against him by his enemies, but there is no reason whatsoever to doubt its authenticity. Zhou is reported to have addressed a working conference of writers in the early 1960s. In a kind of off-the-record chat, during which some participants took notes, he expanded on dilemmas facing Chinese writers—dilemmas Mao's philosophy and Zhou's own loyal actions helped create. The conference was at the time the Party was trying to mobilize intellectuals to get the country's mind off the disasters of the Great Leap Forward. Zhou spoke directly and passionately to the central nightmare the Party had created for writers, and there was no one who knew it better because he himself had helped create it:

> The dictatorship of the proletariat is ravenous, and more fearsome than the dictatorship of the bourgeoisie. In a bourgeois society one can run when one violates the law, but when society is so tightly organized, where can one run to? . . . There is no place for one to vent one's grief and no place for one to submit an appeal. One is afraid that things written down in one's diary might be found out. . . . In our society there is indeed the phenomenon that men are not treated as men.

Such conflicting rhetoric took on flesh among the young people he advanced within the propaganda department, of which he was deputy director and chief architect—people who assisted him in persecuting and hounding writers who strayed from the Party line. Ultimately some of them balked and attacked their own practices, thus forcing Zhou to go to work on them.

When he fell a few years later, only the Party faithful mourned his passing, because his network of deceit was too well known. People may have sneered inwardly at the charges that he had opposed Chairman Mao's "correct line," knowing full well that he was too faithful a follower of that same line and that Mao had to eradicate him when his own thinking and priorities changed. In attacking Zhou, his enemies brought up Lu Xun's ancient and honorable charges against the man, despite the fact that Lu Xun would have perished long before Zhou Yang bit the ideological dust. Chinese people knew this, just as they knew it was nonsense to conclude that Lin Biao and the Gang of Four had always opposed Chairman Mao's correct line even as they rose to high office under his direct patronage. But they were happy to be rid of Zhou Yang, just as they were happy to be rid of Lin and the Gang. In an imperfect world, one takes relief in any guise in which it is offered.

The cycle of inner-Party struggle in China, however, is such that old ghosts who haven't been physically exterminated tend to return to haunt a new generation. Zhou Yang is today back on top of the heap. Not only does he have an important position in the Academy of Social Sciences, an increasingly influential institution affecting many areas of government policy, but in 1979 he made it into the Politburo. He can be heard regularly now advising young writers and artists in China to "speak out clearly and honestly" and "let a hundred flowers bloom." Marx said that when history repeats itself first, it is a tragedy; when it repeats itself again, it is farce.

9

Foreign Games

Nearly all capers between Peking's foreign journalists and officialdom in China begin with a telephone call. This time the call was as brief as it was unusual. The Chinese Foreign Ministry was getting in touch with correspondents based in Peking on behalf "of our friends at the Kampuchean Embassy." It was December 31, 1977, and the official at the other end of the line wanted to announce an important press conference at the International Club on New Year's Day. The Kampuchean Ambassador in Peking, he said, would be making a "significant" announcement.

The pace of events since that day has been so hectic, and so many lives were lost in the intervening time, that it seems surprising to recall what this press conference represented. It was the end of the myth about Communist solidarity in Southeast Asia. Scarcely three years had passed since Communist forces inside Vietnam, Laos and Cambodia had taken over supreme power in their countries. The seemingly monolithic Communist bloc also included the most populous nation in the world, and it didn't require much imagination to summon up a vision of future instability for the area—and, indeed, the whole world. Foreign affairs, however, are never quite what they first seem, and it came as a shock to some people that China, which had substantially assisted the Communist endeavors of its neighbors, now viewed the growing power of Vietnam with even more alarm than did many Western countries.

China's only real ally in the business was Cambodia, renamed Kampuchea by the Khmyr Rouge insurgents when they took over. Under the leadership of a little-known fanatic named Pol Pot, who was appointed first secretary of the Kampuchean Communist Party, the Khmyr Rouge managed to go Hitler one better by attempting genocide on its own people. The full story has yet to be told, but early on it was clear that Pol Pot was the head of one of the most ruthless regimes the world has ever known, a doubly tragic irony if you consider how pacific and gentle most Cambodians are.

From time to time, the Chinese Government discreetly hinted that it did not approve of Pol Pot's "domestic policies"—euphemism for murder and torture—but it has never completely repudiated the Khmyr Rouge, even in their current miasma of defeat, because China's interests were always too actively and intricately involved in the business. Consequently, China is hopelessly implicated in one of the most appalling atrocities of our time. The culpability cuts across political lines: the current crop of pragmatists in Peking have provided support to the Khmyr Rouge just as eagerly as did the repudiated Gang of Four government. Even following the specious logic some Western countries have succumbed to, it is impossible to find any honor for China in the entire Cambodian saga. Peking got involved initially because it keeps tabs on its neighbors and has traditionally supported Communist insurgent groups. With the growing influence of the Soviet Union in Vietnam, the Pol Pot Government also acted as a handy buffer in the larger strategy of containing Soviet "hegemony"—a word the world would come to know intimately before the year was done.

The Kampuchean press conference confirmed reports that units of the Vietnamese Army were moving into Kampuchean territory in raids and direct attacks. The Kampuchean Ambassador barked his words as he itemized the intrusions and announced his country was breaking off relations with Vietnam. Within ten months, the Hanoi Government would begin a successful invasion of that tragic country and establish a puppet regime in the capital of Phnom Penh. A few months after that, China in its turn would also cite border violations as its justification for a costly, punitive invasion of Vietnam. In retrospect, these events appeared to be inevitable results, but at the time it was the sort of day-to-day matter from which journalists make a living. Never in my life had I come across such a mother lode of abusive propaganda as that which was traded between the various "fraternal" Communist parties in Asia, with Soviet *pensées* thrown in from time to time for good measure. Not even the backstage gossip in New York's ballet circles matches it for sheer venom. It kept coming so relentlessly, and there was such a fabric of duplicity and lies created by all sides, it was impossible to sort out basic questions like cause and blame.

That first press conference in Peking was the formal opening gambit of the diplomatic and political warfare that would eventually be transferred to the killing grounds of Southeast Asia. China's bitter confrontation with Vietnam dominated foreign affairs during my time there, and just about every other concern, save the normalization of relations with the United States, was subordinate or related to the feud. The grotesque spectacle of hundreds of thousands of Vietnamese citizens fleeing their land was a harrowing part of the same nasty affair. Some analysts even argue that normalization itself was also tied in and point to the timing of Vice-Premier Deng Xiaoping's historic and successful visit to the United States as proof: the border war between China and Vietnam broke out just a few days after Deng returned from America, where he left the distinct impression that Chinese and United States interests in Southeast Asia were almost identical.

Following the tortured diplomatic battle in Peking had its absurd moments. Shortly after that mind-numbing press conference (which lasted over three hours, because every word had to be delivered in four languages: Cambodian, Chinese, English and French), I received an invitation to attend a special screening at the Vietnamese Embassy which was supposed to show the other side of the quarrel. At the appointed hour, I went off in style with the *Globe and Mail* driver, who dropped me at the embassy and went on to do some other chores. It was my first visit to the Vietnamese establishment, and I was pleased to have the chance to look around and get the measure of some of the officials. At the very least, it would provide an opportunity to compare Communist styles. After the driver went off, I surveyed the Qi (pronounced "chee") Jia Yuan diplomatic neighborhood. It was older than my own district of San Li Tun, and the buildings were less abrasive in design. Nearby was the British Embassy, which had been completely gutted by fire during the Cultural Revolution and rebuilt by the Chinese exactly as it was before. (This annoyed the British, who had made a number of architectural changes during the sixties, which the Chinese refused to reproduce; the British had to do them all over again when the embassy was handed back.) As it was only five minutes before the film was scheduled to begin, I was a little surprised not to see any of my colleagues' cars in the compound parking lot. In fact, the entire precinct looked deserted, except for a lone Chinese army guard who stood on sentry duty outside the gates. I checked the invitation again to reassure myself I had the right day and time. Pushing through the gates, I went to the front door and tried the handle. It was locked.

There was a bell over to the side, so I rang it. After a minute with no response, I rang it once more and also knocked firmly on the heavy doors. Again, no answer. I was just about to turn around and leave when I heard some fumbling at locks from behind the door. Chains were being released and at least two locks unbolted. Slowly, the door creaked open about two inches, and I could make out a pair of eyes peering through the crack.

"I've come to see the movie," I said. There was no response. "The movie," I added. "You sent me an invitation. I'm here now to see it."

Finally, there was a kind of low growl and a bark.

"I'm sorry—I don't understand," I said.

"English," said The Growl. "Not speaking."

"Parlez-vous français?" I asked in what can best be described as desperation French.

"Oui," said The Growl. *"Je parle un peu."*

"Eh bien," I said, gaining confidence in the fact that The Growl's French and mine were probably about equal. *"Je suis le journaliste canadien. Je veux voir le film au sujet de Vietnam. Vous m'avez invité aujourd'hui."*

The Growl opened the door two more inches. Although the interior seemed pitch black, reflected light from outside revealed a nose and a mouth, all set above the collar of a typical Asian Communist cadre's suit. *"Pas aujourd'hui,"* he said flatly. *"Venez la semaine prochaine. Le film au sujet de Vietnam. Venez la semaine prochaine."*

The conversation was going along splendidly, considering the circumstances, but the information was rotten. I understood that he was saying to come back next week, but my invitation clearly stated the film was about to start in three minutes. I was angry at the embassy's mistake, because I didn't know Peking well at that time and would need help in calling a taxi to get back to the bureau. I told The Growl in very uncertain French that it was the embassy's fault, not mine, and I flashed the invitation with a certain measure of self-righteous menace. There was a moment's pause as he took the white card with the Communist Vietnamese crest emblazoned at the top. Then the door opened wide, and The Growl emerged with a look of sheer venom. Without taking his ferocious eyes off me, he abruptly pointed to a neighboring complex of buildings, handed back the invitation, went inside and slammed the door in my face.

I was utterly perplexed and then, deciding the Vietnamese Embassy was bigger than I thought, I set about trying to find the correct entrance. Scratching my head, I walked slowly out of the grounds. The Chinese guard had been observing my little encounter and gave me a half-smile of sympathy. I had the invitation still in my hand and said to him, in Chinese that was worse than my French: *"Tamen buyao wo!"* ("They don't want me!"). The guard clearly didn't understand a word I was saying. *"Shenma?"* ("What?") he asked. Then I showed him the invitation and said my little line again. He started to laugh, marking the first time I had seen an army man laugh on duty, and drew my attention to the crest on the invitation. *"Bu yiyang, bu yiyang"* ("Not the same"), he said as he pointed to the similar-looking crest over the embassy doors. On closer inspection, however, they did indeed turn out to be different, although the basic format of Communist red background and gold palm leaves was the same. It was only then that I noticed the brass plaque behind the sentry's back on the gate pillar. It was the Kampuchean Embassy! Just as The Growl had done, the sentry pointed to the next building, and as I looked down the street I could see one of my colleagues driving through another set of gates.

It was in this way, then, that I discovered that the Chinese Government had placed Kampuchea and Vietnam side by side in Embassy Row. My driver had made an understandable mistake because from the street the complexes look identical—even the trees camouflage the dividing wall. The sites were initially chosen to underline the solidarity of international Communism a few years ago. As often happens in China, yesterday's orthodoxy becomes today's farce, so off I marched to the correct embassy to watch a film of

unredeeming and unrelenting horror, with more maimed and bru-
talized human beings depicted than one would care to see during
a lifetime. The film depicted Kampuchean atrocities inside Vietnam, a charge that would lead directly to invasion ten months later.
Lovingly, the cameras focused on decapitated corpses left to rot in
ditches. At rural cottage hospitals, children with chopped-off limbs
were shown on their cots. You could see that some were screaming
and crying, but since there was no sound except the dubbed-in
voice of the Vietnamese propaganda narrator, the effect was doubly
unnerving. When the lights finally and mercifully went on, several
dazed journalists and diplomats made for the exit even more
quickly than they do at the end of a national-day diplomatic reception. Some of them didn't even give the Vietnamese Embassy's first
secretary a chance to say "Thank you for coming to see our little
film."

Out in the clear air, a French colleague who had long ago hardened himself to this sort of thing turned to me with the consideration an old hand shows for a novice. "Believe me," he said, "as
disgusting as that was, it is only the beginning. There will be double
features every week. I have heard a rumor that the Kampuchean
Embassy will be having its own film show before too long."

I cut him off right there, since I had a scoop. "I've got it right
from the top," I said, finally understanding what The Growl had
told me an hour before. "It's next week. *La semaine prochaine pour
le film au subject de Vietnam.*"

"Really," said the Frenchman. "You're very well informed."

I told him how I had come by the information and he laughed.
Then he frowned. "You can count on them. It will probably be
exactly the same film as we have seen today, only the text will be
changed to say the same things about Vietnam that Vietnam says
about Kampuchea. The only reliable fact will be the dead."

In the end, it turned out to be a different film, but equally
grotesque. I was also able to see the entrance foyer and one small
antechamber in the Kampuchean Embassy, but I was struck by how
few Kampucheans were on hand. Chinese staff, hired for the day,
did most of the entertaining, and The Growl turned out to be the
ambassador himself, whom I had failed to recognize from the press
conference. Some months later, a visiting journalist from a Paris
magazine also had a bizarre experience at the Kampuchean Embassy. He came by after successive phone calls had not been an-

swered, went past the gates and, like me, rang the bell twice with no response. Only this time, he tried the door and found it open. Gingerly, he walked into the front foyer and shouted out a hopeful "hello" in French. No answer. The corridor was very dark, but at the far end a shaft of light came out through a doorway that was slightly ajar. He walked down the hall, trying to announce his presence with several more furtive hellos. When he opened the door farther, he saw a man sitting behind a desk. Apart from the desk and chair, there were only three other sticks of furniture in the vast room.

"Hello," he said again.

The man emitted a low growl. "You must go," he said in French. "You must go now."

"But I want to speak to the ambassador," said the journalist. "I have been trying to telephone him for days and there is no answer. Can you tell me where I can find the ambassador?"

"I am the ambassador," said The Growl, "but you must go, you must go now. I'm not speaking to anyone."

The ambassador's name was Pich Cheang, and he must have been about forty-five years old. We often considered what he must have done to win the confidence of Pol Pot and get this coveted post in Peking, which didn't arouse pleasant thoughts. Before his government was deposed, there was only one other Kampuchean at the embassy. This was the counselor, and she turned out to be the wife of The Growl. A child was born to them shortly after they took up their posts in 1975, and the infant was generally referred to as "the second secretary" by caustic foreign journalists.

The Vietnamese Ambassador to Peking, on the other hand, was a portly, jolly fellow named Nguyen Trong Vinh. A loyal Party stalwart and former provincial governor in North Vietnam, Vinh had to make several trips home to Hanoi as the diplomatic war heated up, but he always bounced back with even more enthusiasm. Although he was away from the Chinese capital during the six-week border war, his embassy stayed officially open, as did the Chinese Embassy in Hanoi—cynical proof that both sides were still eager to make propaganda, despite all the blood that was being shed (neither Vietnam nor China wanted to be the first to break off relations).

Because I was a new man in Peking and a complete novice about Sino-Vietnamese relations, I stayed clear of any controversial reporting on the dispute for some time. On this issue, I was content to report what both sides said and draw no conclusions until I understood the business better. This practice, as it turned out, served me in good stead. Like most of the other forty foreign correspondents based in Peking, I regularly applied for permission to make an extended visit to Vietnam. Since the Communists had taken over the South in 1975, there had been only one resident foreign journalist from the West in the whole country—the Agence France-Presse correspondent in Hanoi. Unlike the other Peking journalists, however, I got permission, and the ambassador told me it was because I didn't have any "anti-Vietnam" articles on my record. Thus, two months before all land and air travel between China and Vietnam was closed in preparation for the border war, I traveled by train from Peking to Hanoi to spend a month touring the country. It was an eye-opener.

Poverty, it turned out, is relative. Having compared the obvious backwardness of India and the hidden poverty of China, I fancied I knew the levels of development in the East and how low people could be forced to sink. I had accustomed myself to the poverty in China, and with increasing experience I could spot little things in the countryside or in cities that indicated regional differences in standards of living. Foreign journalists in China love going to rural stores to compare available manufactured goods and produce. The number of machines or even horses various communes have, and such things as provincial oil and meat rationing, are all important clues. At the initial glance, much of China looks alike, but checking out these hidden things can give you a clear picture of how much harder the life is in Sichuan province than the one enjoyed by peasants in the richer part of Guangdong province. In some places, subsidies from the central government alleviate certain shortages, as in Tibet, but in provinces like Shandong there seem to be large areas that have been ignored for years and simply abandoned to backwardness.

Thus adjusted to China, I found the poverty of North Vietnam a brutal surprise. I was to spend the first two weeks of my visit in the North, based in Hanoi, with several trips out into four different provinces. I had never seen such a poor place. Things I had taken for granted in China, like decent clothing, healthy complexions, sensible organization of paddy fields, basic brick structures and reasonably well-graded roads, were almost totally lacking in North

Vietnam. The whole time I was there, I never saw a Vietnamese male working actively in the fields. No doubt some males do, but I never saw them. The whole domestic burden of the Vietnamese revolution had been placed on the frail backs of the women, and they were the ones I saw toiling away in the haphazard paddy fields of the North. Obviously, this was the legacy of the long anti-imperialist wars, against first the French and then the Americans. The men (and many of the women too) fought, while the women farmed the land, built the houses and produced more children for the war effort. The few men who could be found at work in the countryside were demobilized soldiers, who found country life a bore and barely lifted a hand. On a visit to a model commune, I was taken to a huge field that was being cleared of stumps and rocks to provide more rational and large-scale farming, the sort you often see in China. Out in the field, there were hundreds of women lugging rocks away in sacks slung over their shoulders or held on their heads. At the entrance to the field there were about twenty men; if they weren't playing cards and smoking, they were lolling about on little portable stools and making jokes about some of the women who were slithering barefoot in the wet muck.

Even in Hanoi, most of the heavy construction work I saw was done by women. I got a useful confirmation of this easily observed phenomenon from an English engineer in Thai Binh City. He had been sent out by his company to assist in the creation of a prefabricated jute mill, which the area desperately needed. Of the forty-seven workers under his charge, nine were men.

"They [the men] were useless," he said. "Not only did they refuse to work, but they caused trouble among the women. My girls are pretty frail, and their diet is so poor I can't reasonably expect more than three or four hours a day of concentrated work out of them. But during those hours, they do a good job. You can tell them how to do something, and they will listen. If they get it wrong, you can correct it easily. But the men! They don't listen, and if you try to correct them, they will sabotage the work. They were happiest when they were criticizing the women and beating them for not paying attention to them. I finally told the local officials that I wanted all the men cleared off the site. They refused at first, considering it too great a loss of face. So I had to make some very threatening sounds, and I finally won. Now the project is going ahead without too many problems."

Vietnam had been at peace for several years, but its government had made no accommodation to this peace. Nor had the North Vietnamese men, who clearly knew no other life than combat and perpetual alert. When war with Cambodia and then China finally came, it was clear this suited a significant section of the government and population. How wildly different is the context of the times. I suppose if I had come to Vietnam during the height of the anti-American war, I might have seen all this privation as something heroic in the face of American bullying: it was the common orthodoxy of my generation. I might also have ignored the obvious signs of repression and the history of an exceedingly brutal regime. Or if I hadn't done so, and had reported that the Vietnamese Communists were unrepentant liars and terrorists, I would have been accused of being a CIA agent. But now there was no glorious war of liberation to be fought. The South, as I was soon to discover, was under a far more vicious rule than it had experienced with a succession of American puppet governments, and the true nature of Vietnamese Communist repression could be seen by anyone with honest eyes and ears.

A small group of left-wing French journalists had preceded me by a few weeks on a short visit to Vietnam. In most cases they had been to the country before, particularly during the war, when they had reported favorably on the regime in the North and castigated the American-supported government in the South. They now professed to be horrified by what they saw in the new South and described it as "a vast Gulag," where thousands of people were forced out of the cities and into the so-called New Economic Zones, which were little better than labor reform camps. Had they been more objective about the North in the old days, their horror at what was happening in the South might have been more credible. The Communists in Vietnam cannot be accused of doing worse in the South than what they did in the North. The same totalitarian pall has now descended on the entire country, and the only reason the plight of the South seems more poignant is that the Communists have not had sufficient time yet to whip it into shape.

When I was there, things were still unsettled. I do not propose here to build an argument in defense of the old Thieu and Diem regimes of South Vietnam. The evidence of their corruption and the corrosive effect of American involvement can still be seen everywhere, from bomb craters to abandoned children of obviously mixed racial heritage. But everywhere I went in the South, I received remarkable evidence that the people hated the Communists and longed for something better. The world knows the plight of the ethnic Chinese, and I was in Saigon—renamed Ho Chi Minh City—on the eve of the largest exodus of the Boat People; on long midnight rambles, I haunted all of Saigon's districts and received so many offers for gold or American dollars that I lost count after the first few days. Yet the plight of the Chinese in Vietnam was no worse than that of the ethnic Vietnamese, who had welcomed the arrival of the victorious Northerners for patriotic reasons and found themselves monstrously betrayed. The hazardous option of bribing officials and escaping in boats was not really open to them unless they disguised themselves as ethnic Chinese or were prepared to pay two or three times the sums that were being gouged out of the Chinese.

I had one thing to thank the French journalists for, however. The Vietnamese officials were so incensed at the "slanders" of their former journalistic allies that I was able to manipulate their anger into some interesting revelations. "All lies," said one. "They say there is no freedom of religion and that the prisons are worse than concentration camps. It's just not true."

"I'm sure that's the case," I said, somewhat disingenuously. "I would like to be able to refute these things if they are slanders. Perhaps you will take me to a New Economic Zone and a prison and to rural churches so I can see the truth for myself."

No problem, they assured me. Unfortunately, it did turn out to be a problem, but because Vietnamese Communist officials are such hopeless liars, my trip often descended into tragic farce. They were not, of course, prepared to take me to a real prison. I was offered a Cambodian prisoner-of-war camp instead. Every time I tried to visit a rural church in the North, the priest seemed to be away, and no one else was apparently prepared to act as a guide. In Hanoi and Saigon, the cathedrals still operate as show pieces of religious toleration, but I discovered how the Party works to stamp out religious practice. All one has to do is contrast the "settled" picture in the North with the turbulent situation in the South. Buddhism and Catholicism are still very strong in the South, so the Communists do not close down churches where the community of the faithful is organized and large. Instead, they try to co-opt religion until such time as it is deemed neutralized, and that's when the crunch comes.

In the North, religion has mostly been driven underground, but the South is not supposed to know about it.

For this and other reasons, the border between North and South is now more rigidly controlled than it was during the war. This is eminently sensible. The government doesn't want the Northerners to discover how prosperous the South is (by comparison) because this would put the lie to twenty-five years of Communist propaganda; the government also doesn't want the Southerners to discover precisely how miserable the North is and what is eventually in store for them, because this would undermine "the glorious national reconstruction program."

As in China, the foreign visitor is taken to model establishments. My request to visit a New Economic Zone led me to a farming commune on the outskirts of Saigon, and what a blissful place it was. There were plenty of new Soviet tractors. Each home had a delightful little garden, and in the storeroom of every household there were sacks of grain and a goodly store of canned commodities. These lucky citizens were better off, as far as I could see, than some peasants in Japan. Well, my Chinese experience had taught me how to deal with models: I did not dismiss them, but took them as tokens of aspiration. In China, however, there was never such a huge discrepancy between the models and the normal conditions of ordinary people.

The next day, I was told I would be taken close to the Cambodian border to visit a village that the Khmyr Rouge had attacked and pillaged. It took about three hours to drive there along a superb highway built by the Americans. The countryside was lush, and all along the route one could see sturdy brick farmhouses, relics of the days of free enterprise. Then, very abruptly, all this ended. The highway became a dirt road with a mass of potholes, and the villages and housing looked no better than what was found in the impoverished North. People had the same undernourished bodies, and in their eyes I could see what I called "the Calcutta glaze"— a filmy substance covering the eyeballs, which I attributed to malnutrition. Aha, I thought, the old "free" South had its model districts too. I was happy to have this opportunity to get off the scenic show road and observe that the former South Vietnamese Government had had its nasty backwaters.

We arrived at the village the Khmyr Rouge was supposed to have attacked. It was cordoned off by soldiers, and you could see the few charred remains of some of the mud-and-thatch houses. We were only six kilometers from the border, and it was a very bleak scene. There was little evidence of farming, and the few fields looked as miserable as the pathetic ones in the North. The officials took me to the one remaining house, and I interviewed the family members.

It became quickly apparent that this was a model Cambodian atrocity village. The attack had taken place months before, and this wretched family was being kept there to provide testimony to people like me. A young mother of four children told me the story. Her husband hovered in the background, while her mother-in-law held a baby and whisked flies away from its face. The attack had come at night, she said. The village had been put to the torch and more than twenty people had been massacred. There was no reason to doubt her word: although she was being used as part of a large propaganda campaign, the reality of the attack was very pertinent to her family. She also had a hauntingly beautiful face and a manner that suggested a certain resoluteness. I was a little bit smitten by her, and I asked how long her family had lived in this village. Actually, I asked the question stupidly by demanding "how many generations" her people had been in the area. After this was translated, her face looked puzzled, and I could see she couldn't understand what I was asking.

"Were your mother and father born here?" I asked, trying to simplify the process.

"No," she said, "they were born in Saigon." Well, I continued, was she born here? "No," she said, "I was born in Saigon."

"When did you move here?"

"Two and a half years ago."

I can be remarkably thick at times, and I wasn't taking in what she was really saying, so I pushed on—to the growing uneasiness of the officials who were hovering around the poor woman. "But you moved to a terrible area just a few kilometers from a troubled border?" I asked incredulously. "Why would you leave Saigon to come here?"

Then I got my answer. "It's a New Economic Zone," she said, and with that the interview ended abruptly. The woman was sent packing, and the senior official gave me a stern look and said, "This is *not* a New Economic Zone. Yesterday you visited a New Economic Zone. This is a Cambodian atrocity village."

You have to go a long way before finding stupidity so institutionalized as it is in the Vietnamese Communist Party. I finally realized that in its eagerness to prove Cambodian atrocities, the government had actually brought me into a large tract of land that proved everything refugees were saying about the New Economic Zones. Potential troublemakers were shipped out of Saigon to dangerous areas along the border, where they lived in abject misery and took the brunt of the border conflict. Clearly, the officials accompanying me could not understand why I should confuse a "Cambodian atrocity village" with a New Economic Zone, even when the dumb locals spilled the beans. Over and over again in Vietnam, I would stumble into reality, thanks to Communist stupidity, and from this I learned a significant thing, which my Chinese experience helped me see.

Totalitarianism in China is more pervasive than it is in Vietnam, but curiously, it is less repressive. This requires some explanation. In China, the Communist Party has maintained or co-opted traditional Chinese social customs of group organization and control. While this can bring pernicious and arbitrary hardships to many Chinese people, it nevertheless has its roots in established practice, and it is something the Chinese people understand, even if many dislike it and try to bring about changes. In Vietnam, the social heritage was completely shattered in the long period of colonialism and "anti-imperialist" wars. The Communist Party there had nothing to hitch its appeal to save nationalism, and when it gained power in the North, it imposed a rule that was a direct extension of French colonial power, except that under Ho Chi Minh this power was far more systematically and ruthlessly employed.

The glue that binds Vietnamese people to their government is fear, except for the lucky few who have positions within the Party and power structure (although they too have to watch themselves quite closely, just as Party members in China do). Compared with the Chinese, Vietnamese people have nominally more freedom of religion, and they also have more choice in such things as clothing styles and places of work. In China, the concept of a national family imposes more surface conformity with officially decreed social norms, but this has produced in many Chinese a kind of security from which they can make surprising assaults on the system. It is a question of degree, of course, and I saw many examples of fear in China, but it was nothing compared with the day-to-day terror imposed on the Vietnamese, which was such an accepted thing one almost took it for granted after a few weeks.

My trip came to an appropriate conclusion with an interview at the presidential palace in Hanoi with Premier Pham Van Dong. He proved to be a charming and courtly veteran. The interview began with a stroking session in which he told me he had heard good things about my work and hoped I would return one day to write a book about Vietnam. He would help clear the way for me, he said.

I had been asked to submit questions beforehand, and these received written replies. My "interview" was simply an informal chat during which no notes were to be taken. I remember vividly, however, the last thing he said to me. Rising to considerable passion, he told me that Vietnam did not want one square inch of territory that did not belong to the nation. No matter what I had heard in the past or what I would hear in the future, no Vietnamese soldier would ever be used to attack another country for the purpose of conquest. In a typical Vietnamese gesture, he even held my hand firmly as he said these things, and I confess I was impressed at the time.

Upon my return to Peking, I discovered that the day after our interview, the premier went to Moscow to sign a new friendship pact with the Soviet Union, and within a few weeks, Vietnamese soldiers had overrun Cambodia in a classic invasion. In a less direct style, the Vietnamese also took over Laos. Perhaps the most appalling thing to be said about the entire business is that the Vietnamese conquest has probably brought the Cambodians a less repressive regime than the one presided over by Pol Pot, but in this instance, such contrasts are still killing Cambodia.

Back in Peking, we learned that the Vietnamese invasion had forced Pol Pot to free Prince Norodom Sihanouk from his three-year virtual house arrest in Phnom Penh. He was flown to the Chinese capital and held an amazing and dramatic press conference at the Great Hall of the People. This slightly mad and wholly honorable Cambodian patriot kept foreign journalists transfixed and enthralled for nearly six hours. The former ruler of Cambodia is the only honest statesman speaking for Cambodia today, and because of this and his useful attacks on Vietnam, the Chinese are prepared to put up with his legendary buffoonery. Still, his pronouncements on the Pol Pot atrocities soon became an embarrassment, and he had to be hustled out of the country.

China's concern for Cambodia has nothing to do with the plight of the Cambodian people and everything to do with its own sphere of influence in Southeast Asia. It has seen the Soviet Union expanding into its turf through Vietnam, and there is every reason to believe that matters will become nastier. As for Cambodia, Sihanouk was probably closest to the truth when he said the Chinese Government wants to fight "to the last Cambodian."

It is fear of the north—of the Soviet Union—that governs Chinese foreign policy. On this issue, as with little else, there has been perfect consistency for the past twenty years. Different political struggles come and go, but when the dust settles, the Soviet ogre still looms very large. In 1979, Vice-Premier Deng Xiaoping sounded exactly like Chairman Mao in 1960: "The threat to peace comes from the north," Deng said in a widely publicized speech. "The source of instability and war in the world lies in the north, and should there be foreign aggression against China, it would come from the north."

Western diplomats have a recurring nightmare. The scenario is very simple: the Chinese patch up their quarrel with the Soviet Union in the same dramatic and seemingly abrupt way that the quarrels with Japan and the United States were ended. The resulting Communist monolith would then present an awesome threat to the West, and Doomsday would be near at hand.

The one thing I learned in Vietnam and China was to distrust any theories about monolithic Communism. If it ever existed, it certainly doesn't now. At the moment, the Chinese are far happier in the company of staunch anti- (Soviet) Communists like Prime Minister Margaret Thatcher of Britain or former President Richard Nixon. This is not so ironic as it first appears: the simple philosophy is "thine enemy is my friend," regardless of whether it is the discredited Shah of Iran or the discredited President of the United States. Nothing amused me more than to watch the visiting delegations of European or Canadian Socialist parties in China. The Chinese Communist officials despised them heartily for their softness toward the Soviet Union and their fear of nuclear war. The most successful trips to China were always those by hard-liners who were impressed by China's resoluteness on this single issue. The admiration was always reciprocated.

As a resident journalist in Peking, I saw much of the practice of foreign affairs in Peking through the pompous haze of official state visits. Partly because of my own journalistic background, and also because my newspaper wanted me to concentrate on feature stories rather than ordinary news stories, which were well covered by the various Western agencies, I always took a supercilious attitude toward such visits. Watching Premier Raymond Barre of France stumble through unbelievable banalities was not my idea of a nifty assignment. Much more to my taste was the visit of Ratu Kamisese Mara, the prime minister of Fiji, one of the smallest nations on earth.

The Chinese Communist Government has traditionally made a tremendous fuss over very small countries from the developing Third World. It loves to show that the world's most populous nation considers tiny countries every bit as important as superpowers—at least as far as state visits are concerned. Fiji was the supreme example. In the early seventies it had received independence from British colonial status, and the official propaganda services in Peking went all out to congratulate the national militancy of the Fiji people. Strewn across Chang An Avenue were large red-and-white banners proclaiming, "Firmly support the Fiji people in their just struggle to safeguard national independence and state sovereignty!" At the welcoming banquet in the Great Hall of the People, one of the senior vice-premiers gave a stirring account of the Fiji people's "love of independence and freedom . . . After waging unremitting struggles, they finally won their precious independence."

When it came time for the Fiji prime minister to respond to all this fulsome revolutionary praise, an exceedingly strange speech was heard in the Great Hall of the People:

"Fiji is a young country," he said. "We received our independence [from Great Britain] not more than eight years ago. And here, I am proud to say that unlike a number of countries in other parts of the world, Fiji's movement to independence was happily one of peaceful transition. We sought and were readily given our independence, not as a reaction against oppression by a metropolitan power or resentment against it. In fact, it would be true to say that the metropolitan power itself encouraged the move towards independence, and while we were not ungrateful, we did receive it with a certain air of reluctance. This was because it meant severing political ties with a country with which Fiji had enjoyed almost one hundred years of happy association and which had contributed greatly to the advancement of our country."

You could sense the consternation at the Chinese tables in the Great Hall. This was not how history was supposed to be written, and the confusion, bordering on perplexed embarrassment, was written all over the faces of Party officials as the Chinese translation was read out. Not surprisingly, the Fiji leader's speech was rigorously censored when it appeared in the official press the next day.

All governments succumb to hypocrisy in foreign affairs—it is not so much a sin as a necessity at times. Chinese hypocrisy had indigenous embellishments, however, which never ceased to be fascinating. The Communist Party, for example, is tremendously loyal to any Western leader who has promoted better relations with China. In some ways this is admirable, and the leadership really tries to live up to that traditional Chinese compliment of calling someone an "old friend." That it can carry this to extremes is known to every American by the continued respect Richard Nixon receives in China. As the man who initiated the normalization process with the Shanghai Communiqué in 1972, China is the last refuge for the United States' most discredited president. Dismissing public opinion in America, China has twice invited Nixon to the Middle Kingdom to bask in reflected glory. In Japan too, Vice-Premier Deng made a point of visiting a former Japanese prime minister who was under house arrest awaiting trial on corruption and influence-peddling charges. No matter—he was "an old friend of the Chinese people" and would not be forgotten.

As I said, this can be interpreted as an admirable trait, but when the business gets a bit closer to home, things change radically. If a visiting Canadian or American leader were so foolish as to inquire about the whereabouts and health of his former hostess in Peking —Chairman Mao's widow, Jiang Qing—he would receive the same abrupt reply always made to an inquiry about the Gang of Four. "She's eating well, which is more than she deserves after all she did to China." And that's it. Old-friend courtesies cannot be reciprocated in China.

For me, the old-friend syndrome came to an appropriate consummation during my last month in China. In September 1979, the protocol department of the Foreign Affairs Ministry was strained to the maximum because of three simultaneous and special visits. On the same day, officials had to send former British Prime Minister Edward Heath home after he had returned to Peking from a Tibet trip, welcome Pierre Trudeau, who was on his way to Tibet shortly after the Canadian voters had rejected him as prime minister, and also welcome former President Richard Nixon on his third trip.

Heath had disgraced himself, in the opinion of some observers. He went to Tibet and, according to eyewitnesses, did little but grumble about his accommodations. He saw virtually nothing of the real Tibet. When he returned to Peking he took it upon himself to congratulate Vice-Premier Deng on the good work the Chinese were doing in Tibet, despite the fact that there was much evidence of a repressive colonial regime. As one disgruntled British Embassy junior officer said: "Even if he had made a proper examination of the situation, he was not compelled to make a personal report to the Chinese vice-premier on how the Chinese were behaving in a controversial area the British had some historical responsibility for."

Trudeau, for his part, was a much more acute observer and brought up matters of real concern with Deng when he, in his turn, had talks. "I don't think the answer lies in a perpetual garrison of Chinese troops in Tibet," he told reporters after his meeting with Deng. For a washed-up politician, as he seemed then, he made a far superior impression than either Nixon or Heath. In fact, Trudeau was struck by the comic potential in three abandoned Western leaders' arriving in the Chinese capital at the same time. He pointed this out to Deng during their conversation and suggested that the three of them might have come to get political advice from the vice-premier, who had survived two major purges. Trudeau asked Deng what he should do while he was out of power. Deng smiled enigmatically and then whispered the answer: "Have patience." Good advice, as it turned out. Trudeau's Liberal Party became the Canadian Government again after an election held a few months later. As with Mrs. Gandhi in India, patience has given them the last laugh.

Patience has also been one of the great policies of Chinese foreign affairs, and it eventually won for China worldwide acceptance of the Communist Party's right to govern the Mainland, despite years of United States pressure and economic punishments aimed at preserving Taiwan's position as the legitimate, if usurped, power. The Chinese Communists never budged on this issue, and long after most of the world had accepted the reality, the Chinese Government allowed the United States to use a curious twist in Chinese history to sneak out of some of its obligations to Taiwan and accept the line from Peking. The only point of agreement between the Guomindang authorities in Taiwan and the Communists was that Taiwan was "an inalienable part of China." The debate was simply "Which China?"

Hugging inalienability, over which there was no argument, President Carter extricated himself from the Guomindang with a few formal assurances of protection and then normalized relations with Peking. It had to happen sometime, but, typically, the Americans rode roughshod over the local Taiwanese sensitivities after being so careful and courteous for so many years. The normalization announcement came on the eve of important elections in Taiwan that would have marked a real breakthrough in the democracy movement there. The American actions gave the Guomindang the opportunity to raise the specter of "national security," and the elections were "postponed." Although the American Government had given generous support to Taiwan for years, the manner of its leavetaking was ignoble, and the timing was close to criminal. With the departure of the Americans, Taiwan's distinct perspective was in danger of being totally submerged. By the time normalization was announced, I wanted very much to see this other version of China. When the opportunity suddenly arose, I grabbed it.

10

The Other China

Over the years, Communist China has aimed stunning verbal broadsides at "imperialist" America, the "revisionist" Soviet Union, "militaristic" Japan and "colonialist" Britain. But these attacks, vicious and fanatical as they sometimes seemed, were as inconsequential as dandelion fluff compared with the rhetoric reserved for the "kith and kin" on Taiwan. The tiny Guomindang bastion of Generalissimo Chiang Kaishek and his son Chiang Chingkuo may be isolated in the world, but it remains a stubborn symbol of the unfinished revolution on the Mainland, and its feisty survival irks the Communist leadership as little else does. Since Taiwan was always under the forbidding protection of the United States, the Communists never dared to stage a military invasion, but everything else was fair game. The Guomindang reciprocated with its own special flourishes. The epithets each side used to describe the other stretched even the Chinese penchant for pungent abuse. Depending on which side one was listening to, theirs was a confrontation between bandits and running dogs, hyenas and wolves, paper tigers and bloody murderers, fascist jackals and Communist scum. Here was a unique dialogue between brothers who seemed to know each other's instincts and motivations better than did the world around them or their own people.

Blood and common experience unite the Guomindang and Communist parties as much as they divide them: each one's hero is a traitor to the other side, and the soil of China is rich with the blood of mutual martyrs. So potent was the official hatred between the two that innocent travelers to either place had to learn all the rhetoric, just to survive. In Peking one talked only about "the other place," so that the word "Taiwan" was never uttered. In Taipei, you had to call the Mainland "Red China," and Peking itself was (and remains) Peiping—the old Guomindang name for the city. Both governments adore indulging themselves in the game of "so-called." The rules of this game are very simple: on a visit to either Taipei or Peking, all institutions or officials of the other place must be prefixed with "so-called." In this fashion, officials in Peking referred to the "so-called premier of Taiwan" or the "so-called legislative assembly." In the same way, Guomindang bureaucrats talked about the "so-called People's Liberation Army" or my particular favorite, the "so-called Red China Red Cross." In the past, anyone trying to visit both places had to have two passports, because neither side would grant entry to someone who had been polluted in the other China, although the Communists relented on this sooner than the Guomindang.

Over the years, the propaganda war has become more sophisticated, and as each side became increasingly entrenched in its respective position, a kind of liturgy evolved that became so familiar it was almost comforting. The liturgy managed to survive the deaths of both Chiang Kaishek and Mao Tsetung; in fact, both sides used the departure of their leaders as an opportunity once again to swear eternal, sacred oaths, either to "reconquer the Mainland" or "reunite Taiwan with the Motherland." Then, abruptly, the chant changed on the Communist side. With the formal normalization of relations between Washington and Peking on January 1, 1979, the (so-called) National People's Congress of Communist China sent an extraordinary message to their (so-called) "beloved compatriots" on Taiwan.

"If we do not quickly set about ending our disunity," the message read in part, "what can we say to our ancestors or to our descendants? This sentiment is shared by all Chinese, and who among the descendants of the Yellow Emperor wishes to be branded a traitor of all ages?"

It is almost impossible to describe the shock and amazement this message aroused. The neat reversal of so many years of vitriol was one thing, but here the Communists were invoking both ancestor worship and the Yellow Emperor himself—the mythical, irredeemably feudal founder of the Chinese nation. The Communists announced that improved relations between the two could begin with small things like postal and transportation exchanges. Taiwan could maintain its own kind of government and economic system indefinitely, as well as its own armed forces and police network. All the Guomindang had to do was say it was part of the People's Republic of China and forget the nonsense of perpetuating the repudiated "Republic of China."

Not surprisingly, Taiwan—which was trying to absorb the humiliation and fears that followed the normalization announcement—dismissed the overture out of hand. The Communists don't know how to take no for an answer, however, and pushed the new line relentlessly. Taipei was blitzed with telegrams from every conceivable institution on the Mainland calling for reunion and brotherly love. A painless solution was promised. Our athletes, said the Communists, could compete together against other countries at international events and then return to their own distinctive ways of life when the competition was over.

This new line from Peking was so reasonable and so compelling to outside eyes that Taiwan's adamant refusal even to discuss the possibility of an opening dialogue seemed churlish, belligerent and needlessly dangerous. Can seventeen million people on a small island really believe they can hold out indefinitely against a power representing a billion souls just a few miles away? Even Western pundits who recognized Taiwan's superior economic condition and the advanced level of its productive and technological forces argued that a hookup would be advantageous to both sides: Taiwan expertise and the unlimited manpower of the Mainland could be an almost unbeatable combination. But Taiwan remained obdurate, and I was curious to find out why.

Before I managed to go there in the spring of 1979, it would have been impossible for a correspondent based in Peking to make a trip to Taiwan, get his reports published and then return home to Peking. But the new Communist line, which held that Taiwan was "just another part of China" where normal exchange should be possible, offered a unique opportunity to a Peking-based journalist. There was no problem with the Taiwanese authorities, who were urging Western correspondents in Peking to come and compare the two systems. The Guomindang was quite convinced its version of China would be so much more compelling than the Communist Party's that it professed no fear of comparison. For its part, Peking was anxious to get some sort of exchange going on, and if it had to be foreign journalists first, so be it.

Unofficially, I contacted the Information Department and sounded out officials on the idea. "Well don't let us know in writing what you are going to do," said Chi Ming-tsung with unconcerned cheeriness. "You might simply request permission to travel to Hong Kong. Very easy matter." My formal letter abided by this guideline, but it could not be described as subtle:

> Dear Mr. Chi:
>
> My wife and I are planning a trip to certain Southeast Asian countries and would like to request the necessary permission to leave Peking on April 29, passing through the Hong Kong frontier. We will return 12 days later.
>
> My editor has recently written me expressing an interest in the Government's official attitude to Taiwan in light of the new situation between the People's Republic of China and the United States. Accordingly, I am also requesting at this time the opportunity of speaking to any official who could enlighten me on this matter. I would prefer to do this interview before departing for Hong Kong if it could possibly be arranged.
>
> In the meantime, may I take this opportunity of extending my regards to yourself and your colleagues at the Information Department. Also my thanks for any trouble these requests may give you.

Of course, I knew I would never be given an interview with any Communist leaders on the subject of Taiwan. I didn't even particularly want one, as I also knew it would simply be a repetition of what was carried in the official press. But I did want an obvious reference to what I was up to on the record—not for fear of being refused reentry, but to test the new line on Taiwan.

Coming and going, I made myself thoroughly objectionable at all entry and exit points in both China and Taiwan. In Taiwan, I made sure customs and immigration officials saw I was a resident of Peking; on the Mainland, I opened my passport to the page where the Taiwan stamp was prominently displayed. I couldn't get an angry reaction out of anyone anywhere, and no trip could have been planned more easily. With Hong Kong as the pivotal point, airplane reservations and visas were processed more smoothly than I had ever before experienced. In fact, the eagerness of both sides to let me do what I wanted made me distinctly uneasy: both the Communists and the Guomindang had their own propaganda interests involved in the trip, and it was going to be necessary to remain alert so that I didn't get enmeshed in either side.

What surprises were in store for me! After more than a year in Peking, I had accustomed myself to many conditions that I had assumed were part and parcel of Chinese Communism. It was with some considerable shock, therefore, that I discovered identical things in Taiwan and realized that they were simply a product of traditional China. This experience ranged from the profound to the ridiculous. It was fascinating, for example, to realize that the Guomindang Government has the same distrust of political alternatives as the Communists do and uses much of the same sort of propaganda and police actions to put such heresies down. On a more comical level, it would seem that both sides have developed an identical policy on how to deal with snooping foreign journalists.

In China, I went through an invariable routine whenever I visited a factory. Upon my arrival I would be met by local officials, as well as members of the management, who would unctuously lead me to a conference room for The Official Introduction. The conference room would have chairs, usually covered with lace antimacassars, and from nowhere, it seemed, the inevitable cups of tea would arrive. Since I was accompanied by officials of the central government, it was always a good opportunity for the local crowd to get caught up on high-level gossip, and this whispering banter formed a background to the introduction.

In Taiwan, I visited a steel factory, and sure enough, was accompanied by a government official. Upon my arrival I was met by local party people and members of the management. With precisely the same degree of unctuousness, I was led into a conference room for The Official Introduction. There were antimacassars on the chairs, and tea arrived from nowhere. In the background, the officials gossiped. Then, suddenly, something happened that was different: the lights went out. The Official Introduction took the form of a propaganda film, and I realized I was in the same country I had just left, only updated by twenty years of technological development. The film turned out to be a smoother version of the more primitive

introductions I was used to on the Mainland, but the purpose was
the same.

Just as the Communists used 1949 as a base year for so many of
their statistical miracles, so did the Guomindang. It was a curious
practice that had advantages for both sides. In all the long history
of China, 1949 must have been one of the worst years for production on record. Both Taiwan and the Mainland were torn asunder
by a gigantic civil war, manufacturing had come to a virtual standstill and most peasants in the countryside had to lie low to avoid
getting killed.

Using 1949 as a base economic year to measure comparisons with
current statistics makes as much sense as using 1930—the first full
year of the Great Depression—for the same purpose in the West.
Shortly before I left, the Communists came a bit closer to reality and
started using 1952 as a base year, as well as providing the first set
of extensive and concrete production figures in twenty-five years.
In Taiwan, more sophisticated statistics were available if one really
went after them.

The history of Taiwan under the Guomindang is intriguing. As
on the Mainland, there is so much that is never talked about; one
must ferret and scrounge around for the facts. Local Taiwanese, for
example, are still reluctant to discuss openly the two years that
followed the Japanese surrender in 1945, when Tokyo's model
colony of Formosa reverted to Chinese ownership and the Chinese
name of Taiwan. By the Chinese standards of those days, or even
today, Taiwan was rich, orderly and modernized. In the Guomindang capital of Nanking, Chiang Kaishek was leader of a country
that was exhausted from war and occupation. It was also in the midst
of civil war. Still, there was a broad consensus among the people
that China could stand up on its own. Chiang had a chance with
Taiwan to transform a model colony into a model province with a
potential to affect development throughout the country. Instead, he
allowed Taiwan to be systematically looted and pillaged under the
malevolent authority of one of his closest cronies, Governor Chen
Yi.

There were a handful of Western witnesses to those terrible years
in which thousands of people were imprisoned and hundreds more
executed. The entire island became a carpetbagger's paradise, and
Chiang's own relatives and friends were in the vanguard. Since
Taiwan had been a colony of Japan for decades, the official attitude

in Nanking was that all Taiwanese were potential traitors and were treated as such. To this day, any accurate account of that horrifying time is rigorously banned in Taiwan. The terror, however, has left an enduring legacy. Apart from precipitating a Taiwanese independence movement, which is repugnant to both the Communists and the Guomindang, it has taught the Taiwanese to stay clear of politics as much as possible. Even today, more than thirty years later, Taiwanese parents tell their children to get a good education that will prepare them for solid professions and to keep their mouths permanently shut about government and party affairs.

Although Chiang Kaishek was ultimately forced to have Governor Chen Yi executed, it was not the act of a morally outraged leader. Widespread riots broke out in 1947, and the natives had to be mollified. The tragedy was that they had welcomed the arrival of the Chinese two years before and got bashed for the sentiment. The discontent and turmoil on Taiwan became a crucial problem when Chiang was defeated by the Communist forces on the Mainland and had to stage a massive retreat to the island redoubt. What ensued in the next three decades could not possibly have been predicted. For a variety of reasons, the horrible old Guomindang Party managed to reform itself somewhat, and while its oppressiveness can still be felt by some people on the island today, it has nevertheless become a reasonably effective vehicle for renewal and progress. Initially under the protection of United States military might, which began in earnest during the Korean War, when U.S. policy sought to contain the Communist-held Mainland, Chiang ruled with an iron will and ruthlessness that was allied to his cold (some said Confucian) aloofness. As he got older, however, other forces came into play. On the Mainland, which had a similar problem of old age with Mao Tsetung, radical politics caused unprecedented damage to every aspect of life. On Taiwan, particularly when it became increasingly apparent that the United States could not be relied upon indefinitely, a succession of young reformers began the process of improving life.

Their logic was simple enough and has been proved correct. The key to survival is internal security. The traditional Guomindang solution to this problem was naked threats, but when you are a small island facing Mainland millions, and your people only fear you, this basis of support is extremely precarious, especially when international allies are falling by the wayside. Make life better, however, and people will have a genuine stake in the survival of the status quo. And so, to give one good example, the Guomindang embarked on a progressive land-reform program, which it had never managed when it ruled the Mainland.

The feudal landlord system, which had become unendurably corrupt, was the traditional source of discontent among China's huge peasantry. Sun Yatsen, who led the first Chinese Revolution against the Manchu Court, recognized this when he created the Guomindang Party and suggested various reforms, which were never put into wide practice because he never controlled much of the country. Chiang, his successor, also had land-reform programs, but since the landlords were the principal supporters of the Guomindang, these plans were all left on the shelf. In Taiwan, however, Chiang and his colleagues had no obligations to the local landlords, and with a program called "Land to the Tiller," Taiwanese peasants got their first square deal ever. The dispossessed landlords were compensated for their lost properties and encouraged (that's the polite Guomindang expression; they had little choice) to invest in a new light-industry program.

Luck was on their side, and the new industry boomed, especially with the help of United States aid. The landlords, for the most part, became rich. The peasants got their own plots of land, which they farmed with enthusiasm. The light-industry base became stronger and stronger, thanks to comparatively cheap labor costs, and proved a strong foundation for the establishment of heavy industry. Since the Guomindang has precisely the same use for trade unions as the Communist Party, there has been little labor agitation over the years—which does not say much for the vaunted freedom of the Taiwanese, but it did help get production figures up.

The Guomindang also sought to relieve some of the serious tensions between the two million Mainlanders who came over with Chiang in 1949 and the local population. Land reform and the more equitable distribution of wealth aided in this process, as did a slight lessening of totalitarian authority, although Taiwan still remains essentially a one-party state. The Guomindang Party was modeled on the Soviet Communist Party, the result of a curious quirk of history (Sun Yatsen gratefully accepted Soviet advisers in the early days of his revolution, because the Soviet Union was one of the few nations that expressed support and also returned its "foreign concessions" on Chinese soil to Chinese jurisdiction—the first country voluntarily to do so). Although the Guomindang was committed to free enterprise, the authoritarian Soviet party structure was deemed useful. In time, and only in Taiwan, the Guomindang slowly woke up to the realization that alternative voices need not necessarily lead to its downfall, and a certain degree of genuine opposition is tolerated.

Today, Taiwanese political life is not something Westerners would feel at all at home in, but it is like day from night compared with the restrictions imposed by "the dictatorship of the proletariat" on the Mainland. Increased prosperity and social mobility have aided immeasurably in this process: when a peasant can afford a television set, a motorcycle and a telephone, a lot of primary grievances against an authoritarian state fall away. It is clear that progressive Communist officials on the Mainland recognize this fact, and this is why they have put so much faith in the modernization program. Indeed, some of the fervor behind the new line on Taiwan is a confirmation that the Communists recognize what they could gain economically from the Taiwanese experience. The potential for a model province is once again possible.

When I was in Taiwan, Guomindang officials were vociferous about not having any dialogue with the Communists, of any sort. Despite rumors and a few minor concessions to the contrary, that was still the official line in 1980. This worked its way right up to the premier. In fact, I was scheduled to speak to President Chiang Chingkuo, the son of the old Generalissimo, but the government got so nervous about my being the first correspondent to come to Taiwan who was based in Peking and intended to return there that it canceled the interview. It did not want my trip to be interpreted as a bridge between the two sides, and I was told this very bluntly.

Curiosities of the family feud kept appearing. Both sides pay tribute to Sun Yatsen and his 1911 revolution—the Communists as successors, the Guomindang as inheritors. Sun's widow, Soong Chingling, who was well into her nineties that year, was about the most honored citizen on the Mainland and lives in grandeur in Peking. One of her brothers-in-law was Chiang Kaishek, whose son is now the president of Taiwan. The same son was a much-feared security chief in his earlier days, as was Chairman Hua Guofeng in Peking. During the Cultural Revolution, Chairman Mao was widely referred to as the Great Helmsman, and this is precisely the eulogistic title accorded to President Chiang Chingkuo in Taiwanese newspapers today.

The contrasts and similarities between the two places were a constant revelation, and they came to a mind-boggling peak the day I visited a rural area and dropped in on some farmers. I had been relentlessly briefed on the success of the Land to the Tiller reform program, which I already knew about from independent research. I could see that the farmhouses and lands were well maintained and the peasants relatively prosperous. The only thing that struck me as odd was the smallness of the individual plots.

"Well, yes," said a government official, "that's a problem. You see, so many peasants have so many small plots, it's becoming increasingly uneconomical to farm in Taiwan. There's another problem, too. Because of the success of light and heavy industry, factories in the cities can pay better wages to young people than they can earn tilling their parents' land. So they go off to the factories, and the countryside is getting depopulated. There aren't enough hands to do the work."

"What's the solution?" I asked.

"There's only one solution. Mechanization. It will solve both the problems. We have been encouraging the farmers to pull down the fences dividing their small plots and join their fields with their neighbors'. Individually, they cannot afford to buy the mechanized machinery, and it doesn't make sense for such small plots anyway. But together they can form an organization which could buy the necessary equipment and share it."

"You mean like a commune?" I asked with amused surprise.

"No, not at all. Not in any way. That's communist." The official was quite upset at the obvious parallel. "This is free enterprise. The government is simply encouraging farmers to pool their resources, and we will help out by providing low-interest or interest-free loans to purchase equipment, which will belong to them, not the government."

"Like cooperative communes," I said, somewhat mischievously.

"No, you don't understand at all. That's communist. This is capitalist. It's nothing like that at all."

Maybe it isn't, but consider what was happening on the Communist Mainland. Less than a year before this conversation in Taiwan, the government had accepted reality by recognizing that state farms were not being as productive as they could be, because peasants felt they had no stake in the hard work and had no incentive to do anything more than the minimum amount of labor. To remedy this increasingly serious problem, the government gave back to the peasants small parcels of private land to farm in any way they wanted. The plots were about the same size as the small plots I saw in Taiwan. I once asked a Communist official if this wasn't free enterprise, pure and simple. He looked at me as if I were totally ignorant. "Not at all. You don't understand. There is nothing inconsistent between these plots and socialist theory. You have not understood it correctly."

Perhaps. Perhaps not.

11

The Foreign "Experts"

In the northwest outskirts of Peking, on the way to the Summer Palace, there is a vast complex of dour gray buildings surrounded by a high wall. At the entrance, sentries from the People's Liberation Army stand guard twenty-four hours a day, and the Public Security Bureau is never far away. This forbidding-looking establishment is known as the Friendship Guest House, and within its precincts live a small army of "foreign experts" who work for the Chinese Government as teachers, translators and occasionally advisers. The exact population of the foreign experts is not known to outsiders, but it is certainly over three or four hundred if you count not only the residents of the Friendship Guest House, but also the other foreign teachers spread out in various Chinese cities.

Recently, their numbers have been growing as the Chinese Government seeks to increase contacts with the outside world. English-language teachers are most in demand, and a number of young people in the West have discovered that they can have a unique Chinese experience for a couple of years by becoming instant "experts"—a phrase the Chinese Government applies to the foreigners and which most of them abhor. By Western standards, the pay and living conditions are not great, although they are vastly superior to those any ordinary Chinese citizen enjoys. But really, pay is irrelevant. The experts, for the most part, come to China out of idealism and a desire to serve. Some even resent the few privileges the Chinese insist they accept.

Until 1978, the life of the foreign experts was a deeply shrouded secret to most other resident foreigners in Peking. Diplomats and journalists lived separate lives in districts far away from the Friendship Guest House, and on those rare occasions when members of either group might meet by chance, conversation was usually brief and painful. These were mutually exclusive groups, eyeing each other with suspicion and dislike. The foreign experts, who had more access to Chinese society, regarded the journalists and diplomats as transient intruders with no commitment to China. On the other side, the foreign experts were often dismissed in the diplomatic quarter as stooges and hacks who did the Communist Party's bidding, even when they knew it was venal or arbitrary.

Because of all this, little was known of the life of these unusual foreigners, apart from what emerged in the official press. Among the most prominent was the ubiquitous Rewi Alley, the New Zealander who came to China long before the Revolution and never left. Alley cast in his lot with Mao Tsetung, and for years he has contributed sympathetic and usually lugubrious prose and poetry to government or pro-People's Republic Hong Kong newspapers and magazines. A fantasist who sees only what he wants to see, he is fixated with a vision of revolutionary China that rarely differs from that of the propaganda department. In the past when outside observers talked about the foreign experts in China, they usually were referring to Rewi Alley. He gave them all a bad name in precisely the same way that the legendary writer Han Suyin gave all official "friends of China" a bad name: they seemed to be toadies to whatever faction or party had power in Peking.

Although Madame Han is not a foreign expert and resides outside the country, it has been possible to observe her career closely over the years. Since she fits a type that is now so widely despised, it is useful to look at her more closely.

She was born and educated in China, and since her parents were of different races, she has always had a special insight into both the Chinese character and the Western fascination with China. With the publication of her most successful novel *A Many Splendored Thing,* she has been widely regarded as one of the foremost interpreters of things Chinese. Her numerous books always sell well, and as a strikingly handsome and extremely eloquent woman, she is much in demand on the lecture circuit. Her connections to the Chinese Communist Party leadership are impeccable, and over the years she has been regarded both inside and outside China as *the* foreign expert. I couldn't begin to count the number of anecdotes I have heard about Han Suyin—some true and some, no doubt, apocryphal. She has practically become a mythic figure, and it did not surprise me that she made an appearance in a work of fiction recently, Chen Johsi's *The Execution of Mayor Yin.* My wife remembers her vividly from a University of Toronto "teach-in" during the sixties, when she explained the Cultural Revolution to a generation of Western university students who were eager to learn how to topple authority in their own bailiwick. Elizabeth, along with thousands of others, hooted down a pathetic old English scholar who tried to point out that a lot of nasty things were going on in China, and then cheered Han Suyin, who got up and said, "You don't understand. You are not Chinese."

Part of Han Suyin's power resides in the Western fascination and essential sympathy with the Chinese people. The sympathy has complicated origins—from a perceived guilt for the historical deeds of Western imperialism to a desire to believe in successful alternatives to development as we know it—but it is completely genuine. And, too, ignorance of the Chinese condition and heritage leads many of us to accept at face value any authoritative voice that links up directly with our sympathy.

The unpleasant aspects of Madame Han's career are usually ignored. Beginning as a firm supporter of the Guomindang, she switched her allegiance to Mao as soon as she saw which way the winds were blowing. Throughout the mad, zigzag course of Communist politics, she has always been the outside spokesperson for the prevailing line. If you look back a decade, you can see her fulminating against capitalist-roaders inside the Party; if you can get her to pause for a moment today, you will find her in the midst of a joint Sino-American film project. All along the way, she has profited materially from the Chinese connection.

Among serious Sinologists her views were usually belittled, although I always noted they read everything she wrote because, at the very least, they appreciated her ability to get right to the top of Chinese politics. It was widely known that Mao's wife Jiang Qing liked and respected Han Suyin, who had reciprocated the friendship publicly. There was therefore a certain sense of nausea when Madame Han went on French television a few days after the fall of the Gang of Four and added her knife, Brutus-like, to the others that were in Jiang Qing's back. She even noted that Jiang perspired a great deal, which was presumably a sign of evil intentions. It was this story that helped me appreciate the last anecdote I heard about Han Suyin while I was in China.

Five days before we left, I was invited to pay an official visit to a special journalism class for Chinese reporters, set up by the New China News Agency. The students, from a variety of previous professions, were on a special crash course to improve their English and become either foreign correspondents or domestic reporters who could write news directly for the English-language service of the agency. They were bright and articulate, and after I gave my little talk on the problems facing Western correspondents based in Peking, there was an hour-long question-and-answer period in which they quizzed me closely on many pertinent points. We had different views on the role of journalism, but their sincerity and passion buttressed their outlook. Two days later, I learned that Han Suyin had addressed the same class. She spoke passionately, as she always does, and told the students that they must be fearless as they seek out the facts. Honesty and integrity are paramount, she is reported to have told the students, and I have no doubt she enjoyed speaking to them as much as I did. But then it came time for questions. One of *her* people, as she liked to say, raised his hand. "Can you tell us something about your relationship with Jiang Qing?" he asked. "How much did she influence your work?" According to two eyewitnesses, Han Suyin mumbled something about Jiang Qing's being "a very complicated person" and then refused to discuss the matter any further.

To leave the matter there would be journalistically satisfying, but Han Suyin too is a very complicated person, and her career, far from being atypical, is useful in pondering the dilemma faced by other "friends of China," foreign experts and, indeed, most senior ideologues within the Communist Party itself. The Party believes in the efficacious use of "negative examples" to instruct the masses, and it is an infectious way of looking at things. Han Suyin is notorious only because the stage she played on was large enough to allow many different kinds of observers to take stock of her. Setting aside questions of ego and profit, no one could accuse her of hating the

Chinese people, even if her pipeline was to their leaders and not the people themselves. How many Western commentators and political experts do we suffer willingly who interpret a nation's aspirations exclusively through the perspective of government? How many senior correspondents pride themselves on their connections with leaders and high officers of state? Government is less the manifestation of the will of the people in China than it is in the West because of the nature of totalitarian rule, but it is still some sort of manifestation. Han Suyin gives us an eye into the problem of leadership in China. Her accommodations to the shifting political struggle echo the accommodation millions of Chinese have had to make, either to rise within the ranks of the Party or simply to survive down on the commune.

Like many older Chinese who lived through the civil war and the heroic days of national reconstruction during the fifties, Han Suyin has considered the past and concluded that the present, in whatever form, is better. She is out of touch with the rising generation of Chinese, as I was to learn, but she is symptomatic of the malaise that afflicts much of her own age group inside China. While they have an underlying faith in the Chinese entity, they are incapable of even contemplating a modest philosophical assault on the system, because they believe Party leadership—no matter what monster has grabbed power—is inseparable from that entity. It remains the prerogative of unrepentant individualists and innovators like Mao Tsetung or Deng Xiaoping to wrest control of the leadership, and the sheep will mostly follow.

The only essential difference between Han Suyin and many of the political cadres inside China is that she is a free agent and can come and go as she pleases. Her adjustment to the abrupt changes in Party policy is relatively easy: all she must do is push the new line with sufficient conviction and the job is done. The cadres, on the other hand, have to stay in China and live with the consequences; Madame Han never seems to visit China until a new line is sufficiently established so that she can count on it for a few years. Her enthusiasm, then, is in marked contrast with the halfhearted work of the cadres, who know the rules may be turned upside down again. Most of them will go only so far as they have to in order to survive, and it is this necessary caution that has bedeviled Chinese development on all fronts for decades; the propagandists are always light-years away from current reality.

I had great good fortune during my time in China. Opportunities for travel and contact with Chinese people multiplied with every passing month. Initially, one of the most successful forays was into the world of foreign experts, and when it came, I was amazed at the number of misconceptions I had accumulated—thanks, in part, to my perception of people like Rewi Alley and Han Suyin.

Instead of intolerant hacks, I found a small world of intensely committed people about whom few generalities could be made. Since the country itself was opening up, it was fairly easy to make contact with the new generation of foreign experts, who were mostly my own age and were fascinated with China in the same way that I was. Sometimes I visited them at their places of work, but usually we met at the Friendship Guest House. Although set in a different context, their aspirations and frustrations seemed remarkably similar to mine. the stupidity of the bureaucracy, the forced separation from Chinese, the desire for honest and open relations, the affection for Chinese civility, the annoyance at special privileges designed to keep foreigners at bay. I knew it all in a different way. They were relegated to this hideous guest house, and from time to time the Chinese authorities in charge of the Foreign Experts Bureau attempted to impose the kind of regulations all Chinese people have to put up with as a matter of course. It always struck me as amusing that when this happened there was an instant revolt, and the younger experts never made the connection: they were being honored with equal treatment.

A good example of this phenomenon occurred during the summer of 1979. For over a year, the Friendship Guest House had been going through drastic changes. Because of the shortage of hotel space in Peking, many of the hordes of tourists coming to China had to be put up inside the complex, which had originally been built to Soviet specifications in the fifties to house fraternal Communist experts. When the Sino-Soviet rift broke into the open in 1960, the Soviet experts were recalled, and the guest house became a lonely place for a few years.

The tourists of 1979 meant that access to the complex was easier for people like me. The sentries, for example, would go through the motions of halting each and every car that came through the main gates, but early on I decided that their manner was far too officious and paid them no attention. I would whiz through the gates and leave them flapping their arms in the wind. I was never questioned. Also, most of the new generation of foreign experts from the West resented the summer-camp atmosphere at the place, and after they had settled in they often played loose with the camp rules. Consequently, one day a large official notice appeared in a prominent place, notifying all foreign experts that they had to register every guest—foreign or Chinese—who came to visit them.

The government, as I was to learn in a very direct way, has an absolute horror of Chinese citizens' making friends with foreigners without its say-so. In may naiveté, I had assumed this extended only to traditional spy figures like journalists and diplomats, but I soon discovered it included the experts. This was part of the reasoning behind the notice, which also included other rules, such as the hours when music could be played and the permitted visiting time of guests. The experts were incensed, of course, and since they had been put into a summer-camp environment, they chose childish ways to protest, like staging outside dance parties with loud music beyond the prescribed hour.

I often listened to the complaints of the younger foreign experts and shared my own experiences with them. Sitting in the dining hall of the Friendship Guest House was like walking into a play by Harold Pinter. Conversation often drifted into nothingness, and inchoate hostilities would flare up for no ostensible reason. Most of them longed to be away from the hideous ghetto and live with, or at least next door to, Chinese people in a real spirit of egalitarianism. The biggest shock they had to absorb was that egalitarianism does not exist in China, and people, foreigners included, are placed in categories far more rigid than anything that can be found today in the West.

From the government's point of view, the experts had been assigned an idyllic category, that of senior officials. They had superior living quarters, access to stores with high-quality goods, chauffeur-driven cars—these are perks some Chinese in the Party work a lifetime to achieve. As a result, the government simply doesn't comprehend the experts' discontent. If there is a sadness to their lives, it can be found here. These people are not bitter exiles, pining to be home. They are pioneers who have found something attractive in the soul of China. They want to be a part of this soul and at the same time make their own special contribution, as all the other foreign experts have done. Just as Kang Hsi, the early Manchu Dynasty emperor, sought to keep the Jesuits in their place while obtaining what he wanted from them, so do the Communists strive to control the present generation of foreigners. The gap between the desires of the two sides remains very, very wide.

Even this, however, is only a one-sided look at the life of the foreign experts. Through mutual friends I met the most notorious foreign expert of all, Sidney Rittenberg, who turned out to be one of the most remarkable men I have ever stumbled across. There are few people who have a more fascinating tale to tell. Rittenberg came to China in 1945 and did not leave until the summer of 1979, when he took his Chinese wife to America for a sentimental visit. Since Rittenberg has spent over fifteen of his thirty-five years in China inside prisons, he has a unique perspective on life there, and every time we met he held me spellbound. In another age and another place, he could have been the best stump preacher in history, but his talents and enthusiasm brought him to China and keep him there today. He comes from a well-established Jewish family in South Carolina, where his grandfather was a prominent state legislator and his father was once mayor of Charleston. His own life of social and political activism began during undergraduate days at the University of North Carolina, and one of his fellow students, the American economist Frank Holzman, has given a picture of him then (in a private letter) that still rings true:

> We met as members of the campus left-wing organization, the American Student Union. I was immediately attracted to [Rittenberg]. Behind those incredibly thick glasses there was always a humorous and friendly manner. Even his physical bearing was different—thin, loosely framed, always going downstairs with a hop on alternate steps. We took the Hegel and Marx course together. By this time, the Union began to split into two factions—Communist and other fellow travelers which also included liberals. The uneasy coalition broke up when the Soviet Union invaded Finland. Sid began to work politically outside the university and then left school and ended up with the mineworkers. I heard him speak a couple of times and he was terrific.

In time, Rittenberg overcame a strong antiwar bias and enlisted in the United States Army. He soon fast-talked his way into a specialized training program that led to Chinese-language studies at Stanford University. The idea was to train a number of linguists who would work with Allied troops in the battle against the Japanese on the Chinese Mainland.

As he did everywhere, Rittenberg left a lasting impression on his colleagues at Stanford. An American journalist, Walter Unna, who was with him in the program feels quite simply that he was brilliant. "Ritt became fluent in spoken Chinese while most of the rest of us were trying to form a sentence," says Unna. "He then moved on to written Chinese and then newspaper Chinese, which is quite different. He would practice his characters during military drills by tracing them with his dirty fingernails in the parade-ground dust. His uniform always looked as though he had slept in it. And he probably had. His GI-issue glasses hadn't had the lenses wiped clean in ages, and the rust of the metal rims blended right into his skin. But Ritt knew Shelley and Keats backward and loved life and people. There was always a smile on his face."

Every time I spoke to him, Rittenberg managed to say that he never looks for trouble but simply reacts to life around him. Elizabeth would openly mock him about this, pointing out that anyone who sets himself up as a labor organizer in the Deep South during the thirties and then involves himself in the Chinese Revolution is not exactly a trouble-shirker. I, however, had more sympathy for this line, since Sidney and I share two traits: he can't keep his mouth shut, and he has an insatiable curiosity. He is also an incautious man who is happiest following his own instincts: this is the source of his engaging charm and most of his political problems in China.

The one thing no one can accuse him of is having less than total commitment to the Chinese way of life. He lives and breathes the place, with a passion that is often overwhelming. As soon as he arrived in the country in 1945, he knew he had reached the destination he had been searching for all his life. With his customary lack of restraint, he was poking his nose all over the place and making outrageous demands on his army superiors. One of his first jobs was with a small army department that investigated damage done to Chinese property by United States troops. After the investigation, he would then be required to assess compensation charges. With a commandeered jeep, he was scooting around the Kunming area and quickly became a folk hero to a bunch of enterprising boys who peddled newspapers to both the Guomindang and the Communist parties. It was through these boys that he made his first contact with Communist officials.

Given his own left-wing sympathies and the destitution and horror he saw all around him in China, it was hardly surprising Rittenberg was attracted to the cause of the Great Helmsman. The corruption and cruelty of the Guomindang appalled him, and although the Communists were capable of considerable cruelty too, Mao's forces had by this time achieved heroic status among many Chinese people. The Red Army was, among other things, the first army in Chinese history that never plundered from the masses, and that point was widely noted. Rittenberg was developing his contacts with the Communists when he got a recall notice ordering him to return to the United States.

"I was determined I wouldn't go home," he told me. "China was the only place I wanted to be. So I went to my commanding officer, who was a decent fellow and had a reputation for fairness. When I put my case to him, he said I should simply tear up my orders and refuse to obey any others that didn't say I could stay. So that's what I did, and I snuck out of Kunming and headed for Shanghai. There was no way I was going to leave."

No two people get exactly the same story from Rittenberg; which is not to say he is knowingly deceptive, but his reigning enthusiasms sometimes mean history gets rewritten a little—a trait he may well have picked up from the Chinese Communist Party. In any event, his connections with the Party must have been fairly impressive by this time, because it was the Communists who secretly managed to get him appointed to a regional office of the United Nations Relief and Rehabilitation Administration as an observer. He was expected to mediate in matters that arose between the Communist- and Guomindang-controlled sections of China. Early on, as an UNRRA observer, he met Chou Enlai, who had come to Hubei province as a member of the Communist–Guomindang–United States truce team attempting to bring an end to the civil war that broke out as soon as the Japanese surrendered. In the tiny village of Xuanhuadian the team held a public meeting in the local ancestral temple. "The darkness of the meeting place was relieved only by seven or eight bean-oil lamps placed on the speakers' table in front—each lamp being about the size of a butter dish," recalls Rittenberg. "I sat at the opposite end of the hall. The first words Chou said after we were introduced at the end of the meeting were 'I was watching you. You applauded me loudly, but sat there scowling when the Guomindang general spoke. That isn't good. You have to be more careful. If they find out you are on our side, they may make trouble for you when you get back to Guomindang-controlled areas.' "

Rittenberg said he was impressed by Chou's ability to see in the dark, but the Chinese leader simply said, "Americans are our friends. We have to take care of our friends."

Sidney's anecdotes are rich in colorful details, famous figures and pertinent points. He tells them with relish, and you get swept along as he weaves you into and out of Chinese history. There is no reason to doubt this particular tale—in fact, I never doubted the basics of any of Sidney's tales—but you do have to keep your wits about you nevertheless. When he told me this story, he was preparing for his first trip back to the United States. It was at the time of the normalization of relations between China and the United States, and pro-American propaganda was pouring out of the state media. You also have to keep in mind that there are many Chinese and a number of foreigners who are quite convinced that Sidney was part of a plot during the Cultural Revolution designed to topple Chou Enlai from power. I'm jumping a bit ahead of Sidney's story here, but I learned very quickly that you miss half the nuances and pleasure of his tales if you don't have some background on both current propaganda and past events. Talking with Sidney is a bit like playing chess against a master who knows all the classic strategies: you have to concentrate very hard to make respectable moves before you are inevitably checkmated.

Sidney made his move to the "liberated areas" under Mao's control, shucked his UNRRA job and signed on as an early foreign expert. His job was with the New China News Agency, which in those days did both print and radio work. A natural and enthusiastic propagandist, he set to work with a vengeance and was enjoying himself hugely when disaster struck.

Like many left-wingers in the United States, he had developed a close friendship with the indomitable Anna Louise Strong, the doyenne of American Communism. Miss Strong was in the Soviet Union at the time, and for reasons still not clear, she was branded an American spy during Stalin's final paranoid years. Thrown into prison for a few days, she was subsequently expelled from the country. Soviet advisers were working closely with the Chinese Communists in those days. Particularly in matters of internal security, the Chinese usually did what "Elder Brother" suggested. Elder Brother sent word down that Miss Strong's great chum Sidney

Rittenberg was in the pay of the Central Intelligence Agency, and that was sufficient to send him—without warrant or trial—into prison for five years. When Liberation came in 1949, Sidney pondered the momentous event in a cell.

"It was a terrible mistake," he said. "When Anna Louise was cleared of the charges in 1953, I was immediately released. Both Mao and Chou personally apologized to me, although I really wasn't treated that badly. I could get just about anything I wanted to read, the food was good and the company hospitable. There was no attempt to make me write self-criticisms or confessions. In fact, it was indirectly made clear to me that if I wanted to write off China, I could make a token statement and get expelled immediately. The Chinese seemed to be embarrassed by the business right from the beginning, but Elder Brother had said I was a bad guy, so it must have been true. I refused the chance to leave, of course. There was no way they were going to get rid of me that easily. So I waited and read a hell of a lot of books."

After the official apologies, he was given an important position with Peking Radio as its only English-language foreign expert, and occasionally he indulged himself in some special broadcasting. Life was good in China, and exciting things were happening. Speaking Chinese more fluently than many natives, he was also more at ease with all levels of Chinese people than most Communist cadres. He even became an expert on Chinese art and furniture and had an impressive collection by the time the Cultural Revolution broke out into the open. More important than this, though, he had become —like many converts in many areas of human endeavor—more Chinese than the Chinese. He listened to all the gossip and hobnobbed with the leaders. The community of foreign experts looked to him for explanations of what was going on, and through his own force of personality he began to loom larger and larger. The process of assimilation reached a high point when he married his boss's secretary, Wang Yulin. He courted her in the same way he did everything—full steam ahead, with all guns firing simultaneously.

"Yulin was the secretary to the head of Radio Peking when I first met her," recalled Rittenberg. His wife was sitting beside him as he told this tale, and whenever it didn't jibe with what she remembered, she would jab him in the shoulder. She is a delightful, warmhearted woman, who has stood by her husband even when it meant that she and her children would be cruelly victimized. "She was very bright and independent. I knew I wanted to marry her, so I pursued her relentlessly and recklessly. She was horrified at the idea of marrying a foreigner and let me know it. A Chinese friend advised me to be subtle in my wooing. I must drop all my American directness, he said, and refrain from love letters and forward advances of any kind. Immediately, I sent her a long, passionate love letter and left it on her desk. Before long, she stormed into my office in a real rage and threw a letter of her own in my face. 'Dear Comrade,' she wrote me. 'I have never for one minute considered such a thing as you are proposing. I feel I am far too young to get married, and I hope that you will never again bother me with this kind of talk. The business is finished. P.S. Since I have already agreed to go with you tonight to San Yatsen Park, I will keep my promise.' "

Yulin and Sidney had three children, two daughters and a son. In a way, those children are the finest manifestation of his love for China, and on them, one feels, he stakes much of his emotional legitimacy to be one with the Chinese people. But at the time of their birth, his prime was not yet upon him. That came with the Cultural Revolution in 1966. Since his connections to Chinese people were so diverse and on so many levels, he got wind of the tumultuous changes in store for everyone before most of the people themselves did. At Peking Radio, he was in a particularly advantageous position to monitor factional disputes in the leadership, although the way Sidney tells it the Cultural Revolution just happened along one day, and he had to cope with it as best he could. But certainly he was smart enough to realize early the leveling nature of the storm that was soon to be unleashed by Mao, in which anyone with the least trace of bourgeois propensities would come under attack. Sidney donated his valuable collection of Chinese furniture to the state and transformed himself into a humble proletarian almost overnight. Later, millions of Chinese citizens would perform similar acts on a far simpler level by donning their most threadbare clothing and storing away anything that suggested they were upwardly mobile. The cult of poverty in a land of extreme poverty may seem silly to us, but all things are relative. When Mao Tsetung told the young people of China to "bombard the headquarters" of the Communist Party, he knew exactly what would happen. Many Chinese people were dismayed at the new class of privileged Party cadres who had arisen in their midst, and when things got truly out of hand, such seemingly innocuous things as leather shoes with a hint of style or creases in a pair of pants became targets of furious attacks.

People who hadn't had as much foresight as Rittenberg found that their little collections of traditional Chinese paintings or the few old objects they had inherited from grandparents were signs of their unwillingness to accept the Revolution. Hordes of self-righteous Red Guards confiscated such goods. (A West German correspondent who was stationed in Peking at this time had a field day in the commission stores, where he picked up dozens of priceless snuff bottles for pennies. His fortune was assured when he got them out of the country and sold them, a few at a time, to antique dealers in the West.)

There are a number of foreign experts who concluded that Rittenberg was the most self-serving of their number during this period and cite his efforts to divest himself of bourgeois appurtenances as proof. On the basis of this and other actions it is certainly a valid interpretation, but after I got to know Sidney a bit and watched him operate in today's fast-changing Chinese world, I saw these actions in a different light. He instinctively likes being in the center of things, and since he is a mover and a shaker, he does many things (equally instinctively) to get himself into that position. He is also more of a Chinese than he is a foreigner: when he gets caught up in a cause or a political struggle, he believes in it completely. He can banish inconsistency in his mind, and like many Chinese Party members, he can also shed allegiances without remorse. Although his stints in Chinese prisons have forced him to examine his actions, he is not a naturally reflective person and would much rather be doing things than contemplating them.

At Peking Radio, a storm was brewing. The first serious manifestations of the Cultural Revolution came from the institutions of higher learning. Mao was fighting the entrenched Party leadership he himself had helped to create, and that leadership sought to cool the rising anger of students by sending in investigating, or "work," teams to universities and institutes. Composed of senior Party officials, these work teams collected information on student radicals which became a focal point of contention.

All Chinese people know that one of the worst things that can befall citizens is to have a politically dangerous dossier collected on their lives. It gets into the clutches of both Party and police officials, and every time there is a political campaign unleashed, the dossiers are examined anew for fresh supplies of sacrificial victims. The work teams were putting together numerous such dossiers, and the students, spurred on by Mao's closest allies, who had larger designs, demanded that the dossiers be handed over.

At Peking Radio, there was a journalism institute where the students had been subjected to a work team. As an important aspect of propaganda control, Peking Radio was an early objective of Mao's allies: one of Mao's festering sore points was that he could not get access to major media outlets to propagandize among the Chinese people. The students mounted a major assault on Peking Radio headquarters, and it was in the midst of this volatile scene that Sidney moved to center stage. A meeting had been arranged between the students and the radio leadership, and this is how Sidney explains what happened:

> I arrived early for the meeting, because I wanted a seat up front. My eyes aren't that great. The guy who was handling the dossiers made a self-criticism and said he shouldn't have been so stubborn. Some students who had harassed the People's Liberation Army guards the day before apologized to them. The leader of the students, a very bright young girl, said she was satisfied. But then factional disputes broke out. People began to stand up in their seats and gather advocates around them. Vicious threats were hurled about all over the place.
>
> It was a crazy business, and in the midst of it, I had an idea. I thought I was enough of an oddity to arouse everyone's curiosity—a foreigner who could speak Chinese and was sympathetic to their cause—so I got up on the stage and asked the young girl whether she thought I could help. I just started talking about things, and slowly they all quieted down. It wasn't a very revolutionary speech. I said the students had apologized to the soldiers and that was right. The Party official had apologized to the students and that was right too. So what was all the fuss about? If you just shout, there is no democracy at all.
>
> What happened next was that the speech pleased the powers of the day. The meeting had been taped, and my speech began to be played across the country. I became an overnight celebrity. Soon enough, I began to be asked to give other speeches, and for six months I was one of three members of a rectification committee, set up at Peking Radio. As a foreigner, of course, I was an oddity and stood out in the crowd, but I was never the boss of Peking Radio, as some people have written.

Sidney intends to write a book about his exploits in China, and if he really comes clean, it could be one of the most fascinating stories of the century. Even if he doesn't come clean, it will be riveting reading. At the moment, he doesn't like talking about "factionalism," but unfortunately, to talk about the Cultural Revolution without an account of the complicated factions that were created, and which sometimes resulted in armed warfare, is like pondering the Second World War minus the details of all the battle plans and strategy.

No one has yet provided a definitive analysis of what went on in China during the Cultural Revolution, although some foreigners, like William Hinton in *The Hundred Day War,* have made stalwart efforts. But don't hold your breath waiting for one. Most of the principal Chinese combatants will never be heard from, either because of prudent caution or because of state coercion. It is not a subject on which the Chinese Government today encourages objectivity: the presiding role of Chairman Mao is part of the problem; so is the unfathomable tragedy unleashed on the Chinese people. It is clear, though, that Sidney was a faction fighter of quite remarkable proportions, at least to judge from the tales Chinese friends told me about him. It is certainly true that Chou Enlai considered him a menace, although Sidney hotly denies this. The assumption is based on some statements Chou later made to other foreign experts and the fact that Sidney was not released from his second stint in a Chinese prison until after Chou was safely in his grave.

But I'm jumping ahead again. As far as I was able to learn, Sidney embraced the Cultural Revolution fray with his customary gusto. He delighted in his role as a wheeler-dealer, and contrary to his protestations, he must have wielded considerable influence, for a short period, at Peking Radio. When he fell from grace during a power shift at the top of the Chinese leadership, a Red Guard pamphlet seen in Canton described him as "a counterrevolutionary double-dealer . . . This is a man of doubtful antecedents and one to be suspected. Bourgeois yellow magazines in his home country have cried with pride that Peking Radio is led by an American. What cannot be tolerated if this can be?"

The attack was part of a nationwide campaign to obliterate Rittenberg's influence in China. Ironically, he had achieved one of his goals. He became so enmeshed in the fabric of Chinese life that he was accorded honors normally reserved for only the most prominent citizens who run afoul of the reigning power. It is thought he was with a faction that was pushing for what the Chinese Communist Party derisively calls "ultrademocracy"—a confusing phrase that usually means Western-style, multiparty, directly elected government. He was also a firm and extreme Leftist, so I am not exactly clear about how all this fits together, or the charges that his faction was seeking to undermine Chou Enlai's authority. In any event, Sidney cannot be accused of vacillating in his stance: he stuck with his faction to the bitter end, and before long he was once again in the clink. As he put it himself, he was "a flash that panned." This time, he remained in prison for a total of eleven years, and the first six of them were total misery. He spent much of the time in solitary confinement and was cruelly harassed, both physically and psychologically. Outside, Yulin and the children became pariahs—the fate reserved for all families of official Nonpersons in Mao's time. She is a remarkably brave person and very indulgent of her husband, but she did tell me that she was struck by the loyalty of her Chinese friends and the complete absence of any overt concern from Sidney's foreign friends. What she didn't know, of course, was that many of those friends disapproved of what Sidney had been up to. These were bitter days, and they were made more bitter for Yulin when most of the foreign experts arrested during the Cultural Revolution were released—except for her husband.

In 1973, Chou Enlai hosted a dinner for the foreign experts and formally apologized for their treatment during the late sixties. There are several accounts of what he said about Rittenberg when his name came up for discussion. I know one person who was there at the dinner, and his memory may be imperfect. He thought Chou said Rittenberg had made "serious mistakes," and he doesn't remember his saying that Sidney was a "bad element" or a "counterrevolutionary." This may seem academic, but on such phrases hang life and death in China. Someone who is a counterrevolutionary is usually considered unredeemable; someone who has committed "mistakes," even bad mistakes, has a chance to make a comeback.

It is still a disputatious point, but it is serious business with Sidney at the moment, because when he emerged from prison in 1978, Chou Enlai was the most popular cult figure in New China. It is a role Chou grew into after Sidney was arrested. As the Cultural Revolution unfolded, he seemed to many Chinese the only sane figure in the leadership, and as the masses grew increasingly alienated from the aloof figure of Mao, Chou's paternalistic and calm personality became the source of much adulation. After his death, his memory was invoked by those who overthrew the Gang of Four, and many of the activities of the young democracy activists who emerged in 1978 ostensibly began under Chou's banner.

That's what I meant earlier when I said you had to be up on everything when talking to Sidney. Undoubtedly, he had many conversations and meetings with Chou in his career, and those recollections are particularly useful now that Chou is a cult figure, just as they might have been embarrassing during the Cultural Revolution, when it appeared possible on several occasions that Chou might become a victim himself. Sidney's actions are exactly the same as many Chinese took and continue to take.

Today, for example, in the business of apportioning all blame for the evil past to the Gang of Four, Sidney is second to none. He has worked out a solution to what Chou was supposed to have said about him which is perfectly in line with the sorts of things Chinese propaganda is saying all the time right now. Sidney points out that in 1973 Chou was speaking in the presence of Jiang Qing. By saying that only serious mistakes—not crimes—had been committed, he was in effect saving Rittenberg's life.

"She [Jiang Qing] was gunning for me," said Sidney, on the basis of his most recent research. "She wanted the old spy charges brought up again, and if I had been accused of being a spy, that would have been it for me, brother. I would have been a goner. When people told Yulin what Chou had said, they kept telling her to consider its context, and whose presence he was in when he said it."

It was important for Sidney to get this matter cleared up in his own mind. He was eleven years in a Chinese prison. His mere survival and the retention of his sanity was one mighty triumph, but he also emerged into a newer New China, and it would have been out of character had he decided to slip into the background. Peking Radio wouldn't have him back (although Yulin still works there) because he is still a controversial character, and people retain strong opinions about him. Instead, he was assigned to the translation service of the New China News Agency, a handy vantage point from which to continue snooping on the world and life around him.

On the last occasion I spoke to Sidney and Yulin in Peking, we rambled on and on about current politics and past history. He had had a wonderful time in the United States with Yulin and regaled us with amusing stories that had us rocking with laughter. Perhaps the best was about their visit to Hugh Hefner's Playboy mansion in Chicago, where some thoughtful people had worked hard to cover up every naked female breast in sight—whether in a picture or on the living body of a Bunny—so that Yulin wouldn't be embarrassed. "As a result," said Sidney with an impish grin, and also as one who had missed out entirely on the whole era that *Playboy* centerfolds represented in American culture, "the visit was very boring."

I brought up the subject of Chairman Mao's great concern over the "class struggle." I had been doing some research on the subject and said something to the effect that it still amazed me that Mao, in his position of authority, could have defined so precisely a central dilemma facing Communist regimes today, which is simply that a new class—a privileged elite of powerful cadres and Party bosses—will always rise up to fill the void left by a suppressed ruling class. It has been the experience of many Communist countries that this new class was no better than the one it usurped, and often enough it has been worse.

"Yah, I'm with you," said Sidney, who was clearly not with me at all. "But you know, when Mao talked about the new class I think he made one mistake—he forgot to take a look into the mirror at himself."

Sidney was right there in the vanguard of the most daring thinking in China today, which centers around the role of Mao. He was doing it—and this is important to realize with Sidney—not as a foreign observer with detached wisdom, but as a Chinese participant to whom the very name of Mao still had an almost magical or mystical connotation, for good or evil.

I told this to one of Sidney's best friends, who just shook his head in quiet amusement. "You know," he said, "twelve years ago I talked with Sidney when he was in the midst of the Peking Radio business. He was describing the fierce struggle to me and agonizing at the complexities of life. Sid was the darling of the old leadership at Peking Radio and you know he married the boss's daughter. Well, then there was the business of the students, and everyone was having to make their choices: would they go with the students or stick with the leadership? Clearly, Sidney was in a painful situation as he tried to make his decision. There were tears in his eyes when he spoke, and knowing him as I do, I don't doubt that they were real tears: he is a very emotional man. And he turned to me, with those tears pouring down his cheeks, and said, 'You know, I'm just trying to figure out what Chairman Mao would want me to do, and then everything will turn out all right.' "

Like everything else Sidney has done, this tale is open to fairly wide interpretation, in which serving his own self-interest springs immediately to mind. But by this time I had developed a real affection for the man, and although I could see his flaws and peccadilloes easily, they were also part and parcel of his truly fine qualities. I believe those were real tears too, just as I believe he has convinced himself that his former adulation of Mao was excessive.

I had by that time met a number of Chinese who were just like him, who had been trained by the example of the Party to ignore inconvenient history in the past and go full out for whatever were the particular objectives of the day. It is how the Chinese survive under Communism, and it is wound up in their instinct for endurance. On many occasions it is a wonderful instinct; at times it also causes craven and despicable actions; but in sum, it is the stuff of the human condition, and given similar circumstances, I suspect most of us would be much the same.

Apart from the pleasure of his company, which we valued highly, Sidney was also a special eye we had into aspects of the Chinese character. In time, we were able to appreciate how generous he had been by allowing us to see him whole, warts and all. As I myself became hopelessly involved in the lives of very special Chinese people, I came to understand better his desire to reach out and be a part of the life around him. Sidney's experience also acted as a cautionary tale when I too found myself caught up in Chinese politics and addressing a gathering of over ten thousand people during the remarkable events at Xidan Democracy Wall.

III
Xidan

Prologue

On November 1, 1978, Elizabeth and I boarded a train in Hanoi to return home to Peking. The ancient steam locomotive and rickety cabin cars rarely went faster than fifteen miles an hour, and so the short distance between the capital and the Sino-Vietnamese border took nearly six hours to traverse. I was exhausted and emotionally drained, and while the state of mind of a journalist is usually the last thing his editor or readers want to know about, it is pertinent here because of the amazing events soon to unfold in Peking.

A month in Vietnam had left me profoundly depressed about that sad place. I was by this time no stranger to Asian backwardness and poverty, but nothing had adequately prepared me for the misery I would see there, particularly in the North. Though I had adjusted to the whims and ways of the Chinese Communist Party, the Vietnamese version impressed me with its particular insidiousness. The promise of the revolution had become a hollow mockery, and the wretched Vietnamese leadership, after decades of war, had succumbed to a siege mentality and visited upon its people wholly unnecessary privations; the leadership could not cope with peace and reconstruction, and so it turned to the kind of foreign ventures it had once rallied its own people against.

Crossing the border was like coming home. Contrasting China

and Vietnam, at least in the area of material prosperity, is perhaps unfair because of the long war years Vietnam has been caught up in. The comparison is nevertheless forced on one's consciousness, and China seemed rather impressive. Also, I had just come through a year of rising expectations in the ancient Middle Kingdom, a time of great renewal and hope, when the Chinese people were being given a chance to rise up from the slough of despond, survey their lives and surroundings and, for the first time in years, make plans for the future.

How wonderful China looked, even in backward Guangxi province. Donkey carts, which had once seemed so primitive, were a distinct improvement on the plight Vietnamese laboring women faced when trying to find a means of transporting goods and produce—their own backs. To see young people and old codgers laughing in the streets was suddenly startling, and I realized with a jolt that the entire time I had been in Vietnam I could remember not one soul laughing, except perhaps the nervous cackle of an official at a formal briefing. These sorts of things made me take a kind of year-end stock of the country I was in. Despite all the frustrations, I had to pinch myself from time to time to believe that I was not dreaming about my good fortune at getting such a posting, with all its exotic opportunities for travel and the host of wildly different experiences.

Even my manic efforts at pushing out into Chinese life began to yield a few rewards. Elizabeth and I had struck up a fleeting relationship with a young Chinese girl who was anxious to practice her English, and we would meet from time to time in various Peking parks. It was an innocent but necessarily clandestine business, yet it provided tremendous satisfaction. Here at last was one face out of the crowd that gave evidence of individuality and humanity. Our conversations were rather silly and naive. Without any concrete or consistent evidence to the contrary, I was succumbing to the notion that most Chinese were content with their lot. My initial notions of Communist China had produced a setting in which everyone lurked about the place skulking in fear and trepidation. Nothing could have been less true. We were never able to probe beneath the surface, of course, but clearly any fool could see that laughter and lightness of heart were possible, even in uptight Peking, where ideological and political matters were perpetually paramount.

Since China was so palpably a country in the midst of massive transition at this time, many of the lingering evils of the preceding days were forgiven by outsiders like me, because at the back of your mind, you felt the government was finally trying to change things for the better. I had learned in Taiwan, and even more vividly in Vietnam, for different reasons, that many of the things Westerners thought of as "human rights violations" were really the product of material privation. A Chinese peasant in the countryside, without any means of independent transportation—even a bike—finds his mobility constrained not by state decree, but by the simple endurance of his own legs. That peasant's peer in Taiwan, with a motorcycle and a television set, has a wholly different perspective on the world, even though he also lives under a government with totalitarian instincts and severe ideological restraints. In any examination of human rights around the world, it is first necessary to explore the restrictions imposed by economic necessity and separate them from those things which common sense and civilized decency tell you are insupportable and repugnant.

This task was made easier for me and a few other foreigners in Peking because of the events at the Xidan Democracy Wall, which began to take place shortly after I got back from Vietnam. It was thanks to this truly extraordinary development that I was first able to make contact with Chinese people without the intruding assistance of the Communist Party. In the attendant mood of optimism engendered by the Wall, I was also able to form close friendships with remarkable Chinese survivors, who took me in hand and reeducated me so that I could begin to see a China I scarcely imagined before.

I was an active and willing participant in these events and cannot profess objectivity, nor do I want to. As I write, the Chinese Government has closed the chapter on Xidan by saying it was only the product of "a handful of bad or confused elements." Some Western journalists who never witnessed those heroic days and never had the awesome burden of affection and friendship with Chinese people have also dismissed Xidan with phrases like "the tiny democracy movement." At least one American journalist has dismissed not only the movement itself, but its manifestations throughout the country and the crucial insight it represented as an aberration fueled by the ambitions of foreign correspondents like me. It was a charge that was taken up with enthusiasm by the Party Central Committee.

Many Chinese too were frightened and disturbed by the manifestations of Xidan and what they led to. From these kinds of reactions, poised against one of the great outpourings of independent expression in Communist China's history, there are lessons for everyone to learn. For this reason, and because I was a witness, I want to set down now the events as they unfolded. My own hindsight and the analysis of Chinese and foreigners alike can be reserved for later, because the Xidan phenomenon was above all a mighty drama in which all the players had supporting parts, and the denouement was not known until the end.

I wish with a fervor known only to a few that someone better could do the job. Most of all I wish a Chinese would do it. But the brightest and most eloquent have been either jailed or otherwise silenced, and there is a real danger that the very fact of Xidan itself will disappear. What good is a witness who will not tell his tale? What worth has anyone who, seeing the truth, tries to deny it, not only to others, but to himself? So this is the story of Xidan as I saw it, and you can make of it what you will.

12

The "Tiny Democracy Movement"

I.
Saturday, November 18, to Friday, November 24

"Something big is going on," said Roger Garside, first secretary of the British Embassy. "I can't quite put my finger on it, but my bones tell me to stay alert." I had come to respect the feelings in Garside's bones. He had been posted to Peking first during the Cultural Revolution, and he brought both intuitive luck and analytical precision to his passion for China. Of all the diplomats and journalists I encountered in Peking, his record of prediction was best, and as I had been away from the place for over a month, I blitzed him with questions in order to get caught up.

The setting for our conversation was novel—the first public dance for foreigners in Peking in nearly two decades. It was at the International Club, a curious Chinese-run institution for foreigners in the People's Republic. There is a Western-style restaurant, which serves food bearing the same resemblance to Western cuisine that food served at many Chinese restaurants in North America does to the real thing in China—not much. There are bowling alleys, indoor and outdoor tennis courts, a movie theater and several vast halls where foreign embassies often hold their national-day receptions. Citizens of all nations were welcome—except Chinese, of course, unless they were officials, officially bidden. It was simply an extension of the foreigners' ghetto, and I came to hate it with as much passion as I did all the other things that divided outsiders from Chinese.

The farce of the International Club reached an ironic denouement several months later when the authorities actually started allowing ordinary Chinese into the place. They converted the indoor tennis court into a second Western-style restaurant, complete with instructions on how to use a fork. A special entrance was created around the side from the main doors, and a sign went up saying that this restaurant was restricted to Chinese customers only. "Foreign friends," it added, "should use the main entrance." It turned out that the club was serving much the same food to Chinese as it did to foreigners, only at greatly reduced prices.

Few foreigners would cavil at the price differential: Chinese people, after all, do not earn very much money. But the fact remained that the government had created a segregated restaurant in a club whose motto was "We have friends all over the world." The sign outside the Chinese restaurant was patently insulting, and anyone who knew anything of Chinese history couldn't fail to note the irony. An Australian friend of mine was walking his dog past the club the day after the sign went up and accosted the thickset gatekeeper. "Can I go in there?" he demanded in Chinese. "No, no. It's not permitted. Foreign friends must use the main door," said the gatekeeper. My friend pointed to his pet. "Can the dog go in?" The gatekeeper was enraged. No, he replied, the dog certainly couldn't go in. He apparently thought my friend was slandering the Chinese people, whereas in fact it was the authorities who were insulting them and their history. The incident was an ironic update of perhaps the most famous symbol of imperialist presumption in China's history.

Such absurd aberrations were not apparent on the evening the foreigners had their first ball in Peking since the Cultural Revolution. Garside and I surveyed the dance floor. It was not exactly a disco center, but it was a step forward and another sign of how relaxed life was becoming in China. We were both in an expansive mood. Garside was not just another diplomatic source to me—he was a close friend who shared a natural affection for Chinese people and, like me, rejoiced in the new possibilities that seemed to be everywhere. He knew far better than I did the impatience of Chinese people for change and had been a witness to the dramatic and violent events surrounding the Tienanmen Incident a couple of years previously.

Hundreds of thousands of people had poured into central Peking, ostensibly to commemorate the passing of Chou Enlai on the traditional day of mourning for the dead in China, called the Qing Ming Festival. The commemoration quickly turned into an antigovernment protest, and it was ruthlessly put down. Some people had been killed and many more arrested, while the government declared the entire episode a major "counterrevolutionary" act. It was a few months before Mao Tsetung died, but before he left this world, Chinese people had stood up to oppose the oppression he had either willingly or unwittingly imposed upon them. Garside had also witnessed many of the dramatic events of the Cultural Revolution, and he knew—in those bones of his that when aroused, the Chinese masses were awesome to behold.

"We are pretty sure there are top-level meetings of some sort going on right now," he said, "and there have been one or two posters put up attacking Wu De."

I knew that Wu De was the recently deposed mayor of Peking and a member of the Politburo. I also knew that he had been particularly active in denouncing Vice-Premier Deng Xiaoping when the doughty Sichuanese was disgraced by Mao for the second time in 1976, following the Tienanmen Incident. However, like so many of the other Chinese leaders, he had quickly made the necessary adjustments to the new order after the Gang of Four had been purged, and it had been my understanding that the leadership wanted to have a public show of unity in order to restore calm and stability to the political scene.

I had read many accounts by previous correspondents and Sinologists on the machinations of the Chinese leadership, and while the endless speculation fascinated old China hands, I was convinced they left most educated outsiders bored stiff. During my first year in China I had concentrated on trying to give my impressions of the sights and sounds of a strange land, as well as necessarily oblique pictures of the people. If Wu De was up one day and down another, so be it—the universe was still unfolding as it should, and my newspaper would be only marginally interested, if that. Still, since I had a great faith in Garside's bones, I set about trying to assimilate

—for about the fifth time—the Byzantine political structures of Communist China.

On the weekend of November 18–19, the bureau chief of Agence France-Presse phoned me to say that a rash of wall posters attacking Wu De had gone up on the busy shopping street called Wang Fu Jing, as well as at a wall alongside the bus terminal at Xidan and Chang An avenues. I was seized with a panic I had not known since my first days in Peking, because I didn't know what to do about it. Although the "big-character wall poster," or *dazibao,* was an integral part of Chinese political life, none had been put up during my time in Peking, save for a few personal grievances that were interesting to take note of for future reference but hardly worth a story in themselves. Since I couldn't read Chinese, I wasn't clear as to how one found out what was set down. At that time, I didn't even know it was considered permissible to ask one's government interpreter to translate *dazibao.* Fortunately, Georges Biannic, the AFP bureau chief, and Nigel Wade of the London *Daily Telegraph* took me by the hand and showed me how the business was done. Thanks to them, I got through the first few bewildering days of what was apparently a growing political-poster campaign.

Apart from attacks on Wu De, the posters had been making some veiled criticisms of Mao Tsetung, although there had been nothing very specific. That was something I could relate to easily. It was one thing for outside observers to notice the failings of the Great Helmsman; it was quite another for ordinary Chinese people even to suggest publicly that the great man had flaws. After a few days of taking handouts from my journalistic friends, I arranged for a fluent foreign interpreter to join me on a Wednesday night to see if I couldn't do some sleuthing of my own. We went down to the bus-terminal wall near Xidan Avenue, and the laborious process of checking each poster began. The Wall itself isn't much to behold. It's about seven feet high and made of brick. There are two sections, divided by a roadway between the central cable and telephone office to the east and Xidan Avenue on the west. Behind the Wall, dozens of buses return each evening after the rush hour. On Chang An Avenue itself there is a major bus stop right in front of the Wall. Posters or no posters, there are always a lot of people around this area in the daytime, and the crowds reach their peak at the end of the normal working day, at 6 P.M.

My interpreter friend and I got to the Xidan Wall at about 8 P.M.

Only a couple of dozen Chinese were reading posters, and it was easy to peruse what was up. Although I could read only a few Chinese characters, by this time I knew enough to look for the date at the end of each poster to see if it was a recent offering. Having gone up and down the Wall with Biannic and Wade for several days, I was familiar with which posters had been up for a while, so I went quickly through my paces, looking for something new. There were lots of posters attacking the Gang of Four, which was not very surprising, since the government had been doing precisely the same thing for nearly two years. The day before, Biannic had been the first to spot a *dazibao* that tried to get a bit beyond simple denunciation of popular scapegoats and look at the man who had allowed the Gang of Four to gain such power in the first place. That poster, pasted up by people who said they were workers at a nearby garage, praised the recent efforts of the Chinese Government to rehabilitate victims of the Cultural Revolution. One passage, which had been underlined and attracted considerable attention, read: "Because Chairman Mao's Thought was metaphysical in the last years of his life and for all sorts of other reasons, he had supported the Gang of Four in getting rid of Vice-Premier Deng."

That doesn't seem particularly devastating criticism today, but at the time and inside China, it was startling. What seemed to give people the courage to say such a thing was the reversal of the verdict on the Tienanmen Incident by the Peking Revolutionary Committee the week before. The counterrevolutionary events were now called revolutionary and correct, and with that spur from an official body, people began demanding an accounting. Wu De was an easy target. He had been the official in charge of putting down the demonstrators of Tienanmen in 1976 and had just lost his job as mayor (although retaining his seat on the Politburo).

In a typical pattern from previous Chinese poster campaigns, *dazibao* went up to support the actions of the government. It has always been assumed by everyone reporting on China that no one would have the nerve to paste up a controversial poster unless there was some official backing it. In Canton, three young men put up in a prominent place a devastating attack on the government during 1974. The three used the pen name Li Yizhe, which was composed of characters from each of their names *(Li* Zhengtian, Chen *Yi*yang and Huang Xi*zhe)*. They took a cold look at the campaign to criticize the disgraced former defense minister Lin Biao, who had once been Chairman Mao's closest "comrade-in-arms" and "chosen successor." How could the Chinese people be expected to criticize Lin Biao, they asked, without examining the system that had elevated him in the first place?

Although the poster stayed up for several days, the authors were soon arrested and sentenced to long prison terms. But even here, they had an official behind them who had tried to give them support, and the famous *dazibao* was startling evidence of the fissures within the Communist Party itself at this time, although its significance was dismissed or ignored by most outside observers except for a perceptive few, who were roundly attacked by the "friends of China." By the time the Xidan poster campaign began, the arguments Li Yizhe had used in Canton were part of Communist orthodoxy, although the three were still in prison. It is never very wise to be ahead of your time in Communist China, and there were officials still in power who were directly implicated in the persecution of Li Yizhe.

So my interpreter friend and I were looking for controversial posters, precisely because they were supposed to be either a manifestation of decisions taken at the top levels of leadership or, at the very least, a hint of the kind of debate that was going on. I certainly didn't take them at the time as an accurate indication of the public will. Posters citing personal grievances, such as undeserved arrests or housing problems, were another matter. They fleshed out some of the real problems of living in China, but at the moment they were only peripherally interesting. As we strolled along the Wall I took note of the posters I already knew about and those which were "only another personal grievance," to quote a colleague's government interpreter. Suddenly, we came up to a long poster that had just been pasted up. You didn't have to be Sherlock Holmes to figure this out—the glue was still dripping from the sides. I got out my notebook and asked my friend to start translating. It turned out to be a winner.

"Our country is entering a new historical period," the poster began. "The Chinese people are now thinking of where China is heading. Without a tremendous spiritual revolution in Chinese ideas, our own great revolution will falter, and there will be no final victory. A great spiritual revolution will lead to a great social revolution. We must stand up now and smash our spiritual shackles." Under the general heading "Liberate Ideology" the poster went on to ask four questions about Mao Tsetung that would have had the writer executed two years before. The questions were couched, typically, in fulsome praise for Mao's historical role as a revolutionary leader "whose place is secure in the hearts of the people." Still, said the poster, he had made mistakes. "Try and ask yourself the question: How could Lin Biao rise to such power without Chairman Mao's support? Try to ask yourself the question: Did Chairman Mao realize the true nature of Jiang Qing? Try to ask yourself the question: How could the Gang of Four start an anti-Rightist campaign to topple Vice-Premier Deng from power without Chairman Mao's knowledge? Try to ask yourself the question: How could the Tienanmen Incident get labeled a counterrevolutionary act without Chairman Mao nodding his head?"

There was much more in this vein. When the translation was done, I went into the nearby cable office and sent out a story on the poster to my newspaper and phoned Biannic and Wade. It was silly, I suppose, but I was overcome with relief. No Western correspondent can go it alone in China. There is too much to cover, and you need all the friends you can get. But Western journalism is remarkably competitive, and you have to choose your friends carefully. Both Wade and Biannic worked for news agencies that weren't in competition with the *Globe* or those newspapers which subscribed to the syndicate buying the paper's China copy. By the luckiest of coincidences, they also happened to be the best journalists in Peking. Wade had been the first to unravel the purge of the Gang of Four, several days before the government acknowledged it; Biannic simply ran the most comprehensive news operation in China, with the most extensive contacts possible in those days. At this moment I had a small opportunity to repay them for helping me out during the previous confusing days, and that night I slept peacefully for the first time in nearly a week.

Despite the growing excitement at the various poster walls in Peking, I was similar to many journalists and diplomats in Peking at not taking the business too seriously at first. I loved mixing with Chinese who were reading the posters, and it was bliss just to get away from my normal work pattern, but after the first few nervous days, I could see this poster campaign was a little different from previous affairs, and as I read my predecessors' accounts in the *Globe* files I could see a familiar pattern emerge: meetings at the top, posters from "the masses," changes announced, end of campaign.

It was just a matter of finding out what was going on at the top and the puzzle would be solved.

It was all a bit of a lark, I thought, and nothing underlined my attitude better than my decision to paste up my own *dazibao*. Like many of the absurd situations I have got myself into, it began impulsively, with little sober thought about where it would lead. As a ballet critic in Toronto four years earlier, I had stumbled right into the middle of Mikhail Baryshnikov's defection from a touring Soviet ballet troupe by simply passing on a seemingly innocent message from a mutual acquaintance. Before the business was done, I found myself immersed in the most incredible intrigue; it had overtones of James Bond—right down to secret rendezvous, hide-outs, cryptic messages and a weird break-in at my apartment, which has still not been solved.

On the Wednesday afternoon after the poster campaign began, I had attempted to see if there were any new *dazibao* at the Xidan Wall. The scene was sheer bedlam. As the campaign escalated, more and more Chinese were coming to the Wall to see what the fuss was all about. They knew what a poster campaign could signal, and it was easy to sense the mixed feelings of the crowd. There were those who were enthusiastic and excited; there were also those who disliked disruptions of any sort, especially now that things seemed better.

Unless you have been in the midst of an energetic and excited Chinese crowd, it is a little hard to describe it. In particular, the experience of being engulfed by a *dazibao* gathering can be likened to the lot of a sardine in a tin. In the nonstop mayhem caused by people at the back trying to get up to the front and the people at the front who have finished reading trying to get out, you get twisted and turned in every direction and almost squeezed to death. Just trying to get your arms out in front of you to push a little requires superhuman strength, and there is always the risk that a mass change in direction will cause people to stumble and be trampled upon. It was during such an exercise that I emerged from a *dazibao* crowd to discover that I had lost my gold family signet ring.

At midnight I went downtown to file the day's story, and afterward I walked over to the Xidan Wall and the spot where I figured I had lost the ring. Hardly anyone was around, except for two People's Liberation Army guards on sentry duty at the post office and a few lonely souls who were reading posters while waiting for their bus. Although I knew it would be futile, I got down on my haunches anyway and started looking for the ring by tracing my fingers through the thick dust in front of the Xidan Wall. While thus employed, I aroused the curiosity of two nearby Chinese, who cautiously approached me and observed my strange antics for a few minutes. Obviously I was looking for something, and before long, without a word's being spoken, they too got down on their haunches and started sifting through the dust.

My Chinese is not good, but I usually managed to make myself understood at a very basic level when necessary, and I explained to them I had lost something, but that they didn't have to worry about it because it was my problem. Typically, they first asked me what country I was from and then how old I was.

I knew this game from previous peripheral contacts and quite liked it. "You guess," I said. They smiled. The trick was to guess under the age in order to offer a compliment. They immediately said twenty-five, which was an eight-year compliment, and they naturally refused to believe I was as old as I said I was.

It was now my turn. "How old are you?" I asked. "You say," demanded the elder of the two, who I thought was probably nearly fifty. I said forty and his face broke out in a great, gorgeous smile. "Fifty-six!" he said with pride. "Not at all," I remonstrated, "forty-five at the most." "Fifty-six," he said again, and he added that he had once served in the People's Liberation Army.

Then he pointed to a small piece of paper beneath a large wall poster. I knew from the afternoon visit that it was a notice about a watch someone had discovered at the Wall and turned in at the local Public Security Bureau office. "You can write a poster," said the older man. "The Chinese people will return what you lost."

Brainstorm! Not only would I write a *dazibao* about my lost ring, I could also write a story about writing a *dazibao* for my newspaper. It would be a good way of describing some of the drama and excitement that surrounds a poster campaign, as well as its significance.

The next morning, I prepared the wording—in English, of course—very carefully.

NOTICE. While reading *dazibao* near here on November 22, I lost an old gold ring with the head of an animal carved on it. If any comrade finds it, I would appreciate having it back. [Signed] Fu Ruizhe, Canadian Correspondent, 2-2-31 San Li Tun, telephone 52-1661.

With considerable pride, I took this to Xiao (pronounced "shao") Hao, the *Globe and Mail*'s interpreter, because I wanted it translated into elegant Chinese. It was not just a matter of having it translated word for word. In addition to everything else, a *dazibao* can also be an artistic statement, and the choice of calligraphy is crucial in a country that judges style and personality from the way one wields a brush-pen. Chairman Mao himself worked assiduously to perfect a calligraphic style that was supposed to embody a grasp of history, heroic individuality and his greatness as a leader. You can hear experts discuss the merits of different kinds of calligraphy in much the same way oenophiles rant on about the wines of the Médoc. So I wanted Xiao Hao's support on this affair in order that my *dazibao* would be worthy of the Xidan Wall. Xiao Hao, however, took a quick look at my effort and lodged a criticism: "You can't call this a *dazibao.*"

"Why not?" I asked, somewhat taken aback.

"A *dazibao* makes a political statement or demands justice against false accusations and verdicts or tries to correct a bad situation. This is just an announcement."

"Okay," I said, "you just write at the bottom: 'Long Live the April 5 Movement.'"

April 5 was when the Tienanmen Incident had taken place, the incident that had just been declared a revolutionary act. The date itself had become one of the many magical numbers in contemporary Chinese lore. Chinese months are dated numerically, so that January is "Month One" and December is "Month Twelve." It's a very simple, logical system. A short way, in Chinese, of saying April 5 is simply "four–five," meaning the fifth day of the fourth month. The Chinese have always attached special significance to those days of the month which coincide with the month number. In Daoist mythology, for example, a date like June 6 would be special because that would mean "six–six" or "double six." The Chinese Communist Party has been adept at co-opting popular myth to its own ends, and so you often see major events of the current political calendar celebrated with traditional flourishes like "double eight," which means August 8, the anniversary of the founding of the Chinese Communist Party.

The masses have an annoying independent tendency to play the magic-number game as well, although it took me a few days before I discovered the special significance of April 5, or "four–five."

Nearly a half century before, in 1919, Chinese intellectuals and young people had begun the famous May 4 Movement, which was among the most important events in Chinese history. In addition to throwing off the shackles of corrupted Chinese traditionalism, they had sought contacts with the outside world in order to bring China into the modern age. Out of the May 4 Movement came most of China's greatest writers of this century. On the crest of the sentiments it aroused, the Communist Party was born, and people like Chou Enlai and Deng Xiaoping traveled to Europe to widen their horizons. May 4, of course, is "five–four"—or the reverse of April 5. The connection may seem tenuous and arcane to us, but it certainly didn't to the Chinese people gathering to read posters at Xidan. For them, historical allusion was pertinent and the implications were obvious.

Having somewhat incautiously aligned myself with the prevailing sentiments of the day, I set about the business of getting my poster up on the Xidan Wall. I made a search of the apartment to find some glue. After that all I needed was a bit of brazen gall and a pair of fast feet. *Dazibao* are put up with lightning speed, and those who put them up disappear like dreams at the break of day. This is a wise policy if you don't want to be observed too closely by those whose job it is to observe all actions in China—the Public Security Bureau. Even official support for posters is tenuous, and caution is always the best policy. It is also wise to move fast if you don't care to be trampled underfoot by an excited crowd anxious to be the first to read and copy down a new poster.

Since I was a highly conspicuous foreigner, the moment I brought out my glue pot at the Wall I was surrounded by an extremely curious crowd, which became so thick I found myself being pushed toward the Wall itself before I had a chance to put the glue on the back of my two pristine-white sheets of *dazibao*. There was a very real danger that I would be slammed up against the Wall, with the glue bottle smashing open in front of me, thereby becoming my own *dazibao*. Some order prevailed for a few minutes and I accomplished the deed. Biannic of Agence France-Presse was also down at the Wall at the time, although I had forewarned no one. I was making enough of a media event out of myself without including my colleagues—who, in any event, I was sure would think I was just being silly. Biannic, however, is a journalist for all seasons, and he sent a one-paragraph "color" filler on my actions which went around the world. I soon filed another account (after Biannic had scooped me on my own story), and since I didn't really think I would find my ring, I was quite pleased with the little stir the adventure had caused. I was particularly delighted with the response the poster aroused among Chinese people. They all burst out into laughter when they got to the end. That evening, when I went to the cable office, I returned to the Wall and found several dozen people still reading it. One old type was even digging a little at the earth nearby, looking for the glint of gold. I had not yet learned how much stealing actually goes on in China, and the experiences of other foreigners in the past had led me to believe that if anyone actually found the ring, it would be immediately returned.

In the ensuing days, my poster became quite famous. Chinese staff at several embassies told me it had become a prime topic of gossip in Peking neighborhoods, and there had been several discussions on what the "animal" carved on the ring meant. (It was just the deer's head from a Scottish coat of arms for the Fraser clan.) Biannic's story was widely used throughout Europe, and this filtered back to the foreign community, where I became the subject of much good-natured ribbing. They didn't know the half of it! For one thing, I had unwittingly supplied ordinary Chinese people with the *first* telephone number of a foreigner. Within eight hours, our life at the *Globe and Mail* bureau changed forever. We got phone calls at all hours of the day, mostly from young Chinese anxious to see if there really was a foreigner at the other end and also to practice their English.

I remember one conversation with particular affection.

"Hello," I said, after picking up the receiver.

"Hello," said the Chinese voice in very slow, painfully modulated English. "I read your big-character poster at Xidan Wall yesterday. I enjoy to read this big-character poster."

"That's terrific," I said. "Who are you?"

"I am fine. Good-bye."

Others would regale me with accounts of "Comrade Norman Bethune," a Canadian surgeon who died in China serving Mao Tsetung's revolutionary forces in 1939. Every Chinese seems to know Mao's famous eulogy of Bethune, and any Canadian who comes to China fancies that he has a little extra clout in the country because of the connection—which actually never amounts to more

than a few personalized courtesies. (One Canadian tourist who
pushed it too far exasperated her rather militant Chinese guide,
who demanded of the Canadian: "Yes, that's all very well, but
Comrade Bethune was a Communist. Are you?") Some Chinese
callers spoke very cryptically, indicating that they were happy to
have my phone number and would be back in touch in case there
was some "interesting news" to report.

They were as good as their word in the days to come, and for the
first time in the twenty years since the *Globe and Mail* first opened
a bureau in Peking, ordinary Chinese people started keeping a
correspondent up to date on the passing scene. It slowly dawned
on me that an initially impulsive act was giving me an advantage in
covering China that was nothing short of incredible. I was never
able to convince other foreigners that it wasn't to this end that I had
written the poster in the first place, and they gave me far more
credit for cleverness than I deserved. In fact, I came to feel rather
sheepish because a few days later I actually found the missing ring,
not at the Xidan Wall, but behind some sheet music on my piano,
where I had inadvertently left it before visiting the Wall that fateful
day.

Over at the Wall, however, my *dazibao* was becoming the butt
of local jokes. It is quite common for Chinese to write their opinions about a *dazibao* on the poster itself. Part of the fun of getting
translations done is reading these off-the-cuff comments. Some are
very serious, others humorous. Responses can be long or short,
sarcastic or naive. On my poster one person had written: "The
ground beneath here is very deep. It will require an archeological
expedition to find this foreigner's ring."

A more sympathetic soul suspected the ring had already been
found. "Comrades, have pity on our foreign friend," he or she
wrote, "and give him back his ring, for it may have value to him
beyond the cost of the metal." Then a woman wrote something
very special as a response. It was about ten times as long as my
notice and was written on six pieces of lined notebook paper. In
reading it, you should remember the events that the poster campaign referred back to. The Tienanmen Incident of April 5, 1976,
had occasioned many deaths and arrests. People wanted an accounting and not just the mere reversal of an overall verdict. That was
why they were going after the old mayor of Peking, Wu De, with
such a vengeance. The response to my notice of a lost ring was

signed "A Peking Mother," and it began with five words in English: "Dear friend, how are you?" The rest was in Chinese:

As a Chinese citizen, I shared your concern and felt much pity for you when I saw your notice about the missing ring. At the same time I very much admired your support for the April 5 Movement and the Democracy Wall of Xidan. In spite of the cold and jostling of the masses, you came down to the Wall when the cruel wind was blowing and the dust gets in your eyes, and you lost your lovely treasure. Where was this precious object trod upon? What a pity! Believe me when I tell you that if any Chinese finds it, it will be returned to you and you can be happy again. But you know well the ground below here, and I fear your treasure may never return to the fingers of its master. If you do get it back, that would be wonderful. But if it isn't returned, please don't spend much time worrying about it and don't fuss about such gains and losses. Your poor little treasure, after all, is an inanimate thing with no soul; neither can it cry nor utter any sound at all.

I am thinking right now that you are really not too worried about this ring, but rather are rejoicing with the Chinese people as they seek to free themselves from the cruel times they have had to suffer through. Because you expressed support for the Chinese people and with a view to compensate you for your material loss, I will set down here a poem called "Democracy Wall" which is dedicated to you. Though we are strangers and probably will remain so, still we have had a similar experience. Perhaps, and I know you will agree, my loss was more painful and important than yours. I also lost my treasure near here two years ago. My treasure had a soul, and it was full of life. It could speak and cry and it was of my flesh. It was my poor son. Though we are of different nations and speak different languages, we now have a friendship together through the April 5 Movement.

I have a right to be angrier than you at my loss. My son spoke truly and bravely at an evil time, and when he was called "an active counter-revolutionary" I learned to love those names because I knew my son believed in his country and loved democracy. He was torn from my heart. He was my heart. He was also of the heart and soul of China. So today, like you, I shout at the top of my voice: "Long Live the April 5 Movement! Long Live the April 5 Movement! Long Live the April 5 Movement!"

At this time and in this place we call Democracy Wall, which has been built with blood and tears, we begin a new long march toward a truly democratic life. There is no reason for us to be apart anymore. We can work together in friendship. Let us, through the Democracy Wall, support each other and learn from each other. We both have our strong points to offset our weaknesses, and from our weaknesses we can also learn.

See you, good international friend from the land of Bethune. Please pass on my regards to your whole family. Also, please pass on my regards to the whole people of Dr. Bethune's motherland. Lastly, please accept my ode to the Democracy Wall, observe closely the developments you see here and listen to our cries for democracy. Please accept my Chinese-style homage and allow me to bless you and the people around you.

The response is typical in content and style of a certain type of poster I often saw. Very gushy, it nevertheless has an authentic ring, because Chinese rhetorical passion can often become very sentimental. The Russians can get away with this and so can the Chinese because they have bitter experience to hinge their words together, and you can see the flashes of anger and resolve amid all the heart thumping.

Although I never wrote a story about this response to my poster, being a trifle mortified by the farce of my personal Ring Cycle, I was haunted by the woman's words.

By this time I had started poring over the events of 1976 to try to understand what was going on. Garside had been one witness, and there were a few others still around, although they all said that the Tienanmen Incident had largely excluded foreigners and the few who had tried to push in on the crowds were often beaten up. Perhaps the best picture of what happened comes from the enemy —the official government account of the day. I pulled out the old New China News Agency files for 1976 and read the *People's Daily* version of this "counterrevolutionary" event. Together with two Politburo documents and Wu De's hated speech, it was the same version millions of people all over China read. Many of these people knew exactly what was going on and read the account with rising revulsion. Here it is, in its entirety:

Resolution of the Central Committee of the Communist Party of China on Appointment of Comrade Hua Guofeng to be First Vice-Chairman of the Central Committee of the Communist Party of China and Premier of the State Council of the People's Republic of China.

On the proposal of our great leader Chairman Mao, the Political Bureau of the Central Committee of the Communist Party of China unanimously agrees to appoint Comrade Hua Guofeng First Vice-Chairman of the Central Committee of the Communist Party of China and Premier of the State Council of the People's Republic of China.

> The Central Committee of the
> Communist Party of China.
> April 7, 1976

Resolution of the Central Committee of the Communist Party of China on Dismissing Deng Xiaoping from All Posts Both Inside and Outside the Party.

Having discussed the counter-revolutionary incident which took place at Tienanmen Square and Deng Xiaoping's latest behavior, the Political Bureau of the Central Committee of the Communist Party of China holds that the nature of the Deng Xiaoping problem has turned into one of antagonistic contradiction. On the proposal of our great leader Chairman Mao, the Political Bureau unanimously agrees to dismiss Deng Xiaoping from all his posts both inside and outside the Party, while allowing him to keep his Party membership so as to see how he will behave himself in the future.

> The Central Committee of the
> Communist Party of China.
> April 7, 1976.

Comrade Wu De's speech broadcast at Tienanmen Square.

Comrades! In the past few days while we were studying our great leader Chairman Mao's important instructions, counter-attacking the right deviationist attempt to reverse correct verdicts and grasping revolution and promoting production, a handful of bad elements, out of ulterior motives, made use of the Qing Ming Festival deliberately to create a political incident, directing their spearhead at Chairman Mao and the Party Central Committee in a vain attempt to change the general orientation of the struggle to criticize the unrepentant capitalist-roader Deng Xiaoping's revisionist line and beat back the right deviationist attempt. We must see clearly the reactionary nature of this political incident, expose the schemes and intrigues of the bad elements, heighten our revolutionary vigilance and avoid being taken in.

Revolutionary masses and cadres of the municipality must take class struggle as the key link, act immediately, and by concrete action defend Chairman Mao, defend the Party Central Committee, Chairman Mao's proletarian revolutionary line and the great capital of our socialist motherland, deal resolute blows at counter-revolutionary sabotage and further strengthen and consolidate the dictatorship of the proletariat and develop the excellent situation. Let us rally around the Party

Central Committee headed by Chairman Mao and win still greater victories!

Today, there are bad elements carrying out disruption and disturbances and engaging in counter-revolutionary sabotage at Tienanmen Square. Revolutionary masses must leave the Square at once and not be duped by them.

COUNTER-REVOLUTIONARY POLITICAL INCIDENT AT TIENANMEN SQUARE

[Reported and written by worker-peasant-soldier correspondents and the staff correspondents of the *People's Daily.*]

A few days ago, a handful of class enemies, under the guise of commemorating the late Premier Chou during the Qing Ming Festival, engineered an organized, premeditated and planned counter-revolutionary political incident at Tienanmen Square in the capital. They flagrantly made reactionary speeches, posted reactionary poems and slogans, distributed reactionary leaflets and agitated for the setting up of counter revolutionary organizations. By means of insinuation and overt counter-revolutionary language, they brazenly clamored that "the era of Qin Shi Huang is gone." Openly hoisting the ensign of supporting Deng Xiaoping, they frenziedly directed their spearhead at our great leader Chairman Mao, attempted to split the Party Central Committee headed by Chairman Mao, tried to change the general orientation of the current struggle to criticize Deng Xiaoping and counter-attack the right deviationist attempt at reversing correct verdicts, and engaged in counter-revolutionary activities.

The counter-revolutionary activities culminated on April 5. At about 8 A.M., a loudspeaker car of the municipal Public Security Bureau was overturned, the body of the car and its loudspeakers smashed. After 9 A.M., more than ten thousand people gathered in front of the Great Hall of the People. At its maximum the crowd at Tienanmen Square numbered about one hundred thousand people. Except for a handful of bad elements who were bent on creating disturbances, the majority of people were passers-by who came over to see what was happening. Some of the people were around the Monument to the People's Heroes; the majority were concentrated on the west side of the square, near the eastern gate of the Great Hall of the People. A dozen young people were beaten up by some bad elements, receiving cuts and bruises on their heads with blood trickling down their swollen faces. The hooligans shouted: "Beat them to death! Beat them to death!" An army guard who tried to stop the hooligans by persuasion had his insignia pulled off, uniform torn and his face beaten to a pulp. The handful of bad elements exclaimed: "Who can put this situation under control? Nobody in the Central Committee can. Should any of them come today, he would not be able to return!" Their unbridled, counter-revolutionary arrogance infuriated the masses, many of them saying: "Ever since Liberation, Tienanmen Square has always been the place where our great leader Chairman Mao reviews parades of the revolutionary masses. We will absolutely not tolerate such counter-revolutionary acts happening here!" Several hundred worker-militiamen who went up the flight of steps leading to the Great Hall of the People to stand guard were broken up into several sections by the hooligans. The latter repeatedly shouted reactionary slogans and savagely beat up anyone in the crowd who opposed them. Some of those who got beaten up were dragged to the Monument and forced to kneel down and "confess their crimes."

At 11:05 A.M., many people surged towards the Museum of Chinese History on the east side of Tienanmen Square. In front of the museum, a woman comrade came forward to dissuade them and she was immediately manhandled. At this moment, a bunch of bad elements besieged a People's Liberation Army barrack by the Clock Tower in the southeast corner of the square. They crushed the door, broke into the building and occupied it. A few bad elements, sporting crew cuts, took turns to incite the people, shouting themselves hoarse through a transistor megaphone. Towards 12 o'clock noon, some of the troublemakers proclaimed the inauguration of what they called the "Committee of the People of the Capital for Commemorating the Premier." A bad element wearing spectacles had the impudence to announce that the Public Security Bureau must give its reply in ten minutes. He threatened that if their demands were not met, they would smash the security department.

At 12:30 P.M., the PLA fighters on guard duty at Tienanmen Square marched in formation towards their barracks to guard it. The bad elements who were making disturbances shouted in instigation: "The People's Army should stand on the side of the people!" and "Those befuddled by others are innocent!" Later, they overturned a Shanghai sedan car and set it on fire. The firemen and PLA guards who came to the rescue were blocked, and the fire engine was wrecked. These bad elements said that putting out the fire meant "suppressing the mass movement." Several members of the fire-brigade were beaten to a pulp.

At 12:45 P.M., a detachment of the people's police came as reinforcement. But they too were taunted and stopped. The caps of several policemen were snatched by the rioters and thrown into the air. Some even threw knives and daggers at the people's police. Several policemen were rounded up and assaulted.

In the afternoon, the sabotage activities of this mere handful of counter-revolutionaries became even more frenzied. They burned four motor vehicles bringing water and food to the worker-militiamen on duty or belonging to the people's Public Security Bureau. Around 5 P.M., this gang of bad elements again broke into the barracks, abducted and beat up the sentries, smashed windows and doors on the ground floor and looted everything in the rooms. Radios, quilts, bed sheets, clothing and books were all thrown into the fire by this gang of counter-revolutionaries. They also burned and smashed dozens of bicycles of the Peking worker-militiamen. Black smoke belched into the sky amid a hubbub of counter-revolutionary clamors. Nearly all the window panes in the barracks were smashed. Then they set the building on fire.

The revolutionary masses showed the utmost hatred for this counter-revolutionary political incident. Yet the handful of bad elements said glibly: "It manifests the strength of the masses." They went so far as to claim brazenly that "the situation has now got out of hand and it would be of no use even if a regiment or an army was called in," and so on and so forth, showing their unbridled reactionary arrogance.

See how these counter-revolutionaries, using extremely decadent and reactionary language and the trick of insinuation, viciously attacked and slandered our great leader Chairman Mao and other leading comrades on the Party Central Committee:

"Devils howl as we pour out our grief,
We weep but the wolves laugh,
We spill our blood in memory of the hero,
Raising our brows, we unsheathe our swords.

"China is no longer the China of yore,
And the people are no longer wrapped in sheer ignorance,
Gone for good is Qin Shi Huang's feudal society.

"We believe in Marxism-Leninism!
To hell with
Those scholars who emasculate Marxism-Leninism!
What we want is genuine Marxism-Leninism.

"For the sake of genuine Marxism-Leninism
We do not fear to shed our blood or lay down our lives.
The day modernization in four fields is realized
We will come back to offer libations and sacrifices."

The clamors of these counter-revolutionaries about combating "Qin Shi Huang" and demanding "genuine Marxism-Leninism" were out-and-out counter-revolutionary agitation in the same vein as the language used in Lin Biao's plan for a counter-revolutionary coup d'état —"Outline of Project 571." By directing their spearhead at our great leader Chairman Mao and the Party Central Committee headed by Chairman Mao and lauding Deng Xiaoping's counter-revolutionary revisionist line, these counter-revolutionaries laid bare unmistakably their criminal aim to practice revisionism and restore capitalism in China.

In the past few days these elements not only wrote reactionary poems but plastered reactionary posters. They lauded Deng Xiaoping and attempted to nominate him to play the role of Imre Nagy, the chieftain of the counter-revolutionary incident in Hungary. They talk nonsense, alleging that "with Deng Xiaoping in charge of the work of the Central Committee, the struggle has won decisive victory to the great satisfaction of the people throughout the country." They uttered vile slanders, saying "the recent anti-right-deviationist struggle is the act of a handful of careerists trying to oppose the reversal of incorrect verdicts." They openly opposed the great struggle initiated and led by Chairman Mao to repulse the right deviationist attempt to reverse correct verdicts. Their counter-revolutionary arrogance was inflated to the utmost.

However, the time when these counter-revolutionary elements ran rampant coincided with the day of their downfall. Going against the will of the people, they were extremely isolated. As these bad elements were making disturbances, perpetrating acts of violence and sabotage, many revolutionary people courageously stepped forward to denounce their counter-revolutionary acts and struggled against them. The Peking worker-militia, people's police and army guards on duty at the square and the revolutionary people present at the time worked in close co-operation and fought bravely in defense of Chairman Mao, of the Party Central Committee, Chairman Mao's revolutionary line and the great capital of our socialist motherland. When the handful of bad elements again set fire to the barracks at 5 P.M., the army guards put out the fire at the risk of their own lives. To safeguard the Great Hall of the People, more than one hundred Peking worker-militiamen were injured, a dozen of them seriously wounded. Risking dangers, the people's police persevered in fighting. Six army guards were abducted and many wounded. Although the barracks was besieged and fire engulfed the first floor, leading comrades of the Peking worker-militia command post persevered in the struggle on the second floor. At this critical moment, the switchboard operator calmly reported the news to leading departments concerned.

At 6:30 P.M., after Comrade Wu De's speech was broadcast, most of the onlookers and the masses who had been taken in quickly dispersed. But the handful of counter-revolutionary bad elements continued their desperate resistance and again posted some reactionary poems on the Monument to the People's Heroes.

Three hours later, on receiving an order from the Peking Municipal Revolutionary Committee, tens of thousands of worker-militiamen, in close co-ordination with the people's police and the PLA guards, took resolute measures and sternly enforced proletarian dictatorship. In high morale, the heroic Peking militiamen filed into Tienanmen Square valiantly and mounted powerful counter-attacks. They encircled the small handful of bad elements who were still creating disturbances and committing crimes in the vicinity of the Monument to the People's Heroes. They detained the active criminals and major suspects. In the face of such powerful proletarian dictatorship, the handful of rioters could not withstand even a single blow. They squatted down, trembling like stray dogs. Some hurriedly handed over their daggers, knives and notebooks, on which they had copied down the reactionary poems. Several criminals actually tried to pull out their daggers in a vain attempt to put up a last-ditch fight, and they received appropriate punishment on the spot.

The revolutionary masses and the people of the whole city supported and acclaimed the revolutionary action of the Peking worker-militia, the people's police and the PLA guards.

On the Friday night after the full-scale poster campaign began, Elizabeth and I had invited all the Canadian students studying in Peking to come to the bureau for dinner. It was an exciting evening as we exchanged observations and ideas, although the students noted that the poster activity was not finding much of an echo in the universities—the normal place such controversy began.

We began talking about the Tienanmen Incident and what it meant to Chinese people. As I had just finished reading the above account before the students arrived, I got it out again and read it aloud. There could have been no more eloquent and frightening denunciation than this cold-blooded version of the events, and as I finished reading it, we were all deeply moved.

Then the telephone rang. It was Nigel Wade of the London *Daily Telegraph* to say that a massive sixty-yard-long *dazibao* had gone up in Tienanmen Square, just opposite Chairman Mao's tomb. Thousands of people were reading it, and did I know any translators who could be called at this late hour?

Did I know any? I had ten dining in the next room, all worked up into a revolutionary fervor of disgust at the antics of the Gang of Four and eagerly "re-evaluating the historical role of Chairman Mao," to quote an earlier poster. I came back into the room and told everyone the news, and with ten seconds to grab coats and bags, we were all rushing downstairs for the *Globe*'s Toyota. Two people decided to go on their bicycles and the rest of us piled in —four in the front, six wedged in the back. Off we went into the night to Tienanmen Square to see what the latest "handful" of bad elements were up to. We were not disappointed.

When my mother came to visit us in Peking and first saw Tienanmen Square, she pronounced it "beautiful." The sun was shining brightly, and the yellow procelain roofs of the Forbidden City, at the northern perimeter of the square, glistened magically. Dozens of red banners fluttered in the warm wind of early autumn, and since it was a Sunday, thousands of Chinese—most of them visitors to Peking—were strolling about the vast expanse, many with children flying brightly colored kites. There were long lineups here and there as others waited patiently to have their pictures taken by professional photographers at various vantage points which provided plenty of choice for a backdrop: the Great Hall of the People to the west, the Monument in the center or Chairman Mao's tomb further south, the massive History Museum to the east, or the Forbidden City gates themselves. Despite the golden day, I couldn't resist telling my mother what I thought of Tienanmen Square. It was a horror.

Back in the fifties, the Communists had been hell-bent to destroy the tranquillity and the architectural balance of the original square. The two major new buildings—the History Museum and the Great Hall of the People—were vile Stalinist eruptions that evoked no connection with the Chinese people's traditional or revolutionary past: they were just big and ugly. The revamped square had been designed to hold a million people on those momentous special occasions when Mao would mount the ancient Gate of Heavenly Peace and review a parade at which he, his cronies on the Politburo and a handful of invited guests would be the only observers: the masses were all participants. More likely than not they would be bearing images of Mao himself, so that the Great Helmsman could look upon his people and see his own image duplicated several-hundred-thousand-fold in the form of badges, statues, posters and huge portrait paintings.

In Tienanmen Square, lone individuals were reduced to antlike obscurity. Only when they were massed together did the place take on any logic. An American Sinologist who visited Peking during my time once lectured me on the significance of the planning at Tienanmen Square. It was a perfect contemporary repository, he said, of the enduring Chinese disdain for individuality that you could trace through Daoist mythology and traditional Chinese art, which depicted men as tiny creatures against a massive backdrop of mountains.

My days were often plagued with people like this, who loved to discover in Communist follies the proof of their particular theories and further burden the Chinese people with their curious scholarship. Not content to stick to their area of acknowledged expertise, they patronize the Chinese with their mania for historical consistency, and I put them in the same class as those journalists and writers from the West who prided themselves on their contacts with the Party leadership. They never hesitated to define who the Chinese people were or what their aspirations entailed. The only thing they neglected to do was to check out their theories with the people themselves.

My mother, however, was clairvoyant, because Tienanmen Square did become beautiful to me in time, and the process started that night Elizabeth and I bundled into the car with the Canadian students. Aesthetically, it remained a symbol of empty totalitarian bravado, but peopled with the right Chinese on the right occasion, it really did seem a revolutionary setting where brave words from brave people rang out loud and clear—with the clarity that comes from experience and resolve.

When we first emerged into the square from the north end, I was disappointed because it seemed there was hardly anyone there. "No," said a student, "there's a crowd over by the east wall beside the History Museum. Jesus," he added, "look at the size of that wall poster!"

There was a general hubbub in the car, but the last thing I was going to do was turn around and look anywhere but directly in front of me. Driving in Peking, especially at night before most people were safely in bed, was a sheer nightmare. You are allowed to put on only your parking lights, so that bikers won't be blinded by headlights. There are three million bicycles in Peking, so it is a worthy consideration, but the lack of light and the Chinese dark clothing make driving hazardous in the extreme. In front of the

Forbidden City it is particularly bad because there are all sorts of bikers and pedestrians crossing a width of eight lanes, with no concern about oncoming traffic.

To get to the History Museum, I would have to swing left at the Great Hall of the People and continue all around Tienanmen Square until I could find a safe spot to leave the car. As I approached Chairman Mao's tomb on the right side, I glanced across the square's expanse and saw the extraordinary sight for the first time. On top of a steep, concrete-paved incline was a tall wooden fence that was perhaps a hundred yards long by six feet high. Pasted across most of its surface on huge paper sheets was this remarkable-looking *dazibao.*

When I finally got to the site, it was clear that the authors had chosen the place not for its convenience but for its impact. The steep incline meant that readers had to go up a neighboring lane, climb up some rough steps and walk carefully along a narrow ledge which abutted the fence. One step backward and the reader would be catapulted down at least six feet onto solid concrete. There were several thousand people patiently lined up, either directly on this ledge or in the lineup by the laneway. Hundreds of others milled about on the sidewalk below. It was a happy and very orderly crowd. Perhaps thanks to the physical perils involved, there was no impatient jostling as people read. You had to move along the ledge to read the whole grand affair, and if someone was a slow reader or was making notes, the people behind didn't urge him on.

The Canadian students were extremely conscientious, although, because they were students, they tended to exercise prerogatives journalists lacked. As Nigel and I were flapping our arms, trying to keep warm, we would urge them to hurry up. "My newspaper works on deadlines, you know," Nigel would shout. One student came down to give us a word-for-word translation of a very esoteric poem filled with allusions to historical personalities in Chinese history. Even though I took down notes, I knew this would be of no immediate value, but I didn't want to hurt the student's feelings because he had worked so hard. At one point, he said that such and such a character might mean this or might mean that—the context was difficult to understand. Nigel's chilblains got to him, and he had one of those little explosions for which I came to have a great deal of affection: "My God, man, can't you give us the gist? This isn't a symposium on Chinese literature."

As we started putting the various parts of the poster together in our notebooks, it became clear why the writers had chosen this spot. In Tienanmen Square, Chinese people remembered what had happened two years before when the masses demanded an end to injustice. And the poster had been put up directly across from Chairman Mao's tomb. The poster writers were all artists or authors who had been persecuted during the Cultural Revolution, and for the first time they were telling anyone who cared to read what had gone on during that frightening epoch. In standard fashion, they paid tribute to Mao's role as a revolutionary fighter who had freed the Chinese people from foreign domination and allowed them to stand up proudly in 1949 on their own soil. But he was not a divinity, they added, even if he was enshrined in a crystal sarcophagus across the way. He had also harmed the Chinese people, and these writers and artists summed up their evaluation of Mao's career by saying that he was "seventy percent good and thirty percent bad." The seventy–thirty ratio was repeated several times in the body of the poster and became another kind of magical number that was picked up back at the Xidan Wall. By then, the ratio had been simplified to seven–three. The numbers became a kind of identity mark. If you cited them, that meant you were a person who was able to look at the past without fear, because you could say Chairman Mao had made mistakes. Some foreigners thought this whole seven–three business a huge, irrelevant joke, but they had never read the plethora of bunk that had been written by the propaganda department and dumped on the Chinese people for years. To have even hinted that Chairman Mao could make mistakes could and did get people executed during the Cultural Revolution, even though Mao on several occasions admitted errors and requested that the people be made aware of them. The seven–three ratio also meant that one was capable of discussing the specifics of the "three"— those errors which brought such miseries to China.

As far as the poster writers that Friday night were concerned, most of the "three" was confined to the Cultural Revolution. They talked about the brainwashing of children; the persecution of anyone who questioned the status quo; how teen-agers were transformed into vicious, marauding Red Guards; how the country's rich cultural heritage had been dispatched to a cesspool; how old people had been humiliated; about great artists whose love of China was despised and whose integrity had been their death warrant. To end their poster on a positive note, they reproduced dozens of poems that had been written during the Cultural Revolution but were then too dangerous to circulate openly. Publishing these poems now, they wrote, was an act of faith that things were improving and that the post–Gang of Four government was trying to rehabilitate past victims and atone for the terror of the past.

It was nearly 1:30 A.M. when the last of my copy was processed at the cable office. I decided to go have another look at the huge *dazibao,* because the square was sure to be deserted at this hour. Sure enough, there were only a couple of dozen people left and one foreign correspondent—one of the underlings from the Soviet Tass news agency. I had by this time come to have a horror of the whole Tass operation in Peking, even though I maintained civil relations with the bureau chief, Artur Blinov. The one thing I knew was that its staff weren't journalists. One of their favorite tricks was to tell Western journalists about wall posters no one else could ever find. My favorite was the wall poster someone was supposed to have put up inside Chairman Mao's tomb, attacking Chairman Hua Guofeng. The only corroborating witness was the Cuban correspondent, which didn't provide what I would call sterling proof. We were all looking for any overt signs of discontent with the current authorities, and we hadn't found anything substantial. Some of the less reputable journalists in Peking, however, picked up the Soviet guff and sent it out to their agencies.

One of the Tass correspondents also spoke Chinese and English reasonably well, and his particular stock-in-trade was translating wall posters for lazy correspondents who didn't know Chinese and couldn't be bothered to arrange for trusted translators. His trick was to inject certain lines of his own into the translation which suggested chaos in the leadership. As a result of all this Soviet spoiling, several of us adopted a policy of not writing about any poster we hadn't actually seen with our own eyes, in the company of bona fide translators. Whenever possible, we compared translations and sought clarification of discrepancies. In a crunch, a small pool arrangement was used, but only among the most trusted colleagues.

So as I got out of the car and the Tass man approached me, I indulged in some pleasantries and tried to plumb him for his latest lies. A student friend of mine was up on the concrete ledge to take a more leisurely look at the poster, and as I was talking with the

Tass correspondent, I started witnessing one of the most extraordinary sights I had ever seen in China. About ten official government Shanghai sedans quietly pulled up to the curb directly in front of the poster, and behind them were two small vans. Five or six uniformed members of the Public Security Bureau emerged, along with about a dozen other men.

The Russian was unaware of what was going on right behind him as he was talking, but he must have seen from the expression on my face that something was amiss. He turned around and let out a little squeak. I was amused and condescending about what he then said: "Oh, my God, they are going to end it all this quickly. I thought it would last longer." As things got better and better in the days ahead, I used to tell this story as a sign of Soviet blindness about what was happening in China and the prospects that were possible in what I assumed was a better Communist country. Ruefully, I must now admit his premature speculation was wiser than mine.

In any event, the unfolding scene was dramatic enough. The Chinese people still reading the poster seemed relatively unconcerned, apart from natural curiosity. The uniformed police and the other men gathered in little huddles and then motioned for one of the men standing by the vans to come and join them. The next thing I knew, four more men jumped out of the back of one of the vans, with large, old-fashioned still cameras. Some of their colleagues went to the other van and pulled out four aluminum ladders. Still others rummaged around and came out carrying large battery packs over their shoulders while their hands clutched powerful camera lights on short poles.

The whole scene was quite bizarre until the team, with remarkable precision, set about their work and everything made sense. It was the Public Security Bureau, come to take note of the wall poster for future reference. For the smaller posters at the Xidan Wall and along Wang Fu Jing Street, it would simply be a matter of sending a plainclothes agent to copy down the various posters alongside the citizenry. But this huge *dazibao* in Tienanmen Square obviously required a special effort.

As I watched the men go through their paces, it was clear that the whole operation had been worked out beforehand to the last detail. Two men each worked the four ladders—one at either end. The ladders were placed flat on the concrete incline. As soon as a ladder was in place, a photographer would climb halfway up and take a picture of one page of the poster. On the ledge above, uniformed police had politely but firmly asked readers to move off for a few minutes, and the men with the lights held them up to the page that was to be photographed. Two pictures were taken of each page. Then the photographer would step down from the ladder and it would be moved along the incline to the next page, where the process was repeated. By working in four teams and dividing the *dazibao* into quarters, the men did the job in seven minutes. The equipment took only a few minutes to pack up. As suddenly and anonymously as they had come, the whole team departed.

2.
Saturday and Sunday, November 25–26

Saturday was the official day of rest for the *Globe and Mail* bureau in Peking. Since my newspaper didn't publish on Sundays, the Russians could invade China on a Saturday and I couldn't do anything about it. Alone among the journalists in Peking, I had one day a week in which to breathe easily and catch up at a leisurely pace on anything I had missed. That Saturday became very precious whenever news pressure built up, and Elizabeth and I liked to take trips out to the Valley of the Ming Tombs or the old Summer Palace, where we could go for long and amiable rambles either alone or with close friends. It was to the Ming tombs we went following the escapades at Tienanmen Square, on a clear, bright, cold Saturday morning. It turned out to be one of those rare occasions when you could see the splendid mountains and hills that encircle Peking right from the heart of the city.

We went with the Fritzells, friends from the French Embassy, and had a glorious time tramping around one of the unrestored tombs, where the tourists never come. I know a few very haunting spots in the world and this was one of them. When you climb the wooded tumulus or hill below which a Ming emperor is buried in pomp, you get a spectacular view of the whole valley. It is possible to see the other tombs nestled beneath the mountains on the edge of the vast flat plain. The fields and orchards of the nearby communes are neatly laid out, and the air has a softness I have never noted anywhere else. If you're lucky, someone will be singing nearby, and the echo of the voice dances all around you. Here was as close a definition of serenity and tranquillity as I ever hope to find, and I confess I often succumbed happily to mystical sentimentality in this holy place—holy once only to emperors and now to everyone, Chinese or foreigner, who merely seeks it out.

A visit to the Valley of the Ming Tombs was usually sufficient to keep me flying in the upper altitudes of metaphysics for days on end, but on this occasion I was brought sharply down to earth almost the moment I got back to the apartment. The phone rang, and it was Roger Garside.

"Dear fellow," he said in a tone of voice that I knew from close friendship was maliciously patronizing. "Where on earth have you been? The most extraordinary things are happening and you're nowhere about."

"What are you talking about, Roger?" I was cold and abrupt and play-acting as much as he.

"The Wall, dear boy, the Wall. It was incredible. The masses have found their voice. Everyone's talking. Unless you think you know everything there is to know about China, I suggest you get yourself down to the Wall and have a little chat. There's several thousand people who are bursting at the seams. It's quite the most extraordinary thing I have ever gone through in my life."

"Is it still going on? Should I go down there now?"

"No, you've missed it for today, I fear. But never mind. Several people assured me they would be back to continue discussions tomorrow, so you may be lucky."

I was subjected to two more phone calls, from Georges Biannic and Wade, who poured out even more enticing details. I had missed the event of the year. Apparently, ordinary Chinese people gathered at the Xidan Wall were having conversations with a few foreigners—diplomats, students and journalists—on every subject imaginable, without any discernible fear.

The phone rang again. This time, instead of another breathless account of the amazing events I had missed, it was Robert Novak, the famous syndicated columnist. Novak's principal outlet was *The Washington Post,* which often carried my own dispatches from China. Since he was visiting China on an official trip, he had taken the trouble to get my phone number. Just like every other journalist the world over, he had arrived in a strange place and was getting in touch with some of the locals to find out what was up. He made some flattering noises, which were doubly welcome considering his stature in the journalistic world and my own low mood at the time. Novak asked if we could get together for a talk, so I invited him over to the apartment Sunday afternoon. I added that remarkable things were going on at the Xidan poster wall, and if he wanted to see some of the local action we could go down there after our talk.

The next day Novak arrived promptly at 3:30 P.M., and I opined on the subject of China for nearly an hour, giving him the benefit of my one year's experience. He was particularly eager to have my views on Deng Xiaoping, because he thought he had a very good chance of doing an interview with the powerful vice-premier the very next day.

"That's typical," I said with genuine anger. "You know, resident journalists never get to interview state leaders. They are saved for big shots like you. Someone told me you are fairly anti-Soviet, which means they will love you here. I'm not surprised Deng has agreed to an interview with you."

"Well, I don't know if he's exactly agreed," said Novak with a shrug, "but I've been told to stay ready for an interview all day tomorrow."

"That means you'll get it. But you won't know until the last minute. That's the style here. It's reminiscent of the Vatican during a papal election."

Novak liked the image, and on that note I suggested we go down to the Wall. "You can't come here and just meet the leaders, you know," I said. "You should press flesh with the led too."

What happened during the next two hours still strikes me as a kind of fantasy, but I know it happened because I was there. It took about twenty-five minutes to drive to the Xidan Wall, and as we approached I could see that the crowd was ten or twenty times the normal size. The huge open spaces in central Peking make estimating a hazardous business, but there were certainly over five thousand people, either milling about or reading posters. I believe it was no more than fifteen seconds after we got out of the car before we were surrounded by over a hundred Chinese. A young man of about twenty-five asked me who I was, and I replied in Chinese that I was the Canadian correspondent.

"I live in Peking," I said, "and my friend here is also a journalist who has come to China from the United States for a visit. My name is Fraser and his name is Novak."

I had a business card with my own name and that of the newspaper printed in Chinese on the reverse. Having the cards printed in Chinese and English was one of the little conceits Peking journalists indulged themselves in. There was no need for them in China, as any official you were ever introduced to would know exactly who you were and what you were about. Up until this point we could never have imagined passing one to an ordinary citizen, but we got them printed anyway, and they turned out to be very useful. The card was handed all around the crowd that had gathered beside Novak and me.

This sort of introduction was very important to the Chinese and would be repeated on numerous occasions: being open in identifying yourself was the first step in winning trust. Several times I saw Soviet journalists or diplomats snooping around the Wall, and when Chinese asked them who they were, they would be pathetically deceptive. Perhaps they feared that the relentless anti-Soviet propaganda churned out by the Chinese Government since 1960 would earn them an instant knock on the jaw, but in fact I never saw any Chinese at the Wall—save the police—be rude or aggressive to foreigners, wherever they came from.

We were now in the middle of a large crowd which was growing with every passing second. A young woman wearing braids and thick glasses approached me and in impeccable English said, "We are anxious to ask you some questions about the state of democracy in your country. Will you talk with us?"

"Of course we will talk with you," I said, "but we are journalists and we would also like to ask you some questions. We have never been able to ask ordinary Chinese people questions. This is the first time. It's amazing."

"Yes," she said, bursting with pride, "it is the first time, I think. But you can speak Chinese and many people want to ask you questions and exchange ideas, so can we begin?"

"But my Chinese is terrible and I can't carry on a proper conversation. Won't you please help by translating?"

She looked perplexed and worried, and for a moment I thought I had made a very bad error. I was singling her out, and undoubtedly there were police observers around. She was risking enough trouble as it was by initiating the conversation. How could I have been so stupid? I was forever forgetting I was in a totalitarian country.

"It doesn't matter," I said in English; "we'll manage somehow."

She smiled back at me with such a loving and trusting look, I fairly melted. *"Meiyou pa,"* I said, which was as close to "Don't be frightened" in Chinese as I could come up with. People were closed in all around us and seemed to get the gist. My inept phrase was picked up instantly. Within seconds everyone was shouting *"Meiyou pa,"* and the final chorus was deafening.

"No," she said when things quieted down, "I'm not frightened at all, but my voice is not strong and many people want to hear you. Wait a moment and I'll see if anyone can help us."

She turned to the crowd and said that although she spoke English, her voice was weak. She asked for someone who had a strong voice and who could speak English to step forward. There was some mumbling in the crowd, and finally a burly man in his late twenties worked his way through the ever-growing mass of humanity and joined us. He spoke to the woman for a few moments and her face lit up again.

"We have solved the problem," she said in triumph. "This man does not speak English, but he says he has a voice like a trumpet, and if I tell him what you have said, he will shout it out."

This was explained to the crowd to its evident satisfaction. It was a bitterly cold day, with a fierce wind blowing dust in sudden gusts, but everyone's body was pressed hard against his or her neighbor's, and I couldn't have been warmer. I was now worrying about the implications of what I was getting myself into. This little question-and-answer period was turning into a bloody big political meeting, and I had not yet been invited by the Information Department of the Foreign Ministry to lecture Chinese citizens on Western democracy. Indeed, I was only too well aware of what the Information Department thought not only of Western democracy, but of Western journalists to boot.

I had a brainstorm.

"Mr. Novak is a very famous American journalist," I told the woman. "He has come here at the invitation of the Chinese Government. Tomorrow he will probably be meeting and interviewing Vice-Premier Deng. It might be interesting for Mr. Novak to know what kinds of questions Chinese people would ask Vice-Premier Deng if they had a chance to do such an interview."

Although I was fully aware how aloof the Chinese leadership is from the masses and how structured Chinese society is, it didn't dawn on me until that moment that I was suddenly offering these citizens an unprecedented opportunity to register their aspirations and fears, right to the top of the government, through an independent, neutral and seemingly friendly third party.

As soon as the word was translated to the gathering, fireworks seemed to explode. Suddenly everyone started running toward us from the other groups. From nowhere, people emerged who started issuing orders to the crowd, and within no more than fifteen seconds, those directly around us started sitting down. The instant organizers urged others to do the same, and they weren't satisfied until there were at least a dozen circular rows seated. Behind these, several thousand other people stood. I could not see Chang An Avenue for all the heads, nor the first floor of the cable office. Dozens of youths climbed up into the branches of the trees around us, and over at the Xidan Wall itself many others were perched on the upper ledge. It all happened so quickly, I didn't fully realize what was happening. I turned to look at Novak, and his jaw had dropped.

The meeting was completely out of my hands now. The instant organizers shouted some words, and the woman explained to me that people were being asked to write down their questions for Vice-Premier Deng, then stand up to read them and pass the notes up to the front so we could keep them for reference. Before that, though, they wanted to have some discussion, and once again I was asked about the state of democracy in my country.

"Is it true you can criticize your leaders without being labeled a counterrevolutionary and traitor?" someone asked. "Do you know anything about Soviet Communism? How is it different from China's? Do Soviet citizens have a Xidan Wall?" asked another.

The questions came pouring out and were similar to the ones that had been asked on Saturday. "What do you think about Chairman Mao and his role in history?" "Is Chairman Mao respected in the West?" "Do you agree that although Chairman Mao was a good man, he made mistakes?" "Do people in the West know how much the Chinese people loved Premier Chou?" "A few years ago, did everyone in the world think the Chinese people had gone crazy?" (This one aroused considerable laughter, and the interpreter told me one man shouted that a few years ago the Chinese people had indeed gone crazy.) "What is your opinion of Vice-Premier Deng?"

I skirted all the questions on Chinese politics and political figures.

I tried to explain briefly the workings of the parliamentary system and how the idea of "loyal opposition" had evolved. How little attention I had paid to such things as a student! These were matters one took for granted, and while I could explain the basic mechanism of Parliament as well as anyone, I had never really pondered deeply its strengths and victories. The very concept of a "loyal opposition" seemed suddenly revolutionary in this setting: an escape hatch from a system of purge and counterpurge.

When I finished my little civics course, the decision was made to start the questions to be addressed to Vice-Premier Deng. These too came rolling out in the form of statements, queries and demands:

"First and foremost: we want a proper memorial established for Premier Chou in Tienanmen Square."

"The Chinese people want more contact with foreign friends so that the masses have a means of conveying their wishes to the leaders."

"The Chinese people want a true democracy, true freedom and true human rights. We do not want dictatorship or despotism in any form. We want a true socialist democracy."

"The Chinese people want to be free to examine the events involved in the Cultural Revolution, and we demand that new evaluations be made of the careers of Peng Dehuai and Liu Shaoqi [Chinese leaders disgraced by Mao in previous political struggles]. The rehabilitation of all Chinese wrongly accused of political and other crimes must be expanded and speeded up."

"The Xidan Wall should be made an official place of free speech just like Hyde Park Corner in London."

"We respectfully request that Vice-Premier Deng visit Xidan Democracy Wall and read some of the posters."

"We call upon the people of the West to show support for the Chinese people as they struggle for true democracy."

"There should be an open, fair trial of the Gang of Four that will be televised to the whole nation."

As these questions and statements were being read out and passed up on little slips of paper, there was a fair bit of banter at the center. The whole affair was becoming a bit like a convention. One man stood up and asked a question and was instantly booed and forced to sit down, while his scrap of paper was torn up. I never could find out what he had said, and the woman refused to translate it. "The man is disturbed" was all she said.

When the name of Hyde Park Corner came up, I was instantly intrigued. How on earth had Chinese workers ever heard of Hyde Park Corner and its tradition of unlimited free speech (save treason against the Crown)? "All the Chinese people know about Hyde Park Corner," said the woman. "It's mentioned in a famous article by Marx." Novak asked me who Peng Dehuai and Liu Shaoqi were, and I was able to shine: Peng Dehuai was the former minister of defense and a famous veteran of Mao's revolutionary war, whose plain speaking had won him the hearts of the masses and the enmity of Mao when he criticized the Great Helmsman for his costly errors during the Great Leap Forward; Liu Shaoqi was another Party veteran who became head of state in the period following the disgrace of Marshal Peng Dehuai, but who ended up as the principal victim of the Cultural Revolution.

As I was talking to Novak, the woman started pulling at my coat sleeve insistently. "This question is very, very important," she said. "The woman back there wants to know this. Why is it that factory workers can elect their Unit leaders by secret ballot, but when the leaders of our country are chosen, we have no say whatsoever?" Novak raised his eyebrows: "Damn good question."

More and more people were finding the courage to stand up and pose a question, but the instant organizers started calling a halt to the proceedings, which seemed to be in danger of getting out of hand. Also, Novak had an appointment with government officials back at his hotel and was pressing me to find a way out for him. I was a little taken aback by this. Here he was in the middle of the biggest story to come out of China in years, and he was worried about getting back to a hotel to chat with a couple of government hacks. That was unfair. As I was to realize the next day, I hadn't impressed on Novak the extraordinary nature of what was happening to us: getting an interview with the Chinese masses was infinitely more significant than any number of interviews with any members of the Politburo. I got the impression at the time that Novak thought it was just a part of normal crazy life in Peking to walk down Chang An Avenue and be surrounded by thousands of citizens asking about the state of democracy.

As we said good-bye to the crowd, the woman came to us and said, "The people here and I—we want to thank you for coming to Xidan Wall and talking to us. You will be talking to Vice-

Premier Deng tomorrow, and we earnestly ask you to tell him what we have said and what you have seen. Please present to him these questions from the Chinese people. We also respectfully ask you to come back here tomorrow and report to us about your meeting: otherwise we will have no way of finding out what was said."

Novak said he would try to come back if he could. A man then approached me and said that whether Novak returned or not, I must return and pass on the news. Elizabeth was beside me at this moment, and I could see her eyes widening. "Perhaps we could meet at Tienanmen Square," the man said in English. "I think many people will want to hear you, and there is more room there. Please bring your megaphone."

I turned to the man and said that I would be back at the Wall tomorrow, but as a correspondent to do correspondent's work. It wasn't proper for me as a foreigner, I added, to make political speeches to the Chinese people.

Later, as I was in the midst of typing a story, the phone rang. It was a Canadian student I had become close to, who had gone down to the Xidan Wall after I left. "John," he asked, his voice breaking with incredulous excitement, "what on earth is going on? I'm at the cable office next to the Wall, and thousands of people are saying Fu Ruizhe is going to address the masses at seven tomorrow night. John, have you got an interview with Deng Xiaoping tomorrow or something? People are going wild down here. What is going on?"

I was overcome with sheer panic as I tried to explain briefly to the student what had happened. He kept saying, "Oh, my God, oh, my God," which didn't help matters. "How are you going to get out of this?" he asked. "I'm not joking, you know. There are several speakers all around the Wall, and some of them have megaphones. They are all saying that you are coming down here to speak to them, and instructions are being handed out on how to behave and when to assemble."

"Look," Elizabeth said a little later, "the worst that can happen is that you will be thrown out of the place. Anyway, I think you're safe. Once the police report to Deng what went on, I don't think Novak has a chance of getting that interview. If he does get it and mentions what went on, then you're okay."

Next, Richard Thwaites of the Australian Broadcasting Corporation called. He too had got down to the Wall after we left and had heard the announcement. I told him my fears, and he did his best to reassure me. "There's safety in numbers; don't worry. They've invited all the foreign correspondents to come, and we'll all be there. Even the Russians. They can't do anything to you without doing it to us. Don't panic. It should be interesting."

I thought of phoning the Canadian Ambassador and asking his advice. I also thought of phoning the Information Department and telling them that I was aware of my position as an accredited correspondent and that I was not starting a political movement or campaign. I thought of not turning up at the Wall at all. Then, in a moment of lucidity, I knew what had to be done. I would return regardless, and I wouldn't ask anyone's advice—all I would be told was to drop out of sight. I had said I would be back, and dammit, I would go back. The only person I called was Roger Garside, and he was a perfect diplomat and friend. "You're on your own, John," he said, "but be careful."

3.
Monday, November 27

I had a miserable night's sleep. After tossing and turning for over an hour, pondering the day's events and wondering what course of action would lead to the least trouble, I finally dozed off, only to be wakened at 4:30 A.M. with the insistent buzzing of the doorbell. In Chinese society, the only institution that so rudely assaults people at that ungodly hour is the Public Scurity Bureau in concert with area vigilantes, who unsuspectingly swoop down on neighborhoods to make periodic household checks in order to ascertain who is sleeping under what roof. It is a way of finding out about illegal residents. For foreigners living in Peking, the only institution that seems to act in the same way is the cable office, which unfailingly delivers incoming overseas telegrams immediately. The service is so good and prompt, it drove me crazy. The twelve-hour time difference between Peking and eastern North America meant that cables sent during office hours at home invariably arrived in Peking between 1 and 5 A.M., and while it might take the Chinese bureaucracy years to correct a wrong political verdict, the cable office could deliver a telegram within ten minutes of arrival. The deliverymen were always genial and courteous, although I suspected they swapped stories about the looks on the faces of confused, half-awake foreigners who staggered to open the doors.

After signing the official receipt, I ripped open the cable. "GREAT STUFF STOP KEEP IT COMING STOP LOTS OF INTEREST REGARDS MANLEY," it read. Don Manley was my foreign editor, and there was no more considerate man at the *Globe,* but at that moment I cursed his compliment on my previous day's story. I knew I would never get back to sleep. I went into the kitchen and made some hot chocolate and ambled disgruntledly into the bureau office at the back of the apartment to check if there was anything interesting on the New China News Agency printer. I did not expect to read a Chinese account of the events at the Xidan Wall: I knew better by this time. It would be completely ignored by the official media, because news was what the government decreed was news, not what actually happened. The Chinese people would hear of Xidan from Voice of America or British Broadcasting Corporation broadcasts (in English or Chinese), or, if they were lucky, in *Reference News,* the amazing little government broadsheet published daily and read, one way or another, by several hundred million people.

Reference News reprinted Western journalism. Although it was selected and edited by the government, a great deal of controversial material about China often made it into the columns. Sometimes my own dispatches were reprinted in translation. The newspaper was restricted to a certain class of Chinese—officials, students, anyone with any connection to state affairs, Party members. However, since the circulation was quite wide, anyone who wanted to know what was in it—except foreigners—could find out. Occasionally a copy would slip into my hands, and I was always amused that the government spent so much effort to prevent us from reading what we had already written. But *Reference News* is a kind of miracle, nevertheless, because it allows Chinese more access to news of the outside world than any equivalent journalistic institution in the entire Communist world.

As I suspected, there wasn't a word about Xidan on the agency printer. In China, it is not for the people to find their own voice; it is for the Party to tell them what to say. Still restless, I started browsing absentmindedly through the *Globe and Mail*'s library, which contained an erratic collection of books assembled by seven previous correspondents. The bureau was sufficiently venerable to have become a repository of all sorts of officially forbidden materials: Liu Shaoqi's *How to Become a Good Communist*, a Marxist version of a Dale Carnegie course on ideological self-improvement; Yao Wenyuan's *On the Counter-Revolutionary Double Dealer Zhou Yang;* Chairman Mao's inflammatory directives during the opening blast of the Cultural Revolution; turgid, sycophantic polemics by the late defense minister Lin Biao, the "closest comrade-in-arms" of the Great Helmsman.

As I browsed, I couldn't suppress a certain nausea at all the lies and hypocrisy the Communist Party has foisted on the Chinese people. Consider the clowns just mentioned. Outside of China, their names mean nothing to most people, but inside they are symbols of such abiding duplicity it can scarcely be fathomed. Liu Shaoqi, the original sponsor of Deng Xiaoping, had risen to be president of the republic when Mao described him as "China's Khrushchev" and "the number one capitalist-roader in the Party." He was disgraced and subsequently driven to his death. His little self-help book in the *Globe*'s library is a marvel of orthodox state Marxism, and how anyone could seriously consider him a capitalist spy defies imagination. Yao Wenyuan, on the other hand, was one of Mao's closest advisers and hatchet men. Now he has been dispatched to oblivion as a member of the Gang of Four, while Liu's memory has been rehabilitated and Zhou Yang, the object of Yao's attack in the book mentioned above, is vice-president of the Academy of Social Sciences.

So much of the struggle within the Chinese Communist Party was a result of Mao's changing his mind on various matters, or trying to retain his political preeminence. Each struggle meant that Mao also changed his allies, and because old allies had colleagues throughout the country, vindictiveness became institutionalized. It was not considered sufficient for the ordinary Chinese citizen merely to take note of all this: he too had to be thoroughly caught up in the nonsense about "line struggle" and "revisionism" and "capitalist restoration." Scapegoats and victims were required throughout the entire population, and everyone had to be seen responding to the latest shocking discoveries and militant changes. It was held that this was good for the masses and raised their "revolutionary consciousness." It is safe to say that never in all of recorded history have so many people been plagued and put upon by so few.

This history is a backdrop every thinking Chinese lives with, but

I had just witnessed an amazing event a few hours earlier, and I wanted to understand how it could have come about and what chance it had for success. I started going through some of the more thoughtful studies of the Cultural Revolution, which tried to show how a new generation of Chinese had taken advantage of an unprecedented political experiment to voice their grievances against an overweening bureaucracy and a society still stuck in a feudal rut. There was passion and eloquence in the early documents of the Cultural Revolution, especially some of the Red Guard newspapers, that was similar in tone to some of the things emerging from the Wall. I also picked up Edgar Snow's classic *Red Star Over China.* Although it is still read by many would-be revolutionaries all over the world, it is considered outdated now, and the *Globe*'s copy was worn and tattered. I had perused it once before, but on this occasion it made compulsive reading.

Learning about the Chinese leaders in their younger days put some of the inequities entrenched in current realities into perspective. Snow can be fairly accused of glossing over a number of totalitarian tendencies which later came into far greater focus. But through his investigations it is possible to see, at the source of the Party's experience, a decency and vision, which I thought could still be observed in some of the better things that had endured in a Communist-controlled society. I also realized, with some disquiet, that I had ceased being a neutral, dispassionate observer. I was getting caught up in the events around me, and I wanted things to be better for those people I had met at the Wall.

Shortly after noon, Novak called to tell me that he had seen Deng and obtained a highly successful interview.

"Fantastic," I said, feeling the first real relief in several days. "What happened?"

"Oh, he was in good form," said Novak. "I told him what happened yesterday, and he said that he thought the Xidan Wall was a good thing and could go on forever. At the end, I put some questions to him the crowd had asked. I couldn't get them all in, but at least I've got something you can report back to them tonight if you still plan on going."

"Of course I'm going," I said, a touch mystified. "Aren't you coming too? With this news, it should be spectacular."

"Unfortunately, I can't. I'm committed to a dinner with the officials of the Information Department, and I don't see how I can get out of it. I'm off the next morning bright and early for the oil fields of Daqing [pronounced "da-ching"]. But you tell those people Deng thought the Wall was good and I'll give you the rest of what he said. And please apologize to them for me for not coming."

What a relief! As long as I spoke exclusively on those things Deng had said in response to Novak's questions from the Wall and didn't get carried away, there was nothing to worry about. I set about writing down a short speech.

During the afternoon, the word had got around the foreign community that Fraser was going to make another spectacle of himself in the evening, and the phone never stopped. I refused to talk to anyone except Biannic and Wade, and I was hardly coherent with them. Finally, it was 6:30 P.M. and we got into the car and headed for Xidan.

The scene awaiting us was unlike anything I had anticipated, through all my trepidation. There were well over ten thousand people assembled. Some estimates put it closer to twenty thousand. They filled the area directly in front of the long wall completely and spilled out onto Chang An Avenue itself. Every nearby vantage point was occupied: there were people in tree branches and on top of the wall itself, and at the periphery of the crowd other people were standing on their parked bicycles to see over the vast sea of heads.

It was already dark as we approached, but several Chinese people recognized me and passed along the word. The atmosphere was electric, and I suddenly found myself walking toward the center of the crowd through a pathway made by the masses themselves. Seated on one side of the circle in the middle were all the foreign correspondents of Peking, including, to my amusement, a full contingent from the East Bloc countries. The Communist journalists' reaction to me, in several notable cases, was hostility tinged with utter confusion at what was unfolding before them.

At the center there was considerable confusion at first. My arrival had set off a mad scrambling among the people to get a good vantage point up front. Organizers, who once again seemingly sprang from nowhere, worked hard to calm everyone down. They kept shouting things like "Everyone sit down and be quiet"; "We must maintain discipline, comrades"; "There are foreign friends here tonight, so everyone must take special care"; "How can we say we are ready for democracy if we cannot maintain order and discipline at this meeting?" At one point, the organizers apparently decided that the interest in actually seeing my face was so intense that it had better be assuaged. Before I could protest, I found myself hoisted on the shoulders of two burly Chinese men, who paraded me around so that the people in the back could see.

Finally, after about fifteen minutes, the organizers restored discipline, and everyone relaxed after a very inspired bit of crowd control: a man simply started singing the "Internationale," the stirring anthem of the world's working classes. It was sung in Chinese, but I knew the first lines of the anthem: "Arise, ye prisoners of starvation/Arise, ye wretched of the earth. . . ." Everyone sang lustily. I have never heard such singing, never heard a song so moving. I saw what had first seemed a ragtag, disorderly mob transformed into a melded whole, and I got a vision of what "the masses" really meant. The force of their singing was a symbol of the force of their power. In such large numbers, they provided each other with the most useful protection in China today—anonymity in the crowd. After the "Internationale," they broke into the Chinese national anthem, which was sung with equal fervor, and when this was done, there was a great expectant silence.

By this time, some of the organizers had approached me with a translator. I explained that the meeting with Vice-Premier Deng had taken place, and although Novak could not be here tonight, he had authorized me to give a report, which I was prepared to do. I kept emphasizing that it was a report, not a speech, but I believe this was lost in the translation. This crowd had turned up to see what was in the political wind, and the very fact that I had come with news from Deng Xiaoping, the favorite son, was already a harbinger of victory.

The system adopted to pass on the report went like this: I would read a sentence and the translator would then provide the Chinese version to a group of about six "trumpet voices," who would fan out and shout the word and return to get the next sentence. While all this was being arranged, I was amused to watch my colleagues distribute their business cards like pretzels and peanuts at a cocktail party.

Finally, it came time to give the report and I began, sentence by sentence:

"The American journalist Novak met with Vice-Premier Deng this afternoon in the Great Hall of the People.

"Journalist Novak apologizes for not being here tonight, but he was detained on official business and asked me to make the following report.

"Journalist Novak told Vice-Premier Deng that he had talked to a large crowd of people at Xidan Democracy Wall and that the people had given him some questions to ask the Vice-Premier.

"Journalist Novak then told Vice-Premier Deng some of the things we spoke about last night, although there was not time to ask everything.

"Vice-Premier Deng said that he thought Xidan Democracy Wall was a good thing."

As soon as this was said, pandemonium broke out. I heard the phrase *"Xidan hao"* ("Xidan good") ring out all around me. People at the back started pushing, which caused everyone in the carefully seated rows in front to stand up instantly in order not to be crushed. It took about five minutes for the organizers to restore calm, and they did it once again with the singing of the "Internationale."

"However, Vice-Premier Deng also said that he thought some of the things the masses were saying and writing at Xidan Democracy Wall were not correct."

The mood suddenly became frighteningly somber. I was not fully aware at the time how much importance was being attached to each phrase that I spoke and how much these people were counting on the Vice-Premier to defend and back up what they were doing. It was a pivotal point for the future development of the Xidan Democracy Wall because while people were looking for nominal encouragement from the new leadership to speak out freely, it was now clear that something was started—for whatever reasons, either covertly official or spontaneously from the people themselves—that could not be easily turned off. Consequently, people strained to hear the next sentence with particular interest.

"For example, Vice-Premier Deng said that he did not agree with the seventy–thirty evaluation of Chairman Mao's historical record. He said Chairman Mao was better than seventy–thirty.

"On the question of Marshal Peng Dehuai, the Vice-Premier indicated that his memory and record would be rehabilitated shortly.

"Journalist Novak told the Vice-Premier that whenever the Vice-Premier's name was mentioned, the people cheered their support.

Vice-Premier Deng said that he did not approve of this because his record was only sixty–forty. He added that Marshal Peng Dehuai's record was also only sixty–forty.

"When Journalist Novak asked about the rehabilitation of former President Liu Shaoqi, Vice-Premier Deng made no response at all to this question.

"This is the report given to me by Journalist Novak. Now that it is finished, I have nothing more to say, and I think it is proper that I leave."

With that, a pathway miraculously appeared, and I left the center quickly. My head was pounding from emotion. As I went down the escape route, Chinese people stepped out to shake my hand, and several actually embraced me in warm bear hugs. Someone shouted in fractured English, "You are a brave man, Fu Ruizhe. The Chinese people thank you." I had never felt less brave in my life, and I was overwhelmed by the expectations all around me.

Having made my way successfully out of the crowd, I drifted around the periphery, enjoying instant anonymity. I couldn't tell what was going on, except that some other speakers—all Chinese—were addressing the crowd. Suddenly, everyone started to move, seemingly at once. I sprinted off quickly in the direction of the cable office to be ahead of the surging crowd. In its midst, unbeknownst to me at the time, Elizabeth was accidentally knocked down and was nearly trampled to death. Thanks to some large Chinese men who got her up and held her steady, she escaped without too much damage, although her coat looked as if a thousand people had walked over her. One or two other foreigners, unused to Chinese mass gatherings, had also been knocked down, and they too had tales of Chinese people struggling to help them get up and maintain their balance. It was that kind of night.

When we collected ourselves, we could see, looking out onto Chang An Avenue, that the evening was far from over. The crowds had taken over literally half of the broad street and were forming into ranks ten to fifteen people wide. With complete order and discipline, they started marching in the direction of Tienanmen Square, singing the "Internationale" and the Chinese anthem. What an extraordinary sight it was! Traffic came to an astonished standstill. Public Security Bureau traffic police along the way looked on in disbelief.

The march—the various estimates of the crowd ranged between ten and fifteen thousand—went past the gates of Zhong Nan Hai, where many of the Party leaders live and where Mao's Peking residence had once been, then on to the Great Hall of the People. The ranks held firm until everyone reached Tienanmen Square, where most people went up to the central monument. Others, however, formed into circular groups of several hundred, and for the next three hours a huge symposium on the nature of democracy in China was held. It was impossible to keep track of everything that was said, and I decided it would be best to stick with one group. Three rather wonderful English-language students hitched themselves to me and provided excellent translation services for most of the time.

The entire scene was like something out of an old film on the Russian Revolution—in black and white. It was very dark, and the eerie light from lamp standards around Tienanmen cast somber shadows everywhere. Some of the windows were lit up in the neighboring Great Hall of the People. In the huge square, the crowd didn't seem nearly as large as it had at Xidan, but it was certainly of an impressive size, especially when you consider the sorts of things people were saying.

In our particular group, there was a discussion of the press in China. I was with an Australian diplomat who was a fluent Chinese linguist, and the exchanges were extremely lively. There was criticism of the fact that the Chinese press was completely under the control of the Communist Party.

"So you do not believe everything that is written in the *People's Daily,* then?" I asked.

The response was interesting.

"It is not a question of believing," said a middle-aged man who must have been an official of some sort, to judge by the better cut and cloth of his coat and the Japanese digital watch on his wrist. "The Chinese people know that the *People's Daily* represents the direct thinking of the Party. When they read it, they are looking for news of the Party and the direction in which the Party wants to lead the country. We are very happy to have this information. But we would also like a newspaper that expresses the thoughts and interests of the people themselves. We do not have such a thing. The favorite newspaper of the people at the moment is *Reference News,* which prints translations of foreign news agencies, but it tells us only what foreigners think of China—it is not our newspaper and does not express our views. This is only one of many deficiencies in our system which must be corrected."

I was asked to explain how the Western press operates, which I tried to do. Foreign correspondents were by then held in such high regard that, while stressing the importance of the independence of the press from government in the West, I felt compelled to inform them that not everything was simply wonderful.

"Most newspapers are very bad, and only a few live up to principles and are prepared to risk the serious wrath of governments or advertisers. Sometimes huge monopolies take hold of newspapers, and they do not always serve the people's interests."

I couldn't do anything wrong at this juncture, and my response won me hearty compliments for my modesty and understatement.

"We all know," said one young man, "that an American newspaper was able to remove a head of state from power."

We then got into a discussion about Watergate, and once again I tried to explain that it had been one newspaper and two reporters who had been tenacious in getting to the bottom of the scandal. In time, some other newspapers had joined in, but for the most part the vast majority of American newspapers ignored and disliked such journalism.

"Honestly," I said, "you would be surprised at how bad some newspapers are." My stock soared ever upward.

"The Chinese people know," said another, "that Western journalists are uncrowned kings. We all admire you very much."

After a bit more of this, I took my trinity of translators over to the big symposium at the Monument. On this Monday night, I did not hear too many major speeches there. One or two people read out what I had said at Xidan as well as the official account of Novak's interview, which had been carried by the New China News Agency. These items were repeated over and over again, and people were urged to go off into smaller groups to discuss issues. As I looked over the square, I could make out about six such groups. In some cases, young men had mounted the permanent television camera stands built in the square for the big state occasions. The wind was quite strong and the speakers leaned into it, talking through battery-operated megaphones. It was another scene from a great film.

I ran into Biannic, who had already been filing on his telex to

Paris and was back to get the latest. We exchanged notes. He pointed out that in Novak's interview, as reported by the official government agency, there had been one ominous note.

"You know what he said, don't you?" he asked me. "He said some of the things being written and spoken at Xidan were against stability and unity. That's not a good thing to say."

"Yes, but for God's sake, Georges," I said with some irritation, "the man clearly stated that he thought Xidan was a 'good thing,' and the police certainly aren't making any effort to stop this business. The crowd at the Monument have just been told that there will be meetings again tomorrow night."

"Yes," said Georges, "and it will be very interesting. But you and I both know that what these people are struggling toward is not a certain degree of free speech and democracy. It is the real thing. Either there is free speech or there isn't: you can't put a qualification on the word 'free,' and Deng has put on a very strong qualification. These people do not have an official sponsor at the top, no matter how much they idolize Deng today. He is protecting his territory with qualifications. At best, they have only very wary support. As for the police, they never act fast on this sort of thing. Even in the Tienanmen demonstrations, it was several days before the repression began."

I wrote a dramatic account of the evening, since the event itself was the most important thing. Analysis and speculation could wait. Late at night, I drove down to the cable office. At the time, I was unaware of the singular fact that Bob Novak had preceded me there after concluding his official dinner. He had finished writing his interview with Deng and had walked right past the last remnants of the crowd at Xidan—now three blocks away. Later he told me he had vaguely wondered how I had got on. In all the excitement, I had forgotten to get in touch with him, and he was in total ignorance of the events for which he had been the catalyst. The next morning, he was whisked out of the city to visit the northern oil fields, and no one could get hold of him. Before he was able to return to Peking five days later, he heard all sorts of wild rumors from his Chinese hosts, including one which held that I had been carried down Chang An Avenue on the shoulders of Chinese dissidents! Novak thus became yet another Western journalist who discovered to his chagrin that you can be in the center of things in China and oblivious to the biggest story of the day. His hotel, where he had dinner with the officials of the Information Department, was a two-minute walk from the Xidan Democracy Wall.

4.
Tuesday, November 28

The telephone at the bureau had gone berserk. Newspapers, television stations and China experts around the world all wanted to know what on earth was going on in Peking, and phoning the *Globe and Mail* appeared to be the easiest solution. Around 8:30 A.M. Biannic called to say he had been restless and had been out scouting the town. He reported that a new wall poster had gone up announcing the first edition of an "unofficial" magazine called *April Fifth Journal,* which would be available for sale at the Xidan Democracy Wall the next day. The journal's manifesto had been posted, along with the announcement:

> Our official slogans are "Long Live Democracy," "People Should Be Their Own Masters," "Servants of the People Really Should Be Servants" and "Without Free Elections, Servants Will Become Masters."
> Conditions necessary for elections: (1) Electoral law. (2) All levels of the Communist Party must play a role in guaranteeing fair elections. (3) Elections must be for positions from the top to the bottom. (4) There must be more candidates for office than positions available. (5) Scrutineering should be anonymous. (6) There must be secret ballots.

Biannic was still wary about Deng's caution on "stability and unity," but because he was a good journalist, he was concentrating on what was actually happening, not what might be. In this way he controlled his deep pessimism; by a reverse method, I tried to control my optimism and reminded my readers that a previous manifestation of free speech and criticism—the Hundred Flowers Campaign of 1956—had led to widespread repression. Biannic also reported that the magazine said a future issue would make suggestions for social change in China.

"Not bad, eh?" he asked. "It's the first underground magazine in China I have heard of for some time—since some of the Red Guard magazines during the beginning of the Cultural Revolution."

Something bothered me about what he had just said, and we got into an argument.

"Georges, we can't start calling it an underground magazine when they are advertising it openly at one of the biggest intersections in the city," I said. "We can't call them dissidents, either. A lot of what they are saying is just an extension of the government and Party attacks on the Gang of Four, and I haven't heard anyone calling for the downfall of the government—or the Communist Party, for that matter. I'm calling them 'activists,' and until they are driven underground, which I doubt will happen, that's the way I'll think of them."

At the time, I couldn't express the real reason I was worried by the kind of labels being flung out by some of my colleagues. The night before, a Reuters correspondent had fulminated at my madness by attacking Novak's role in the business. The journalist said that we had become involved with and were encouraging "Chinese dissidents."

"Anyway," he added for good measure, "this whole business isn't serious. It's just a bunch of kids."

I wasn't predisposed to debate the point. It struck me as hilarious that anyone could dismiss a movement in China because there were just "a bunch of kids" involved. In the first place, it showed a desperate ignorance of Chinese revolutionary history. If this wasn't "serious," the May 4 Movement, the early years of the Chinese Communist Party and the Cultural Revolution itself were not serious. In the second place, it showed a remarkable lack of observation. Quite a number of middle-aged people had been present at Xidan. Indeed, one of the most intriguing speeches at Tienanmen the night before had come from a distinguished-looking gray-haired man who knew a great deal about foreign policy. He had called for a scientific approach to all aspects of government and used foreign policy as an example. He pointed out that all countries place national self-interest ahead of any ideological considerations. Had the Chinese Communist Party taken a logical and scientific approach to its relations with the Soviet Union, it would have discovered that Stalin always worked for Soviet self-interest first, even if it meant betraying a fraternal Party. He expanded on the point:

Because the American imperialists were our enemies, we understood clearly their national self-interest; but because the Soviet Union was supposed to be our friend, we failed to make a proper examination of things when we were first liberated. We should have normalized our relations with the United States right away. It could have been done despite the American Government's resistance had we only thought things out properly and made certain concessions. That would have prevented the Taiwan problem. Instead, we trusted the "internationalism" of the Soviet Union, which was a trick. In the process, we also adopted the Soviet model of government, and we copied it right down to the last detail. And what did this get us? It got us a Stalinist, fascist regime which nearly destroyed our country. Only now are we trying to set things right, at a time when many people have lost their faith in the Communist Party. The people and the Party have paid a grievous price for this bitter lesson.

From my understanding of Chinese history and culture, I also knew it was a mistake to confuse issues with the Western understanding of the word "dissident." At least, it was at this point. This is a complicated business and is the same kind of problem that is involved in discussions of "human rights" in China. To our minds, I think, a dissident summons up a very concrete image of a lone individual standing up against the faceless, oppressive might of the state. We think automatically of Soviet dissidents. The Chinese people I saw marching down Chang An Avenue did not see the state as inherently wicked or something to be challenged as such. The state was, in fact, the extension of the Chinese family, and they felt as much a part of it as the most powerful leading cadres.

The Communist Party has always adopted the role of *paterfamilias* and allied itself to this presiding sentiment. The Xidan crowds were more patriotic and concerned for the well-being of the larger Chinese family than the average citizen, who tried to avoid trouble and confrontation. One can argue that if you examine famous dissidents in the Soviet Union or the West, you will find much the same emotions when you scratch the surface of the rhetoric and make allowances for cultural differences. To some extent this is true. But if you call it dissidence in China, you have to include the fact that the most ferocious dissidents were right at the heart of the body politic. The reason the Xidan crowds wanted the approval of Deng Xiaoping was that that would mean their grievances had a chance to be aired and their aspiration an equal chance of being fulfilled.

It was explained to me at Xidan that in China to have no access to power is to be cut off from the possibilities of change and dissent.

In this light, Deng Xiaoping himself was one of the great dissidents, and the secret of his durability resides in the fact that he has solid power bases throughout the country, such as important elements in the army and regional administrations. Without these power bases, his resistance to Mao during two decades would have been pointless, and this was something that seemed to be understood by everyone we met. It was becoming clear at Xidan that Deng's record of opposition provided an aura of hope for those who wanted to push improved conditions further and faster than they were already going. They were working for an ideal through very practical means. When these means came under attack, many people lost heart and felt betrayed.

One of the people at the Wall called me shortly after Biannic hung up the phone.

"Hello," said the voice, and I knew what I was in for immediately. "I am a Chinese friend. Did you find your ring?"

"No," I said, paying my daily penance for that damned poster. "Who are you?"

"I am a worker. I would be very interested to talk to you and practice my English. I speak English very poorly."

"Not at all," I said, playing the game and paying him a compliment. "You speak it very well."

"Oh, no," he said, "my education is very backward. But do you think we can have a chance to talk? Will you come to Xidan Wall again tonight? We can talk safely there."

"I'll be there. Do you know what I look like?"

"Yes, of course. All the Chinese people know the famous, brave correspondent Fu Ruizhe."

"That's great," I said. He'd outcomplimented me. "You try to find me down there and we'll have a talk."

No sooner had I hung up the phone when it rang again.

"Hello, is that Fu Ruizhe?"

I nearly slammed down the receiver, so blasé was I becoming about Chinese phoning me at random. But I didn't, thank heaven. In terrible, halting English, the voice said, "I get letter for dinner, thank you."

Sweet Mother of God, I had nearly hung up on Huang Anlun —but I had better go back two months to explain. As part of the normal work of resident journalists in Peking, I made periodic requests to the Information Department for formal visits to various institutions. From the opening of the *Globe* bureau, these requests, sent in letters, were part of the formal farce correspondents were required to take part in. In most cases, the letters weren't even acknowledged by the Information Department. When you actually got a special visit—to a commune or a factory, for example—it wasn't because you had requested it, but because the authorities wanted you to go there. On several occasions, I would be told that I might visit such and such a place, and perhaps I might send along a letter requesting the visit. In this way, the Information Department felt it was "complying with the requests of our foreign friends from news circles." Communications with the Department improved steadily in my time, and although they were far from ideal, the contrast with what had gone on before was remarkable. The United States journalists who arrived in China as permanent residents in 1979 never knew what had preceded them, and when they complained bitterly of the slowness and unhelpfulness of the Information Department, they didn't get much sympathy from the rest of us, who knew things were considerably improved.

In any event, I received permission from the Department to make an official visit to the Peking Ballet School to meet the team that had produced a new Western-style ballet called *The Little Match Girl,* based on the story by Hans Christian Andersen. I had requested such an opportunity and was delighted to get such a swift response (two months).

The ballet itself, which I had seen some time before, was nothing special in itself. It was certainly good to see the Chinese breaking away from the Jiang Qing "model revolutionary" stereotypes, and it was fascinating to observe that the dancers had somehow maintained their excellent technique, which was based on Russian style with Chinese acrobatic embellishments. In the context of China, it was a very encouraging show; but I am a former ballet critic with occasional tendencies toward snottiness, and I couldn't help observing that the pedestrian choreography was of the most banal type.

The music was another matter altogether. The composer, whose name meant nothing to me, had taken some themes by Edvard Grieg and woven a magical score that was romantic but unsentimental. As ballet music it was impeccable, giving the dancers strong direction for their work and adding a rich, dramatic structure to the tale, which both foreigners and Chinese responded to enthusiastically. It made the ballet seem better than it was. Naturally enough,

I was delighted to discover that the team I was meeting included the composer himself, Huang Anlun. He and I were nearly the same age, we had both been married for about five years and we shared the same problem with eyeglasses which slipped down our noses when we talked too much.

After the formal interviewing was done and we toured the school, I found myself off in a corner with him, along with Xiao Hao, the *Globe*'s interpreter. I had been arousing some laughter with my attempts at Chinese, and Huang Anlun spluttered out his English, which was worse. In the interview, he had said how much better things were in China for artists like himself now that "the Gang of Four has been smashed," and I took this with a grain of salt. I had become a trifle cynical about everything wrong in China, including the spit on the streets, which was blamed on "the pernicious influence of the Gang of Four." Would that we in the West had such an all-purpose scapegoat. When Huang Anlun therefore blamed the poor quality of his English on the machinations of the Gang of Four, I cut him off short:

"Well," I said, "I speak crummy Chinese, but I'm afraid I can't blame the Gang of Four. It's because I'm stupid."

He looked straight at me for a moment and let out such a whoop of laughter he got both me and Xiao Hao laughing, just from the explosiveness of his mirth. His hearty, warm laugh made me like him straightaway. Because I liked him, I finally found the courage to tell a Chinese what was really in my heart. "Look," I said, "you told me upstairs that things are really better in China now, but for me nothing is normal. I have been here for nearly a year and yet it is not possible to have any sort of decent relationship with Chinese people. I'll believe things are better when you can come to my home with your wife and we can go to your home. In my country we would be able to get together and discuss music and life in general, but such things have never been possible here. To me that's not normal—that's strange and unnatural. I would like to see you again, but I know we won't have the chance unless I come back here officially, and that makes me angry and sad."

We were interrupted at this point by other people, and the endless business of saying good-bye to Chinese hosts had begun. Sometimes it takes up to fifteen minutes of extravagant promises to preserve Canadian–Chinese friendship and undying amicable solidarity before you can make your getaway. Just as I was about to get into my car, however, Huang Anlun came running out, waving a piece of paper. He was in a state of high and nervous excitement.

"Here," he said, thrusting the paper in my hand, "I have written down my address and the phone number of my father. I'm very busy during the next few weeks, but after that why don't we get together to discuss music?"

In a state of stupefaction, I accepted the paper with a meek, "*xiexie*" ("thank you"; pronounced "shay-shay") and got into the car. Privately I concluded that nothing would come of it. Just in the short period I had spoken to Huang Anlun, I knew that he was impulsive, and by the time he had checked out his actions with his leaders, wiser counsel would prevail and I would hear no more of the matter. Still, I wrote him a letter weeks later. I was sure I wouldn't hear anything, especially since I had invited him for dinner in the foreigners' ghetto, where no Chinese without very official authorization was allowed to enter. Now, here he was on the phone. I told him to hold on while I got Xiao Hao on the office extension to translate. This was something really important, and I didn't want any misunderstanding.

The upshot was that when we asked what night would be convenient for dinner, he immediately said, "How about tonight?" And so it was set for 6 P.M.

Because of the events at Xidan and Tienanmen, none of this really registered on me until later in the day. It was becoming clear that a very high-level meeting of the Communist Party was going on, and the future direction of the country was being charted. Most observers dismissed the Xidan movement as part and parcel of this leadership deliberation, and because there was such a concentration of attention on the role of Deng Xiaoping, it was generally felt that Deng's faction had encouraged and even whipped up the masses to provide some grass-roots support to back up his struggle within the hierarchy.

It was certainly obvious that the many changes and rehabilitations in the national life were profoundly disturbing to the Old Guard, who had followed Mao religiously. These people were entrenched in the bureaucracy, and it doesn't matter how enlightened the leaders of China are if they can't persuade the huge ranks of middle-level officials to go along with new programs. The middle and lower bureaucracy keeps China going, in whatever form. Their members had seen the political pendulum swing from left to right and right to left countless times in their lives. As in all swings, the

Any foreigner, including me, is conspicuous in a Chinese crowd. The key to survival is turning that conspicuousness into the advantage of easy access to the warm affection of Chinese people, even during the bitter cold of a Peking winter.

My wife, Elizabeth MacCallum, with Lao Chen, the cook of the *Toronto Globe and Mail* bureau in Peking. Whenever we were angry about the regime, we had to remember Lao Chen's history and what the Revolution had meant to him.

(All photos by Elizabeth MacCallum unless otherwise noted)

Peking in 1939, on the eve of the Japanese occupation. This picture was taken in the old shopping district below Tienanmen Square. *(Wide World Photos)*

The same area 30 years later during the Chinese New Year celebration. Life is a lot less harsh than it used to be for Chinese people, but they still suffer from an undue share of bitterness and poverty thanks to the cycle of corrosive political "rectification" campaigns.

Peking is a city of bicycles. Millions of them are on the streets during the working day and make driving a car a hazardous but far from boring experience.

In Chengdu, the capital of Sichuan province, a local sculpture emporium turns out pieces like this one which is supposed to depict the misery and hardship of life before the Communists took over.

Directly outside the sculpture emporium, however, you can still see many people harnessed to wagons and carts as beasts of burden. The sculpture is an example of "socialist reality" in art; the man is simply an example of reality.

Chinese people in Taiwan and Chinese people on the Communist Mainland both have to deal with totalitarian governments which seek to control what they think and say. Still, most people manage to survive thanks to a combination of ingenuity and caution. Above, a small crowd watching a Communist Youth League performance in Peking; below, another crowd watching a Daoist religious parade on the streets of Tainan City, Taiwan.

Tibetans are now a minority in their own capital thanks to the Chinese Government's policy of bringing thousands of colonial settlers from the interior. On the streets of Lhasa, Tibetans in traditional garb are beginning to look out of place.

In 1979 the Communist authorities reopened the Drepung Monastery on the outskirts of Lhasa. From the darkened interior an old monk looks out on the valley and mountains beyond.

The mystical city of Lhasa, capital of Tibet, is awesome in its physical grandeur. From the roof of a temple in the old town, the imposing official residence of the Dalai Lama—called the Potala—presides over the entire valley.

Images of Tibet: Top, two old countrywomen have come to Lhasa for medical treatment. At left, two nomads from the highlands who have come to Lhasa on a pilgrimage because they have heard the temples are open once again. Below, two brothers from the old district of Lhasa.

Vietnamese prisoners of war at a Chinese camp in Guangxi Autonomous Region. This group is made up of teen-aged peasant boys recently recruited by the Vietnamese. They are undergoing thought reform, monitored by Chinese officials. Eventually, most will say openly that the 1979 border conflict was caused by their own country, not China.

At the turn of the century, there was a notorious sign in a Shanghai park which said, "No dogs or Chinese." This was taken as a burning symbol of foreign arrogance in China. Eighty years later, the Chinese government put up another sign on the gates of the International Club which was an ironic reminder that arrogance isn't confined to one race alone.

Sidney Rittenberg, the most notorious foreign "expert" of them all. He spent the Liberation in a Chinese prison, and during the Cultural Revolution he was considered sufficiently dangerous to be imprisoned again for eleven years. He is shown here in his Peking home with his Chinese wife, Wang Yulin (right), and daughter Xiao Xiang.

Dr. Han Suyin. In the late sixties, she helped explain to the West why the Chinese Government was seeking to eliminate "capitalist-roaders." Fifteen years later in Peking, she announces at a press conference that she is aiding a Sino-American film project for friendship and profit.

January 1, 1979, was a historic day in Peking: the United States and the People's Republic of China normalized their diplomatic relationship after three decades of hostility, misunderstanding and bitter propaganda. Here U.S. Ambassador-designate Leonard Woodcock meets the Western and Chinese press corps on normalization day. On my right is Nigel Wade, correspondent of the London *Daily Telegraph*.

Wall-poster readers in three Chinese cities. These *dazibao* are a traditional means of communicating grievances and aspirations in China, but when people took to them too enthusiastically in 1979, the government banned all but those approved by the state. Top, the Xidan Democracy Wall in Peking, where you could read posters as well as unofficial magazines. Center, Shanghai citizens read about the plight of unemployed youth. Below, Cantonese learn that a famous trio of earlier activists—known collectively as Li Yizhe—have been freed from prison.

People who pasted up wall posters were risking official wrath, so they usually worked quickly. The safest time to put one up was when a big crowd was around. The masses protected the *dazibao* writers from overt, immediate police action and also provided quick and needy camouflage when the deed was done.

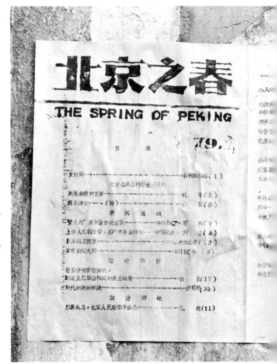

Peking Spring was one of the many unofficial magazines that circulated widely during the happier days of the "tiny democracy movement." Copies were few, but the contents of most issues were posted on the Xidan Democracy Wall, where many people spent laborious hours copying them.

In Tienanmen Square one wintry morning, I met the human-rights activist Ren Wanding for the first time. He is in the middle of this group with two of his colleagues. A shy, naive and surpassingly decent man, he was arrested on April 5, 1979, for putting up a wall poster two blocks away from this scene at Xidan. He was never given a trial and is thought to be in a labor reform camp now.

The poor peasants of China who came to Peking seeking justice for their grievances march down Chang An Avenue in central Peking. On the left, clutching one side of a protest sign, is Fu Yuehua, the young woman who helped organize the peasants into a major force. She was arrested by the Public Security Bureau on the eve of Vice-Premier Deng Xiaoping's historic trip to the United States. Her subsequent trial and three-year prison sentence was a travesty of justice.

A legal, government-sponsored demonstration in Tienanmen Square, ordered to show "mass support" for the decisions taken at a meeting of the National People's Congress. In the forefront is an older Chinese woman whose feet were bound in her youth, a reminder of women's treatment in China during the very recent past.

The poor peasants sit down and protest at the ornate entrance to Zhong Nanhai, the very seat of power in China. An old man kneels before a somewhat uncomfortable soldier to request that a petition be taken inside and presented to the Chinese leadership.

Symbols of an authoritarian state. Above, the ubiquitous Hong Zi, or Red Flag Limousine, of a state leader. Uniformed members of the Public Security Bureau stand guard, while a flunky with dark glasses waits inside for the official to return. At right, a plainclothes policeman puts out his hand to block my wife from photographing the poor peasants at Zhong Nanhai. Below, the ''little policemen'' at work. The younger boys are offspring of policemen who are brought in to upset demonstrations and harass and insult foreign journalists. The bully in the forefront is a police officer who organizes them. *(Bottom photo courtesy of Francis Deron)*

Traditional Chinese art takes its inspiration from the haunting beauty of the land. This is Wanshan, a mountain area beloved by centuries of painters.

Ancient sculptures abound throughout China. If most people don't know much about their meaning and history, they are nevertheless a source of affection and often pride. On the negative side, they still have the power to induce iconoclasm, as the damage done to many of them by rampaging Red Guards during the Cultural Revolution proved.

The Imperial Observatory in Peking, overlooking a new apartment complex (for foreign residents). The observatory was saved from Red Guard excesses, but because of poor conservation it was badly damaged during a summer storm in 1979.

Chinese actors playing Westerners on the stage. This kind of fare was banned for more than a decade by Mao Zedong's wife Jiang Qing.

The return of traditional Chinese opera in 1978 was a cause for national rejoicing. Here, two actors in one of the favorite scenes in the repertoire: *T-Cross Junction*.

Comrade chic in a Shanghai department store. Although Pierre Cardin held a fashion show in 1979 and clothing styles are not nearly so rigid as they were during the Cultural Revolution, the Chinese authorities still frown upon too much individualism in dress.

The pleasures of the people include from top to bottom; ice skating in Peking's Drum Tower district; picture taking in Shanghai; a bit of privacy in a Canton park and card playing in Chengdu.

In the West, Chinese people under Communist rule are often thought of as brainwashed blue ants. In reality, the diversity and individuality of Chinese people is one of the wonders of the world. Clockwise, from top left: a summer in Qingdao, Shandong province; an old woman still putting in a day's work on a rural commune; grandmother and child on the periphery of a government demonstration in Peking; a father and child in a Nanking park.

safest policy was to show nominal support to the current presiding powers while preserving one's position with as little agreement and activity as possible. Deng and his forces, who had control of most of the official media, were constantly carping at the slowness of officials to adapt to the "new reality," adding that this slowness would be the death of the Four Modernizations.

I culled from the official press any hints and gleanings that could be found and then made the rounds of political officers at various embassies to get their thinking. I myself believed that it would have been unprincipled and foolish to dismiss what was happening, although this was what many of my colleagues were doing. I knew from my reading of the Hundred Flowers Campaign and the Cultural Revolution that while the leadership might start and encourage certain mass manifestations, people, being what they are, have a tendency to exceed the bounds laid out for them and take matters into their own hands. The history and practice of the Communist Party in China was such that only a fool could encourage criticism of past errors and misdeeds and not expect it to rebound on the present. Unless, of course, the whole thing was a fraud and the masses were once again encouraged to speak out only so that the police could identify the malcontents and "bad elements" and dispose of them accordingly.

There was also a third possibility, which some Sinologists use when discussing the Hundred Flowers Campaign. In this scenario, Mao is depicted as genuinely soliciting criticisms of Party failings after a period when the Party was seen to be doing constructive and widely popular work. The post-Liberation work of reconstruction in China up to the Hundred Flowers Campaign is thought by many to have been a miraculous period of Chinese history, a time when people throughout the country worked hard and sincerely to make a better life. To his horror, however, Mao discovered that a number of intellectuals dared to question the right of the Communist Party to be the sole and final arbiter in all things and the only real political presence in the country. In this interpretation, Mao lost his nerve and cracked down on them, convinced that the physical revolution had to be followed by a spiritual revolution which would turn the citizenry into a militant force that would "never forget the class struggle."

In the days to come, I was to hear foreigners dismiss Xidan and the things that were being said there because they involved only relatively few people "who didn't represent the population as a whole." This kind of line infuriated me for several reasons. These self-appointed spokesmen for "the population as a whole" were eschewing the first opportunity to have an honest conversation with any Chinese in thirty years. Also, it was clear that the Communist Party wouldn't dismiss the importance of such a manifestation. Who would know better the potential power of a small, idealistic group who wanted to change the course of Chinese history for patriotic reasons? As the Tienanmen Incident and the Hundred Flowers Campaign proved, Party propaganda might dismiss activists as "a mere handful of bad elements," but the government never hesitated to use all the resources of the state to control and suppress them. The old Guomindang Government had always referred to the Communists as "bandits" and, in the beginning, dismissed them as small and unimportant, though it too tried to destroy them.

Apart from all this, Xidan was such a good human-interest story. Many things were emerging from the Wall that put the lie to a multitude of pat theories—and not just those of Party propaganda. When the Party controlled all access to the people, it was very easy to have consistent theories because there was no one to say you nay. Now the nays were becoming explosive, and the Xidan Democracy Wall was the first significant eye into China foreigners had had in a long time. It was for these reasons that a few of us—Nigel Wade, Georges Biannic and Francis Deron of Agence France-Presse, Philip Short of the British Broadcasting Corporation and Richard Thwaites—haunted the Wall at all hours and most days. Personally, I never had another easy day in China unless I had either directly checked out the Wall itself or, at the very least, reconnoitered with several of these colleagues.

On this Tuesday, of course, the Wall was still all the rage. In between blitzing diplomats and fellow journalists on the kinds of speculation that were beginning to emerge, I made a visit and was eminently rewarded by the letter-and-poem response to my own impromptu *dazibao* about the ring. The poem still haunts me, even though some people suggested it was probably a fraud and had been written by one of the nameless, unknown organizers of the movement. Fraud or not, one of the verses has never left me, and as much as anything during my two years in China, it defined the new opportunities that were available to everyone, Chinese or foreigner:

Love of democracy and truth finds out the best of friends.
Here, random tours need no guides,
Interviews need no surveillance,
To make a friend needs no acquaintance:
The only introduction is an open, honest heart.

As the time for Huang Anlun's arrival approached, I wondered what was going to happen at the gate, where I knew the PLA guards would stop him and closely question who he was and what he was up to. I thought at first that I should just leave this problem as an internal Chinese matter and let the guards and Huang Anlun thrash it out while I watched impotently from the window. Then I got mad. Dammit, I thought, he is an invited guest, and if they are going to humiliate and interrogate their own people, they will bloody well have to do it in front of a witness. In principle, those guards were supposed to be there for our protection, although everyone knew their main purpose was to keep Chinese at bay. So down I went, five minutes before the appointed time, and to my chagrin I saw that Huang Anlun was already there at the gates and showing his identity card and the letter of invitation I had written him. I went running toward this little confrontation, but he didn't seem in any way flummoxed. As soon as the guard saw me coming, he quickly handed the papers back to Huang, smiled nervously at me and made no further trouble. In this way, I discovered that if I physically accompanied any Chinese through the gates, he would not be questioned, and this was a practice I followed throughout the rest of my time in China.

We made a few grunts at each other which sounded like "Hello" in Chinese and English, but we were both too nervous to talk coherently in any language. A few seconds later, we were up in the apartment and sitting down in the living room. Elizabeth and I stared at Huang and he stared at us and we all started laughing.

"I never thought such a day would come to pass," he said, shaking his head in disbelief.

Neither had I, for it was a momentous occasion. For the very first time in the twenty years since the *Globe* opened the bureau, a Chinese friend of a correspondent—I was the eighth—had come visiting. Questions and answers came spilling out, and the conversation was just a jumble for quite a time because we were so overcome by the experience. He told us that, as I had suspected, he had given me his name and address on an impulse and also to check out whether or not the Party was being sincere about life's becoming more normal.

"In the end," said Huang Anlun, "I did ask permission to visit you, after getting your letter. There must have been a bit of Gang of Four in my heart, because I got very nervous, so I went to our Unit leader, who gave the permission."

He told us his wife and whole family, especially his father, were anxious to meet us and that the next time we got together, it would be at his home. His father, we learned, was Huang Feili, head of the conducting department at the Peking Conservatory. His whole family was musical. His mother taught music to children, his wife was the piano accompanist at the Peking Ballet Academy and one of his younger brothers played in an orchestra. His youngest brother had had musical aspirations too, but the education system had been in such tatters and his family had faced so much trouble that he had never been able to learn music properly and was now "an ordinary worker."

This was a situation that was to become very familiar to us. We would meet someone in his or her mid-thirties and learn that he or she had a good job at a university or laboratory or in the bureaucracy. "And your brothers and sisters," we would ask: "what do they do?" The list would come out: teacher or technician if they were older, factory worker if they were younger. You could tell the ages without asking. The older ones had got some education before the Cultural Revolution, but the younger ones hadn't stood a chance. Even when their parents had tried to teach them privately, the former government had relegated them to menial tasks. Of course, this refers mostly to educated city families, in which the parents had had a good education and had suffered accordingly during the Cultural Revolution.

That was the start of our friendship with Huang Anlun. He and his wife, Ruili, became our dearest friends. Mutual curiosity and the drama of the times had brought us together in the first place, but we soon passed that juncture and entered into a relationship in which unspoken but mutually understood things were the most eloquent of all.

After dinner, we made him sit down at the piano. He had told us a bit about his family's ordeal during the Cultural Revolution. We were to learn much more later—how his father's music library had been destroyed, how he had lectured his younger brothers on the "correctness" of the mass criticism that was expected to descend on his father. At the time, we knew only that in common with so many other gifted and bright Chinese, he had seen his talents despised during the Cultural Revolution and his patriotism distrusted. He had wanted to be a concert pianist, but he was dispatched to the countryside—miles away from any piano. His father had advised him not to forget music and try to become a composer. The peasants to whom he had been sent to learn soon learned to love him as we did and arranged for him to have time off from manual work to continue his self-help studies. In an abandoned Christian church being used for grain storage, he had found an old pump organ, and on this he had played out the products of his imagination. During this time, he actually had the nerve to send off a piano composition to Peking to be considered for publication. It was pronounced "pure garbage" by the authorities in the Cultural Department, which was in the thrall of Jiang Qing's theories on revolutionary art. It also got him into trouble because it was assumed, correctly, that such garbage must have cut into the work he was supposed to be doing—picking cabbages. After he played a Beethoven sonata for us, we asked him to let us hear "the garbage."

I can't vouch for the piece—only for the moment. I was suddenly overwhelmed by all the events that were swirling around me. I had longed so much for Chinese friends and now one was here in my own home. I loved music and here it was, being played with passion and conviction. I loved China and here was a symbol of the country that did not seem to disdain me. Most of all, I believed that the strength of the human spirit—regardless of nationality—can overcome most odds and here was living proof of someone who had been to hell and back, a kind of hell I only vaguely understood at that point. Elizabeth's eyes and mine caught each other. We were both weeping.

5.
Wednesday, November 29

These were great days for journalists, or the "uncrowned kings," as the Chinese had started calling us. Among the crowds at Xidan and even with a few officials, we were the repository of considerable esteem and some envy. In general, Western journalists are differentiated clearly from the East Bloc Communist journalists, who the Chinese know are caught up in the business of their governments just like their Chinese counterparts. We are the beneficiaries of contrast. Our reports are often carried in *Reference News,* and when these are stacked up against official state-controlled Chinese journalism, we can't possibly lose. No matter what our particular affiliations are, or our particular biases, we are not in the pay or under the control of the Chinese Communist Party, and so there is an automatic willingness to believe us, whether it is merited or not. It was also evident from the more sophisticated members of the crowd at the Xidan Democracy Wall that they believed our reports were noticed and closely read by the leadership and senior bureaucracy. Thus by getting ideas across to us now, they felt that they had a kind of access to the top which was unique in their experience.

I had just found out something else that was very interesting about journalism in China. Chinese television had shown two films recently in which the featured roles had depicted the lives of independent journalists. In most countries it would be foolhardy to place much significance in a couple of television shows, but in China television has been so uniformly awful, banal and venal for so long, anything remotely out of the ordinary can have a profound effect. For the past few months, the television authorities had begun to improve programming. The mercilessly tedious ideological talks had been shortened and softened in tone. There were more viewing hours, and efforts to vary the fare were, in Chinese terms, impressive.

In the cities, anyone who really wants to see some television can do so despite the scarcity of sets. There might be a set to serve an entire apartment building, for example, or perhaps it's down at the factory recreation room. Even in the countryside, many communes will have at least one television set for group watching. A West European diplomat told me that he had been invited into the home of a local official in the port city of Tianjin—an almost unprecedented courtesy—and was told the large, three-story house had once belonged to the official's family before 1949. He and his wife and children lived on the top two floors, while the first floor had become a television-watching hall for the neighborhood. This is apparently common practice.

Three weeks before, the state television network had showed the first of four screenings of a Japanese film called *Looking Home,* made in the mid-seventies. Any foreign film attracts incredible attention in China because Jiang Qing had banned them for years. This one became instantly notorious with many of the older generation because it told the story of a Japanese prostitute and included some scenes of nudity. In a deeply conservative and often prudish society, the film had considerable shock value and was instantly championed by the young people, who had never seen anything like it. The film had a strong moralistic base and told the story of the prostitute through a series of flashbacks. She was depicted as a victim of a decadent society, and as the film progresses, we see her rise above the evil around her until the moment she realizes she has been used and begins to fight back. Ideologically in China, it was impeccable, and the television network won high marks for showing it complete with nudity (which was very brief and utterly harmless by Western standards). The prostitute, however, tells her story to a Japanese journalist. It is the journalist who treats the woman kindly and gets her to analyze her past. The journalist is depicted as considerate and concerned, pointing out to the prostitute that if she tells her story to the press, it could have a salutary effect on the conditions she despises.

The other film, which I never saw, was screened only twice. The first time was on a Sunday morning. It was a Chinese film from the early fifties. One diplomat who saw it assured me it had the same kind of excellent quality one could see in most Chinese films during those days. The Shanghai studios had been very fertile, productive places. Film directors and actors had identified strongly with the new regime and tried to bring their best talents to bear while, at the same time, remaining true to their individual artistic standards, which were very high. The Party had not yet come down heavily on film content, and evidently people felt a great deal of freedom in what they created.

Even the overtly propagandistic films were good. A fine example was *Dragon Beard Ditch* by the popular novelist and playwright Lao She (best known in the West for his pre-Liberation novel *Rickshaw Boy*). The cinematography, in black and white, is brilliant, and the strongly etched characters are beautifully portrayed by leading actors of the day, who had wide experience in playing roles naturally, articulating the pungency that so identifies Lao She's best work with ease. Even the upright Communist Party cadre, the moral center of the film, which depicts a poor Peking family on the eve of Liberation, is portrayed with wry humor. The film provides a staggering contrast to the wretched products of the Chinese film industry during the late sixties and seventies.

The Chinese film that was seen by many of the people who gathered at Xidan was about a poor man living near Nanking, the old Guomindang capital. He has been cheated and persecuted by his landlord and tries in vain to get justice from the corrupt government. Defeated and dejected, he is on the verge of suicide when he meets a Nanking journalist, who takes up his cause and starts an investigation. The landlord turns out to be involved in a conspiracy with local Guomindang officials, and the journalist fearlessly exposes the whole game in his newspaper. It was made in a more innocent time, before the Communist Party had had a chance to show it could be as arbitrary as the horrible old Guomindang. Many Chinese people now either have direct experience of Communist officials' abusing power or have heard shocking accounts (sometimes from the official press). As propaganda, the film rather backfired in the late seventies because the Guomindang officials did not seem so different from some of the horros currently foisted on the masses. The independent journalist, on the other hand, who could cut through red tape and corruption by exposing wickedness in his newspaper, evidently made a stunning impact on the new audience.

Anyway, kings we became for better or worse, although the antics of some of my colleagues allowed room for a certain amount of skepticism. For nearly thirty years it has been impossible for outsiders to get a real chance to have honest, open conversations with Chinese citizens. The Xidan phenomenon was barely half a week old before some journalists and other foreigners started tiring of it, making jokes about "the masses" and talking about people there as if they were some species of strange animal that could do cute, humanlike tricks.

This week marked the beginning of a four-month period during which Elizabeth and I virtually dropped out of the foreign community. We started by turning down dinner invitations because we wanted to be as free as possible with our time. In total, there were to be three journalists (Wade, Biannic and Deron), four diplomats and about five foreign students whom we would have anything much to do with during this period, and that was because they shared with us the desire to make as much contact with Chinese society on any and all levels that we were able to.

The "democracy symposium" at Tienanmen, as it was now being called, continued on Wednesday. There were some fine speeches, although the best one made the salient point that for democracy to spread in China, it could not be confined to brave words at the Wall or Square. The speaker seemed to be about thirty years old, and there was an air of urgency in what he said:

> Never in our lifetime has there been a better chance to obtain the things we have dreamed of for so long. We are all fighting for a true democracy in our socialist motherland. It is unacceptable to the Chinese people that only the bourgeois West can enjoy the freedom of thought and action which is also our right as human beings and as Chinese citizens. But this democracy will not be handed to us, nor will it come just because we marched down a street and make speeches at Tienanmen. We are going to have to fight for it, and the struggle will be very hard and perhaps very long.
>
> But today, right now, we have a better chance than we ever had before. All of us must take the spirit of these evenings, the spirit of the "democracy symposium," to our individual Units and make it come alive there too. We will need the same discipline that we have shown here and the same fortitude we showed under Lin Biao and the Gang of Four. Here, from the same Tienanmen, where the blood of our brothers and sisters was shed on April 5, we will begin to fight for true democracy in our motherland. If we let this opportunity pass by, we will stand condemned by the suffering of the past and the expectations of the future.

There was a great cheer for this, and when it was later announced there would be another meeting the next day, I wondered how long the business could last.

Curiously, a significant proportion of the crowd seemed to change each night. I met a number of people who said they had just heard of the meetings and had come down to see what was up.

There were a few stalwarts, particularly among the speakers, and it was clear there was a small core of well-organized and highly motivated activists, who had been responsible for giving a focus and impressive discipline to all of the proceedings. They were also notable for their Chinese patriotism. Every attack on past and present evils was couched in a desire to serve the country and the masses.

It was a style that was certainly sincere, but it was also lifted straight from the Party propaganda manuals. The method of organizing such large numbers of people and the rhetorical embellishments of the speeches were a weird replica of orthodox Party practice. I suppose it was because this is the only style that is known; it was also tremendously effective—a tribute to the Party's strong roots in the collective Chinese psyche as well as an obvious indication of how it can be manipulated and controlled by its own devices.

6.
Thursday, November 30

Suddenly, everything changed for the worse. My very first unofficial Chinese sources told me that a mild clampdown was under way to take the wind out of the sails of the Xidan movement. Individual Units passed along the word to all citizens of the city that the "democracy symposium" was against "stability and unity," and citizens were urged to avoid it. Biannic's fears had been confirmed, for the word apparently came from the very top, which in this matter almost certainly meant Deng Xiaoping. I learned this in the late afternoon, so I was naturally curious to see what effect it would have at Xidan. The most hopeful thing was that the spirit of the movement had not been condemned, just the disruption of traffic and public order which the marches and speeches had inevitably caused because of sheer numbers.

Despite the unanimous agreement among all the Chinese sources about the reality of the clampdown, there were still several thousand people gathered at the wall by 7 P.M. This was the familiar pattern: gather at the Wall, march to Tienanmen and hold discussions and debates for a couple of hours. Elizabeth and a friend went toward what seemed to be a large group a distance off, and I waited at the cable office with our car. I had been talking with the doctor attached to the French Embassy, Bernard Fritzell, for a few minutes when I noticed that Elizabeth and Fritzell's wife, Chantal, were walking very quickly in our direction, with a crowd of about three or four hundred Chinese following them just as quickly. Actually, it was quite a funny sight: they looked like a pair of female Pied Pipers marching along at double time.

As Elizabeth got closer, I could see from her expression that something was very wrong, but for the life of me I couldn't figure out what it was. The Chinese crowd following them seemed much younger than on previous days, but they were in good spirits and everyone seemed to be either smiling or laughing outright.

"Get going," Elizabeth barked as she approached. "Something screwy is going on. These are awful people."

Naturally, I assumed that Elizabeth was exaggerating and the crowd might have caused her to panic. For four days we had had no problem whatsoever with far larger crowds than this. The crushing on the second night had been an unfortunate product of a sudden move in a massive audience, but even in the midst of the short-lived chaos, discipline and concern for foreigners' safety had set things right in a few minutes. Only one person had been seriously hurt. So I started to talk to the crowd, and Elizabeth grew frustrated and annoyed.

"It's no use, I'm telling you. This is a bad lot."

Within seconds, I saw what she was talking about. This was a different set of people altogether. They started pulling at our clothes and laughing at us when we tried to talk. I may not speak Chinese well, but coarse laughter is universal and this bunch was out to make trouble. The first thing was to get away.

Fortunately, we were standing in the small parking lot in front of the cable office, so with the crowd all around us, I slowly started pushing our way toward a parked car. The idea was to force the crowd to split on either side of the car, and I told Elizabeth and Chantal to get ready to run into the cable office and head for the very back, where the telex machines were. Bernard and I would keep the crowd at bay for a few moments and then try to join them.

The plan worked perfectly, and at the last moment, just before we were surrounded again, Bernard and I bounded up the cable-office steps and entered the main foyer. To my considerable chagrin, the crowd followed us right in. In the distance, I could see that Elizabeth and Chantal had just made it to the telex-room doors, and we headed through the foyer and into the main telegraph room.

The cable office resembles an old-fashioned train-station waiting room, with its huge vaulted ceiling and chandeliers. At one telegraph window, a couple of American business people whom I had met a week or so before were trying to file a cable. There were about forty other Chinese in the hall, but it was so large the place seemed almost deserted. At first I didn't look behind me as we headed straight for the safety of the telex room, but the American couple—a man and a woman—suddenly turned from the window and stared in my direction. The sheer horror on their faces startled me. I turned around. The whole front foyer was filled with our crowd, and when I turned around, they laughed and jeered, and people in the front even spat on the cable-office floor. What was going on?

The people who work for the central cable office are among the nicest I ever encountered in China. I had met most of them on my late-night rambles and had got to know their shifts. I liked them all and was impressed by the speed with which they worked and the accuracy they maintained in sending long and complicated news cables. It was often possible to engage them in ordinary, civilized conversation, and during the past few days I had become something of a celebrity with the younger members of the service, while the older ones had all read my articles on Vietnam and would ask me very good questions on the situation there from time to time. At the end of most working days in China, these were the last Chinese people I spoke to, and I couldn't have chosen better companions anywhere. On this night, they turned out to be real friends.

When I made it back to the telex room, the senior official came in to talk to me with a very worried expression on his face. When he saw it was I, he smiled briefly and shook my hand. I tried, as best I could, to explain what was happening, and other staff members gathered around. One spoke English fairly well, so I explained things to him in more detail and he translated. After this, the senior official stormed out into the hall and went down to the crowd gathered in the foyer. He spoke to them for a few minutes, then returned. By this time, other staff members had brought everyone a cup of tea and we were all trying to figure out what happened. The senior official said that he had got the crowd out of the building, but they were milling about outside and we should wait a few more minutes before leaving in our cars. I asked him if he had discovered why they had tried to frighten us, and he said he didn't know the answer, but he was clearly very much annoyed at something and for a moment I thought it was I.

"I'm sorry," I said, "to bring this trouble to you."

"You are not the cause of the trouble," he said very firmly. "You are a friend of the Chinese people. The crowd has some bad elements."

"Bad elements" is a universal term of denunciation in China, and

I have heard it used by the Communist Party to refer to activists and by activists to refer to members of the Communist Party. We went home shortly afterward without discovering precisely what sort of bad elements were involved, and I got to the bottom of the mystery only six months later, when a friend asked me if I remembered the night the crowd had come after us and I said I remembered it only too well. It had been a bad business, he said, adding almost as an afterthought that I must not judge all of the Public Security Bureau from this incident.

"What do you mean?" I asked. "I don't understand."

"It was the police who chased you in there," he said.

"The police?"

"Yes. They use their recruits and also the children of police officials to make trouble at the Xidan Wall. They were trying to break up the meetings and frighten foreigners from coming to the Wall."

Suddenly, it all fitted together. By that time, I was beginning to see how the police operate among the masses. Increasingly during those later days, peasant and democracy meetings would get rowdy and disorganized despite the best efforts of the people who were trying to maintain order. If a Western photographer tried to take a picture, he might find himself—or herself, in Elizabeth's case—jostled from behind. One Scandinavian correspondent had his camera smashed into his face when he tried to take a picture. In this way, the police sought to disrupt meetings and put the activists in a bad light without showing their uniforms. Chinese people knew who they were from their actions and would contemptuously refer to them as "police recruits." Eventually, even this practice proved inadequate and the state ordered in the uniforms—first on the anniversary of the Tienanmen Incident, and then definitively after we left China in October 1979.

I couldn't see into the future as I drove home that night, but I knew that the "democracy symposium" as I had seen it during the past few days was over. But the government couldn't turn the clock back; of that I was certain. I had seen too much and learned too much ever to go back to the old ways. Now I knew a bit about the people in the city around me, and I was determined to find out a lot more. I had made friends and would make more.

Apart from Huang Anlun and his family, all the Chinese friendships I was to form in the months to come were to result either directly or indirectly from the Xidan Democracy Wall. Because of the Wall, I was to make easy connections in other cities throughout China—even as far away as Baice in the Guangxi (pronounced "guang-she") Autonomous Region, bordering Vietnam. Interest in and concern for what the Xidan Democracy Wall represented was my passageway into China. Other outsiders have had different ways in and correspondingly different perspectives: students have lived with Chinese and seen life through that world; some foreigners have married Chinese and thereby gained remarkable social access; foreign experts and friends have had the chance to observe official-dom close up; while a lucky few have even been able to live with Chinese for short periods. I had the Wall, and there is more than passing irony in this.

Longtime residents of Peking with a sense of history will tell you that it is an "old-style city." By this they mean that it has an abundance of walls, behind which the life of the city throbs in a manner most outsiders normally can only guess at. Walls hide government ministries and humble homes, plastics factories and graveyards, schools and police stations, forgotten Buddhist monasteries and the very seat of government itself at Zhong Nan Hai. These walls are, first of all, a simple fact. It is very difficult for even a curious Chinese to get behind them if he does not in some way belong to the business going on inside. These walls define precisely the nature of the contact possible for outsiders with the reality of China.

I knew better than most that as much as is humanly possible, foreigners are restricted to an official view of China. The Communists did not invent this system, any more than they conceived of that apotheosis of artificial barriers, the Great Wall. But the Communists did recognize a national penchant that was useful to their purposes, and therefore sought to co-opt and perfect it. Consequently, all those walls became a symbol of a fortresslike mentality that still seeks to order what shall come in and what shall be kept out.

Once you have lived in official China for a while, you gradually realize that all sorts of Pooh-Bahs and lackeys, and even ordinary folk, have erected walls around their own thinking and personalities. "Are we talking about the same thing?" has been a question foreigners have puzzled over for centuries when trying to analyze an unfathomable conversation with a Chinese. The easiest answer has always been to assume that no, you were not talking about the same thing. If you accept the comfortable notion that Chinese people are essentially different from Westerners, a notion buttressed by a unique history and cultural legacy, then things become very easy. All sorts of woes and tribulations can be dismissed as being "Chinese" and alien to one's experience, while the triumphs and successes of the Chinese people, which might lead us to reexamine some of our own bland orthodoxies, can be observed at a safe remove and laid aside as inappropriate to our circumstances.

And even if it is essential to come to terms with Chinese history and culture, they too can become a kind of wall before which one is prepared to accept, almost without question, the theories of professional experts and Sinologists while instinctively doubting the wisdom of ordinary common sense and the evidence of one's own eyes. A unified nation of a billion souls is so far beyond our ken that we dismiss single voices crying in the multitude which insist upon their individuality and common humanity.

Yet it was a wall that led me into China, and perhaps, in the end, this was more appropriate than ironic. Chairman Mao had admonished the Chinese people to "Make the old serve the new" and "Make things foreign serve things Chinese." Does this not also work in reverse? I was new and foreign to China; yet one of the oldest symbols of Chinese durability and secretiveness—a wall—opened my way into the interior.

7.
Friday, December 1

The Communist Party's definition of "stability and unity" was going to be harder to enforce than anticipated. On this day, new wall posters continued to go up. Across from the Xidan Democracy Wall a huge banner proclamation was pasted on a long wooden fence. You could read it all the way over at the cable office. For me, it was of more than passing interest: "Firmly condemn those bad elements who frightened foreign friends at Xidan."

IV
Inside
Looking Out

13

New Friends

"**I**'ve read most of what you've written since you came to China. Until last November, many of your articles were very ignorant, don't you agree? Does it embarrass you to think of what you once wrote?"

The question was belligerent, rude and, worst of all, directed at me. Yet the fact that it came from a Chinese during an intimate luncheon among friends made it symbolic of the distance I had traveled during the two months since that momentous week at the Xidan Democracy Wall. There were more than a dozen of us at this gathering in a public Peking restaurant. My wife and I had been bidden at 10:30 A.M. on a Sunday morning because that was the only hour for which our Chinese friends had been able to book a private room. Although we were the only foreigners there, I had by this time assimilated an initial and overweening sense of pride at actually having real Chinese friends who seemed to like us and for whom we already had an inordinate affection. It now seemed a normal thing to talk openly to real Chinese people.

The questioner was a confident man close to my own age of thirty-four. He was a political cadre, and thus a Communist Party member, from an important government institute. Since he was an old friend of our friends, he was automatically acceptable, even though I had never met or heard of him before. However, had there been any other stranger in our midst, Chinese or foreign, the conversation would have been stillborn, just as it died whenever a waitress came into the room with a plate of food. Our company was based on trust, but it was hardly conspiratorial and included one or two other Party members, a government inspector, a teacher, a dramatist, an interpreter for a literary organization and a scattering of university students. Some of the students had close relatives—usually parents—who had important positions, within either the government or the Party, and these connections were presumably what gave them the confidence to arrange an open luncheon party with someone as distrusted by their government as a foreign journalist.

It was a festive lunch, organized by our friends to repay hospitality received at our home as well as to celebrate the strangely exciting fact of our friendship. Although the conversation ranged through politics, the arts, sports, life-styles (a subject of mutual and insatiable curiosity) and even the weather, the delicate aura of courtesy and formal etiquette which many Chinese like to maintain had been carefully observed. That is, until this rude question came tumbling out. The question was clearly seen as being rude by the other Chinese. You could tell from their faces and reactions: some looked shocked and others giggled nervously. I was not only being challenged; I had also just lost face and had to set about recovering it—no easy feat.

"I agree," I said, not agreeing at all. In fact I was rather proud of my first year's efforts in China, although I was the first to admit that the Xidan phenomenon represented a professional quantum leap into the reality of the country and the thinking of many Chinese people. "Much of what I wrote before the posters went up last November was based on official propaganda or on things I did not understand well. But how could it have been otherwise? It was not possible to have conversations with Chinese people such as we are having today. The barriers were solid and insurmountable. Perhaps you can tell me why it has taken nearly three decades for the Chinese people to find the courage to speak to foreign friends and talk about those things which really matter."

I could feel the tension lessen as I shot my modest barb. Our friends were pleased with the response. The parry was acknowledged by the questioner with a wry smile, and we were all left free to carry on our amiable banter and gossip until the happy occasion drew to its reluctant close. It was here, though, that I discovered for the first time how much intelligent young Chinese like these resent the condescending platitudes of those Western observers who come to China, see and learn nothing they are not already disposed to learn and serve it all up as insight into the inscrutable. Like academics and theologians, journalists have a horror of inconsistency, and for the handful of writers, diplomats and students who actually took advantage of this unprecedented opportunity to make real Chinese friends, loyalty to previous theories was the first thing that had to be shed.

Nothing happened slowly or undramatically during this period. Every day seemed to bring a new shocker: the announcement that China and the United States had agreed upon normalization; the first press conference ever given by a chairman of the People's Republic; the Vietnamese invasion of Cambodia; the Boat People tragedy; the startling reemergence of Cambodia's "lost" Prince Sihanouk in the Great Hall of the People, where he denounced Communism while Communist officials sat on either side of him; the Chinese invasion of Vietnam; the arrival of thousands of improverished peasants from all over the country, protesting hunger and injustice at the very seat of the central government in Peking; the arrests of the most vocal of the democracy activists; the unlikely (and unwelcome) arrival of types like Pierre Cardin and Bob Hope, with their luggage of self-indulgence and institutionalized ignorance; the historic visit of Vice-Premier Deng Xiaoping to the United States; the decision to let China's brightest students study freely in a dozen Western countries. On top of it all were the new possibilities of contacts with Chinese—unprecedented in three decades of Communist rule.

After that first warning from the authorities to cool down all the expectations and public gatherings, there was a short lull in which people caught their second wind. That second wind, when it came, was one of the wonders of our time, because it signaled the first meaningful, complex and emotional relationships foreigners had been able to have with the Chinese people since 1949. Ironically, many of my colleagues dismissed the events at Xidan as a brief aberration and gratefully returned to the standard kind of reporting on China which had hitherto prevailed, from interpreting government propaganda to filching whatever thoughts and observations resident diplomats or visiting foreigners might have. But for a few of us, life changed more remarkably than we had ever experienced before. Cautiously at first and then with rising optimism, we were bidden into a very different China from the one we had known.

The people I got to know well in Peking (and later, in Shanghai, Canton, Wuhan and even Chengdu in Sichuan province) were not really radicals. The democracy activists I came into contact with were never friends, much as I admired some of them. The reasons for this are quite complicated, of which more later. Yet China is a very big country, with a remarkably diverse population, far more diverse than the uniformity of clothing and life-styles would at first lead you to believe, and when the government eased up on its pervasive repression on contacts between foreigners and Chinese, there were many people—although certainly a small minority—who decided to take every possible advantage of this unexpected leniency. Each consummated friendship was an act of conspicuous courage, and friends came from all circles of city life, a fact which a number of other foreign residents in Peking refused to believe, since they assumed only well-connected Chinese would have the nerve to sustain any connection with a journalist. Of our circle of intimates in the three principal cities of Peking, Shanghai and Canton, only a few people could claim important government or Party relations, and in each case, they studiously declined to ever let me know just exactly what that connection was. From this inner circle, I met many others, and it was through all these eyes that I started to look at China again. It was not so much a newfound place that I discovered as a country come wildly alive and vital.

The actual mechanics of meeting people in those days was not particularly difficult. We were all experimenting and exploring in a new world, and as various taboos seemed to collapse—such as the entry of unofficial Chinese into the three foreigners' compounds—we foolishly assumed that an acceptable practice had been established. With hope and optimism as your armor, it is amazing how quickly a new situation can be accepted and almost taken for granted. I suppose in the back of all our minds was the feeling that this might backfire, which brought about a certain amount of caution. Unconsciously, for example, I initially eschewed the company of those Chinese who had no use whatsoever for anything in the Communist Party—which was hypocritical on my part, because I certainly would not want to live under any of the Communist governments that are today in power around the world. Nevertheless, I admired most those Chinese who could look objectively at the Party and government, but whose strong patriotic sensitivities led them to believe there was a way of adjusting the system.

One night, for example, I tried goading Lao Jiang on this subject. Jiang was a remarkable person who was more than a trifle rash in what he did and said. Imprisoned briefly for attacking the old Gang of Four government, he had recently been fully exonerated and praised, but he still spoke out in his weekly political meetings with such vehemence that some people refused to remain in the same room with him for fear of being contaminated by his arguments in the future. He had a marvelous and often wicked sense of humor and adored mocking the bourgeois embellishments of our lives. The first time we offered him a chocolate mint, called "After Eight," that we had imported from Hong Kong, he asked us the derivation of the name. I said that eight o'clock was the fashionable hour to eat dinner in the West and, since these were fancy after-dinner mints, they were given a fashionable name. He broke up. In China, he said, they would have to be called *wu dian yihou* ("after five o'clock") because that was the "fashionable" hour for the masses to eat dinner. "I suppose," he added, "the taste is more exquisite three hours later."

Lao Jiang never hesitated to rail away at the stupidities he saw around him. At times he reached such a ferocious level he even frightened me a little, and I would once again grow vaguely worried that our living room was bugged, although he had said he didn't care whether it was or not. One day, I told him Elizabeth had met a young man in Tienanmen Square who had no use for the Communist Party at all. As far as this person was concerned, I reported, the Party had been an unmitigated disaster from the beginning and had brought nothing but misery and privation to the Chinese people. All he wanted to do was get out of the country by any means possible. He had made three attempts so far to get to Hong Kong—unsuccessfully, although he had never been caught.

"I wish he would go tomorrow," exploded Lao Jiang, "or even today if it could be arranged. If he has so little understanding of his country's history, he should go as soon as possible. If he has so little courage and imagination that he cannot conceive of working here to improve conditions and helping the lot of the Chinese people, then I despise him. I wish he were not in this country."

Well, this had a touch of bombast, perhaps. He was sincere, though, and I respected and admired him, especially since he was so objective about the problems facing the country. He had already suffered for his thoughts, and behind his opinions there was a steely resolve, backed up by endurance and struggle.

Lao Jiang was also responsible for one of the weirdest encounters I ever experienced. We had arranged a gathering at our home for several friends, including Lao Jiang and two Western diplomats whom we liked and trusted. One was a trade official at his embassy, and since Lao Jiang was keenly interested in economic matters, I thought he and our friend might have some interesting discussion. I was not disappointed.

"True communism can never occur under the historic conditions present in China today," said Lao Jiang to the trade official at one point. He loved opening a new avenue of discussion with a shocking statement, and I could see a hint of his wicked grin emerging from the lines on his face. He was a formidable scholar of Marxism, and unlike many Chinese, he had easy access to the complete works of Marx, Engels and Lenin. The masses get only tightly edited versions, which change according to the needs of the current ideological line; such editing also applies even to the works of Mao Tsetung himself. "Consider the background. There was never a real capitalist class in China, just a few compradors in the cities, who generally worked in collusion with the imperialists. Suddenly, we start instituting all sorts of economic theories based on the assumption that the working class had triumphed over a sturdy but discredited capitalist class. This was theory, not fact. In reality, we went from feudalism to an aberration of Marxist communism, without going through the necessary intermediate stages, and that's why our economy and productive forces have been in such a mess. If we really want to establish a true communist state, we must allow capitalism to run its natural course."

I could see the shock on the trade official's face. He spent his days in China ruminating over statistics and basing his theories and predictions on the central planning of a completely socialist state. Everything was apparently finite, and the economy of a billion people seemed to him ultimately amenable to such central planning. I knew Lao Jiang much better than the trade official and quickly decided to be his devil's advocate.

"How many years do you think China should have a capitalist economy, Lao Jiang?" I asked in rank humility.

"Oh," he said, feigning deep contemplation, "not too long. Perhaps one or two hundred years. Long enough to get the peasant population up to advanced world levels. Maybe three hundred years. That's a very short time in China's history."

"You're crazy," blurted the trade official. "You must never abandon central planning. Your economy couldn't stand the shock, and terrible inequalities in society would emerge."

Lao Jiang suddenly became very serious. "The inequalities exist today. You have never lived in the countryside. The only thing that has equalized is the lack of opportunity, except within the Party. There have to be other ways to harness ambition or else the suffering and hardships the Chinese people have endured for so long will count for little."

Political theories and rhetoric were only a small part of our conversations with our Chinese friends. I had to spend a great deal of time explaining how daily life operated in the West: this was the willingly paid price of finding out equivalent facts about China. There was talk of love and marriage, of women's liberation, of average incomes and working conditions, of death and dying, of faith and religion, of movie stars and Margaret Trudeau, of President Nixon and the mass suicide of members of the People's Temple. Xiao Liu, another friend, was particularly interested in women's liberation, a subject of much blather in Chinese propaganda circles.

"Chairman Mao said that women hold up half of heaven," she once said, "but sometimes I think our half is heavier." I was fully aware of how backward, or "feudal," attitudes toward women still were in China, although the almost daily sight of old women with bound feet was a constant reminder of the improvements that had already been accomplished in some people's lifetimes.

Xiao Liu had an interesting and important job. She was a Party member and, until recently, had been an inspector of small rural industrial enterprises. She knew better than most the absurdity of trying to insist that these sideline efforts fitted into a rigidly defined national model, because she had traveled extensively as a representative of the central government, insisting on just such absurdities. When the post–Gang of Four government started espousing the new policy of letting local conditions and needs dictate policy and method, she had had to find a new line of work, but no one could have been more pleased than she. Often, she said, she would studiously overlook certain things of which she knew the central authorities would disapprove but which made great sense locally. She ended up spending more time covering up than enforcing, and her bitterness showed when she talked about "Gang of Four policies." She also had higher status and more pay than her translator husband, Xiao Wang. Nevertheless, it was she who did all the housecleaning and marketing and most of the rearing of their four-year-old daughter.

Xiao Wang, the husband, was articulate, bright and handsome. His job prospects were good, despite his current rather lowly position, for his father was a senior official who had already arranged good housing for him and his family. When asked about his own role around the house, it became quickly clear that he had never lifted one domestic finger and had no intention of ever doing so. However, he was amused to see that I helped carry out dishes to the kitchen and that washing them was not the exclusive preserve of women. Eventually when they visited us, he would vie with me in doing the most work, but his actions did not faze his wife. She told Elizabeth, "He's only doing this to impress you. At home, his big excuse at the moment is that he is studying for exams. Actually that is true enough, and that is why I let him alone. But many Chinese husbands help out around the home now, and when his examinations are over, I am determined to have a modern husband!" Months later, with the exams successfully out of the way, Elizabeth asked him if he had begun "pulling his weight" around the house. He let out a loud laugh and we knew the answer instantly. His wife looked at him with a combination of affection and cynicism. "There's still some lingering influence of the Gang of Four in our home," she said, and that broke everyone up.

We saw all our friends as individuals. In the area of helping wives, for example, Lao Ouyang was a model husband. He had been a soldier in the People's Liberation Army and thought nothing of sewing patches on his two kids' clothing, and because he had a fetish for neatness, it was he who was constantly sweeping out their modest apartment. Also, just walking through the streets of Peking, anyone could see that many Chinese fathers idolized their children and showed them more overt affection than you would ever see in the streets of Western cities. It was a source of constant delight to see swarthy, rough-hewn types cuddling tiny bundles in their arms and checking every five seconds, or so it seemed, to see if the baby was all right.

Our friends forced me to stop seeing the Chinese people as "the masses." Now that we were sharing with them the individuality and complexities of their lives, we were never again able to walk down a street full of people without searching for familiar faces in a crowd. Only on a few occasions did I ever meet someone I knew, but the act itself meant that I was looking at all Chinese people from a new perspective. I suddenly started noticing tiny things, like the minute variations in clothing styles. Someone's hat cocked at a jaunty angle seemed to be a symbol of personality; the variations in the way people walked, or even their reactions to me as a highly visible foreigner, were automatically compared to things I was gradually learning from our friends. I was always an outsider in China, but now I felt more a part of the passing scene because I knew something of what was passing.

When foreign friends asked me if I thought the Chinese I knew were typical, I always responded by saying, "No, I don't know what a typical Chinese is anymore." But actually, I was always trying to discover if there was some common denominator with the Chinese I was meeting. This became more and more difficult to see as our circle widened, and through friends in Peking I was able to meet other Chinese in Shanghai and Canton. On one occasion, I had an interesting discussion with Xiao Wang on this matter. He suggested that the people who would be most interested in having contacts with Westerners would be "Right." Ever the novice and because his English was not strong, I became confused and asked if he meant that these Chinese—like himself—were "correct" in their attitudes. "No, no," he said, laughing. "Right–Left, Right–Left. Politics. Do you understand me?"

In Chinese politics to be a rightist meant that you were an adventurer, a disturber of the status quo. In the ranks of the so-called radical Left were the Bible Belters of China, those who clung to the holy writ of Mao Tsetung, believed every word and felt that others who veered from the straight and narrow path were doomed to the materialistic damnation known as "revisionism." It was the Right which had been suppressed so forcefully during the Cultural Revolution and had come back to power with such vigor after the death of Mao. Xiao Wang surmised that no one from the Left would want to be contaminated by contact with a foreigner. It is a curious phenomenon that in the West when a young person bucks the system, he or she usually espouses leftist sentiments, while in China the reverse is often the case.

In any event, the Right–Left factionalism in Chinese politics was a source of real and pressing concern to people like Xiao Wang. I would be quizzed closely on concepts like "the loyal opposition" of British parliamentary tradition, and I could see Xiao Wang physically agonize over the difficulty of fitting Western political practice into the Chinese experience.

"It is very complicated," he said. "You know that the distance between the theories and practice of the Gang of Four and Vice-Premier Deng is considerable. Maybe it is even more than between some of the political parties in your country. But this opposition between the two lines actually exists within our one Party, and the struggle between the two lines has been the source of much suffering for millions of people. You know, when the Gang of Four was in power, no one ever knew the thinking of people like us in the Right. We did not exist, except as something to attack. And yet we were very strong. Today we control the government, and as a foreign journalist you can travel throughout China, but you will never find a Chinese citizen who will tell you he is a leftist and thinks the government is making many serious mistakes. But don't think they have all vanished. They are silent now, as we were under the Gang of Four. So we have to ask ourselves: are we today creating the same conditions leading to the return of the Left as the Left did with regard to the Right?"

Xiao Wang was, above all things, a pragmatist. He had been born into Chairman Mao's world and knew nothing firsthand of the "miseries and bitterness" of pre-Liberation life that the Party propaganda machine told him had existed. For him, bitterness and misery were associated with the Cultural Revolution, when his father had been disgraced and as a thirteen-year-old boy he had been abandoned in the countryside with his schoolmates. He had thought about things deeply from that time on, and unlike his own father, he felt no sentimental allegiance to the Great Helmsman. That same harassed and victimized father—to Xiao Wang's continuing annoyance—could never bring himself to utter a criticism of Mao.

"My father," he said once, "respects the ultimate integrity of the

Party, despite all the suffering our family underwent, and he will not be drawn into any discussion of Chairman Mao's failings or errors. I do not discuss politics with him anymore. It is too frustrating and annoying." Still, as a pragmatist, Xiao Wang accepts the Communist Party as a fact. Like so many Chinese, he does not want to see the country riven apart by civil war, and so he follows a middle road which holds that the Party can be changed and adjusted from within. It is his hope, for example, that an existing institution like the National People's Congress can be transformed from its present status as a rubber-stamp parliament to a genuine forum for real political debate by popularly elected representatives, a forum which would minimize the factional disputes that cause such ruptures to Communist China. "The Left," he says, "must not be allowed to plot in darkness, as we were. There is no hope for China that way, only a continuation of the cycle of repression and purges."

I had come to think, initially, that all serious conversation in China—once particular curiosities had been satisfied—came down to political considerations. From this I concluded that China was the most politicized nation in the world, and I received support for this theory from my Peking friends. The Cultural Revolution, they said, had changed the way millions of Chinese regarded government. That unprecedented social experiment had, in some way or other, touched every Chinese and showed people they had a direct stake in whatever was going on among the central authorities. It paid to stay alert. And yet, as I branched out, I came to discover that the presiding role of politics took on different hues in different places, at least with the people I got to know.

For example, in Chengdu, the Chinese I spoke to on several visits always came back to the material hardships of life. Although the capital city of Sichuan province, like most major Chinese cities, had its controversial poster wall, the concerns expressed there had much more to do with the problems of employment and working conditions than the specifics of free expression or contacts with "foreign friends." There were no great ideological debates. I got to know some people there moderately well, but our contacts were fleeting, conducted in parks for the most part, and I knew they never could amount to more than that. From such people I learned that Chengdu's beggars were all shooed outside the city limits whenever large groups of foreigners came to town. By the same token, I also learned how conditions had improved during the previous year, when a new provincial administration had been set up, and how efforts were even being made to allow citizens to reestablish small cooperative enterprises so that their own industry could be more directly rewarded than was possible using any of the crazy, pseudo-socialist schemes dreamed up by the Gang of Four.

Since these people said there were improvements, I believed them, but there was much in Chengdu to sadden the heart. Once I was taken to a crafts factory, where I saw clay sculptures that purported to show pre-Liberation "bitterness." I remember one such depiction vividly. A young man had been harnessed to a cart like an animal and was wincing under the burden. When I emerged from the factory, I looked out onto a street and saw six young men similarly hitched up. Inside, the victim was modeled out of clay; outside, they were carved from flesh and blood. After thirty years of Communist rule, men and women were still needed to act as beasts of burden in China.

Again, I had to learn to keep such scenes in perspective, as unpalatable as they appeared to me as an affluent Westerner. One Chinese friend in Chengdu assured me that the work was hard and as miserable as it looked. "But they are paid better than the average worker here," he said, "and they have a more generous allocation of food coupons." Had an official told me this, I probably wouldn't have believed him, but my friend made a point of taking me up to one of the laborers, who confirmed the account. So there had been an improvement, and it was good to know.

In Shanghai, I encountered my first strong dose of proletarian snobbery, which seemed to be a direct descendant of traditional Chinese snobbery. Shanghai people, if you push them very far, just don't like dumb northerners. They are considered stupid, crude, filthy and uneducated. This attitude has prevailed despite the vast leveling of society carried out by the Communists, particularly during the Cultural Revolution.

In Shanghai, the major concern I heard about was the problem of unemployed youth—the young people who had been shipped off to the countryside, but who had returned illegally to the better life of the city. Parents were concerned about this serious social problem, and officials were so vexed that they made no effort to cover up but tried to address the problem head on. It was a problem that became the source of many lively discussions on the differences between the quality of life in the cities and in the countryside, and for the first time I got a small glimpse of the reason behind Mao Tsetung's annoyance at traditional urban Chinese attitudes toward the great mass of the peasantry.

I had friends who considered the average peasant subhuman, and talk like this upset me as much as when Torontonians joked about ignorant Newfoundlanders, among whom I had lived and worked for four years. I was later to discover in a very profound way that the Chinese peasant, like Shylock, will bleed if you prick him, and he is not insensitive to the nature of the wound or the manner in which it is inflicted. Endurance, stoicism, self-interest, even docility —these things can be found in the Chinese people; but they cannot be automatically equated with unquestioning acceptance or indifference. Chinese peasants have a strong and ready sense of basic justice, and when they detect even an ounce of decency in their governors, they strive to demand that justice in a way which startled even the more knowing citizens of Peking, who thought they knew everything there was to know about the peasantry.

Farther south in China, in Canton particularly, it is difficult to find the hard core of patriotic acceptance that you could discover in the north. Canton is too close to Hong Kong, and even those people who are reasonably satisfied with life inside the People's Republic know that the possibility exists to escape it, in one way or another. Quite literally, every person in Canton either has a relative in the British Crown Colony or knows someone there. The tangible proof can be seen in their better-quality footwear, or their wristwatches, or the television and radio sets in their homes. A simple comparison between Canton's poverty and Hong Kong's wealth is certainly not fair, but it is one that Cantonese often make. Nor are the Hong Kong relatives who return home for short visits any help. They always come laden with gifts—indeed, they are expected to come with gifts—and they never tell their Canton cousins how hard they have had to work in Hong Kong to save the money that they now dispense with such largesse.

The images drifting in from Hong Kong, either through travelers' tales or on illegally connected television sets, depict a world of glitter and ease, far removed from the reality of ordinary life for Chinese there. In fact, in many ways, life in Canton is superior. Most salaries are guaranteed by the state, working conditions are often better and housing costs are stupendously lower. Food is not a serious problem in Canton, and there are certainly no two-hour rest periods around lunchtime in Hong Kong.

Looking at the two cities completely objectively, one could say that for some Chinese in Hong Kong, the restraints imposed by material privation and excruciating working conditions are more onerous than anything the dictatorship of the proletariat has imposed on the people of Canton. The only thing that is substantially lacking in Canton is the possibility of independent endeavor. What Communist ideology always forgets, or chooses to ignore, is that people often prefer taking risks to settling for certainty. It is in the nature of the human condition, and it seems to transcend politics often enough to become a kind of law. Herein lies the main reason for the daily flow of illegal immigrants to Hong Kong from the Mainland. Even those Chinese who are patriotically inclined toward the Motherland are often driven to seek escape, and it is not so unusual to hear Hong Kong Chinese who have fled Communist rule maintaining that they felt they could do more for China from the outside. It is one of the tragedies of China today that truly innovative spirits are driven underground or out of the country altogether.

Canton strikes me as the saddest place in China. People know too much there and have too many contacts with the outside world. Revolutionary ardor, particularly during the immediate post-Liberation reconstruction period, did much to raise the pride and self-reliance of the Cantonese, but successive mass political campaigns of increasing mindlessness transformed many people into raging cynics, and one can often sense the tiredness and frustration of the people. Not surprisingly, one of the first open attacks on the official ideological stupidities foisted on Chinese people in the wake of the Cultural Revolution came from Canton.

This was in November 1974, when the activist trio Li Yizhe put up their huge wall poster at a main intersection of the city protesting the massive injustices Chinese people faced as well as the mania of the latest ideological campaign. They were very quickly arrested. It was not until well after the fall of the Gang of Four that they were released, although their rehabilitation to this day has not been particularly generous. Primitive communications and pervasive censorship meant that the Li Yizhe trio were not well known outside of Canton, but in the city itself they were a *cause célèbre,* and their subsequent release was an occasion for unofficial civic rejoicing. Because we had good contacts with Chinese people, Francis Deron of Agence France-Presse and I were the first to hear of their release. Deron was a keen student of China and spoke the language well. Li Yizhe were not just any group of protesters to him. Before he joined the French news agency, he had translated their famous wall poster and had it published in the West. Thanks to him and the Belgian writer Simon Leys, more foreigners knew about the case of Li Yizhe than Chinese. He was determined to see the trio, and he pulled off the feat with amazing panache.

Taking a plane to Canton, Deron was met at the airport, as everyone is, by a lowly Canton representative of the China Travel Service. The standard routine is for the guide to ask you what you would like to do in Canton: see an opera, visit a park, look at a model commune and so forth. As soon as the hapless guide asked the question, Deron said he had come to Canton for one reason and one reason only—to meet with Li Yizhe. The guide paled visibly. He began to stutter. "Don't panic," said Francis, who was taking a considerable gamble with this venture. "The government has released them, as you know. You should be able to reach them at the Fine Arts Institute. But first have your leader phone the Foreign Ministry in Peking—here's the telephone number—where you can check me out. The Ministry should give you permission, and then you can arrange the meeting. I am staying at the hotel until I hear you have arranged everything, and I'm not leaving until I meet them." A few hours later, he was talking to Li Yizhe in the garden of the East Wind Hotel, and they heard in detail, for the first time, about his efforts in their behalf.

Back in Peking, things rarely went as smoothly as this. People like Francis and me had to learn to keep professional instincts and our new Chinese friends clearly separated, although this was the cause of some heated discussions at times. Xiao Zhou, for example, was a very bright student at one of Peking's major universities. He had worked as a schoolteacher for a number of years and only recently had been allowed to take advanced courses. At twenty-eight, he had seen and experienced quite a lot. Since he came from a bona fide poor-peasant background, he helped us to a broader understanding of problems in the countryside. He was an utterly openhearted man who spoke plainly what he felt. We had met him at the Xidan Democracy Wall, but he had been there mostly out of curiosity and our first conversation was clearly only an effort by him to practice his English. Our friendship grew out of shared jokes and his insatiable desire for knowledge, which usually far exceeded my ability to deliver. He knew very well the risks he might be taking by talking to me: there was the immediate possibility that he might lose his university position which he had struggled so hard to get. Other repercussions we could only imagine. I never pushed or urged him to do things he did not carefully consider first, and he always made the decision as to whether or not to come to our apartment.

In February 1979 the Public Security Bureau arrested a woman named Fu Yuehua, an organizer of the poor peasants who flocked to Peking during the preceding months, seeking redress for past injustices. She was arrested just as Vice-Premier Deng Xiaoping was leaving for the United States. I had seen her in action a couple of times and met her once briefly at the Wall, and like most of the foreigners who were seeing Chinese at this time, I was shocked by her arrest because it burst the bubble of security we had erected around our own dealings with other people.

Several weeks passed and nothing more serious happened to any activists, leading many of us back into the old false sense of security. One day, Xiao Zhou and I were discussing the plight of these poor peasants, and I noted that the official press appeared to be backing them up with the first set of honest reports to come out of the countryside. Xiao Zhou was immensely pleased with the new kind of coverage of peasant conditions. They conformed to what he knew about life from his native village, and he took this progressive journalism as an extremely positive harbinger.

"I suppose that woman, Fu Yuehua, will be released soon," I said.

"Fu? Not a chance," he said. "She's a very bad type."

"How do you know this?"

"Everyone knows," he said matter-of-factly. "She accepted nylon stockings from foreigners, and it has been proved that she slept with an American diplomat."

"This is an extraordinary bit of news, old friend." I was quite perturbed. "Has there been a trial already? I haven't heard a word about it from anyone."

"No, there has been no trial. The police are still collecting evidence. But she's a bad type, take it from me. She makes false accusations, she'll sleep with any man and she only got involved with the peasants to advance herself."

I exploded. It was the first time I had raged at a Chinese, and as I look back on the scene today I realize I was really raging at myself and my own naiveté, although Xiao Zhou was just as stupid as I was.

"You're just spreading rumor and gossip that the police have passed on. That's how they get at people. They spread shocking stories, and by the time the trial starts, the gossip is so widespread most people believe it is the truth. Suppose the police arrest you tomorrow?"

"Me?" he said, genuinely alarmed. "Why would the police arrest me? I haven't done anything wrong."

"You know you haven't done anything wrong. I know you haven't done anything wrong. But we're the only ones. Do you think the PSB will ask me to be a character witness? I would be proof that you are evil. And then we would start to hear the stories: how I weighed you down with expensive presents to get secret information from you; how my wife enticed you to bed with her; how you made the Chinese people lose face because you actually sat down at our dining table. And maybe before they had done with you, you would start believing those stories yourself."

The outburst turned out to be somewhat prophetic. A few days later, a wall poster went up at Xidan telling of a meeting among senior officials of the municipality of Peking in which contacts between Chinese and foreigners were damned for the first time. The poster writer said that these "municipal harangues" had been opposed "by the masses," but the implicit threat remained. One of the charges made by a senior city official was that when a Chinese entered a foreigner's apartment and partook of foreign hospitality, he made the Chinese people "lose face." Casting scorn on this, the poster writer asked rhetorically if the Chinese people had lost face when Vice-Premier Deng Xiaoping sat down to dinner with President Jimmy Carter in the White House the month before.

As the weeks went on, it became clearer and clearer that the government would not tolerate such unofficial relationships. At one point during this period, I was invited to a discussion between foreign correspondents and senior officials of the Academy of Social Sciences who were drafting China's first wide-ranging criminal code. It was a hopeful endeavor, this proposed criminal code, because it would set down for the first time in a comprehensive way what the state considered permissible behavior. Previously, there was no such direct guide for the citizen, which was by design because in this fashion illegality could be determined according to the specific ideological needs of the day. My friends were very much on my mind when I went off to this meeting. I asked the Chinese officials whether the new criminal code would contain guarantees to protect Chinese citizens from state reprisals if they had friendships with foreigners.

"No," said one official, "such a thing wouldn't be in a criminal code. Friendship is a normal thing and does not need laws. During the reign of the Gang of Four many pernicious things happened. If a Chinese citizen was seen talking to a foreigner, he might be accused of any sort of crime. That was a terrible thing, but that period has passed, and now, while there might be a bit of reluctance on the part of some citizens who still fear the influence of the Gang, the government considers such friendships entirely normal."

Reluctance! What a euphemism. Only Huang Anlun, our composer friend, who was from the relatively apolitical world of music and dance (only recently apolitical, mind you), had had the confidence to go to his Unit leaders and ask permission to see my wife and me. All the others, without exception, were convinced that if they sought permission, not only would it be denied, but their lives would become hell on earth. In the case of those people whom the authorities knew I was seeing, they were approached in a variety of ways and given quite explicit instructions as to how to end the relationship and what would happen to them if they didn't.

After the first major crackdown came, at the end of March 1979, I was never again able to see these Chinese friends in my home or go to theirs. Because of our concern for their safety and future, I hardened myself and tried to make final meetings as easy for them as possible. For some it was an intolerable situation, and I was able to remain in contact through a variety of ways. Although it became an unpleasant, furtive business, I nevertheless was the recipient of a kind of courage I had never before witnessed, and there was no single thing that changed me more profoundly than these seemingly small acts of affection and elemental courtesy, which could have cost them so much. Even today as I write these words, I fear for their safety. What if the police go after some of them, even if they weren't the ones whom we continued seeing? Silence and self-censorship is the safest and most prudent answer, but I am under an obligation. As Xiao Jiang said to me once: "The Chinese people appear docile to foreigners. We are not docile. You must tell the truth. We want you to write about friendship. Maybe our leaders will see it is not sinister, that we learn from each other. This must begin somewhere, so let it begin here."

That said, I am also forced to account for my friendship with the Huang family and their circle. These were my official friends. After that extraordinary evening with Huang Anlun in the midst of the Xidan events, I had gone to his father's modest apartment and met the other members of his family: his parents, his brothers, his wife and child. I also met other members from his institute. Throughout all the troubled period, when activists were being arrested and unofficial Chinese who visisted foreigners were being described in the *Peking Daily* as "traitors" and "the scum of the earth," I was able to see the Huangs without let or hindrance.

It seems absolutely absurd to feel any gratitude whatsoever to a government that actually seeks to order with whom people shall make friends, but it is nevertheless what I feel, even today. Given the background of violent taboos on relationships between foreigners and Chinese in Communist history, this was a step forward, and I came to feel as close to the Huangs as I do to anyone outside my own immediate family.

The focus of our gatherings, either at the *Globe and Mail* apartment or at the home of Huang Feili, Huang Anlun's father, was music. We were a motley collection of amateur and professional musicians, and the kind of fun we had those evenings can scarcely be imagined. One time, Mama Huang was singing a Schubert *Lied* with surprising gusto. Her voice had gone long ago, but that didn't deter her in the least. She had been a beloved music teacher at a primary school and radiated an earthy warmth that transcended all other considerations. As she was straining for a particularly high note, which had escaped her capabilities years ago, her youngest son suddenly ran up behind her with a large fan and started fanning her like mad. "She'll faint if she ever reaches that note," he said, his face lined with mock concern.

There were serious moments too, and they were haunting. Any Chinese over the age of twenty has stories to tell of the Cultural Revolution, and it is here more than anywhere else that lines are drawn between outsiders and Chinese. We cannot even begin to imagine fully what these years meant to so many Chinese, and after hearing the worst of the tales, I always marveled at the resiliency I saw around me. When the Cultural Revolution first exploded, Huang Anlun was sixteen—the best age to be a Red Guard, or one of those "little generals," as Mao's wife Jiang Qing called them. His father was the head of the conducting department of the Peking Conservatory, and as a front-line artistic institution, it was soon to feel the cruel effects of iconoclasm and mass hysteria.

"I can never forget that time," Huang Anlun said one evening. We were all together—mother and father, wife and son, foreign and Chinese friends—everyone packed into the tiny living room, which also served as a bedroom by night and a piano practice room by day. "I had always been close to Papa, but I was overwhelmed by the events that were happening. I took my two younger brothers on my lap, and I told them that Papa was probably going to be dragged before the masses and criticized, and that the masses would be correct. I expected this to happen daily; maybe even a part of me wanted it to happen. My brothers cried and cried. They could not understand why I would say such a thing. Today I have my dreams and memories to live with. I go over and over this period in my head to try to figure out how I could ever think such a thing. The masses, as it turned out, had more care for Papa than I did. He was never publicly critcized because he was kind and good and had a big reputation for always being fair with everyone."

There was more to the story than this. Although he wasn't publicly humiliated, all of Huang Feili's music library was burned; books and sheet music and records he had scraped and saved to purchase went up in a night of flames. The whole family was shipped off to the countryside, and the chosen career of my friend Huang Anlun was dashed: he had wanted to become a concert pianist and had already shown prodigious talent. His father was the first to face reality. In the countryside, he said, there would be no pianos on which to practice, but the music in his soul could not be destroyed. And so he became a composer. Today he is among the most popular in China.

One of Huang Anlun's friends who was there wanted me to have a more comprehensive picture of the Cultural Revolution. It was not enough, he said, merely to consider the betrayal of parents, the burning of books and the denigration of the best in traditional culture. The friend was called Tang Ming—a name that intrigued me because it seemed to be composed of two imperial dynastic reminders. For weeks I thought his parents must have been the most recklessly foolish people in China to name their son this way after the Communists took over. It was like calling someone George Hanover in the United States immediately after the American Revolution. I discovered later that only the sound was the same —the actual characters in written Chinese are quite different.

Tang Ming's father had been disgraced during the 1950s. As an engineer he had protested the single-minded dependency the government was placing on Soviet Union experts. He was proved correct by 1960, but the Communist Party in China—until very recently—had an absolute horror of reversing past injustices, even when official policy acknowledged them. Because of this, Tang Ming's family had suffered many wrongs, both trivial and great. His father, accused of being a "rightist," had only recently had his good name restored. When Tang Ming spoke, I listened with respect.

"Many of us," he said in a more serious moment, "consider that some of the causes of the Cultural Revolution were valid. They are still valid today. There was a strong feeling then that the bureaucracy had become a terrible burden and that things had been established in the years since Liberation that could not be changed. Most people had had some sort of bad experience, and when Chairman Mao spoke out about the matter, he spoke straight to the heart of what many of us were thinking. Most of what happened afterward was terrible, that is true. The Cultural Revolution was a bitter experience for all of us, but the fact that the methods used to attack the problem were wrong does not mean that the issues were invalid. How can they be? We still have the problem, although now people are trying to solve it in a more sensible way, without the terrible destruction of everything."

The Huangs also had strong political views, as was made clear to me one day when I was driving Mama Huang up to our apartment and we passed the Xidan Democracy Wall. This was before the first major crackdown, and I was still in an ebullient mood. As we drove by, I pointed out the Wall and asked her, *"Hao buhao?"* ("Is it good or not?").

"Buhao," she snarled ("Not good"). She said it so forcefully, I was taken aback.

"Why not?" I asked.

"It has been only a short time since the fall of the Gang of Four.

Already there have been a great number of changes, but some people seem to want everything all at once. Those wall-poster writers are doing nothing but stirring up trouble. Most of the young people who listen to the speakers and read the posters don't really know all the problems China faces. I think we have to rally behind Deng Xiaoping and the other leaders at this moment. They need lots of support for the changes they are making, and those people [meaning the wall-poster writers] want too much too soon. Have they forgotten all the work that has to be done to improve conditions in the countryside? We have many privileges, living in the city, that most Chinese people will never have, but some people forget this and take it all for granted. They feel no responsibility for the good of the whole country. If it was up to me, I'd pack the whole bunch off to the countryside. I know what I'm talking about. I've worked in the countryside, and you learn a lot there. So would they."

This ended that particular discussion. We were very fond of each other, but she was not about to take any lectures from me on the philosophical underpinning of the new democracy movement. Her husband was working again, and the music from her son's soul was making impressive connections with audiences throughout China. She had not thought to live long enough to see such things happen, and consequently was not prepared to tolerate anyone who was only "stirring up trouble." We were poles apart and never discussed the issue again. Those troublemakers seemed to me the very conscience of New China and the hope of the future.

14

The Activists

Who is ever going to tell the stories of wonder and horror and promise of New China? It can't really come from outsiders, no matter how much their sympathics lie with the Chinese people nor how involved they become with Chinese realities. Such accounts will always lack the crucial element of simply being written by Chinese. Even those books by foreigners which have come closest to identifying with the Chinese soul, such as Pearl Buck's *The Good Earth* or Jonathan Spence's *The Death of Woman Wang,* are ultimately compromised by a sense of externally perceived poignancy.

To manipulate William Butler Yeats for a moment, the observations of other people's rooftops never have quite the same force as the careful and knowing depiction of the thatch over one's own home. When the artificial barriers separating Chinese and foreigners are removed, there is nothing preventing anyone from entering into warm and complex relationships. Having thus entered, however, a foreigner is constantly made aware of how different his friends' experiences have been; differences which, when tied to enduring Chinese conditions, account for a special perspective on so many universal traits of human nature, such as courage, cowardice, fidelity, cruelty, compassion and stubbornness.

In China, one confronts basic considerations very quickly, without the often convoluted detours we are accustomed to make in the West. I have lost count of the number of evenings I spent hashing over individual accounts of the Cultural Revolution. I was in the midst of a constant dialogue with hardy survivors, and everyone had a tale to tell that was imbued with the kind of passion only a bloodied participant could summon up.

For many Chinese, the Cultural Revolution was the supreme trial by fire. There were tragic victims and fierce heroes; in between were the majority of Chinese, who simply tried to survive the enveloping storm. For those who are now in their late twenties and early thirties, this fearsome social experiment was a brutal coming of age in which innocence and idealism were manipulated in a stunning fashion. Cut off from the discipline of formal schooling, and when the productive forces of the nation were grinding to a halt and anarchy was on the loose, this extraordinary generation was suddenly confronted with the possibility of acting out the wildest fantasies. The brutality meted out to teachers, out-of-favor officials, intellectuals and "class enemies" was one thing; against this has to be played the unprecedented chance for young people to travel anywhere in the country, like figures out of a picaresque novel, as well as the dizzying prospect of playing with affairs of state. These were stupendous experiences, reached at the most formative stage of a young person's development, experiences that form the basis of the way this vast generation now surveys life both in general and in particular.

The variety and complexity of responses the Cultural Revolution aroused can scarcely be imagined in the West, for several reasons. For one thing, we never had a Mao Tsetung actually encouraging us to "bombard the headquarters." Nor have we gone through such a profound and quick cycle of promise, exultation, betrayal and repression—our own campus revolts of the 1960s pale in comparison. Also, we have traditionally been reluctant to see in the Chinese a mirror image of ourselves. At best, we have taken Maoism as a romantic alternative in the fields of education and social development. At worst, we have simply ignored China altogether. Why not? After all, we are affluent and they are poor; we have a tradition of evolving liberal democracy and they have an enduring familiarity with tyranny; we encourage individuality and they appear to put a premium on conformity. Thus does the variety in the human condition and experience—part of our universal heritage—

lead us into the fallacy of denying the condition itself to a quarter of the world's population. Today, there are few more fatuous conceits than this. Some academics, Sinologists and foreign-affairs analysts maintain a lively profession by reinforcing the queerness of the Chinese, buttressed by Communist propaganda and the propensity of some journalists for latching on to every outlandish event which supports the notion that "they" are somehow a separate species from the rest of us.

For so long, the Great Silence from the masses acted as a kind of endorsement for those on the outside who urged us to suspend common sense and common decency when we sought to understand what was going on inside China. Most of us were prepared to do so because there was much that seemed inexplicable, although the silence itself should have warned us that the whole tale was not yet told. Even the Tienanmen Incident, which was clearly antigovernment, was quickly ignored and forgotten. Until the phenomenon of the Xidan Democracy Wall, in which foreigners were invited to participate, the Great Silence ruled supreme. Until Xidan, nothing was published in Communist China unless the state gave its permission. Those brave but wretched souls who provide the few notable exceptions were mostly hounded, quite literally, to death.

It is in the nature of the Chinese political condition that the full story behind the events of Xidan may take many years to come out, but they will emerge eventually. Take the Cultural Revolution, for example. It has been shrouded in mystery for over a decade. Communist propaganda first touted it as a Good Thing; now it is officially a Bad Thing. This abrupt reversal of the prevailing line has brought forth a flood of accounts, statistics and analyses from the Chinese themselves which have expanded our understanding tremendously. Eventually, the same process will apply to Xidan. Even though I was in the midst of it, it was impossible to understand much of the larger machinations that were going on. Ironically, since Xidan helped to unravel some the secrets of the Cultural Revolution, it became possible to see the connection between the two events, despite the fact that the former was played out in the huge arena all China became, while Xidan hardly had a chance to breathe.

As a preliminary hypothesis, I have come to accept the idea that when the posters first went up in November 1978, they had the tacit, if cautious, approval of a variety of groups hitched to the rising star of Vice-Premier Deng Xiaoping. Indeed, there was probably some high-level support for a bit of grass-roots politicking from the masses to back up the controversial changes that were being imposed on the Chinese body politic. We now know, too, that Xidan occurred at a crucial moment in the negotiations over normalizing relations between China and the United States.

Xidan had a phenomenal impact on public opinion in the United States. The spectacle of Chinese people speaking out freely and openly for the first time in most people's memory was so encouraging to a country officially concerned about human rights that a potentially damaging major report from Amnesty International which appeared at the same time was effectively neutralized.

Based on solid research and presented in as low-key and unhysterical a style as possible, Amnesty's report drove home the point that in China the Communist government had foisted an oppressively regimented regime on citizens whose basic rights—rights recognized in the Chinese Constitution and by the United Nations, of which China is an active member—were regularly denied or trampled upon. The Amnesty report on China contained nothing that was particularly new, but the accumulation of data was daunting. Had Xidan not occurred, uncomfortable truths like those presented by Amnesty, as well as unease over the abandonment of support for Taiwan, might have been sufficient to stay President Carter's decision on a quick resolution of the normalization question.

But if Xidan had official backing for a short period—and Vice-Premier Deng had told Robert Novak that it was "a good thing" —it was also a damned nuisance. Many of the senior and middle-level officials who were back in power had been victims of earlier wall-poster campaigns during the Cultural Revolution, and there must have been some haunting memories in the corridors of the Great Hall of the People as poster writers developed their skills and started really examining the society and government around them.

As the Hundred Flowers Campaign of 1956 and the Cultural Revolution itself showed, what is initiated from on high invariably begins to take on a course of its own when those below get hold of it. The government could not have predicted the actions of someone like me, who inadvertently showed ordinary Chinese a novel means of directing their aspirations and frustrations to their own leadership. On the other hand, the authorities—especially veteran authorities—had had sufficient experience to know that there would be some Chinese who would not remain content with the official explanations of the Communist Party's past errors, nor with a simple and rigidly defined exorcism of the Gang of Four. You do not urge people, as the government relentlessly did, to "emancipate their minds" and "search truth from facts" without preparing yourself for the effects of this emancipation.

Under such ostensibly liberating slogans, was it surprising that some Chinese not only would examine the facts surrounding the Gang of Four, but would push on toward a punishing analysis of the system that had allowed the Gang to gain such power in the first place and hold on to it for so long? All this came to pass with clockwork precision, as did the inevitable official reaction. This time, though, the "bad elements" were not intellectuals, "rightists," confused students or Party careerists. Xidan was a genuine manifestation from the masses, based on the experience of the Cultural Revolution and the Tienanmen Incident. It had its own logic and progression, and there were historians who saw in Xidan the same spirit that had aroused Chinese youth in the epochal May 4 Movement, begun in 1919. To attack these offspring of Chairman Mao's own era, the authorities had to devise a new label—and thus the epithet "newborn bourgeoisie" was conceived.

Conditioned to the seeming docility of the Chinese people, quite a number of foreign observers—certainly some of those stationed in Peking—were genuinely shocked to discover that citizens were able and eager to voice the most diverse kinds of thoughts, criticisms and aspirations. To travel from the absurd paeans of praise for "the wise leader Chairman Hua," pouring forth from the official media in 1977, to the eloquent manifestations of the Xidan Democracy Wall was to travel from duplicity and surreal fantasy to the very conscience of a generation that had lost its innocence at an early age.

The Wall was neither a handsome nor a heroic-looking place, but it had for me and others the luster of a mighty symbol. I went there day and night, speaking only rudimentary Chinese and reading virtually none. Translations came from Chinese eager to practice their English, as well as a few trusted diplomats and students who were as caught up in the phenomenon as I was. The whole story of China was not Xidan, of course, but what was presented there was a part of the story that had never been heard before. Those people who belittled the Wall—both Chinese and foreigners—were to be pitied. It was, as a Communist official said to me one day, "a remarkable eye into China."

To communicate to people who were not there the flavor and substance of the Xidan Democracy Wall, it is necessary only to let the poster writers speak for themselves. To this end, I have assembled some excerpts from those *dazibao* which impressed me the most. In any one day, one would not expect to find all of the following in a single session, although each item was published during a six-week period at the beginning of 1979 and after the authorities had made their first attack on the Wall. Also, the prevailing tone of these excerpts is angry and extremely critical, whereas in reality there were many posters which took a cautious approach, skirted controversy and often merely asked questions. Other *dazibao,* which were sometimes revealing in a different way, dealt only with personal and specific grievances, such as unfair housing allocations or certain injustices meted out by local officials. As with letters to the editor, there was also a fair share of crank contributions, and like the editor himself, I am exercising the prerogative of choice.

What follows, then, is the best of Xidan, and I didn't get it as easily as you are about to. The weather was usually bitterly cold, and sometimes a whole poster might require over an hour to be translated. That is a minuscule complaint, though, for these are the words and thoughts of people who knew the risks they were taking and the price they might have to pay: indeed, three of the authors are already in prison.

The Guomindang rule has gone away for thirty years, and it is unnecessary to cite repeatedly the misgivings of the past to praise and defend the present. The Chinese Government has armed its borders to the teeth to keep out everything different from the Chinese version of Marxism-Leninism. Under such conditions, the propaganda against "the abuses of the capitalist society" rammed down the throats of the Chinese people has been rejected long ago and has lost its charm to induce self-delusion.

———————

It has been reliably learned that Jiang Qing is now in Qincheng Prison. The first thing she said after her incarceration was "Reprisals have been made and favors extended where they were due. I shall die without regret." However, when she discovered that her name had been placed third in the list of the Gang of Four, she asked, "Why wasn't it first?"

It's reassuring to know that she has retained her humility, always her finest trait.

Every tiny portion of genuine democracy has been stained with the blood of martyrs and tyrants, and every step forward was met with strong attacks from reactionary forces. Democracy has been able to surmount all these obstacles because it is highly valued and eagerly sought by the people. Therefore, this direction is irresistible. In a battle, Chinese people have never feared anything. As long as they have a clear purpose, the forces of tyranny no longer look undefeatable, despite their size. Is the struggle for democracy what the Chinese people really want? The Cultural Revolution was the first occasion for them to demonstrate their strength, and all reactionary forces trembled before them. Because the people then had no clear purpose and the democratic forces did not play the main role in the struggle, the majority of them were bought over by the autocratic tyrant, led astray, divided, slandered and finally violently suppressed. . . . Today, twelve years later, the people have finally learned where their goal is. They have a clear purpose and a real leader—the democratic banner. The Xidan Democracy Wall has become their first battlefield in the fight against reactionaries, and this struggle will certainly be victorious. . . . There will be bloodshed and suffering, and we may be covertly plotted against. However, the democratic banner cannot be obscured by the miasmal mists. Let us unite, then, comrades, under this great and real banner and march toward modernization for the sake of the people's peace, happiness, rights and freedom.

Tolerance

> The Chinese people are very tolerant.
> They know how to avoid trouble.
> Even though their wives are raped
> They try to understand.

In China, people who question the authority of Marxism-Leninism and Maoist Marxism-Leninism are branded "class enemies." Unfortunately, those who have come forward today to challenge the Marxism-Leninism and Mao Tsetung Thought are precisely the young people brought up during the Mao Tsetung era. We as a group are taught, conditioned and directed since our birth to pledge loyalty to Marxism-Leninism. As faithful disciples, we worshiped it blindly. Awakened now by the disappointing practices of its followers, we realize that to love our country and work for the happiness of the people, we must not lose sight of our own sensibilities and the true purpose of life. We are no longer willing to submit ourselves to this cold ideology we do not understand.

The citizens of China demand that a national referendum be held to elect state leaders as well as the leaders at all levels, in various areas. Deputies to the Fourth and Fifth National People's Congress were not elected in a general election involving all the people. This was a scathing lampoon of "socialist democracy" and makes a mockery of the basic rights of 970 million people.

According to the laws of history, the new will not come until the old is gone. Now that the old is gone, the people are rubbing their eyes in eager expectation. Finally, with God's blessing, they got a great promise—The Four Modernizations. Chairman Hua, the wise leader, and Vice-Premier Deng, an even wiser and greater leader in the people's minds, have defeated the Gang of Four. The very eager hope for democracy and prosperity by those who had shed their blood at Tienanmen Square seemed soon to materialize. . . . However, to the people's great regret, the hated old political system has not changed and even any talk about the much hoped-for democracy and freedom is forbidden. People's living conditions remain the same, and the "increased" wages are far behind the soaring commodity prices.

We have just received a report from our Tianjin correspondent, which follows:

"Since the beginning of the year, many people continue to experience long periods of unemployment or else considerable hardships and difficulties in their livelihood. For these and other reasons, they are driven to sell their blood in order to gain a little cash. In 1977, 1,068 people sold blood; in 1978 that figure was increased by 1,510. Among these were 116 unemployed youths and 48 educated youths; 568 of the people were between 20 and 26 years of age. According to law, no one under the age of 20 is allowed to be a blood donor; however, some youths below the age of 20 borrow other people's residency cards and sell blood under someone else's name. The law also prohibits one person from donating blood more than once a year, but in 1977 and 1978 some youths sold blood up to 15 times in a two-year period."

Self-Portrait

Since I began to observe people coolly,
Nothing on earth has stirred my emotions.
Reality is not what I have pictured it to be
Nor can it shed any light on my gloomy soul.

When I summed up the experiences of life
I gradually lost my poetic innocence.
For a society in which black is called white
I no longer have a light heart to play my fiddle.

Everyone is born destined to seek freedom. Wouldn't anyone enjoy freedom and leisure and the pleasure of doing what he likes? To enjoy freedom and do what one likes are basic freedoms. Of course, such rights are subject to limitations of time and material conditions, but there will never be a time when human beings voluntarily turn down opportunities to do their own thinking and manage their own lives. If the Chinese Communist Party were to announce to the Chinese people tomorrow that they can think and explore what they like, as long as they don't resort to violence and disturb public peace, do you think that the people would feel let down and start crying like babies abandoned by their mothers? Mao Tsetung and his followers used to spread shocking propaganda to justify their attempt to compel people to believe and abide by a single doctrine, a single ideology. After thirty years, if the Chinese people have not become more resentful of such coercion, at the very least they are as resentful as ever.

These writings speak well enough for themselves, although there are some interesting subtleties. The poem called "Self-Portrait," for example, makes a reference to a society "in which black is called white." Most Chinese would understand this allusion immediately. Before the Cultural Revolution, Deng Xiaoping had been in an argument about the best ideological approach to production. Was it better to be "red" or "expert" in dealing with such things as agricultural development or the manufacture of steel: in other words, should a higher premium be placed on revolutionary zeal than on actual working knowledge? The Left faction in Chinese Communist politics held that there was no point in having expertise unless it was allied to the correct political outlook, that it was better to have less production, as long as the ideological goals—such as class struggle—remained paramount. In time, the faction argued, there would be plenty of people who were "red *and* expert." The Right faction, under people like former head of state Liu Shaoqi and Deng himself, thought this debate the epitome of metaphysical stupidity. "White cat, black cat," said Deng. "What does it matter, as long as it can catch a mouse?" This line came back to destroy him during the Cultural Revolution and was used as prima facie evidence that he was an unrepentant "capitalist-roader" taking "the revisionist road."

The poem was originally written in the early seventies when Deng was still in deep disfavor. It was posted at the Xidan Wall and published in the unofficial journals sold there because in the past such works had been strictly prohibited. It was a timely reminder to many people that for years those who believed so fervently in the cause of Deng Xiaoping had been the dissidents of their day. Indeed, from this perspective, Deng himself was the biggest dissident of all.

The other poem, called "Tolerance," was the angriest thing I ever read in China. On the surface, the prose polemics seem far more devastating, but they are hinged to specific problems of institutional Communism. "Tolerance" is directed at a perceived national psyche which highly values endurance in the face of adversity. One of the great symbols of this endurance is the bamboo tree, which bends in the fierce storm only to stand up straight in better weather. It is a symbol worked out in the literature and art of this ancient land, and it served many people in good and bad stead during the Cultural Revolution—the most onerous national assignment any Chinese ruler has put his people through since the Emperor Qin Shihuang (pronounced "chin-shur-huang") first conceived of the scheme to build a Great Wall along the entire northern border of China.

By the time I discovered "Tolerance," I already knew that the symbol of the bamboo tree bending in the storm had become for many young people the focus of intemperate scorn. When I asked about a particular member of the Politburo, for example, they might say that he or she was the object of considerable hope, or they might dismiss the individual by making a curious hand gesture. The movement was nothing more than a brisk waving of the hand from the wrist, and at first I thought it was a simple dismissive gesture. Later, I learned it represented the swaying of the bamboo tree, by which they meant that the particular leader had hedged all bets and taken on the coloration of whatever was the presiding ideological line. The contempt for such "shifting bamboo trees" was immense. The anonymous author of "Tolerance" is evidently a member of the most intolerant and demanding section of the Cultural Revolution generation, who is furious not only at the way his peers were tricked and duped by the Communist Party leaders, but also at the way the same leaders have been able to take advantage of traditional Chinese endurance. It is a generation that also despises the way Chinese people avoid confrontation and much of the nation's misery is attributed to this trait.

This generation has a number of other factions. There were the pragmatists and optimists. They still believed in the art of the possible from within the system. There were those who rejected the system altogether and wanted either to clear out of China or to clear the Communist Party out. There were also those who had become thoroughly disillusioned but saw no way out. This last group accepted the status quo because there didn't seem to be a choice, and some of them even entered the ranks of the Party itself with the well-known theory that the unbeatable should be joined. Others, robbed of the blind faith they once had and also of a kind of pride and self-worth, which was an undeniable product of the Cultural Revolution for some people, resorted to either lassitude or violence.

Contrary to all the theories of lawfulness in China, there was a considerable amount of crime and physical violence stalking the country. With Deng Xiaoping's less repressive regime and a comparatively more open society, many of China's social divisions and fissures became more obvious. The Cultural Revolution, it turned out, had bequeathed China a permanent and not insignificant population of thugs and gangsters. Some of these hooligans have put themselves completely beyond the pale and will receive no mercy if they are ever apprehended. Others, as I was to discover at the Wall, have had their propensities harnessed by the police and were used to confuse and upset those Chinese who at the time had a constitutional right to assemble and air their thoughts.

The business of the Constitution and legality in China had a direct bearing on the course of events at Xidan. The right to put up wall posters and hold open debates was written into the Constitution. In fact, Chairman Mao's own words were used in the pertinent paragraph. It is a generally well-understood fact that Communist countries produce some of the most eloquent constitutions in the world and that they don't mean anything. The Constitution in effect in China throughout 1979 (it changes according to the needs of the day) was a model of this sort of hypocritical document, but it was promulgated at a time when there were unbounded expectations for the future, expectations that were being backed up daily by articles in the official press and by the actions of the leaders. The widespread effort to redress past injustices was impressive, and the talk about setting up the country's first comprehensive criminal code, in which citizens would actually see for the first time what the state defined as criminal behavior, supported the prevailing aspiration that true legality was finally going to get a fair chance.

To give the Communist Party its due, the Constitution had escape clauses everywhere: there is freedom of speech, for example, but it is unlawful to question the presiding role of the Communist Party or the doctrine of the dictatorship of the proletariat. The state also reserves the right to define the term "counterrevolutionary"—a catchall designation which is the worst label that can be pinned on a Chinese citizen. Many of those who believed in Deng Xiaoping in the past were pronounced counterrevolutionary by the Gang of Four, and some lost their lives as a result. Today, those who persist in Chairman Mao's obstinate struggle to perpetuate class struggle could conceivably be labeled counterrevolutionary, as some of the people have been who agitated for reform and change at the Xidan Democracy Wall. But these escape clauses and Catch-22s were the furthest thing from people's minds during the happier days of Xidan, even though the government reiterated them as it became uneasy about the Wall's direction. In retrospect, it is easy to see why the leaders got so nervous.

With China's primitive communication and transportation systems, an outburst of wall posters in Peking could conceivably be contained without too much difficulty. It had been proved in Canton a few years before that a scorching public essay which left a city of millions wide-eyed in wonder was relatively unknown elsewhere in the country. But things had changed since then. Not only were there far more travel opportunities, but there was a considerably less repressive atmosphere about. When the activists at Xidan started forming into groups which produced provocative and regularly printed magazines—however crude the format and publishing materials—the movement took a large step forward. Even at its most primitive level, however, a wall poster alone had an amazingly wide readership. One Chinese told me that if one poster goes up and stays for at least a half hour and only a few Chinese actually read it, within a few days anyone in Peking who wanted to know what was on it could find out.

When the state controls all the principal forms of mass communication, unofficial lines work remarkably well. This can be observed in all totalitarian countries. Since Xidan initially was allowed to function with little overt repression, people traveling to Peking often went to see the Wall and make extensive notes on the posters as well as purchasing the magazines. A few even had small cassette recorders and dictated posters into the contraptions.

Once, on a train trip, I got into a brief conversation with a railway security worker who lived in a remote part of the country. He was clearly delighted to meet a foreign journalist. I asked him if there was any poster activity in his city, and he laughed. "None at all," he said with a rueful laugh. He lived in a city that was part of a strategic military area, and the People's Liberation Army kept a very short leash on any public activities. "Are you aware of what has been going on in Peking at Xidan Democracy Wall?" I asked. "Of course," said the man. "Many people in our city know everything that is going on." I asked how this was possible. There were two means, it turned out. One was courtesy of the Voice of America, which broadcast reports about the Wall as they came out to the West via the resident correspondents. Some people had shortwave radios, and it was no longer a crime to listen to either VOA or the BBC. The other way people found out was far more intriguing.

"Our train travels to Peking every ten days," said the railway security worker. "When I arrive in Peking, I always head straight for the Xidan Wall. Of course, I take these off [he pointed to the red tabs on his jacket collar, the badges of his office]. I write everything down, purchase magazines if I can and take everything back to my home. You know, railway people are the messengers of China, especially if they are on a regular run to Peking."

The mobility of the railway workers and others who had the means and opportunity to travel aided the internal and national growth of the activist movement. Taking strategy from the Cultural Revolution, a number of the activists fanned out around the country in "linkup" groups to bring the word of Xidan to other cities, where there were willing listeners among friends and relatives. The numbers were not great, but no one knew better than the old revolutionaries in the Communist Party the effect of a few well-disciplined and highly motivated people spreading propaganda all over the place. Such tactics eventually helped give the Party the governance of China: what worked once can always work again.

When the first major crackdown came the following spring,

poster walls were censored and activists arrested in most major cities in China—as clear an indication as anything of how seriously the Party viewed the threat. The crackdown was aimed at "the handful of bad elements" who were "sabotaging the stability and unity" of the country. This was true to a certain extent. Any serious questioning of the role of government and its practice is going to upset the status quo. Rather than viewing Xidan as a safety valve to measure the discontent of the people, even Deng Xiaoping was forced to lower the boom. Inherent in the actions was the fear every institutionalized Communist government has of the judgment of the people.

The saddest thing of all to contemplate about the whole business is that if a national direct election had been held at the time, Deng would probably have received an overwhelming confirmation in his post. But he is trapped in a system in which he can be neither confirmed nor, without a purge, rejected. His "retirement" in 1980 still left him in the commanding position, of necessity. Other recent efforts to ameliorate this situation—by widening the franchise for the rubber-stamp parliament a little, for example—are well worth watching in the future, but precedent and practice are not on his side. Nor is there any evidence that he even approves of the direct popular election of state leaders, even as an ideal. The most outspoken of the activists, Wei Jingshen, thoroughly considered the precedent and practice and decided that the Communist Party's record was sufficiently awful to argue for radical alternatives. He tried to engage the Party in an open debate on the issue, through wall posters and his magazine *Explorations.*

Like the other journalists who established contacts with the activists of Xidan, I had an ambivalent attitude toward them, which was reciprocated. It was a dangerous thing they were doing, and they knew this better than we did. In fighting to change China, they were completely cut off from the public media. Even Canada's three minuscule Communist parties (allied to the Soviet Union, China or Albania) are allowed free, country-wide access to television during national elections. Such exposure is their ruination, and it might well have happened that an equivalent exposure for the democracy activists would lose them their sting. There are lots of Mama Huangs in China. But the Communists, using the same terminology as the Gang of Four administration ("a handful of bad elements"), chose repression. When the old Guomindang Government tried to suppress the Communists, it referred to them as "a small group of bandits." *Plus ça change, plus c'est la même chose:* eventually even the clichés become part of the farce.

Since they were cut off from the official media, the activists developed a three-pronged strategy: create their own press, spread the word around the country and stay available to the Western correspondents (or at least those journalists who were interested). There are those, both inside the Chinese Government and among foreign observers, who have pushed the theory that the activist movement could not have existed without the foreign correspondents. That is praise indeed for six or seven people at the most. But the accolade can't be accepted, for we too were pawns and were useful in spreading the good news of freedom of speech throughout the world when it was helpful to the government. When such reports ceased being helpful, the government reacted as if we didn't exist. It is also curious that the majority of those arrested during the first crackdown were not in Peking, but in cities like Shanghai, Canton, Chengdu, Wuhan and Sian: for these people, both the struggle and the repression were carried out without benefit of Western news coverage.

The flowering of free expression in China began in the bleak midwinter of Peking, but because of the passion, warmth and expectations it created, many Chinese referred to it as the Peking Spring, since it had similarities to the Prague Spring of 1968, when the Czechoslovakian people briefly shook off the fetters of tyranny. Ever the optimist, I disliked the phrase "Peking Spring" because of what had subsequently happened in Prague when the Soviet troops marched in to obliterate the horrifying spectacle of a people actually trying to work out their own destiny in a free atmosphere.

No Soviet troops would be marching into Peking, that was certain. If the Chinese people wanted to dismantle some of the structure of totalitarianism around them and this was receiving the support of an enlightened Communist Party leadership, there was very little the Soviet Union could do about it. Even when China was in chaos during the first years of the Cultural Revolution, the Soviet Union was not tempted to make serious trouble. As Chairman Mao once said, Soviet troops were welcome to invade China and go as deep into the country as they wanted; they were not, however, welcome to leave. If the Soviet Union was so stupid as to want to control a quarter of the world's population against its will, it would receive a terrifying lesson.

But as the real spring of 1979 approached, it was becoming increasingly clear in Peking that the leadership of the Communist Party was no longer taking an indulgent attitude toward the Xidan movement and might apply stringent curbs of its own. Shortly before Vice-Premier Deng went to the United States in the New Year, Fu Yuehua, the woman activist who had been organizing poor peasants in the city, was arrested. I once saw her in action in front of the gates of Zhong Nan Hai, next to the Forbidden City, where the central offices of the Communist Party and the government are located, along with the homes of many of the leaders. Against a backdrop of ornate roofs which were a reminder of the might of imperial China, and the slogan "Long Live the Glorious Communist Party" (which was a reminder of current realities), Fu Yuehua was leading several hundred poor peasants in a series of chants that decried injustice and starvation.

The sight of the poor peasants, all victims of past political campaigns, who had come from all over China to protest their plight, shocked the relatively affluent citizens of Peking. The sorry state of these people, all suffering from malnutrition and many crippled from various diseases, put the lie to a lot of propaganda. To the credit of the government, it did not directly attack the peasants, although the reasons for this were somewhat complex, as I was to discover later.

Early in 1979, however, they represented a phenomenon into which we were unable to probe very deeply. Late at night on the day I saw Fu Yuehua leading the chants, I drove to the central cable office to file a dispatch. Driving past Zhong Nan Hai, I saw that the peasant protesters were still there, although their numbers were somewhat depleted. Leaving the car at the cable office, I walked back toward the site on the opposite side of the street and lurked in the shadows to watch what was going on.

There was still some sporadic chanting, but it sounded tired and pathetic. Suddenly a young child started to cry out. I guess the cold had become too much and the peasants' appalling rags were not much protection. At this point, I saw Fu Yuehua run toward the child, open her coat and enfold the sobbing youngster next to her body. The child was probably about five or six, and its head popped out of her coat. With her arms around the child and still on her knees, she swayed back and forth. The sight overwhelmed me. I vowed then that somehow I would find out more about the business.

A few days later, Fu Yuehua was arrested under mysterious circumstances, and we heard about it only through a wall poster. A friend of mine who knew her well told me much later that he had had a discussion with her shortly before the arrest in which she had expressed frustration at not knowing what to do next. The marches to Zhong Nan Hai had brought attention to the peasants' plight, but this didn't seem to bring about any further action, and she frankly felt at a dead end. She was close to despair.

On top of this were her own personal problems. Some years before, an official at the place where she worked had tried to rape her, but when she pressed charges it was the official who came off scot-free, while she was subsequently victimized and ostracized at her work. A lot of her passion and commitment had arisen from the central injustice of her own situation. When the peasants came to Peking to complain about their own battles against injustice, the logic of joining forces with them seemed obvious and compelling. Fu Yuehua set about trying to organize a kind of united front. Their grievances were just, they felt, the times were propitious and she was clearly a woman with a mission. As far as I was concerned, her threat to the state was epitomized by that simple act of common decency, when she shared her coat and body heat with a frozen, frightened child: it was humanity versus institutional obduracy.

I never got to know Wei Jingshen well either. Like Fu Yuehua, he was in his early thirties, but after that, all similarities ceased, except that they were both Chairman Mao's children, raised in New China after the Liberation in 1949. A number of details of Wei's life were widely known to many Chinese and some journalists. He was an electrician at the Peking Zoo, but during the Cultural Revolution he had been a ferocious Red Guard and later had been inducted into the People's Liberation Army. His father had minor Party connections. By Chinese standards, he was better off than most. He was also blessed—or rather, cursed—with extraordinary intelligence and equally extraordinary courage.

I met him once, briefly, during the Xidan week in November, but the only vivid detail I remember about him was the smoke stains on his fingers. What I know of him is what anyone who read his polemics knows. In his magazine, *Explorations,* Wei editorialized about the most remarkable poster to appear on the Xidan Democracy Wall. In his article, called "The Fifth Modernization," Wei argued that unless true democracy—and not a sham facsimile—were instituted in China, the much-touted Four Modernizations would never come about. Wei thought it farcical to believe that China could take the technological gains made in the West without evaluating the system which allowed a free atmosphere for research and debate; that atmosphere may have been the reason for the gains in the first place. Without the fifth modernization—true democracy—the other four would come to nothing.

By any critical standard, he was the best political essayist China had produced since Lu Xun, China's greatest writer in the twentieth century. Indeed, Lu Xun may well have been Wei's model, for they shared the same style, which combined logic with remorseless sarcasm toward the things they attacked. It is a style that hits home directly with Chinese people, who enjoy a spirited, pungent debate. There may be better political writers in China than Wei, but they have not been heard from. Certainly no one inside the country has posed a more direct and eloquent challenge to the Communist Party. He had no army and only a few close followers. His only armor was his wit, his only weapon a pen—the most ancient equipment of people with independent, inquiring minds.

As has happened so often before, the state panicked and arrested him. It was apparently incapable of answering his arguments, so it silenced him, even as it was making a conscientious effort to rehabilitate all those who had been unjustly and unfairly victimized in the past for doing the same thing.

The arrest came in March, along with many other bad tidings. On March 16, Foreign Minister Huang Hua announced that the Chinese punitive expedition into Vietnam was over and the troops were coming home. The end of the Vietnam caper, which was proclaimed a great success by the leadership, but which clearly had brought about mixed results, seemed to be the signal to start another punitive expedition against the activists. Four days later, we heard from Chinese sources that Vice-Premier Deng had made a strong and uncompromising speech to a vast throng of officials in Peking. The gist of what Deng was supposed to have said was that certain troublemakers had to be dealt with firmly. It was an echo of the speech reported on the Xidan Democracy Wall made by a Peking municipal official a couple of months before. Deng was said to have denounced antigovernment posters as "counterrevolution-ary," and he called upon citizens, officials and the police to put an end to them. The police, as it turned out, were the only group to respond with unequivocal enthusiasm to the challenge. Municipal edicts were declared, and antigovernment and anti-Party posters were duly prohibited. As April arrived, it was clear that the move-ment for free speech and unhyphenated democracy (which the authorities hyphenated anyway, calling it "ultra-democracy") had received a serious setback, but it was not certain how far the crack-down would go.

It was during this period that I last saw the activist I knew best. His name was Ren Wanding. He was somewhat older than the others, and less well known. I met him first in Tienanmen Square because it was he who had signed his own name to a big human-rights poster at Xidan. We talked hurriedly, but in the open. I learned that he was head of the Chinese Human Rights Alliance, and that he and his group had met with people earlier in the day and answered questions about their controversial poster. Several people were concerned about his call for an end to anti-Soviet propaganda. Ren had responded by saying that China was now friends with Japan and the United States, two formerly bitter ene-mies. After twenty years of relentless vitriol about the Soviet Union, he added, perhaps it was time to reconsider foreign policy in this area, especially if the country was searching for peace and stability. I gathered that the answer was greeted with an acknowl-edgment that this was a good argument, but one person said Ren and his group were nevertheless naive about Soviet aspirations for global domination.

Naiveté, I suppose, was part of Ren's character, but he hardly represented a serious threat to the state. It was his basic premise that human rights would be good for China, that a proper respect for them might have prevented the machinations of the Gang of Four. Eventually the state tried to answer his challenge. It wasn't impres-sive. The *Peking Daily* announced one day that "human rights" was a "bourgeois, European concept" that had no meaning in a country where the people's basic rights were "respected and protected" by the Communist Party. Therefore, the article concluded, any harp-ing after bourgeois human rights was "anti-Party" and "anti-Chinese."

This was exactly the kind of argument, employed with such contempt for the basic intelligence of people, that identified the Gang of Four period in China. It was also the sort of thing that led someone like Wei Jingshen to point out that the tiger had merely changed his stripes, but his fangs were just the same. "I beg you all," he said on a Xidan poster, after reviewing the mind-boggling shifts in Party ideology over the years (which nevertheless didn't seem to lift the totalitarian pall that hung over the Chinese people), "do not let these political swindlers cheat you again!"

Ren Wanding had acted alone in making the decision to sign that first poster with his real name. He had heard the charges the government was making about "underground" activities, so he decided to nip that one in the bud by being so aboveground that no one could accuse him of covert activity. Before long, other groups decided this was a wise policy and even started publishing their headquarters' addresses. During this period, the groups operated under the hope that the Party and government would recognize that this signal act of good faith on the activists' part was a token of their patriotic credentials.

Psychologically, it may have stymied the government for a short time, but the activists also lost all of their cover. They were terribly exposed, with virtually no protection. Perhaps they thought that the scrutiny of the Western journalists might help, but this applied only in Peking—if it applied at all—and was no help to the others in faraway cities. After Wei was arrested and the ban on "anti-Party, anti-government" posters was officially proclaimed at Xidan, Ren Wanding tried to sort things out in his troubled mind. Part of his problem was that he neither liked Wei nor agreed with many of his arguments.

On the night of April 3, we spoke for a long time. He had come to a resolution. The third anniversary of the Tienanmen Incident of April 5, 1976, was rapidly approaching. His group had a magazine published to commemorate the event, but there were no unduly provocative articles in it as far as he could see. The magazine simply traced the historic roots of young Chinese people's democratic aspirations, starting with the May 4 Movement of 1919. He had also decided that on the following morning, he would put up a poster at Xidan protesting the action of the municipal authorities in arresting Wei Jingshen and restricting free speech at the Wall. "It is against the Constitution," he said firmly. "Surely the Constitution of a country has more force than a stupid civic ordinance."

That was Ren Wanding—naiveté and faith. It was obvious that the municipal authorities would never have undertaken such an overt act of repression without the explicit approval of the central government, and Deng Xiaoping's speech was proof that this approval not only was there, but probably originated from the top.

"Don't go down to the Wall tomorrow," I said. "There's sure to be trouble. The police are openly pulling down posters and monitoring everything that goes on."

"I must go there," he said. "There's no choice. If we become silent the very first time there is a serious attack on us, then what we have said over the past months stands for nothing."

He wanted to give me a copy of his new magazine and reached into his satchel to get one. Other papers fell out, and he bent down to pick them up. His glasses fell to the tip of his nose, and as he tried to push them back, more papers came tumbling out. He swore at himself and then laughed.

The next morning Ren went to the Wall at about ten o'clock. After he had glued up a page or two of his *dazibao,* two plainclothes policemen took him away, pinioning his arms behind him. Thugs and hooligans who had obviously been brought to the Wall by the police jeered at him as he was taken away.

I wasn't there to see the agony of this decent, kindly man. I was on an airplane heading home on a brief trip to Canada to receive an award for my reports on how free speech had come to Peking the previous November. I felt I had taken part in a miserable fraud.

15

The Police

Gonganju. The name doesn't mean anything to someone outside China, but inside, the mere mention of it can summon up the
most intense fear and loathing. This is the Public Security Bureau,
the national police force responsible for enforcing "the dictatorship
of the proletariat," and for three decades its all-encompassing powers have grown so sweeping that even its nominal master—the
Chinese Communist Party—has found ample reason to be wary of
its might.

The nature of any nation's police force is the easiest thing to
gauge: all one has to do is mention its name in normal conversation
to a sufficient number of citizens from various walks of life and take
stock of the answers and reactions. This is as true of the Public
Security Bureau as it is of the FBI, Scotland Yard, the KGB or the
RCMP. For a foreigner to bring up the subject of the PSB in polite
conversation with Chinese is very bad form, roughly analagous to
belching at the tea table.

Ironically, democracy activists had the most to fear from the PSB,
yet they were the ones who conscientiously and succinctly tried to
explain and define the role of the police in Chinese society. Along
with a few brave and independent-minded people in the Party, they
were among a minority of citizens who were trying to test and check

the police system to discern whether it had learned to abide by some sort of legality or was simply continuing to follow the current political line. Mentioning the PSB to government cadres, most Chinese friends or ordinary citizens encountered on official visits leads to a dead end of extreme nervousness and tongue-twisting platitudes supplied by government propaganda.

There are always exceptions. Shortly before leaving China, I was talking to a shop clerk at one of the Peking stores for foreigners, where Chinese customers are strictly forbidden. Although he wasn't a friend and had always been completely correct on the few occasions when a political subject arose, he nevertheless enjoyed practicing his English and had a lively, open mind on many matters. We had developed an amusing, bantering relationship, and he was particularly wry on the subject of the dramatically rising prices of the products sold in his store. "Just think of it as your personal contribution to the Four Modernizations," he said one day as I winced at the tripling of a particular price. There was a sardonic smile on his face.

At our last encounter, however, I asked after the whereabouts of a colleague of his who hadn't been at the store for several months.

"Gone," said the clerk.

"Gone where?" I persisted. Had he been transferred? Was he sick? This other fellow also had a nice manner, although his English was weak.

Carefully and very slowly, the clerk looked over both of his shoulders (the most clichéd of furtive movements, which never failed to arouse intense anxiety in me throughout my time in China) and said quietly, "He's in trouble. He accepted [foreign] books from a diplomat. They used to meet at Bei Hai [a popular city park] from time to time."

"But what kind of books?" I asked. "What had he done wrong?"

"English books," said the clerk. "He wanted to practice his English—but I don't think they believed him."

I asked the clerk how "they" found out, and he fixed me with such a withering gaze that I thought he was going to spit in my face.

"How long have you been here?" he demanded. The question was asked with more belligerence than I had ever experienced from any Chinese. When I told him it was now over a year, the belligerence turned to exasperation. "How can you ask such a question? They're everywhere."

"They" are the Gonganju, of course, but the name never had to pass either of our lips, and they are indeed almost everywhere. I wasn't quite as dense and naive as the clerk thought, but unlike many Chinese people, I had to be reminded about the omnipresence of the police. Not conditioned from youth to consider the political and "security" implications of everything I did or said, I was guilty of occasional forgetfulness.

Heaven knows, there wasn't much excuse for forgetfulness. It is possible for a foreigner in China to go through the entire time there without any untoward awareness of the Public Security Bureau. An overseas student with his or her nose stuck permanently in a book, business people who singlemindedly pursue sales and eschew any contact beyond their regular spheres of activity, journalists who are content to let the official Chinese news agency do their work, or a diplomat who hides behind protocol and a heavy work load—none of these will ever run afoul of the Gonganju. They may not even have to apply personally for a travel document to get outside Peking if they have Chinese staff.

But if a journalist actually tries to be competent and professional, he or she will inevitably encounter the police, no matter how indirectly, thanks to a multitude of ill-defined but sacrosanct taboos and prohibitions. If that same person goes further and commits the cardinal sin of making Chinese friends, then a nightmare world of secrecy, treachery and fear is suddenly revealed. It is a world that many Chinese have been conditioned to accept as natural, and they have learned many of the tricks necessary to keep it at bay. But the first encounter for an outsider is always memorable.

I had lived a relatively peaceful life in China for the first year, and I had fallen into a familiar pattern of being a professional onlooker in the inscrutable East. I had warm but carefully correct relationships with the household staff and a few Chinese employed at embassies or the Foreign Ministry. Although my nature is such that I never failed to try to make some sort of human contact with Chinese I met in stores or on official visits, it is clear now that I had unconsciously begun to accept the impossibility of having a real friendship or a genuine exchange of opinion and information. I suppose I didn't like accepting this reality, so I never openly admitted it. But it was true enough.

After the events at the Xidan Democracy Wall, however, I was inundated and overwhelmed by the brave new world of possibilities. So it was with a light heart and a great deal of excitement that

I drove to the Peking Hotel one day toward the end of November 1978 for an early rendezvous with a new Chinese acquaintance. The sidewalk outside the hotel had seemed a perfect place to meet. There were always plenty of foreigners about, and Chinese hotel staff walked into and out of the grounds without a care in the world. Or so it had seemed for a year. This particular day was one of great expectations.

Overeager, I had arrived at the hotel fifteen minutes early and parked the car in the ample lot directly in front of the newest section. It was a crisp, cold day; the sun was bright, and the air was unusually clear—so clear, in fact, that it was one of the five or six times a year you could easily see the beautiful Western Hills from Chang An Avenue, a double reminder of the antique splendor of Peking's natural setting and the density of uncontrolled pollution which normally affronted the city's atmosphere.

After five minutes of self-satisfied communion with the glorious day, I saw a Chinese come up to the parking entrance from the street, automatically pull out an identity card and show it to one of the two army guards on duty. I had seen this before in my own apartment compound, and while I had taken note of the fact that Chinese had to fully identify themselves before being allowed access to the forbidden precincts of foreigners, I had never registered the reality. There had been no reason to. Indeed, it was at least another two minutes before it slowly dawned upon me that I was inside the hotel's compound and that my new Chinese friend would never be able to get past the guards.

I shudder now at the series of impulsive actions I took at that juncture. In sight of one of the guards, I drove the car out of the lot and onto the street, backing it up almost to the same guard's station. This action alone had aroused his curiosity, and when I got out and started walking up and down in front of the hotel, I saw out of the corner of my eye that he was taking careful note of my license number. Then, in quick sequence, I started noticing a lot of other things. At the nearby corner of the street there were two uniformed policemen. In addition to the army guards at the hotel's entrance, two other soldiers walked up and down the sidewalk in front of the hotel. Crouched in a corner of a neighboring wall and partly hidden by shrubbery was a thickset young man who seemed keenly interested in my movements. In time, I learned to recognize all the telltale marks of a Chinese plainclothes policeman: the arrogant stance, the leather shoes made in Shanghai, the expensive watch, the better-quality haircut.

This familiar corner of Peking suddenly became completely strange to me. Where before the building and grounds and the passing masses had seemed a familiar, even comfortable, sight, they were now entirely erased from my vision, and all I could see was the custodians and apparatus of "security." Even peasants from out of town who gawked at the massive building from outside the long iron fence were given short, sharp commands to move on. It all came over me so quickly I had no chance even to react when I saw my friend coming.

Although I was to be in far more delicate and dangerous situations in the days to come, I don't think I ever again felt as frightened as I did at that moment. Not for myself. I had my newspaper, my embassy and my special status to protect me; my friend, who was fast approaching, had nothing save the cold embrace of the dictatorship of the proletariat. In an instant, I realized he could never adequately explain the spontaneous and simple mutual curiosity that had drawn us together the first time. I was so utterly transfixed with fear on his behalf that I stood dumb and mute on the sidewalk, unable to move in any direction.

The matter resolved itself easily, and I learned my first and the most important lesson in any relations between Chinese and foreigners. Quickly and astutely, my friend sized up the situation and saw that our splendid meeting place was in reality a badly disguised booby trap. I learned later that the police keep a particularly close watch on the Peking Hotel to separate unsuspicious tourists and unsophisticated Chinese who are under the illusion that friendship or simple acquaintance can be extended beyond a simple "Hello" and "How are you?" on the street to a cup of tea in the hotel cafeteria. If the tourist and the Chinese actually make it past the army guards at the street entrance, they will be stopped at the building entrance by plainclothes police, where the Chinese will be asked for his name and Unit number. That is more than sufficient to send him packing fast, while the disillusioned and shaken tourist stumbles into the hotel lobby to see that huge red-and-gold sign which says, in Chinese and English, "We have friends all over the world."

My friend, obviously, was not unsophisticated. He simply walked past me, without breaking stride, almost imperceptibly giving a little negative shake of the head. Not this time, not this place. When in any doubt about relationships in China, I always took my lead from the Chinese. Even when certain precautions seemed absurd beyond belief, I always did as bidden: they knew their country and its institutions far better than I did.

Given the continuing feudal legacy of China and the devastating fascist period it went through during and after the Cultural Revolution, it is perhaps important to realize that the Gonganju is not as despicable and ghastly as the Nazi Gestapo was or the Soviet KGB is, although the Chinese police can certainly use Gestapo and KGB methods when called upon. Unlike the Soviet Union, however, where political power largely rests with those who can gain the ascendancy over the police apparatus, power in Communist China has increasingly been held by those who had confident connections with the People's Liberation Army, an institution less ominous and more fully integrated into everyday life than the police.

This distinction is no doubt lost on many citizens who have become victims of the strong arm and arbitrary actions of the Public Security Bureau; but theoretically at least, it does hold out some hope that the Chinese can one day progress beyond a police state more naturally than can other Communist countries. Also, there are genuinely progressive people within the force, who are trying to bring about changes in police thinking. Allied to this is a healthy, almost anarchistic, disrespect for the police among the masses, which registers itself in the most unusual ways.

Six months after we arrived in China, we went to an exciting soccer game at the Workers' Stadium a few blocks away from our home in San Li Tun. We usually walked to this stadium because it was close and, more important, because it was possible, for however brief a time, to immerse ourselves in the happy crowds under the cover of night and forget that we were foreigners. The stadium holds eighty thousand people, but the reality of such a figure doesn't hit you until the end, when the entire throng, almost at once, makes for the bicycle stands and bus stops. It is an incredible tidal wave of humanity that surges out of the main entrance, and if you are near the head of it, you can see wise Chinese scurrying away from its path.

There are always large numbers of uniformed police at these games, and it struck me as curious that they did so little to direct and control the dispersing crowd. Then I discovered the reason. On this particular night, a young officer had got trapped in the middle of the wave. I caught glimpses of him every now and then as I too was being pushed along by the dense crowd. His hat had been tossed up and lost long ago, the red cloth badges on his white collar had been torn off and his face was contorted with pain. I had no idea what was happening to him, and it was impossible to stop and make inquiries. Eventually we got outside the stadium gates and off to one side of the crowd. Then, very suddenly, I saw the officer propelled from the crowd, much the way a baby porpoise is propelled out of its mother's womb.

He lay moaning and rocking on the ground, clutching his genitals with both hands, until a pair of other police officers saw him and came running over to carry him away. The pummeling he got must have been ferocious, and at the time, I was genuinely shocked, not only that the crowd had had the nerve to do this, but also because, as far as I could see, it had been unprovoked. It wasn't until later, as I repeatedly observed the number of picayune and despicable ways the police intrude upon the ordinary citizen's life, that I realized such mass occasions afforded a unique opportunity to settle scores with a hated symbol.

When I first came to China, I loathed the phrase "Chinese masses." This was partly because of my own individualistic and Western upbringing, but it also had a great deal to do with the unconscionable use made of the term by the Party propaganda department in any number of political campaigns. In thirty years of Chinese Communist history, there have been more despots and charlatans unctuously wrapping themselves in the infallibility of the Chinese masses than anyone could possibly begin to count. What took time to learn was that in their masses, the Chinese people really are quite a force to reckon with, for good or evil, and no one knows it better than the Chinese themselves when they are in the state of being amassed. It is for this reason the government fears any large gathering it has not ordained and over which its forces are not in full control. This fear is always manifested by the presence and work of the police, either openly or covertly, but the Gonganju rarely allows itself to be caught in the kind of spontaneous trap the soccer crowd so successfully set.

Although frustrating, it would be less depressing if one could report that this view of the police was confined to difficult foreigners who don't know their place and undisciplined "bad elements" among the Chinese. But the sad truth is that police work in China is so hopelessly caught up in political struggle that the police have difficulty in distinguishing genuine crime from natural curiosity and political debate from treason. It was not always this way, and a great deal of the blame can be attributed to the capricious use made of police power under Mao Tsetung's rule.

In the first years after the Communist victory of 1949, when the Party set about to consolidate its power and began the arduous task of reconstructing a broken and ravished country, there were many examples of arbitrary police actions against both innocent and guilty parties, but they were restrained in comparison with the corruption and atrocious cruelty of the Guomindang forces of law and order. Contrast alone gave the Communists wide leverage in consolidating their power, and in a number of cases, the police may well have been a restraining influence on people eager for more blood from "class enemies" than the government thought prudent. Mao's great experiment in reeducating the masses and raising their consciousness did not usually call for police intimidation, and it was not until the regime's failures started producing widespread discontent, in the late fifties, that the Gonganju became inextricably involved in political coercion.

Early foreign experts, who came to China long before the Cultural Revolution, talk wistfully of the friendly, open nature of relationships then, and the common aim to rebuild the country which united so many people from different sections of society. This is something of a nostalgic myth, but it at least represents an accepted standard much higher than today's. In fact, early on the government had institutionalized the wretched business of putting "black" labels on people, and Party policy was systematically snuffing out alternative voices in the nation's cultural and political life. Increasingly, the methods employed required the use of the police, and the Gonganju was more than willing to take on an expanded role.

Its first major test in a large-scale political campaign after the reconstruction period was the nationwide Anti-Rightist Campaign of 1957, when hundreds of thousands of people were imprisoned, driven to suicide or hounded out of their jobs. Even with the best of police forces, such a vast action, carried out in a blaze of publicity and the white heat of the political leadership's maniacal rhetoric, would have resulted in abuses. In a country without a systematic and comprehensive code of laws and only the most nebulous guidelines for correct behavior, the Gonganju simply went wild and began a pattern of activity that would be repeated many times thereafter.

Because these campaigns were political in nature—part of Mao's never-ending class struggle—the whole concept of crime was transformed, and the police soon learned that there were few barriers to their actions. Certainly, police investigators were cautious when treading in the territory of powerful state leaders, but before the Cultural Revolution was formally brought to an end, in 1977, they were fully aware that while state leaders come and go, the police go on as always. One of the most significant struggles of the Communist Party in the post-Mao era has been to try to prevent the police from intruding into internal Party matters. You can be sure that when the game was played on that high a level, the repercussions in more humble hearths were even more deadly.

I was constantly shocked by the triviality of police snooping in China. In the early days of the democracy movement, I was so far from being cynical as to warrant classification among the simpleminded. One incident, in retrospect, stands out as another act of unthinking folly and carelessness, which I bitterly regret.

Two of my friends were hoping to become writers someday. Both of them were in their mid-twenties, and they were among the earliest friends I made as a result of the open talks at the Xidan Wall. They were often invited to our apartment, and nothing in the world could have been more open or natural. Anyone who wanted to know who they were could have found out with a minimum of fuss. They wore their school pins on the outside of their jackets, and they always took a bus directly back to their institute after a visit.

One day, at my suggestion, we took some pictures of each other as a souvenir of friendship. Picture taking is a great ritual in China. The formal and often hilariously ludicrous posing takes a long time, while the very fact that you are committing your friendship to the permanency of photography is a statement of considerable import. Our friends were obviously proud to have a record of a friendship with a foreigner, and I was beside myself with pleasure that they had accepted me as a fellow member of the human race. So the pictures were taken, and I asked them if they thought it would be all right if I had them developed at one of the Peking photo shops. Of course it was, they said. They even acted a little taken aback that I should suggest getting them sent to Hong Kong, where the developing could be done "more safely."

Two months later, I discovered beyond any doubt that the Gonganju had visited the photo shop, having been tipped off by one of its numerous underlings who, in this case, worked there. The police had come to formally demand extra prints for their own files. I look at the pictures now, and the transparent innocence of everyone makes the whole thing seem that much more pathetic. As far as I know, the police have so far not even approached my two friends. Nor have they gone to their institute to register an indirect warning —all of which makes you wonder why they bothered having a record of such a trivial, personal nature.

The answer is very simple. As the police have watched the ebb and flow of political debate in China, they know that today's innocent action can be useful ammunition in tomorrow's political campaign. Given another Anti-Rightist Campaign or even a small-scale "internal correction," one can be absolutely certain that the police will have an ample and ready roster of new victims to serve up to satisfy the leadership that it is keeping on top of things. Mao once said, in a much-quoted statement which has won the endorsement of Chairman Hua and Vice-Premier Deng, that "ninety-five percent of the people are good and only five percent are bad." With a population hovering around a billion, this means that a minimum of fifty million people are officially up to no good, whether they know it or not. With statistics like this, any police force would find itself hard-pressed to keep up with events, even one as overstaffed as the Gonganju. (Statistics are not available on the full size of the force, but it always seemed to me that there were at least twice as many uniformed police on duty in any Chinese city as in cities of the same size in the West—and this estimate obviously does not include plainclothes police or their spies, bullyboys and contacts.)

Curiously, though, the Public Security Bureau is not very good at some of the most basic work all police forces are expected to do. Perhaps it is not fair to give a foreigner's perspective on this, because I saw the police through very distorted lenses. If there is a theft or an act of violence inside one of our compounds, for example, the police may take note of the event if it is reported, but they will rarely do anything about it. The state of lawlessness inside the compounds is a scandal, but in this area at least, the Gonganju are under strict guidelines from the government on relations with the foreign community.

In Chinese domestic quarrels and other small social problems

that require police attention, the police have a decent enough reputation among the people and can even be a help. Their role here
is simply an extension of the neighborhood or commune committees, and they are called in only if the problem requires some
reinforcement more compelling than the local authorities can summon up. I witnessed one such action in January 1979 in Peking's
Drum Tower neighborhood. A fourteen-year-old girl had become
deeply troubled because of the incessant bickering between her
mother and father and decided she would run away from home. For
two days she hid out at a friend's house, on the pretext that her
parents were away and she didn't want to stay alone at her home.
The worried parents approached her schoolteacher, and the teacher
made investigations and soon tracked the girl down, but she was
adamant in refusing to return home. Eventually the local police
were brought in; a sympathetic officer arrived, did a creditable job
of discovering the roots of the problem and persuaded the girl to
go home.

Because this was China, the matter didn't stop there. The police
officer returned to the girl's home several times during the next
month and even took it upon himself to visit immediate neighbors
to get them involved. He discovered that the girl had received
regular clouts from her father, who was warned that any repetition
would land him in serious trouble. I'm not so sure we in the West
would like this business of involving everyone and his neighbor in
private family affairs, and heaven knows, both the police and the
neighborhood committees can be monstrous snoops, with no good
intentions. But in this case, certainly, the system worked for the
girl, and the police work was laudable.

In the case of "irresolvable contradictions among the masses"—
that is to say, robbery, murder, graft, rape, bashings—I rarely heard
anything but expressions of contempt for the Gonganju from Chinese. Xiao Qi, a friend who worked in a bicycle factory, was beaten
up by a street gang one night, a short distance from his home. He
was brought to his knees and kicked so severely in the head that
he needed sixteen stitches. More than forty people watched his
ordeal and did nothing to help him. He was robbed of a few yuan
and left bleeding on the street. The police hardly investigated. For
one thing, such gangs—which have been widespread in many Chinese cities for several years and are part of the legacy of the Cultural
Revolution—are bad publicity for socialism in China and have only

recently been acknowledged. So many bashings were administered in public with official approval in the past that the wisest citizens stay clear of involvement.

Xiao Qi is a rather special person and a genuine humanist. After he had absorbed the loss of face of being bested in the assault—an enduring Chinese trait—he told me he was no longer angry at the thugs; they were products of their background and the system. But his contempt for the police and their inability to properly investigate his case or cope with the overall problem was considerable.

"The Gonganju are very clever in spotting foreign journalists and foreign students talking to Chinese," he said to me one night, his head still wrapped in bandages from his bashing. "They can see that the foreigners' clothes and facial features are different from Chinese, so they know something evil is going on. Really! They are first-rate at being able to tell the difference between a foreigner and a Chinese. But they are not very good at protecting people from ordinary bandits."

So many tourists have come to China and marveled at the unlocked hotel rooms that it is a little hard to convince them of the reality of crime in China. The "used razor-blade saga" has entered the mythology of our age and found such universal approval that no one really wants to know the truth. (In this saga, which has countless variations, a tourist tries to discard a used razor blade, but his cheerful and utterly honest Chinese guide or floor boy brings it to him, just before his departure. It could also be a discarded ball-point pen or an empty throwaway lighter. I once heard of a used condom being washed—a Chinese practice—and returned, but I decided the tale was apocryphal because it was too appalling, even if true.) Just as the Western press and folklore screen out good news and deeds in favor of the malefactions of the human race, so the official Chinese propaganda used to screen out bad deeds, except when they were useful as "negative examples." If he is secretly or openly sickened by the seeming selfishness and material avariciousness of fellow Westerners, there is no more willing dupe for this kind of Chinese propaganda than the jaded middle-class tourist or cleric or academic expert: the easily observed mania of all Chinese to lock every drawer, cupboard or bicycle notwithstanding.

In fact there is a great deal of petty thievery in China, or at least that's what we would call it. For Chinese, the theft of a few yuan or a sweater and a pair of leather shoes, or especially a bicycle, can be an economic debacle that we would have to translate into jewelry, automobiles or credit cards to understand the degree of annoyance and frustration. It's almost the case that a Chinese man is not properly attired unless he has at least five or six keys dangling from a short chain attached to a belt loop. Many Chinese have things stolen from them and report it to the police; I have never heard of anyone who has ever managed to retrieve the stolen goods. Chinese do not steal from foreigners as a rule because if they are caught, the repercussions are known to be hideous; but they often steal from each other, and they usually get away with it because the police are usually too busy with class enemies to bother about ordinary criminals, who, in any event, are not supposed to exist in any significant numbers.

The Communist Party has begun a campaign to reorient the Gonganju from being an enforcer of political thought to being a more effective custodian of law and order, but it's going to be a long, uphill struggle. There is every reason to believe that the police establishment will successfully resist too great a change because it knows that a one-party totalitarian state always needs a political thought enforcer eventually.

Still, the opening salvos of the campaign to upgrade the Public Security Bureau were fascinating because they provided the first important glimpse into the philosophy and practice of the police from the inside. After the purge of the Gang of Four, the Party slowly began the process of regrouping its shattered forces. There was an immediate understanding that the police had become so enmeshed in the Party structure that it was almost impossible to breathe without inciting suspicion. Stern warnings went out that the Gonganju must stay completely away from internal Party debate. It has done so, but not because it recognizes the error of its past ways. A European foreign expert who established a good relationship with a middle-level police cadre for a few months explained it this way:

"The Gonganju was needed to mop up after the decision had been taken to get rid of the radical Maoist faction. This was natural work for them, and when the new government, which was determined to bring sweeping changes to the country, decreed that the police stay clear of future internal squabblings, they did so because they understood clearly what the order meant: stay clear until we need you again. When it became necessary to keep tabs on Chinese meeting foreigners or crack down on democracy activists or flatten the enthusiasm of strike-prone Shanghai workers, they were completely ready for the job. All police forces get buffeted from time to time, but they know one thing: through revolutions, political-line changes and the fall of governments, the police are eternal. Throughout the world, there is a built-in historical perspective on the function of police, and the Gonganju is certainly no exception."

The buffeting can get rough, though. As the Communist Party sought to reassert its moral authority, it became absolutely necessary to redress the grievances of the past and rehabilitate those Party veterans and other loyal citizens who had been victims of grievous injustices through no real fault of their own. This included high-ranking state leaders who were humiliated or even driven to suicide during the Cultural Revolution, as well as hundreds of thousands of ordinary people who had had to be served up as victims during such witch-hunts as the Anti-Rightist Campaign because the system arbitrarily demanded a quota of villains, whether they existed or not.

The police were not originators of the campaigns and persecution, but inevitably, they were the most visible enforcers. Consequently, as all these people were being rehabilitated, there was a natural focus on recent police history, and the Gonganju began smarting. In September 1979, the *People's Daily* carried a remarkable report on a regional-level police conference held in the capital under the auspices of the Public Security Bureau leadership. The article quoted the police establishment's own internal magazine, *Public Security* (never before heard of by Westerners) as proof that there was a deep-rooted malaise inside the force, particularly over the number of rehabilitations, which reflected badly on the Gonganju's work. The nation's chief police official, Liu Jianfu, delivered a modest self-criticism (not itemized), and the *People's Daily* said that the anger of certain officials at the publicity surrounding the rehabilitation process was a sign that the police had not made a correct adjustment to the new course the country was set on. The official paper of the Communist Party went on to quote the president of the Supreme People's Court, He Lanjie, who said that it was imperative that the police start making "a clear distinction between criminal actions and ideological work."

As with so many of these brave utterances during the post-Mao period, practice quickly belied the theory. Within weeks of this statement, the Gonganju was marching four abreast to the Xidan Democracy Wall to arrest people for their political thoughts and censor theoretical essays on wall posters because they had been deemed criminal (or "counterrevolutionary"). The police aren't the villains here. They are just the police. When the government itself is unable to make "a clear distinction" between criminal actions and political debate, however ideologically uncomfortable, there is not a hope in heaven or hell that their minions will be up to the job.

In May 1979, I learned indirectly that I had received a kind of backhanded honor. The Gonganju had put a cap on me. "Cap" and "label" are the terms Chinese use when a person has been defined as a bad element of some sort. If, as a Chinese citizen, you have been thus capped, life can become hell because the business will affect your work, your private life and your security. A cap is to be avoided at all costs. The police had given me the cap of "international spy." This was announced at a large meeting of PSB officers earlier in the spring. The curious thing was that it didn't directly affect me. The cap was simply for "internal reference." My relations with the Foreign Ministry continued as before, and I experienced no problems in getting travel visas for trips around the country. But with that cap, I knew I was marked.

Wherever and whenever the bureau car traveled, its license number was well known. I began going out of my way to avoid neighborhoods where I knew certain friends lived, because I didn't want to give them trouble simply by passing by. When I went outside Peking, word was obviously passed along, and for the first time, I started noting that I was being trailed on my rambles through other cities. This all reached a ludicrous pitch in Qufu (pronounced "choo-fu"), the birthplace of Confucius, where an inept PSB plainclothes officer made such a dismal show of tracking me that even the peasants in the street started having some good laughs. Back in Peking, the final word came from an Australian journalist, Richard Thwaites, who had been active in his work and had good Chinese contacts but hadn't been capped as an international spy. "I'm outraged and humiliated," he said about his exclusion. "This is a slander against my work, and I've got a good mind to write an official letter of protest to the PSB."

A foreign journalist gets a very one-sided view of the police in China. In the less frantic world of the countryside, where most of

China's population lives and where the strains and threats come from different quarters, the police are a more natural and less oppressive part of the setting. They fit into a more traditional picture, where the enduring struggle to make the ground produce sufficient food takes precedence—except on those occasions when political mania overwhelms everything.

16

The City Versus
the Country

The Peking Railway Station, just a few blocks from Tienanmen Square, was one of the ten great civic construction projects undertaken in the capital by the Communist government during the 1950s. Hundreds of thousands of Peking citizens labored night and day, and they utterly transformed the ancient face of the city. The most famous project was the Great Hall of the People, which, like the railway station, was completed at breakneck speed. Altogether, they represent an amazing achievement in such a poor country, and most of the people who worked on the projects look on them today with real pride. They are all very ugly buildings, in the Stalinist style, and their construction often necessitated the destruction of ancient monuments and sites whose loss is tragic for Chinese culture. But the buildings have such an aura of permanence that one thinks they have been there forever.

I liked the railway station best because it was always a hive of frantic activity. At almost any hour of the day or night, you could go to the railway station and catch a glimpse of the pungent, colorful variety in Chinese life. City residents went off to visit relatives in other cities or in the countryside; young soldiers on new assignments tried to strike poses of self-importance and purposefulness; officials on assignments set off to go all over the nation. The atmosphere of adventure and expectation is always at a high pitch at the railway station, and the numbers simply add to the excitement.

Foreigners who come to China and think everyone is dressed the same and looks the same should be required to spend an hour at the railway station just gawking. If you take a simple walk around the perimeter of the grounds, the diversity of what you will see is remarkable. The railway station is not just a place of departure, of course; it is also where thousands of Chinese citizens arrive each day. Trains from Sichuan province or Guangxi Autonomous Region disgorge hundreds of people, who find themselves suddenly mingling with sharp-eyed Shanghai types and the lumbering, solid souls from Shandong province.

There are also huge numbers of people in transit, who camp outside the station building itself, waiting for the next train connection. As you walk from the freight and customs section to the east of the main entrance, you have to pick your way through a stream of people scurrying either in or out, and also be careful not to trip over all the bodies sitting or squatting on the pavement. Some even lie down, their heads propped up by bedrolls. Children scamper about, and there, in a corner, you might catch sight of a pretty young peasant woman carefully going through her hair with a wooden comb to hunt out some tenacious lice, or an old codger sucking away on his long-stemmed pipe. Suitcases, dunnage and huge bundles carried on shoulder poles define squatting territory, and families often build small enclosures with their belongings to pen in the smallest children. Hot buns, fruit and bowls of rice gruel are sold by vendors who bark out their products' virtues, as lineups quickly form beside their small stalls. Always, it seems, there are a couple of old women pushing along dilapidated white carts, each containing a large, cold thermos jar full of watery-tasting popsicles, sold for only a few pennies.

Inside the station, the loudspeakers are kept at maximum volume and blare out jaunty airs and train announcements. The vast central concourse is dominated by two long escalators and several huge paintings depicting either historical revolutionary events or socialist construction projects. A few slogans, usually printed with white characters on a red background, urge the masses to do such things as "Work Full Out for the Four Modernizations"—pretty tame stuff compared with the fire-and-brimstone slogans of the Cultural Revolution.

Not everyone in the station is there on travel business. Overlooking the main concourse is a large gallery which you reach by taking an escalator, and as often as not you will find dozens of street-smart city youths leaning over the railing, talking and laughing in an extremely animated way. They are watching what they clearly think is one of the best shows in town, something we might call "Country Peasants on the Escalators." Ranged along the gallery railing, the youths try to spot the most awkward and simply dressed country folk coming through the main doors. When they see a likely-looking specimen, they will quickly shake their friends' arms and shout, "*Laile, laile, laile*" ("Coming, coming, coming"). Then their eyes will widen and they will watch the progress of the unfortunate soul —or better still, a whole family—as he or she approaches the bottom of the escalator with mounting trepidation. For many country people coming to Peking the first time, the railway station is probably the biggest building they have ever seen, and these moving staircases are obviously a source of both wonder and fear. With a surging crowd behind them, there isn't much choice but to keep moving along, and when an inexperienced peasant balks at getting on the escalator, it causes a chaotic traffic jam all the way back to the main entrance. The youths upstairs, who can see the whole concourse below them, love the sight of this disruption. And this is just Act One.

Although they have obviously seen the routine before, the youths break up at the sight of Act Two: often a peasant man lifts one leg way up, waiting for the right moment to bring it crashing down on the first moving step he has the nerve to mount. This action thrusts him onto the escalator like a missile released from a catapult. Sometimes he falls under his own overexertion, and at the very least, he has a hard time keeping a precarious grip on his unwieldy luggage. It takes a little while before he realizes that simply by standing still, he is moving. The youths watch all this with wicked glee. It's terrific sport, and the more often the show is repeated, the funnier it is.

Because the escalators are very long, the victim has usually recovered his equilibrium halfway up and the youths prepare themselves for Act Three—getting off. It is particularly good fun if the peasant is carrying his belongings on a shoulder pole and there are a few young children who have to be watched as well. As the victim nears the end of the escalator run, he braces himself, his pole and his children for the landing. You can see the concern on his face, made all the more acute because the escalator doesn't stop to give him a chance to work things out. A leg is brought up again in preparation for the exit, and this time it is really raised high. The climax of the whole show as far as the youths are concerned is here, and as the peasant is hurtled off the escalator, they are practically on the floor, rolling around with laughter. On a really good day, the peasant will stumble to his knees as soon as he gets off, causing chaos all the way back down the escalator.

Watching simple peasants confront big-city ways at the railway station is evidently a good source of amusement for at least an hour. Later, when many of these same smart alecks get a little older and find themselves sent down to the countryside to learn what life in China is really like for the overwhelming majority of the population, the joke will be reversed. It will be the turn of the peasants to laugh at the spoiled and pampered offspring of the cities. Unless they have well-connected parents, or manage to get the kind of education that will allow them to find jobs in the city, these young people will discover that the route to the countryside is as inevitable as the run on the escalator. The population of China's cities is rigidly controlled, and until the birthrate becomes static and the industrial base substantially expanded, redundant city youths will find themselves drawers of dung-water and hewers of cabbages.

"I hated life in the countryside," said Xiao Gu (pronounced "shao gu") one day in his own home. Gu was an extremely amenable and interesting fellow who along with his classmates had been sent down to a rural commune about two hundred miles from Peking in 1974. He had completed his middle-school education and knew, in those days, that he had no choice. He was luckier than most, though, because he had an impeccable class background, thanks to his peasant grandfather, who had been an early supporter of the Communists. His parents had low-profile but solid positions in the bureaucracy, and he was confident that he would be back in Peking within a few years. That confidence was rewarded when he was accepted as a student at Peking University in 1978.

Life in the country had changed him. Initially he was horrified at how backward things were, especially since they were in such sharp contrast to the confident propaganda that was a part of his elementary and high school education. But he had learned self-reliance in the countryside and came to respect the practical attitudes and hardy resourcefulness of many of the peasants he met. In this he was unusual, since most educated youths don't bother to disguise their contempt for country people and ways.

"It was a horrible life for someone used to a city," he said, expanding on his favorite subject, "but I shall always be grateful I had the experience. And I am luckier than most. I am back in the city. The most important lesson I learned was that conditions have to be improved in the countryside, and as quickly as possible, or else China doesn't stand a chance in the future. We will be destroyed by our own backwardness. The contrast of living conditions between the city and the countryside is too awful, too great, and the people know this. When I hear my parents' friends saying that the wall posters at Xidan are 'undermining stability and unity,' I just want to laugh out loud. The biggest threat to stability and unity is the poverty of the peasants. I have learned that lesson well, and it is in my blood now. Somehow, I want to work to improve conditions when I graduate. I see it as a duty."

Xiao Gu was not one of those who criticized the Communist Party as a matter of course. Nor had his experience in the countryside, at such odds with what he had been told to expect, turned him into a cynic. He had faith in the Party's ability to eventually solve many problems, provided it went about reform and development in a logical and concerned fashion, always taking into account peasant concerns. Perhaps he could be accused of false optimism because he enjoyed many privileges denied to most Chinese. His family's apartment, while hardly opulent by Western standards, was nevertheless comfortable. His university education and his father's connections buttressed his aspirations. Yet he also had a strong conscience and could be brutally objective when discussing the failings he saw around him—no matter what the source.

His ambivalent feelings were also reflected in the fact that he chose to maintain our friendship in dangerous times, long past the period when he could cite naiveté as an excuse to the authorities. By continuing to see me, he was jeopardizing a university career and thus his whole prospects for a relatively happy and secure future. When I tried to discuss this with him, he consistently downplayed the risks and possible repercussions. We had taken certain necessary precautions after the first crackdown, of course, but in the end, these were rather feeble when you consider how conspicuous any foreigner is in an informal relationship with any Chinese. Only someone with an official job dealing with foreigners could feel safe in such a relationship, and then, by definition, the relationship would be of a very shallow nature. (With us, the Huang family of musicians was the only exception.)

"The situation is ridiculous," Xiao Gu recounted. "My parents told me that before Liberation, they had good relationships with foreigners. Even when the Party took over, it was not considered such an evil thing to know some of the foreigners who stayed behind. There was never this horrible fear of consequences. From what I understand, the problem really began with the Anti-Rightist Campaign [1957], when contact with foreigners and foreign ideas became automatically suspicious. And during the Cultural Revolution, it was proof that you were an unrepentant counterrevolutionary. Today it is better, but there are still many problems. So you and I are a bit in advance of what must become a normal situation before too long. It is ridiculous that we are not supposed to be friends, don't you agree? And your job is silly if you don't have the chance to talk to Chinese people and hear what they have to say. Many members of the Party still have a feudal attitude on this matter, although believe me when I tell you that most young people like me long to have a normal relationship with foreign friends."

It was from Xiao Gu and his small circle of close friends that I first started discovering the reality of life in the countryside. They prepared us for the initially astonishing spectacle of the poor peasants' protest marches in Peking and gave us tips on what to look for in any rural communes we might visit as we traveled around the country. Most of all, they helped us to see the vastness and complexity of the Chinese peasantry, and from this we developed some sympathy and appreciation for what the Communist Party had been able to do during its more progressive periods. This was a good antidote to my often arid and impotent feelings of outrage, brought out by the crackdown. It also helped me see a truer picture of China.

At the same time as the Public Security Bureau was arresting Wei Jingshen, the government was also lashing out at the mindless political campaigns that hundreds of millions of peasants had been forced to take part in for several decades. Replacing the wretched bombast about blissfully happy peasants reading the works of Chairman Mao, and thereby learning how to obtain better grain production and raise fatter pigs, stories like the following one began to appear in the national press—a sure sign of how serious discontent down on the commune was. This report, carried by the New China News Agency on March 13, 1979, was printed by several national newspapers and was backed up by some of the most detailed descriptions of actual life in the countryside ever published under Communist rule:

"Morale-boosting posters and slogans painted on boards, quotations from Chairman Mao carved into hillsides, multitudes of red flags planted on construction sites—these things did more harm than good to production," said peasants in Dangtu county of Anhui province.

"We want a substantial increase in both collective and personal income along with growth in production, not a lot of display without substance," they told the New China News Agency recently.

Some of the country's leading officials developed a habit of boasting and doing things arbitrarily under Lin Biao and the Gang of Four. They put up unrealistic slogans such as "Try Out New Things Every Year," "Always Think Big and Do Great Things," and "Think of Ways to Double the Output and Even More Than Double the Output When Drawing Up Quotas."

"We did try out new things every year," said a veteran peasant in the Hongxing [pronounced "hong-shing"] Production Brigade. "Our living conditions, however, remained the same year after year."

In 1974, the peasants there were mobilized for a project to "rearrange the rivers and mountains." They were asked to make the rice paddies into neat squares, even though this would not bring in better harvests. Then they rebuilt a dyke because it had a curve in it. In that winter, the brigade was ordered to build underground irrigation ditches after they were built. Again, in the following year, the peasants set about rebuilding the ditches with concrete. The project stopped halfway to completion when the production brigade ran out of funds.

"We had to put on a great show of working at night when we rebuilt the rice paddies," said the old peasant. "Busloads of visitors were brought in to see how socialism should be built. The county authorities had their vanities satisfied, but we peasants suffered the hardship. Some production teams ran into debt and were unable to pay their members."

"We hope the leading personnel will drive only to points where the roads become too narrow for their cars," said a commune Party secretary. "They need to mix with the people to learn first-hand what the people think and want. From now on, people who like to make ostentatious gestures must be criticized or, if necessary, made to pay for the expenses they have run up. As a final resort, the law must be invoked to punish serious offenses."

It is always a wise policy to follow the lead of many Chinese people when reading anything from the state-controlled press: be suspicious. Even in this blunt and refreshing account of the complaints of peasants, it is important to remember that the government and Party are pushing a new ideological line, and this requires a full dose of abuse for the line it is replacing. The new policies, as far as I could see and learn, were generally popular. Peasants were outraged when their private plots were confiscated by the state in the 1960s, while the increasingly arbitrary actions taken by the central authorities brought about a deep-rooted malaise in agricultural development.

When I traveled to Sichuan province in 1978, a top Party official told me that this amazingly fertile "rice basket" of China was reduced to such chaos and inefficiency by the early 1970s that it had to import grain to feed the people. If a province as agriculturally rich as Sichuan had to import grain, it doesn't take much imagination to realize how terrible conditions must have been in much poorer areas, like Anhwei province.

Ironically, the chaos arose from something at the core of Maoism that was fine and noble. Mao Tsetung was a peasant himself and understood better than anyone else that the only successful revolution in China would be one that rested solidly on a peasant base. It was he who raised the peasant consciousness of China and reversed the social order so that peasant lineage became the definition of a respected class background. Mao consistently argued that unless the peasants were included in the benefits of the revolution, that same revolution—no matter how successful initially—would be doomed to failure.

His policies in the "liberated areas" of northern China before 1949 were concrete proof of the soundness of this approach. They were also in stunning contrast to the slough of corruption, ineffectualness and greed to which the Guomindang Government of Chiang Kaishek had sunk. In the six years following the Communist takeover of the whole country, the government undertook the most far-reaching land-reform program ever known in China's long history. There was broad support for this program, and the Party was held in very high esteem.

"We were all working together in those days," a candid official in Guangdong province explained to me once. "The Party was anxious to show its leadership but had cautioned all the cadres not to impose regulations and plans that went counter to what local people thought was sensible. We were leaders rather than disciplinarians, and we had real prestige among the people. If we tried out something new that didn't work out—like a different system for planting—no one searched for a scapegoat; we just worked very hard to find the correct solution that would do the job properly. It didn't have to wait for approval from Peking.

"By 1957, the working style had started to change for the worse. There was a lot of talk about enemies—like the Rightists—and many cadres stopped listening to the wishes of the people. The most important thing for them was to give a good 'report card' to their superiors, who in turn wanted to send good 'report cards' to the central authorities. Instead of trying to deal with problems, officials had to show how central orders were being enthusiastically obeyed by the masses.

"Mao became impatient to see his revolution expanded and neurotic about those who disagreed with him. This new system required a whole network of lies to support theories that had never been properly tested. During the Great Leap Forward, there were so many lies that even people on the job weren't sure what the truth was.

"Today, the prestige of the Party is very low in the countryside. There have been too many changes in policy and very little honest contact with the people. Even Chairman Mao started taking the peasants for granted. He began to speak on their behalf without speaking directly to them, or if he spoke to peasant leaders, he heard only what he wanted to hear. Right now, the peasants' big demands are consistency and fairness. If the Party meets these demands, then its prestige will once again be high."

Since Mao was given to "metaphysical thought" in the last years of his life—this is the polite phrase some Chinese use—it may have come as a shock to him, if he ever realized it, that raising the peasants' consciousness—historic achievement though it was—did not as a matter of course raise the standard of living. Indeed, for many people during the Great Leap Forward and the Cultural Revolution, the standard of living fell below some Guomindang levels. In religious, rural Chinese households during the old days,

Daoist deities were honored only as long as they delivered the goods. Come bad times or misfortune, a once-favored god could be cast out of household worship with a ferocity that often mystified the students of comparative religion in the West. Mao himself became something of a deity in his time, and came to be regarded by many with precisely the same deference—or lack of it.

The new government of Hua Guofeng and Deng Xiaoping can be credited with learning a few lessons from the malpractice of the past. The new policy of once again "letting local conditions" come into force harks back to those initial post-Liberation reconstruction years, and the practical policies now being carried out have started producing welcome results in the form of renewed enthusiasm and better production.

A colorful symbol of this change for the better can be seen in any of the so-called free markets, which are once again being enthusiastically encouraged in all of China's cities and towns. These markets are outlets for the produce peasants grow on their private plots. It is perhaps wrong to call them "free" in that the state monitors prices and practices very closely, but they do offer Chinese peasants a practical and immediate return for their extra labor. For those customers who purchase food at the markets, there is the blessed relief of not having to use ration coupons, which is well worth the slightly higher prices than those charged in the state stores. Some of the sideline sales at these peasant markets are fascinating because of the evidence they provide of the supreme ingenuity of Chinese peasants if given half a chance. Its most tangible form is the simple children's toys hawked either at the food stalls themselves or by itinerant peddlers who amble throughout the crowds selling their wares.

A large free market was established on the outskirts of Peking in 1979, near the Friendship Guest House. It stretched for a long city block, and the atmosphere was much like that of a medieval European village fair. Shoe repairmen set up shop at one end, right next to a donkey cart full to the top with bales of garlic. Squatting in another place would be a peasant woman with her display of eggs spread out all around her. There would be a few chickens in a crate beside her, and sometimes she would also sell some clay roosters she had made and painted in an imaginative range of colors in her spare time. Baskets of tobacco and herbs filled the air with pleasant aromas, which nevertheless had to fight the omnipresent odor of the nearby latrine. Nearly every bit of human waste in China goes back into the fields, and in case foreigners ever forget this, a random tour of any city street or commune village will eventually remind them of this central and odorous fact.

The toys sold at these markets really were marvelous. Give Chinese peasants some sticks of bamboo, an elastic band and a bit of paper and they will come up with some of the most miraculous gadgets you will find anywhere. My favorite was a double paper windmill on a bamboo stick. When you wave it around in the air to make the wheels move, the action sets off two little paper drums rat-tat-tatting. I have yet to find a Chinese or Western child (or adult, for that matter) who has not become mesmerized with delight at the way it works. Another favorite was a slithery paper snake on a stick which practically rattles with menace when you shake it.

One of the other delights of the markets was to see country types in the city. For so long, the Chinese Communist Government was hell-bent on presenting a particular picture of life in China, and anything that didn't conform to propaganda was kept rigorously hidden from a foreigner's view. When a foreigner went to a model commune, people would be dressed in their best clothes, a fact lost on many tourists who never noticed the contrasts in Chinese clothing—which have more to do with the quality and age of cloth than the particular cut or style. While this policy no doubt sprang from an understandable desire to show the best picture, and Chinese people themselves would want to put their best foot forward when they were being visited by foreign guests, it was nevertheless imposed from above and often degenerated into rather crude theatrics. But at the peasant markets, citizens from the countryside came dressed as they were in their own homes and places of work.

In China, one has to learn to stop making judgments on people based on the way they dress. The seeming uniformity of clothing necessitates, first of all, a concentration on the individual. Even when one is able to start detecting better quality clothing, it is not always a criterion of position or status. Senior officials or their offspring might well prefer to wear rather humble garments, on which patches are displayed as badges of humility. This practice was rife during the Cultural Revolution when a cult of poverty was actually foisted on a people who had known little but poverty—an amazing feat when you consider that Communism's big promise is material advancement.

The dark side of Communist theory and policy as it affected the countryside is all too familiar, and it is a struggle to see any of the positive accomplishments. For one thing, city youths who have been sent down to the countryside and then later manage to return to the cities will rarely give an enthusiastic account of life on the commune. They are too keenly aware of the striking contrasts between the standards of living in the cities and the countryside, and for every person who makes an adjustment after the move and settles into contentment in rural life, there are hundreds fulminating in rage and frustration.

Peasants, who are born and brought up in the country, naturally view the business in a different light. Everyone who has traveled to China and visited a state commune has heard how grateful the peasants are to Chairman Mao and the Communist Party for improving their standard of living. At the model communes, and also at many of those that aren't models, this is undoubtedly true for the majority of people over the age of forty. The lot of Chinese peasants has been sufficiently onerous for so long that the new dignity conferred upon them by the Communists means a great deal. Those model communes are real models, however: the symbol—not the reality—of better things to come. In thousands of hamlets and villages where foreigners are not normally bidden and where the state has made few inroads, save raising the flag and dispossessing a few landlords, the bitterness of peasant life continues.

The urban West has come a long way from its own rural roots and is prone to view life in the countryside through a nostalgic, often romantic haze. We have lost touch with our ancestors who struggled from dawn to dusk to make the soil produce. Karl Marx saw nothing noble in being harnessed to a plow, and because he could so effectively evoke the drudgery and mindlessness of being tied to the land, he won converts all over the world.

Throughout history, Chinese peasants have never asked for a great deal, but when the burden of their work becomes too great and the return too little, they can be easily coerced into revolt. An aroused peasantry led by crafty men has punctured the seeming serenity of the Middle Kingdom for ages, causing the downfall of dynasties and, most recently, the rise of a new social order. This is one of the reasons the Chinese Communist Party works so hard to co-opt peasant discontent.

The government that sprang up in the chaos of the Cultural Revolution forgot this, and the Party was very nearly destroyed. A symptom of the malaise can be seen in a number of stories about Vice-Premier Deng Xiaoping, which have a lot of currency, even if they might be apocryphal. The one that is apparently known best in the countryside—I heard it in five different provinces—concerns the time when Mao first purged Deng, during the Cultural Revolution. Part of the price he had to pay was exile to his native village in Sichuan province, a place he hadn't set eyes on for decades. Upon his arrival, he made a quick tour of the place, and before long, villagers were treated to the surprising spectacle of this usually resilient man overcome by tears. He is said to have been appalled at how little change there had been, despite nearly two decades of Communist rule, and he took the village's enduring poverty as a huge indictment of the Party as a whole. Whether the story is true or not is irrelevant. The importance of it is that many Chinese people know of such places and feel that national leaders should be mortified.

A life in the city, though, insulates many from harsh realities. City dwellers will never have any problem in arranging a visit to country relatives. They can make the arrangements almost as easily as can someone in Toronto or New York who wants to see his grandparents down on the farm. The authorities know that city people won't linger longer than necessary and that there are no enticements in the country that will keep them away from their legal places of work and residence in the city, where services and commodities are in comparative abundance. But let an adventurous peasant youth have an itch to see the big city and problems will immediately arise.

There is no law in China prohibiting country folk from traveling to Peking or Shanghai, but there are indirect restrictions in day-to-day procedure that make it almost impossible, except for those with family there or who are high enough up in the pecking order to be included in once-in-a-lifetime holiday trips.

Let's suppose, just to start off, that our eager peasant lad has saved enough money to pay the train fare to Peking. Since he has no relatives or friends there, he would have to see his Unit leaders to get an authorization to stay at the simplest of hotels in Peking, as well as some special food coupons that can be used outside his own province. In theory, he could get all this, but the very act of asking permission to make such a trip would instantly mark the peasant as a possible troublemaker.

My friend Xiao Gu saw this happen on one occasion in 1974. The local Party secretary decided that the youth making the travel request was clearly up to no good and hounded him and his family for months. The youth's head had been filled with visions of what life was like in Peking, visions supplied by city youths who had been sent down to the countryside. Moreover, he knew that many Chinese young people had traveled extensively in the country during the opening blast of the Cultural Revolution, when he had been too young to take advantage of this unprecedented opportunity. He had an itch to see things for himself, that was all. Before his ordeal was done, that itch had been scratched by every Nosey Parker in his village. The youth, said Xiao Gu, was unusual in that he had shown such interest in the first place. "Most peasants don't see beyond the next meal," he said, in more frustration than contempt.

The contempt, however, is felt by many city dwellers when they contemplate the rural peasantry. In part, it results from the sheer gratitude felt at not being stuck on a commune. I talked to many officials and Party members in Peking who had to undergo stints in the countryside from the Cultural Revolution onward, and the louder they talked about the joys of manual work, the more we knew how much they hated it. And they, at least, had a real stake in such endeavors, which had been institutionalized in the so-called May 16 Cadres' Schools. It was Party policy, until recently, to send cadres down to the countryside "to learn from the peasants." At first, they actually worked alongside ordinary folk, but this was such a shock for them, and produced so much contempt from the peasants, that the policy was quickly adjusted to mean that the cadres should go to special communes where they would have to work only among themselves. This policy now applies to most of the educated youth who are sent down, and this institutionalized segregation—similar to the way the Han Chinese operate in the national-minority areas—makes a mockery of learning anything from anyone. If the cadres had worked reasonably diligently and hadn't committed any serious errors, they would be back in their old jobs before too long. In time, the procedure became so routine it resembled the annual retreats of Catholic priests. Reports of cadres' commitment to the joys of rural endeavor had an almost hysterically hollow ring.

Among the most dramatic events that occurred in Peking during 1979 was the arrival of some of the most oppressed members of the rural population at the very seat of the central government, in

Zhong Nan Hai. The first hint I got of what was going on came from a Chinese friend who had walked along a street near Tienanmen Square toward the end of December 1978. What he saw shocked him to his core.

"It was a terrible sight," he reported shortly afterward. "I didn't think such people existed in our country, and I feel ashamed talking about them. A short distance from the Peking Hotel, there were hundreds of them, dressed only in rags. They were keeping close together to share their warmth in the cold, and all their belongings were in small bundles at their feet. I could not believe these were fellow citizens. I can't describe the shame I felt. When I tried to speak to a few of them, a plainclothes policeman came quickly up to me and asked me what I was doing and who I was. When I said I simply wanted to find out who these people were, he got very angry and started shouting at me not to intrude in affairs I knew nothing about. I left the place quickly after that."

The Xidan Democracy Wall provided the first concrete information. Posters about these poor peasants, and later by them, started appearing, and from these we learned that they had come from all over China to protest the injustices and privation they had lived under "for years." But what injustices? What privation? How many years?

Several days after the first posters went up, the peasants marched along Chang An Avenue from the Peking Hotel to Tienanmen Square and later to the gates of Zhong Nan Hai. During these marches and meetings and, later, for a few furtive moments at an encampment the city authorities had made available to them, it was possible to piece together the story.

All these people, and there were certainly over ten thousand in Peking by late spring, had come to the capital city seeking justice. In one way or another, they had all been victims of various political campaigns in the past. Word had filtered across the land that a just government had taken power in Peking, and so they had come, in a fashion nearly as old as China itself, to the seat of that government to seek this justice for themselves.

The sight of them all together was truly awful. Everyone was badly undernourished, and this came as a shock to both Chinese and foreigners in Peking, who had thought that no matter how poor the country was, people weren't starving anymore. These "petitioners," as the government was to label them, made clear that the history of New China under the Communists had had its fair share of periods of starvation, especially in the early sixties and early seventies, when "we had to eat the bark of trees"—the final food of desperate people on the way to death.

Many citizens of Peking responded to their plight with sympathy and concern. I was with one Chinese office worker on the day of the second march to Zhong Nan Hai in January 1979. His English was far from perfect, but together we managed to have a talk with an old man that left us both shaken. The man in question, whom I would have put at seventy, turned out to be only forty-seven. He had terrible bandy legs which might have been crippled by rickets, and that caused him to pull away from the marchers along the route for a rest. That's how we managed to talk to him.

Born in rural Anhwei province, he had left his native village at a young age, after his father died. There were too many mouths to feed in his family. He eventually ended up in Canton, where he did journeyman work, putting his hand to any odd job he could find. By the mid-fifties, he had managed to build up regular work and even tried to find himself a wife. Then, at the end of the decade, disaster struck. Crop failures and chaotic economic planning had left China with a city population it couldn't possibly feed, and the drastic action of sending many people back to their native villages was taken.

Sent back to his village, which seemed to him as bleak and hopeless as when he left it, the man quickly realized that there was no work for him, nor did he have any family that cared to acknowledge him. There was no call for his skills, and he was reduced to foraging in garbage and begging for handouts to feed himself. His presence was resented from the beginning, and since his affairs were never normalized, he avoided contact with officialdom as much as possible; thus he had little protection.

As an indigent, living on the periphery of life, he was easy prey during the intensive ideological campaigns that ensued, and was gratefully served up by his fellow villagers as a class enemy. One almost got the impression that the villagers kept him alive to be a perpetual sacrificial victim.

As the story emerged, tears began coming from the man's eyes. He would grab impulsively at his rags to emphasize a point, and we noticed with horror that they started to disintegrate at his touch. He had come to Peking to have his situation corrected so that he could live like a man again. Pulling out a few coins—perhaps six fen (about 3 cents)—he said this was all the money he had in the world. During the past fifteen years, he added, he never had more than three mao (20 cents) cash in his pocket.

This was too much for the Chinese man I was with. He pulled some money out of his own pocket and tried to press it into the hands of the man, but the effort was refused with anger. By this time there were about a hundred people around us.

"I came for justice," said the man, his eyes blazing through the tears. "If I wanted to beg I could have remained in my village."

This had a profound effect on everyone who was listening. I wondered how on earth such a destitute soul had managed to make it all the way from Anhwei province to Peking. It seemed an impossible feat. In the end, I didn't ask him to explain because the mood wasn't appropriate for such a question. But I discussed this with quite a number of the petitioners, and they explained that it was just a matter of keeping alert and coming. Some bought platform tickets to get into railway stations, thereby managing to sneak a ride part of the way. Others simply walked most of the way, foraging as they went. Sometimes they would be lucky and get a short lift on the back of a transport truck. All of the petitioners were victims of ideological struggle of one sort or another. Some even carried the tattered pages of some ancient self-criticism they had been forced to write.

The effort to organize the petitioners beyond marches failed after the arrest of Fu Yuehua. Not long afterward, however, the government finally acknowledged their presence in the city and, through the New China News Agency, issued a statement from no less a personage than Chairman Hua himself. The petitioners had "just grievances" which had to be corrected, he said. It was an amazing acknowledgment from any Communist Party leader, but Hua went further by issuing specific commands for correcting the situation, such as urging the legal bodies in the city to hurry up the process of reversing the old political labels that had been put on these victims.

But the wheel of justice, if it moves at all in China, turns very slowly. Six months later many of the petitioners were still in Peking, still protesting injustice and still waiting for the verdicts to be reversed. By this time the government had lost patience on two fronts. The petitioners, said an editorial in the *Peking Daily,* were now causing China "to lose face" in the eyes of the world by their rowdy demonstrations. It was ordered that those demonstrations be halted, and the forces of the militia and Public Security Bureau were employed to this end.

The government also issued another statement criticizing the slowness of the judicial process in reversing the verdicts. Even when some of the petitioners got a favorable verdict, they were reluctant to return to their villages until the central authorities had notified local representatives of the change. Some peasants had gone home in March and April after getting satisfaction in Peking, only to find themselves victims all over again—this time for stirring up trouble against local officials. To remedy this problem, the government announced that it was going to send special work teams under the authority of the Central Committee itself to go to local villages and ensure that the Party's policy was properly carried out.

"I think we can begin to see how useful the petitioners are to the government," Xiao Gu said, after he learned about the special work teams to be dispatched throughout the country. "You know, even Chairman Mao often felt frustrated at his inability to get his orders passed through the bureaucracy. These petitioners may turn out to be a key into the countryside for the new policies of the government. The work teams can use the petitioners' problems to examine the working style of local officials who are reluctant to make changes. People who are not supporting the new policies can be accused of following the Gang of Four. I think this will be good, don't you?"

Good or not, one thing was clear. If the government was sincere in trying to bring about fairer policies for the rural peasantry, this had to be backed up by elemental and reliable justice. That would require more than a few brave speeches in Peking and adjustments in ideology. China's future stability and strength, more than any other country's, depend on how it meets this challenge.

Back in the early fifties, most peasants were eventually convinced of the logic of abandoning their traditional farming practices in favor of collective efforts on communes, because they could see better results. The propaganda work to raise their consciousness and self-esteem was part of the process of transforming agricultural production. The benefits to the state were obvious to the government; more important, the benefits to the peasants were also obvious to the peasants. United, they had protection against natural calamities, which had been the cause of unspeakable tragedies to millions of Chinese for centuries. The flooding of the Yellow River, for example, caused so much damage throughout history that you can still hear the mighty waterway referred to as "China's sorrow." Most of all, in unity the standard of living began to rise appreciably.

In the early years of Communist rule, peasants could make a clear distinction between the necessity of cooperative efforts and their own strongly felt desire to control part of their destiny in small private plots. When that distinction was arbitrarily eradicated by the state, the goodwill and practical resourcefulness of the Chinese peasantry were forfeited. Living standards became static or even fell. It is for this reason that the Communist Party is being forced into the current course of action. The past cannot be reversed. With luck, though, it can be neutralized by consistency in policy and fairness in practice. Without these essential ingredients in a predominantly rural and peasant society, the Four Modernizations will be a farce of tragic and stupendous proportions.

17

The Pleasures of the People

During the formative years following the establishment of the People's Republic of China and in the ensuing period of mass ideological campaigns, which culminated in the Cultural Revolution and its sordid aftermath, a strange notion about Chinese people became firmly rooted in the Western consciousness. It was simply this: being Chinese was all work and no play. If you were a defender of the regime, the work took the form of "building socialism." There have been endless stories in newspapers, books and magazines about all those millions of busy beavers working full out under Chairman Mao's benevolent gaze, trying to "fulfill and even overfulfill" the latest state targets for production in agriculture or industry. To the detractors of Communist rule, only the mindless drudgery of day-to-day work and endless political rectification seemed evident. For both groups, the enjoyment of leisure seemed confined to Party-supervised activities, which received fulsome pictorial coverage in the pages of propaganda magazines like *China Reconstructs*. An ideology that insisted on perpetual class struggle, it appeared, left little time for the pursuit of simple private pleasures.

From time to time, stories would appear in Western newspapers to reinforce both views, like the time during the Cultural Revolution when a few elderly citizens of Peking were physically assaulted by Red Guards and later officially criticized for their seemingly benign hobby of training songbirds to sing. The old men used to bring the little birds in homemade cages, delicately constructed out of sorghum and bamboo sticks, to public parks. This habit was ostensibly to give the birds an airing in the outdoors, but the Red Guards knew better. Songbirds were a "feudal" hangover from decadent days. The old men were wasting valuable time in training the birds, time that could have been devoted to the study of Chairman Mao's Thought. Moreover, there was a secret competition between the men to prove who could produce the best songbirds —a competition proletarian fighters could no longer afford to ignore. The cages were smashed and the birds either killed or set free. On such tales were Western theories of Chinese leisure built.

It was a surprise, therefore, to discover that the vast majority of the people throughout China had a hobby or a pastime that was pursued with a passion far exceeding their enthusiasm for their daily labors in building up socialism. It is true that during the Cultural Revolution many of these hobbies were put aside or kept indoors until the storm subsided, but they never disappeared entirely from view. By the time I arrived, they had returned with a vengeance, so much so that one Hong Kong acquaintance of mine who made regular trips to see relatives in Canton, Shanghai and Tianjin had concluded that the whole nation was riding a vast hobbyhorse.

"No one wastes much effort at work," said the Hong Kong man, who was a typical Chinese denizen of the Crown Colony in that he went full out from dawn to dusk to make as much money as possible. "Why should anyone work hard? There's no real incentive. Until recently, if you tried extra hard to do a good job, you might be accused of putting profit ahead of politics. When I arrive on a visit, all my relatives—and most of their friends—stop work altogether for a week or so, citing illness or some other excuse to their Units. We all have a marvelous time playing cards or going for outings. One cousin is a painter, and I am always obliged to bring some better-quality paints with me. That's the only importance of my trip to him, aside from the fact that he too uses my arrival as an excuse to take time off. But he never wants to talk to me. He'll disappear for the whole week with his paints, and I'll discover later he has been off on a trip with some fellow painters.

"Who needs to go to the theater with the entertainment available in Chinese families? Someone will be sure to be a musician of some sort. Another cousin can do remarkable gymnastic tricks on his bicycle, and we can waste a whole afternoon watching him perform. Some of the younger relatives think they would like to come to Hong Kong, and I always tell them they are crazy. You're living like kings, I tell them. Their salaries are guaranteed, even if they are low. They always seem to have a good two-hour break for lunch and a rest during midday. Their Unit looks after housing for them, and there is plenty of spare time to pursue hobbies or sports.

"In Hong Kong, it's a dog-eat-dog world, and everyone has to fight hard for every penny earned. My father has a small factory in Hong Kong, and he used to hire Chinese who had managed to cross the frontier. But no longer. Socialism has spoiled all the younger people. Even if they have the courage to flee China, they aren't prepared for the hustle and fight of life in Hong Kong. Some even go back to China, knowing they may face punishment for a period. That crazy Communist government is talking about modernizing the country and bringing it up to 'advanced world levels.' In leisure, China is already far ahead of the West—they are in the twenty-first century already. If arts and crafts were a menace to the world, we would never get an easy night's sleep from the threat of China today!"

It is an exaggeration, of course, but there is some truth interspersed in all the sarcasm. Although many Chinese toil very hard for their daily bread, especially in the countryside, improved working conditions and chronic overemployment in most jobs has left a lot of people with an inordinate amount of time on their hands. For some time to come, it seems, the traditional drive and ingenuity of individual Chinese will be directed toward private pleasures and pastimes, except perhaps in those areas where state policy coincides with them. An example is national fitness, from which derives the amazing mania for jogging and Tai Chi Chuan (the ancient, slow-motion version of Chinese shadow boxing) which so impresses foreign visitors.

All this is no doubt a source of frustration to a pragmatic government determined to get a reluctant nation back to hard work, but for a foreigner living or traveling about in China it is also a source of constant delight and fascination. It is also proof of the essential humanity of Chinese people, something outsiders must constantly be reminded about if they are to survive the deluge of ideological propaganda coming from both the Party and those foreign observers who hope somehow to find in the basic propensities of Chinese people something radically different from their own experience and values.

Even foreigners who have no particular axe to grind, one way or another, often swallow the old propaganda whole. I remember vividly the reaction of a correspondent who had worked in Peking during the early seventies and came back for a trip in 1979. In a candid conversation, he and a young Chinese official had rehashed many of the events of those earlier days. On some issues, the official was unclear about certain pronouncements of the government which had been repeated in the press so often they had become cemented in the journalist's mind forever. For example, he will probably go to his grave with the ideological implications of the campaign to criticize the traditional Chinese novel *Water Margin* as his last worldly thought. (This was a campaign that convulsed the entire country, or so foreign observers thought, as the Party leadership sought to use the old novel to get at current enemies.)

"I didn't pay much attention to that campaign," said the official blithely. "It was like so many others, and in my group, we just stopped listening. Anyway, we were too busy reading Western novels like *Love Story* to concentrate on the propaganda."

"*Love Story?*" blurted the journalist. "How on earth did you get your hands on such a book during those days?"

"Oh, in the cities it wasn't very difficult. Quite a number of people had access to restricted materials, or else overseas relatives brought them in. Such books passed quickly to many people. And of course, during the Cultural Revolution many libraries were raided by Red Guards and the first thing they went for was restricted books from Western literature. I could read English, so I was at a great advantage in one way. On the other hand, my knowledge became a heavy burden because I was always under considerable pressure to make translations for friends."

The journalist was flabbergasted. The country had seemed so monolithic to him then that he couldn't even have conceived of such an action. Laughing at himself, he turned to the official and said, "It's stupid, but I feel betrayed. I really thought you were all studying the works of Chairman Mao and looking for class enemies." Commiserating, the official said that everyone *was* studying the chairman's words, so he shouldn't feel so betrayed. "After all," he said, "you had to be able to quote Chairman Mao to survive, so we studied the Little Red Book very diligently. I memorized sixteen new quotations during the time I was reading *Wuthering Heights.*"

A superb place for observing the Chinese at leisure is Ritan Park, which is just a few blocks from the diplomatic compound located in San Li Tun. Ritan Park was a place of worship in ancient days, when emperors ruled from the Imperial City. As in all the city's parks, it was hard until recently to find a single blade of grass, and when one actually did appear, there was sure to be some quick-eyed park worker to snatch up the intruder by its roots. Grass had been declared a breeding ground for mosquitoes twenty-five years before, and with typical thoroughness, nearly every blade in the city had been done away with. The numerous flower arrangements, a bountiful supply of trees and a number of water pools and fountains, however, have made Ritan Park a welcome refuge from the busy streets nearby. A couple of little hills crowned by fanciful pavilions vary the perspective, and to the west there are some handsome traditional buildings which occasionally feature exhibitions of professional and amateur paintings. A larger pavilion to the east, next to a crudely fashioned soccer field, is a favorite haunt of older people, who liked to sit there in the cool shade during the oppressive heat of summer.

The best fun at Ritan Park occurs early in the morning. To see it, or to participate, you have to be prepared to rise at 5:30 A.M. If you arrive as late as 7:30 A.M., the fun will nearly be over. Between those hours, Ritan is a magical place—a jousting ground of the Chinese imagination. The first hint of what is going on inside comes as soon as you pass through any of the three gates. A strange array of sounds fill the air, some shrill and loud and others echoing softly from far away. These are the musicians, both vocalists and instrumentalists. As one walks around the park, they appear in the most unexpected places: behind shrubs, leaning on trees, squatting in a tiny glade. Some of the singers are belting out Western-style songs and arias; others strain their voices to extremity to master the intricate, high-pitched, staccato lyricism of traditional Peking Opera. Flutists and trumpeters abound, and against the piercing shriek of a traditional opera buff, you can often hear a bit of Mozart or Shostakovich being played with wild abandon. Violinists try very hard to find some uncacophonous corner to themselves, being mostly exuberant romantics who prefer solitary trysts with nature and their music.

Nearly everyone is an amateur in the best sense of the word: nonprofessional but extravagantly enamored of his or her choice of endeavor. It is always practiced with single-minded determination, which helps to explain why there are so many good amateur singers in China. But not all are amateurs, and the exceptions provide the best show in Ritan. Over at the eastern pavilion, retired Peking Opera veterans gather once or twice a week for a semi-impromptu jam session. The group at Ritan varies between ten and twenty people, and there are always four or five instrumentalists to accompany the singers. Traditional Chinese instruments, such as the pipa (a bit like a guitar) and the shrill-sounding two-stringed erhu, are carefully brought out of battered old carrying cases. The regulars start things off with a few favorites from famous operas, and within a matter of minutes, a large crowd gathers at the pavilion. The high ceiling gives a nice resonance to the sound, and the old singers soon get right into their former roles with facial grimaces and wild, expository gestures. These sessions are a boon to the amateurs who hover on the sidelines. They know all the roles the old singers used to perform, and they pay close attention to style and delivery, sometimes trying to copy details exactly while singing along under their breath.

After the old pros have made their mark once again, they start calling for amateur volunteers from the crowd. What ensues now is a delightful scene of reticence and ambition. Someone will request a particular aria, and the old singer will turn around to the person who spoke out and say something like "I'm not quite sure how it goes. My mind is getting feeble. Perhaps you could sing it, and then I will have a go at it," or "Well, I'll sing it if you'll take on the part of so-and-so, and then we can do the whole sequence." This request sets off palpitations in the amateur. "No, I sing very badly," one might say, or "It is not proper that I sing in the presence of really good singers like you. I have a terrible voice." This goes on for a few minutes.

You have to realize that the amateurs are all dying to sing in this crowd, especially because of the chance of having really good instrumental accompaniment. The old professional singers try some gentle encouragement, and the crowd starts playing its designated role. *"Lai bulai?"* says someone ("Are you coming or aren't you?"). Sometimes the amateur will be literally pushed to the fore-front, protesting all the while. Once up front, he or she makes a great to-do of self-effacement before the instrumentalists and professionals. Nerves may become too much and the amateur will try to sneak back into the crowd, but no one will make way. If this courting scene goes on for too long, one of the veterans will say, "Let's start together." Invariably, the amateur will begin singing to a wall in the pavilion, with his back resolutely to the audience. As he or she gains in confidence and the old professional steps out of the limelight, the singer will eventually turn around bearing a face wreathed in exultant satisfaction. Cheers will greet the conclusion, and another cajolable victim will be brought to the center.

Strolling away from this happy place toward the soccer field, you will probably find a game in progress, although the ball will rarely be regulation. Soccer balls are expensive, and Peking youths seem able to have fun kicking around any old thing, even a metal tin. Walking through a nearby woods, you eventually get to a clearing where some martial-arts fanatics have set up shop. Both young men and women go at each other with swords and spears in intricately choreographed patterns. Usually an older practitioner is around to offer tips and make corrections after he has done his daily Tai Chi Chuan exercises. Tai Chi can be seen all over the park. People do it either on their own or in groups, and it is particularly popular with older citizens because of its gentle pace.

Those old reprobates, the songbird fanciers, are lined along the pathways where park benches are located. Their feathery friends are in their cages, either on the bench itself or hung up on the branch of a nearby tree. Occasionally, a youngster walking by will try to engage a bird's attention with a sharp whistle or even poke a finger into the cage. This will bring a howl of abuse from the bird's owner, and the youngster will scamper away, delighted at all the fuss he has caused.

At any of the particularly picturesque spots in Ritan, there are always bound to be a few amateur artists hard at work. They sit on small stools in front of their work and never seem to mind the small crowds that gather behind them. If someone openly comments about the good quality of the painting under way, the artist will invariably mutter something to the effect that he is a very poor painter, has never had the chance for proper training and doesn't know why he continues in his hobby when the results are always so bad. Curiously, the style preferred by most amateur painters is impressionistic. This is in startling contrast to the rigorously realistic art pushed by the cultural arbiters of China until very recently. Some amateurs will even force a bit of absurd pointillism into their work, and I imagine this is a bit of a belligerent statement against state-approved art.

Ritan Park, like nearly all the parks of China, is an unending source of fascination early in the morning. Several thousand people are there, but the grounds are large enough to prevent undue crowding. Now that leisure activities are not monitored to the same stifling extent as they were a few years ago, much of the activity is relatively uninhibited, and people are at their most relaxed. A foreigner who is prepared to shed a few inhibitions and enter into the spirit of things can partake fully in the mood. Since everything is out in the open, there is less fear of happenstance contact. Meeting a friend in a park by arrangement can be fraught with trepidation and danger, because there always seems to be someone around who makes it his business to check out any contacts between Chinese and outsiders. Impromptu participation, however, does not appear to threaten anyone—indeed, it is often a chance for Chinese people to show their ordinary courtesy and kindliness. As one who benefited from both qualities on many occasions in Ritan Park, I came to look on the place with almost mystical affection. From experiences there, I also learned to search out the Chinese at their leisure pursuits wherever I went in the country.

In the seventeenth century, when the early Jesuit missionaries were trying to spread the Gospel in China there were various attempts made to make the Mass more Chinese. The Jesuits replaced the ringing of bells when the Host was raised heavenward with the loud crackle of firecrackers. The purpose was the same—to draw attention to the miracle of transubstantiation, when the bread and wine become flesh and blood—but the practice drew the ire of the Jesuits' superiors in Rome and was soon ended. "It was a pity," said Mr. Fei, a former Christian who still enjoys the occasional theological wrangle with foreign diplomats and who now teaches foreigners how to speak Chinese. "All the Chinese people love firecrackers."

Indeed they do. The Jesuits were not the only ones to try to co-opt the practice of setting off firecrackers to celebrate important events and festival days. Three hundred years later, the Communist Party always makes sure a bountiful supply of fuses and powder is made available to the masses on appropriate occasions—usually to celebrate Party deeds. The most spectacular efforts could always be seen at Tienanmen Square on the Chinese national day, October 1. It was quite simply the best fireworks display in the world. But that particular show has been retired for a while. The government of Hua Guofeng and Deng Xiaoping has evidently decided that the annual national-day ceremonies, including the evening fireworks extravaganza, were a pompous display of empty posturing. Now the concentration is on the enjoyment of the holiday, and the major public parks grant free admission all day, as well as simpler entertainments and diversions.

The march-pasts won't be missed, but the fireworks are, and to make up for this lack, the traditional Chinese New Year celebrations made a major comeback in 1978. Throughout the years of the Cultural Revolution, celebrating the New Year—which, after all, was a lunar event and therefore, by definition, superstitious—was distinctly frowned upon. Celebrations didn't end, but they were driven indoors and took the form of quiet, low-key banquets among family members, who went about the business in a somewhat conspiratorial fashion.

China taught the world long ago how to celebrate the coming of the new year with mirth and boisterousness and familial civility, so the restraints imposed on the festival during Mao's declining years were yet another indication of how mean-spirited and petty-minded the people's masters had become. This restraint must have been a particular grievance of many people, because when the word was sent out in 1978 that it was all right to indulge in a (relatively) old-fashioned New Year's celebration, they took to it with a fury that can scarcely be imagined. I happened to be in Canton during the New Year's Festival of 1978. It was a joyous occasion. The crowded downtown streets were a blaze of pyrotechnical mania. Teen-agers seemed to have taken strategic positions on every roof in town. Rockets swooshed upward into the dark sky, and loud cannon crackers were thrust down on unsuspecting pedestrians below.

It was all a bit frightening for a foreigner brought up under the distinct impression that firecrackers were potentially lethal missiles.

The spirit let loose that night might properly be described as benign anarchy. There had been special flower exhibitions in all the parks and on many of the streets, so the Canton air was fragrant. Every ten or twenty seconds, another rocket would light up the night, while the steady din of the cannon crackers and sizzlers never let up till well past 3 A.M.

New Year 1979 brought no abatement in the celebration. In Chien Men, the long shopping street directly south of Tienanmen Square in Peking, there was open warfare. Early in the morning only the real firecracker diehards were left—several thousand of them. Nearly everyone had joined one or another of the factions grouped at various strategic spots along the road. The small hand rockets were the main weapon, and they would be aimed at factions across the street. You needed the courage of a martyr just to run a few steps to new cover under a store portico. I was amazed at the seemingly unlimited firepower of all the factions until I saw that at regular intervals along Chien Men Street, there were special booths, at various stores, that were selling packages of the hand rockets for a few cents.

Every now and then, some poor worker heading off to a night shift or, perhaps, returning home would actually risk cycling down the street—no-man's-land itself. When this happened, all factionalism ceased and the rockets were aimed at the cyclist's wheels. The poor victims never caught on fast enough. There were only two possible defenses: either get off to the sidelines quickly or pedal at double time. The second defense usually had catastrophic results, because the factions were on opposite sides of the street for about a mile down the way and the cyclist would ride into ever-increasing firepower. Occasionally a rocket would get caught in the spokes of a wheel, and there would be a spectacular whirl of flashing sparkles until the cyclist literally jumped off the bike and let it come crashing down.

Undoubtedly, this carrying-on must result in some tragic accidents, although I never actually saw any, in either Canton or Peking. In Hong Kong, the colonial government has banned all firecrackers because of such accidents, and this is certainly a sensible, sane policy. There was some muttering in the *Peking Daily* during 1979 that the same measure might be taken in China, and of course that too would be sane and sensible. But something would be lost in the process. Firecrackers seem to ignite a very specific element in the Chinese soul, at least among many of the young people. There's intrinsic magic in fire, of course, but more than this, fire-crackers unleash an animated fury and wildness in stunning contrast to the order and discipline that the state, as well as the traditional values of Chinese society, puts such a premium on.

In Nanking, the old Guomindang capital in the days of Genera-lissimo Chiang Kaishek, my wife and I set out one early evening to look for a place to eat some local-style food. Eventually we found a likely-looking restaurant far away from our hotel and made our way through an unusually large crowd gathered outside. The down-stairs was packed solid with as many as three hundred diners, and no one seemed in a hurry to leave, which was also unusual. I had been in plenty of Chinese restaurants where expectant diners stand right behind someone sitting at a table and literally glare the eater out of his place after he has gulped down the last morsel.

"We'll never get seated here," I said to Elizabeth as we pushed our way through the crowd.

"Well, let's ask anyway and get ready to run."

The running was necessary if the senior restaurant official was one of those who ordered Chinese diners to vacate a table for "foreign friends." It was a hateful business I refused to be part of, although I suppose it stems from a desire to make foreigners feel welcome and well treated. It had precisely the opposite effect on me. Imagine going into a restaurant and asking for some food, only to find that as many as ten people are told to leave a table so you and your wife can sit down in solitary splendor facing a roomful of eyes watching your every move.

The larger restaurants in China usually have a few private rooms, and foreigners are whisked off to these areas quickly. This is not a pleasant experience either because one would prefer to eat with Chinese citizens, but at least you aren't responsible for some poor soul's being dispatched to a sidewall mid-dinner. Many foreigners think these rooms are specially created for them. They are wrong. Chinese with status are the principal users of the private rooms—cadres, army men, senior bureaucrats and the like. A private room is a major luxury in a crowded restaurant, and many Chinese simply do not understand why some foreigners resent being segregated in this fashion. They are being given the same privileges as the best-connected people in their country.

At the Nanking restaurant, we were inevitably taken off to a large private room, but because of the unusual construction of the old building, I quickly realized that we were being given a unique opportunity to do some unfettered snooping. Consequently, I spared our hosts the usual protest about being excluded from the masses. The restaurant took up all four floors of the building. There was a central courtyard around which the building was constructed, so that every floor featured a generous-sized balcony, each crammed with tables and diners. Our host, who was in an extremely good-natured and jolly mood, soon said that the restaurant had been entirely booked for over a month, except for the room where we would have dinner alone at a table that could seat twenty. Since most of the diners (the restaurant could seat over 1,200 at one time) seemed to be ordinary citizens, and since ordinary citizens in China would never think, or even be able, to book a table, I was considerably intrigued.

"It's the marriage season," said our host. "You have come to Nanking at a happy time." Chuckle, chuckle; nudge, nudge. We got the gist very quickly. Every table featured a bride and a groom, and our host was practically beside himself at the thought of all the consummations to be achieved that night. I asked him to choose some of the restaurant's best dishes for us to eat, insisting that we didn't want a feast. All foreigners in China, it seems, are thought capable of consuming anywhere from ten to sixteen courses at a meal, and you have to be very firm at some places if you don't want to end up bloated like a pig at the slaughterhouse gate. "No problem," he said, and went off. We were left to our own devices, and we started to fan out around the place fast.

"Come quickly," said Elizabeth. "I think there's going to be a speech."

I was never able to figure out the logic of the building and concluded that the architect had been a delightful madman. One interior window, located in a short vestibule just outside our room, overlooked a small, subsidiary courtyard, and across the way, on the floor below, I had a terrific view, within easy listening distance, of a smaller private room where about sixteen young people were seated around a large table. Their ages can be safely guessed. The Chinese Government frowns upon marriage until the man is twenty-eight and the woman twenty-five. This is for reasons of birth control and the shortage of housing for married couples. The merrymakers looked as if they had all turned twenty-five and twenty-eight the day before. One of the men was standing up with a little glass of liquor in his hand and was talking in a very extravagant way.

It was not a toast to the bride. It was a challenge to the other men to fill up their glasses and see if they could keep filling them up longer than he could. Some of the women giggled a little and bent their heads while this great display of manliness ensued. After six fill-ups, the man sensibly stopped without achieving a decisive victory. Perhaps he realized that there was a finite supply of booze, or perhaps he saw the concern on the faces of two of the women who were becoming increasingly less amused.

On the other side of our own room, there were two doors that led out onto different parts of the surrounding balcony. From there could be seen hundreds of diners on various levels partaking in the New China version of a bacchanalian wedding feast. With dozens of brides and dozens of grooms, there was more than enough cause for celebration, and there are few sights more compelling and infectious than watching Chinese in a festive mood. Nearly always, food is central to the occasion, whether it is a simple meal or a mighty banquet or, as was the case at most of the tables in the Nanking restaurant that night, something in between.

The average meal in China would not be very appetizing to most foreigners. It would certainly be a downright disappointment if they were accustomed to their favorite Chinese restaurant back home and thought Chinese cuisine revolved around sweet-and-sour spareribs. Whether on communes or in the city, an enormous amount of food is produced by canteens and eaten quickly—especially the all-important midday meal. It is usually a large bowl of vaguely nutritious slop: a glutinous conglomeration of some vegetables, an occasional piece of meat and a lot of gluey sauce. Starch comes either from a bed of rice at the bottom of the bowl, especially in the south, or from sticky *mantou* (steamed buns), which are a favorite of northerners. The evening meal at home may have more substance if a family can afford it and can secure the produce at a store or market.

What is generally described as ''Chinese cuisine'' in the West is the kind of meal most Chinese would aspire to only a few times a year; but they *do* aspire to it, and therein lies the principal difference between Chinese and Western eating habits, with the notable exception of the French. Chinese people, almost all of them, know what good food is. They don't like soggy vegetables, and they put a high premium on taste and presentation of food when and if they can. Almost nothing, though, goes to waste, certainly not anything even remotely edible. There is a great deal of misunderstanding about this in the West, and some of us shudder at the thought of eating chicken feet, bull's penis and sea slugs, ascribing Chinese enthusiasm for such things to inscrutability or some other appropriately mysterious trait. The simple truth is that if we had as many mouths to feed as China does, we too would suddenly discover that all sorts of food hitherto considered inedible can be consumed.

It is for this reason that the Chinese make such an effort to talk up a particular delicacy which we might consider revolting. The more potentially unpalatable something is, the rarer the sauce it is served with. The more humdrum and ordinary a particular bargain at the market, the greater its advertised benefits will be. I have sat at the table of Chinese friends and had a rather weather-beaten pear described to me in such glowing and magical terms—its aesthetic symmetry, the quality of its juice, its historical antecedents, its ability to bring happiness—that I was salivating before I had even consumed a morsel. The banter reached such a pitch I scarcely noted that it was pulpy and spoiled by several brown spots.

Through food, one begins to see how the Chinese have developed the art of necessity, which is an integral part of the Chinese way of doing things. If given a choice between a perfect pear and a mangy one, no Chinese would hesitate to reach for perfection. But that choice seldom exists, and so a lively imagination is brought to bear on the imperfections of the world. It is perhaps from roots like this that the Communist Party has been able to enjoy some of its success in China from time to time: it too is a product of necessity and has got away with fanciful descriptions of potential good while serving up bleak reality. That said, it should also be pointed out that it is possible to see a Chinese in a Peking "fast food" restaurant smash down his bowl in disgust at the dreck that has been handed him. Food, like politics, has to begin with the premise of the possible.

Gongxian (pronounced "gong-shian"), a town near Loyang in Shansi province, is preparing to become part of the foreign tourist circuit in China. It will take a few years before this comes about, however, because hotel accommodations are primitive and the principal attraction of the area, the Sung Dynasty imperial tombs, are too difficult to get at for large tour groups. The town is one of the poorer ones, but it could not be described as destitute (although I did see three dead rats for sale on the street and never got an adequate explanation for this). Moreover, the atmosphere is good and it is possible to take careful stock of the popularity of recent political changes. One peasant assured me that the local stores had far more produce and products available than had been the case for years, and the town's free market was bustling with animated excitement.

My reason for going to Gongxian was to see the Sung tombs. As wonderful as they are, they did not end up as the highlight of the trip—an evening at the opera earned this distinction. By this time, I had become an *aficionado* of traditional opera. My time in China had coincided with the return of this much-loved fare after over a decade of the dreary, mind-numbing "model operas" like *The White Haired Girl*—propaganda fare of the Cultural Revolution which, despite the revolutionary themes, seemed to take its style from the kitschiest Hollywood musicals of the thirties. A year before, in Chongqing, I had witnessed one of the first revivals of traditional opera in Sichuan province, and it had been a miraculous evening. Famous actors and actresses who had been banned from the stage since 1966 made their first reappearance, and people throughout the audience stood up in their places and whooped out joyous welcomes. It was an evening for the survivors, both in the audience and on the stage, and one had the impression that the performance itself was a kind of announcement that normal times had at long last returned.

In Peking, I went to traditional opera as often as I could. To fully appreciate traditional Chinese opera—Peking Opera is only one style, and regional differences can be quite startling—requires a bit of work. Like any art form, it has its own traditions and aesthetics, both of which have to be appreciated before you can get its full measure. Unless one respects the conventions of Western ballet or opera, the events on stage can seem utterly ridiculous, and this is the same for traditional Chinese opera. For those Chinese old enough to remember traditional opera as a normal part of their lives, the conventions are a matter of fact rather than something to be appreciated. When Jiang Qing attacked the art as "feudal" and said that Chinese people, apart from a few "bourgeois elements," hated it, she perpetrated another monstrous cultural fraud. Everywhere, I saw only wildly enthusiastic audiences. Even in Peking, where people can be very picky and rude if they don't like a particular performance, they flocked to see any traditional fare put on the stage.

In Gongxian, I learned that there was to be an evening of traditional opera at the local outdoor theater and pleaded with our willing guide to get us some tickets. Although I had seen a version of this opera before in Peking, I was interested to see what kind of audience turned up in such an out-of-the-way town. When we arrived at the theater I got my first clue from the many wagons hitched up to tractors or animals on the street outside. People from all over the nearby countryside had come, and because there was the threat of rain and this was an outdoor theater, everyone seemed to have either a plastic raincoat or an umbrella.

It was quite a scene. Every spare inch inside the theater had been taken up. We arrived late, but because we were foreigners, a couple of places had been saved for us on a bench that had the best view of the stage. We were given towels to sit on, since the seats were damp from the slight amount of rain that was falling. Looking around, I could see that it was a family night. The presence of three, and possibly four, generations could be felt everywhere and was nowhere more obvious than on the stage itself. Twenty or thirty people had managed to give the ushers the slip and were seated on the sides of the stage's apron. Particularly wrapped up in the action were a grandfather and his five- or six-year-old grandson, who sat on the outstretched legs of the old man. They were dressed in rough country clothing, and I saw their heads in profile throughout the whole performance. The child was the spitting image of his grandfather. Chinese opera provides a total package of entertainment: singing, drama, gymnastics, fantasy, tragedy, comedy, spectacle—you name it and most traditional operas have it. The fascination of the young boy with everything he saw was infectious, and he constantly turned to his grandfather to ask for explanations, which appeared to be patiently rendered.

From evenings like this, one can see that traditional opera in China is not so much an art form as it is another expression of the soul. A half century ago, when people were led off to public execution, a real test of their courage was whether or not they could remain sufficiently calm to sing a favorite aria before the fast-approaching final reckoning. Such a scene is depicted in *The True Story of Ah Q* by Lu Xun, the best story written in China so far this century in the opinion of many Chinese literary buffs. A generation was cut off from this heritage during the Cultural Revolution. In Gongxian, it was interesting to observe that young people were once again being taken to opera as a matter of course.

In Peking, the atmosphere is somewhat different. The audiences there are the toughest, meanest and rudest in the world. Unless someone is absolutely top-notch, a Peking audience will barely applaud. Curtains cannot usually close fast enough before people are stampeding out to catch a late bus or get to their bicycles. Everyone coughs and spits during the actual performance, and if a performer does something wrong, God help the poor soul—he or she is usually laughed off the stage. Even the major sign of approval is disconcerting: an outstanding performer or sequence will immediately get everyone talking excitedly. Chatter, rather than silence, is an indication of attention and involvement, and sometimes the din of approval can be deafening. In this earthiness and liveliness, despite all the hacking and coughing about you, there is further proof, if proof is needed, of the normality with which Chinese people treat their culture. It is as natural as buying vegetables.

North American audiences who attended the productions of the Peking Opera troupe during a 1979 tour would have seen a young extrovert named Tan Xiaozeng (pronounced "shao-zeng") perform in an opera called *Uproar in Heaven*. The opera is about the most beloved mythical creature in all Chinese literature, the Monkey King. Those who saw Tan on stage would hardly believe that he was only thirty-one because he played the stately role of the Jade Emperor. This is a *laosheng* ("venerable old man") role, and Tan plays equivalent stately old men in many other operas. What is truly remarkable about him, though, is that he is the fifth generation of Tan males to play *laosheng* roles. His father competes for the same parts, and his semiretired grandfather teaches the roles at the opera academy. The art was handed down to him in direct descent from his great-great-grandfather.

Sichuan, China's most populous province, has been kept closed to most foreigners for thirty years. As a traditional source of rebellion and discontent in China, it is not surprising that during the

Cultural Revolution and right up to 1975 it had been a notorious center for factional warfare. An American friend who had been in Chengdu (the provincial capital) many years before remembered the teahouses there as something quite special, and he asked me to see if they had survived. In pre-Liberation China, teahouses had been favorite retiring spots for young and old. They were a focus of all sorts of things, from political debates (and plotting) to the haggling over the price of a bride. One of China's better plays, by the Peking writer Lao She, is called *Teahouse,* and it traces the changes in Chinese society and fortunes through several generations at the same emporium. The Chengdu teahouses were said to have a unique Sichuanese ambience, in which pungent and fiery argument was the normal thing.

Some of the teahouses were still going strong, although I learned that most were closed down during part of the Cultural Revolution, having been deemed dangerously fertile ground for "bourgeois counterrevolution." From what I could see, they were all fertile ground for enthusiastically played cards and checkers—both national manias. There are various kinds of card games played in China. If you really want to show what an advanced thinker you are in the cities, you play bridge. During the Cultural Revolution, one of the proofs that Deng Xiaoping was a "capitalist-roader" was that he loved to spend an evening playing bridge with his cronies. Accordingly, with natural and universal reverse logic, many people then took up bridge privately with a passion: what is prohibited is doubly appealing, a fact of human nature that seems forever beyond the comprehension of the hard-liners in the Communist Party and those who would rigorously enforce strict limits on social behavior.

If card playing was generally frowned upon for a period, though, it was a hard pastime to put down. A Chinese version of poker seems to be the most popular game of all, and it is often played with homemade cards. Any tourist can take in the action on most street corners or village squares in the country. The game is played with a gusto that would shame the enthusiasts of Las Vegas, although foreigners are always told that it is never for money.

"It's just a game," said one of the men who had set up a card table in front of the steps of a former church in Chongqing. I had heard shouting on the street outside, and because I was curious to see what use the church was being put to, I ventured past the high wall and the gate at the entrance. Usually there was a doorman at all such entrances to shoo away people like me, but this time the post was empty. The reason was soon self-evident: the gateman was playing poker. The church was now a factory producing various kinds of nails, but it was closed for the day, and only the caretaker staff were on duty—or off duty, as it turned out. I was bidden to join them in some tea, which I did, and they explained very precisely how it was all just good, clean fun, with no decadent gambling of any sort. I concluded that the church must have been Methodist in the old days, and its pious influence could still be felt. In fact, it is the Communist Party that has adopted Methodist views, and so frowns on any sort of gambling. It is this kind of ethic which has won the Party the enthusiastic support of many old Methodist missionaries forced out of China when the Communists took over. Gambling does in fact go on, but on a very modest scale. This might not necessarily take the form of actual cash, but could involve services and "back-door" products—"the back door" being the euphemism for all things arranged and procured contrary to official state regulations and procedures.

Gambling or not, Chinese card games are a remarkable feature of everyday life in the country. When the temperature soars, people hit the streets, especially in the cool of the evening. To play cards outside at night requires only three things: a pack of cards, willing players and lights. There is never a problem in locating the first two prerequisites. The third item, light, is something of a vexatious issue. The obvious solutions in cities is street lights; thus do card mania and necessity team up to create a potential traffic hazard of unique proportions. In Peking, street lights are on only one side of a road, and card players move their little stools right out onto the street to be directly below the best light. On the other side, cyclists glide along without benefit of reflectors or lights of any sort.

Between the two come cars hurtling down at great speeds, and since it is against the law to use anything other than parking lights on the road (bright lights blind cyclists and one is supposed to flash them on for only a few seconds, in particularly dark areas), it is possible to see the potential for tragedy. The worst road in this regard in Peking is the one from the airport. Chinese and foreign drivers alike love to speed their cars along this road, which is relatively wide and goes for several miles through farming country. It is one of the few roads you can use to put a car through its paces. In summer, card players from the neighboring communes are lined along the whole route, and each group has its clutch of onlookers. Their presence does not seem to impede the speed with which drivers continue to zoom down the road.

I traveled this road regularly and felt I knew it well. Since foreigners are allowed to drive their cars only in Peking and its environs, the road was a nice change from the usual snail's pace in town, where you had to pick your way through cyclists and carts. One hot summer night I was driving at a fair clip. Suddenly, a few feet in front of me was a donkey-drawn cart which was almost completely hidden in the dark. I didn't even have time to flash on my lights. Swerving quickly to the left, I escaped a crash, but before I had a chance to whistle from relief, I found myself bearing down on a card player out in the middle of the road who had very abruptly jumped up and backward out of his seat.

I missed him by about one inch, and although everything happened so quickly, I knew exactly what had taken place. When a player gets a particularly good card, one that definitively finishes off a game, he smashes it down on the ground with ferocious gusto. This one must have been the card of the century, because the young man had hurled it down with such force that he lost his balance and stumbled backward, almost in front of my car. I quickly stopped by the side of the road and walked back to the players to make sure he hadn't been hurt.

The players, including the near-victim, were perfectly oblivious to the danger that had just passed them. They were still shouting about this spectacular card when I reached their encampment, and my sudden presence didn't faze them one whit. When one of the older players caught sight of me, he pointed to the card on the ground and then gave me a grand flourish of two thumbs-up—the most acclamatory sign of approval in China.

Shandong is a marvelous province. It is easy to get to by train from Peking, and I went there several times. There's a saying in many parts of China that all Shandong people are "big and stupid," but since we always had such splendid times there and were treated more normally than in any other place in China, I consider this a monstrous slander.

Shandong is poorer than many parts of China, and like Anhwei province, it has seen much misery, both before and since Liberation. In Qufu, the birthplace of Confucius, you get the feeling that time stopped centuries ago, and there is little overt evidence that life is better under Communism. Shandong has a number of famous historical sights, none more beloved than Tai Shan, one of Daoism's famous five holy mountains. I felt no less a sense of awe than the "ten thousand generations of worshipers" who had preceded us. I went the way Confucius did 2,500 years ago, all along the *panlu,* or "Pilgrim's Way."

Tai Shan is the mythical home of the benevolent Green Dragon, "the lord of springs and streams." As a result, peasants and emperors alike came annually to invoke blessings and pray for rain or relief from floods. The mountain rises five thousand feet out of the broad Shandong plain, and climbing it has been the happy duty and challenge of millions of Chinese for several millennia. Its beauty and popularity transcend creeds or ideology, and Mao Tsetung found himself as inspired, once at the top, as Confucius did.

It takes about seven hours to traverse the wooded pathways and climb the steep stone steps of Tai Shan. The reward at the end is not only a spectacular view, but also a transcendent feeling of satisfaction. First of all, it is a physical challenge. It is also an ascent through Chinese history and mythology. Finally, Tai Shan offers one the chance to come to terms with oneself and one's surroundings—as true today as it ever was—and this is why the rite of passage is still called the Pilgrim's Way.

In high spirits, I had taken the overnight train from Peking, which arrives in the small town of Taian at the foot of the mountain shortly before 6 A.M. After breakfast at the local hotel, a group of us assembled the few things that we would need for our overnight stay in the Pilgrim's Lodge at the top of the mountain. This lodge has been built right next to the temple of Yu Ti, which was reserved exclusively for the worship of the Jade Emperor, the supreme divinity in Daoist mythology.

The Pilgrim's Way has been artfully contrived over the years to provide the wayfarer with a variety of experiences and vistas: natural splendor, serene little wayside chapels, lacquered-wood teahouses, suitably inspiring inscriptions carved into rocks to spur the weary on, babbling brooks and mighty torrents, all sorts of wild flowers and trees—the simple pleasures just go on and on. The first half of the journey is easy. The ascent is gentle and gradual. Tiny villages along the way consist of sturdy stone homes for some of the most genial people in all of China. A Shandong peasant is one of nature's aristocrats, with a highly confident sense of his or her own place in the world. Foreigner, high-ranking Party cadre or fellow peasant—it makes no difference to Shandong peasants, who treat all with a gruff good humor that is as invigorating as the crisp air.

Since there is only one way up and the same way down, the guides from the China Travel Service do not feel obliged to dog your every step, and the fact that this was the first time I had been allowed off the leash when in the countryside added to the prevailing mood of exhilaration. All along the route, I met people young and old who had managed to come from various parts of China to be able to say that they had climbed Tai Shan. Some younger people even jogged up, a feat that seemed more impressive the harder the ascent became.

The various stops along the way have delightful, evocative names. Once you get past the First Gate of Heaven, one of three ceremonial arches, you can pause for a few moments and survey Peach Orchard Valley. If the morning mist is rising, the delicate contours of the East Hall of Bright Vision will emerge on a neighboring hill. By the time you reach a bustling little way station, ominously called Where Horses Turn Back, thoughts of lunch naturally occur.

Mercifully, Chinese coolies no longer have to carry the heavy burden of fat pilgrims up the face of the mountain on awkward sedan chairs, but all supplies, from food, coal and furniture to large concrete blocks for new edifices, still have to be lugged up on the sturdy shoulders of Shandong peasants. These porters at Tai Shan belong to an ancient profession which is still passed on from father to son. Young boys are initiated with relatively light loads, but soon enough they are competing for heavier burdens. By Chinese standards, they are now paid well for their work, and the cruelest exploitation (competitive downward bidding for services by merchants and pilgrims, as well as the need for opium to keep undernourished limbs moving) has been eradicated. Nevertheless, it is still exhausting work, and their exhaustion can be seen in their faces when the going gets tough.

After the midway point at the Second Gate of Heaven, the climber's work begins in earnest. (For those who feel enough is enough, there is a lodge at this point, where you can stay overnight and wait for the return of friends who insist on pushing to the top.) During the last half of the climb, seven-foot-wide stone steps rise vertically in dozens of flights. The steps are uniform only in steepness, and many people can't manage more than twenty without taking a breather. The last eighteen flights are a nightmare. After the leisurely and exquisite rests at the lower-level teahouses, the gossip with the midway villagers and the ambience of serenity, the final, sheer climb up is killing. The only thing on your mind is to get it done and not admit defeat.

Once up, of course, you find the pain is quickly forgotten, although there is still a mile to walk along the crest of the mountain. The old sages knew all about the feelings that overtake everyone once this point has been reached. "Enter with awe this region of beauty," reads the last stone inscription at the top of the steps. As you walk along the Pathway of Heaven, you understand what Dorothy must have felt as she approached the Land of Oz. The sun was fast setting, and the vistas all around produced a panorama of spectacular grandeur. In the past, the occasional Daoist mystic became so intoxicated from both the climb and the final spectacle that he would hurl himself over the precipice to reach the bosom of the sun. For those of us on a somewhat lower mystical peak, the emotional response—a mixed awareness of both the littleness of humanity in the face of God's grandeur and the uniqueness of our species in conquering and appreciating it all—is still strong: Daoism and Maoism intertwined.

The air is brisk here, and the wind at the top is fierce. The lodge provides quilted greatcoats, which you wear all the time during the colder months. At sunset, after a fine dinner of steaming-hot food in the freezing dining room, I went to bed. The one remaining adventure before the descent begins is to be awakened at about 5 A.M. to see the sun as a fiery red ball shooting up through the horizon over the ancient state of Lu below. When Confucius saw this sight, he noted with irony that "the kingdom of Lu is not so big." When Mao Tsetung saw it, he observed that "the East is Red." No doubt, the Jade Emperor would have smiled at both. His power, imagined or real, ignored or respected, still draws the Chinese to his hearth. To have climbed Tai Shan is regarded as a major accomplishment and a duty fulfilled.

Dancing, like bridge, has made a real comeback recently in China. It had been strictly prohibited for years as the very essence of Western decadence, another mighty hoax foisted on the Chinese people by the puritan busybodies of radical Maoism. Who enjoyed a dance more than Mao Tsetung himself during the Yenan years, before Liberation? Maybe only Premier Chou Enlai and Marshal Lin Biao. The entire Communist leadership loved to fox-trot and waltz away the evenings, and the practice carried on until the sixties. Wives of resident diplomats used to vie with one another at state functions to get a chance to dance with the elegant Premier Chou, but from 1963 to 1978 dancing was strictly taboo, branded "decadent and bourgeois."

As life relaxed in China, the first tentative two-step was tried. Typically, those in the forefront were cadres' children, who practiced in the privacy of their homes and enlisted their parents' memories to teach them what it was all about. Before long, the foreigners' International Club announced that the weekly "ball" was being reintroduced, and suddenly all of Peking was dancing.

During the Xidan period, my wife and I were in considerable demand as dancing teachers, despite the fact that we were rotten dancers. We also couldn't play bridge, a fact that disappointed a lot of people. If you actually *were* a "capitalist-roader," the least that was expected of you was mastery in bridge and dancing. For a while, we danced in private homes, at Peking University and at night spots like the Nationalities Hotel. It was an experimental business, and you could take Chinese friends to such places as the hotel if they had the nerve to come. The government had concocted a seemingly foolproof scheme to keep ordinary Chinese quietly out of places frequented by foreigners. The admission price was a whopping ten yuan (about seven dollars), and the authorities knew no Chinese would be so foolish as to waste so much money on dancing, even if he or she had ten yuan to spare. What they didn't count on was the fact that foreigners would buy a bunch of tickets and simply give them to Chinese friends. Eventually, the government got around this problem by bringing in approved Chinese— mostly members of folk-dance or ballet companies—while requiring all other citizens to register their name and Unit at the entrance. That did the job of screening out undesirables overnight.

But if Chinese were not encouraged to dance with foreign friends, the government nevertheless allowed them to dance among themselves, and all sorts of places were opened up to dancing parties. The long-closed Drum Tower suddenly became a hive of happy souls tripping the light fantastic, and before long, individual Units could even rent rooms in the Great Hall of the People for a dance party. A number of curious difficulties emerged. The sycophantic and slimy head of the International Club, Mr. Fei, resolutely announced that "there will be no rock-and-roll" ever heard in China. That was going too far!

The intended snub to Western sensitivities didn't bother most foreigners: we knew the Africans would take care of the matter in short order. The Chinese Government was still swallowing Jiang Qing's remarkable thesis that rock-and-roll and jazz were decadent and American. After the first somber "ball" at the International Club, the Africans staged their own cultural revolution, and the authorities soon discovered that everything from jazz to disco was built on a base of "Third World" revolutionary fervor. But what might be appropriate for blacks was certainly not going to be appropriate for Chinese youths. The government was well aware of the fact that many young people were far too keen to see what all the fuss was about. Dancing was accepted back into China as a "healthy" activity if kept in proper bounds. It was discussed in the press almost as an adjunct to physical fitness. And men and women too shy to dance with the opposite sex felt no strangeness in dancing with the same sex.

Theater and films all over China became much more interesting and provocative after the fall of the Gang of Four, and perhaps the most fervid and fertile place to see the changes was Shanghai, China's most Westernized city. Despite thirty years of strict Communist rule and the rigid exclusion of Western influences, Shanghai is still a place apart in China. When foreigners from the West first walk along the famous Bund by the waterfront, they usually get the feeling that they have stepped back forty years into their own cities. The Bund was the old financial district of Shanghai, and the gray, solid thirties-style skyscrapers could be a perfect set for a period film about New York or Chicago or Toronto.

Shanghai seems, at first glance, a city caught in amber. If you have adjusted to China, however, Shanghai also seems instantly special because there's something approaching a hustle among the citizens that you don't find in the other cities, and people walk about the streets more confidently. Peking seems an enlarged village in comparison. Again, a newcomer might think everyone was dressed the same, but all Chinese and resident foreigners know differently:

Shanghai is the manufacturing center of China, and you will see more leather shoes and different shirt styles there than anywhere else. Since there are so many more services, diversions and products, "the back door" forms an important part of many people's lives; thanks to relatives and friends, the "Shanghai connection" to some of the better things in life touches many parts of China.

Shanghai also has a true proletariat, one that occasionally tries to stand up for workers' rights. It is not possible to have a strike in China anymore, because nearly everyone works for the state, and a strike, by definition, would be antistate and therefore counter-revolutionary. During the Cultural Revolution, however, Shanghai workers taught the nation how to work-to-rule: you just stop your job and assiduously study the thoughts of Chairman Mao for weeks. Eventually someone figures out there is a grievance.

Shanghai is everything a great city should be: controversial, a little uncontrollable, a playground for dreams, a place to get lost in and a place to be found. The Gang of Four's fortunes started here, and when they were overthrown no place rejoiced louder. Shanghai is also the breeding ground for some of the most creative talent in China and the intellectual capital, despite the best efforts of the Communist Party to make Peking, where controls can be arranged more effectively, the focus of such things. Even during the Cultural Revolution, travelers noted that things strictly frowned upon elsewhere in China—like holding hands with your girlfriend in a public park or curling your hair—could be seen in Shanghai. The place is simply too big to completely control, and with a population somewhere between ten and thirteen million, there is a lot of safety in numbers.

Shanghai is the place to meet Westernophiles, Chinese who love to soak up Western culture and ideas. The most recent phenomenon in this regard is the eager group of young English-language students who blitz the Bund from dawn to dusk, waiting for tourists with whom they can strike up conversations. Sometimes on Nanking Road, the famous shopping street, you can hear two or three Chinese in the midst of an animated conversation entirely in English as they stroll along the sidewalk. It is mostly pretentious chatter to show off their language skills. However, one friend in Shanghai told me that when he and his friends are having a serious political discussion, they drift naturally into English as a modest form of protection from prying ears.

Movie studios in Shanghai used to produce wonderful films, both before and after Liberation, but the Cultural Revolution was particularly hard on the arts and public entertainment there. Many of the older professionals, hurt in too many ideological campaigns, are refusing to have anything to do with the new breath of fresh air. They are waiting quietly for the next reversal in the line struggle, and this time they don't intend to get caught out on either side. They have retired from that world entirely.

Since politics still rules the roost in moviemaking and theatrical production, there has been a great deal of emphasis on approved Western farc, both on the stage and on the screen. Now that the people can decide for themselves what films and plays they can go to, a dud doesn't stand a chance anymore. When the government started allowing screenings of foreign films, Shanghai was the first testing ground, although the results could surely not have been in much doubt. Ticket lineups stretched for blocks. Charlie Chaplin had a revival such as the world had never seen. Millions and millions of people took to him with unrepressed delight, and a year after his old films were put in general release, he was still drawing packed houses everywhere. On the other hand, a Chinese-made epic on the struggle to control the flooding along the Yellow River, which had cost several million dollars to make and featured a cast of thousands, was withdrawn from circulation after barely two weeks. This was in spite of a national propaganda campaign to give the film top billing. Word of mouth killed it dead.

The Chinese love movies, and most people don't ask for a great deal, but they won't accept propaganda unless it is done well. The most popular indigenous films in China today are the older ones, especially from the fifties, when censorship and a good Party profile were less oppressively enforced. If a good Hong Kong film makes it past all the current ideological hurdles and into general release, then there is nothing more popular in all the land.

In Shanghai the theaters are well built, and some are even air-conditioned during the summer. This is quite a contrast with the film shows in the countryside, where a cinema team will set up shop in the middle of a field and people bring their own stools. But there are constants in China, despite all the differences between town and country and between the educated elite and the rural peasantry: the Yellow River saga was a flop on the communes too. After all, acknowledged a Chinese film magazine, it was supposed to be a story about peasant endurance, and when the peasants themselves thought it hollow and false, something was wrong.

It is inaccurate to think of the Chinese as cringing in daily fear of their totalitarian government. The varied pleasures of the people are proof enough that this is not so. Most Chinese people accept the status quo, and in many of the areas where they do not, they have found unique ways to get around it. Nothing is quite as it first seems to outside eyes in China, but pleasures are pleasures, and the Chinese appear to get more satisfaction out of theirs than we do out of ours, despite our material affluence. I was always convinced that their satisfaction arose not only out of the necessity of acceptance, but also as a reaction, conscious or not, against the inequalities and arbitrariness of so much that rules their lives.

18

The Burden
of the Masses

By the time Vice-Premier Deng Xiaoping made his historic
trip to the United States in early 1979, some amazing things had
begun to appear on Chinese television. Accustomed to the same
dreary regurgitation of propaganda on the screen that they had to
suffer in print and at regular political meetings, many Chinese had
tuned television out of their lives. Transmissions were only a few
hours a day anyway, and since only a tiny handful of people had the
privilege of watching television in their homes, the medium held
out few charms, save simple curiosity for electronics enthusiasts.

During 1978, the authorities started countenancing much
broader programming, and interest, not surprisingly, began to pick
up. More sports features were aired, along with popular productions of traditional opera and even the occasional foreign film or
feature. Communal television sets became, for the first time, a lively
focus of social activity, and as the pace of events in China quickened, millions of people started tuning in regularly to see what the
latest surprise would be.

They never had to wait long. In line with the new state policy
of gently wooing Taiwan back into the embrace of the Motherland,
for example, the first positive depiction of everyday life in the
Guomindang bastion was screened on national television. After

years of being fed propaganda about the dire conditions on the island, Chinese people suddenly saw with their own eyes tangible visions of prosperity in modern Taipei. Here were fellow Chinese enjoying all the better things in life. The film was a Japanese travelogue which depicted none of the uglier aspects of Taiwan—Guomindang suppression of human rights, urban blight or the tawdry, pathetic red-light district. The superior economic realities of life on Taiwan were known to many educated Chinese, but even on them —as well as those who had bought the old propaganda whole—the little half-hour film had devastating effects.

A few weeks later, Vice-Premier Deng set off for the United States and a Chinese television crew accompanied him. The footage sent back for home consumption had an even more profound effect than the Taiwanese gambit. Anxious to put a good light on the new Sino-American friendship that had so recently been formalized by the establishment of normal diplomatic relations, a picture of abundant prosperity and hope in the land of the former Number One Capitalist-Imperialist Enemy flickered across the length and breadth of the Middle Kingdom. Was this really the place where workers cringed under merciless yokes and millionaire gangsters controlled the government? (The Chinese propaganda authorities are not often guilty of subtlety. An enemy has traditionally been painted in the most lurid colors, while friends and allies are wreathed in unspotted halos.)

In going to America, Chinese television made no effort at objectivity and even went so far as to film "a typical American home," which turned out to be the residence of a junior executive at IBM. Not very surprisingly, a crisis of confidence ensued as many Chinese started asking themselves about the lies they had been fed for years. If what they saw on television was an example of the horror of capitalism, it compared dramatically and favorably with the joys of Communism, which they knew only too well. Realizing the error in their tactics, government propagandists attempted to correct the record shortly after Mr. Deng returned.

Articles began appearing in the press differentiating between alliance and emulation. Explanations were provided for the startling contrasts between the affluence of America and the poverty of China. Not illogically, these explanations revolved around the historic conditions each country had inherited. The Chinese press once again dug deep into its files on the images of exploitation in

America, from the lack of broadly based health care to the continuing slavelike conditions of blacks.

In the official media, the attacks on American values and conditions were fairly tame, especially considering the frantic hyperbole that was so beloved during the Vietnam war. Typically, however, propaganda meant only for domestic Chinese consumption verged on the hysterical. Traditionally under Communism in China, pep rallies for youth groups, delegations of workers and other organizations take a much more flamboyant line than can be found in official pronouncements. A lot of license is encouraged in order to elicit the enthusiasm of the masses. Accordingly, the presentation of America was relatively balanced on one level, but for internal references, the country was nothing less than "a capitalist hell." That was the phrase used by the vice-president of one of Peking's major universities when he gave a report on his two-month trip to the United States. The official, Zhang Guangdou of Qinghua (pronounced "ching-hua") University, told delegates attending a Communist Youth League meeting in Peking that "on the one hand, there is theft and oppression" in the United States, and "on the other there is arduous labor." Zhang told of weddings that cost over a million dollars and said that "capitalists lead a life of debauchery and waste." Furthermore, he added, "If a son goes to his mother's house to eat, he must pay money. If the mother goes to the son's house, she must also give money. I am not joking in the least. A family invited me to eat dinner. Four of them invited me, and after eating, and in front of me, they took out a calculator and calculated who owed what."

Despite all the talk about human rights in America, he said, none really existed, and the political system was a fraud. "There is a great deal of [political] activity, but in reality the capitalists are in the background controlling everything. What freedom of speech do the common people have? I looked and I didn't see any freedom of speech. Take a hard look at the United States. When can a black ever be president? The United States Congress is without blacks. Is this truly one of the human rights? . . .

"Before, we propagandized that the American workers didn't get enough to eat. But then we went abroad to look, and we saw that all Americans have cars—workers have cars—and they have nice houses. We cannot deny that their living standard is higher than ours. On the other side of the coin, wealth in the United States is very unevenly distributed. Workers are very nervous and worried. Money is still not ample. . . . Those who admire the lives of capitalists and want to go abroad have had their heads filled with ideas that are based on myth. They are naive. We must talk to them and explain things as they really are."

Scurrilous as the speech is, both in its content and in its intended purpose, it is absurd to debate it on the same level. In fact, some Americans may well have paid a million dollars for a wedding, and while blacks do get elected to Congress, there are not many of them. (But could it be true that some miserable family actually does charge money during family meals?) The point is that we know this is not a true general picture. If you want to balance it, though, the American vice-presidential candidate George Bush could be cited. In 1980, he told a campaign audience that his years in Peking as chief of the United States Liaison Office (precursor of the U.S. Embassy) had made him more aware than ever of the benefits of the American way of life.

Mr. Bush cited the manner in which Communism had destroyed the Chinese family as one example. If any Chinese people had heard this, they would have laughed out loud in scorn. The family is stronger in China today than it is anywhere else in the world. Part of the proof can be seen in Zhang's speech. The anecdote about a son's charging his mother money for a meal and vice versa just seems silly to us, but it would be shocking to many Chinese. The masses have great burdens in China, but they also have developed remarkable resources to evade or alleviate those burdens. In coming to terms with the tricky question of human rights, those burdens have to be seen in the light of both Chinese experience and universal values.

Foreign journalists are not normally taken to places of detention in China. Occasionally the authorities will permit a visit to a model prison, usually in Shanghai, but generally information about conditions in prisons and labor reform camps comes from ex-inmates who have managed to leave China. The most famous account is by Jean Pasqualini in his book *Prisoner of Mao.* The author's mother was Chinese and his father a Corsican. After Liberation in 1949, Pasqualini's continuing relations with foreigners earned him the suspicion and enmity of the authorities, and he was eventually arrested and tried as a spy. With his dual Chinese and French nationality, he was the lucky recipient of state amnesty when the government normalized its diplomatic relations with France in 1964. After a decade in various camps and prisons, he was set free and permitted to leave the country.

Those reading his book and expecting to discover the Chinese equivalent of the Gulag Archipelago in the Soviet Union will be confused and possibly disappointed. Life in the Chinese Communist penal system, at least during the fifties and early sixties, was certainly no picnic, but it wasn't so radically different from the lot of ordinary Chinese in normal society. In fact, Pasqualini's experience showed that life in prison may well provide a model for the kind of supremely ordered and disciplined life that the authorities feel is appropriate for all Chinese. The concentration on thought reform, with its emphasis on improving prisoners' social consciousness and revolutionary world outlook, was a clearer indication of what the Party's ultimate ideological strategy has been than the often compromised efforts on the outside. Some atrocious things occurred, like the summary execution of a homosexual barber, but there were also atrocious events on the outside. Living conditions became very bleak following the failure of the Great Leap Forward, but they were bleak in the country as well. Life inside, suggests Pasqualini, was much like life outside—only more so.

Sidney Rittenberg, as well as a Chinese acquaintance released in 1978 after eight years of prison, said that the Cultural Revolution had brought havoc to the prison system. Rittenberg simply shudders when he remembers the first years of his second incarceration: mindless physical and mental brutality were commonplace, and thought reform took on even deeper Orwellian implications than the comparatively tame version previously practiced. Pasqualini even talked wistfully of some of his jailers during the earlier period. The best, he said, were good men who were conscientiously trying to improve the outlook of their charges and deal fairly with legitimate grievances.

He likened these exemplary cadres to Catholic priests who worked for conversions with a combination of faith and moral rectitude. Just as the Church had its share of bad priests, so the Party had its share of bad cadres. The best, though, were honorable and decent. These were precisely the sort of people who were put down during the excesses of the Cultural Revolution. Having generally been faithful to a Party line that had been discredited, they were now defenseless, and some were incarcerated in the same places they had once been in charge of. By the time I arrived in China, the prisons were reverting to the pre–Cultural Revolution system, which was presumably a boon to all prisoners.

Outsiders have no way of knowing how many people are imprisoned in China for offenses ranging from hooliganism to political dissent, but the figure may not be as high as is often thought in the West. Thanks to the extensive nature of state and Party controls, potential and known felons can be closely scrutinized in everyday life. The Chinese Communist Party does have a genuine desire to reform, and in cases that do not directly constitute a grave threat to national security, a complicated series of measures are often pursued before someone is actually sent to prison. The most important of these measures is the surveillance of such individuals by fellow workers and even family members.

Thanks to these government controls as well as China's poverty and primitive transportation system, it is not possible to roam at will the way one can in North America. Thus surveillance is fairly easy to ensure, and in this light, prison is simply an extension of the system—or a closer surveillance employed when necessary. On the surface, such a system compares very favorably with ours if the acknowledged evils of many Western penitentiaries are taken into account. For this, the Communist Party should be given full credit. Under Mao Tsetung and, to a somewhat lesser extent, today, the Party has developed an all-encompassing and comprehensive view of Chinese society: prisoners, no less than high state cadres, are referrable to this view.

This may make surveillance and incarceration in China sound rather benign. They aren't, of course, but the fact remains that prison life is closely allied to the overall lot of the Chinese, whereas in our systems inmates are set quite aside from the community, psychologically as well as physically. One doesn't have to hunt very deep to discover the evil animus that governs all this. The other side of the coin is the ordinary lot of the Chinese which is allied to prison life. If it is wrong to think of Chinese people cringing in constant fear of the authorities, it is equally wrong to dismiss all the dangers they have to face in conducting their lives.

It is only recently that the government has seriously tackled the problem of creating a proper criminal code. For thirty years, citizens have never had a clear definition of what the state considers lawful or illegal. This is for the simple reason that the Communist Party, and thus the government, as well as what has passed for a judicial establishment, keeps changing positions. Certain basic felonies, like murder or arson or rape, have usually transcended such ambivalence, but in a country where political crimes cover such a wide area and vary from year to year, a precise criminal code would have been a perfect nuisance. The history of New China is littered with newer crimes which are never identified until after they are committed. When the Hundred Flowers Campaign backfired in 1956, it was suddenly discovered that millions of "rightists" were threatening the state. When the Cultural Revolution unfolded, "revisionists" appeared from nowhere, all over the country.

Today, when ordinary crimes and political disagreements—still linked together as criminal activities—continue to exist, a new classification has been created to cover those people who were born under socialism and Maoism, but who nevertheless resist their blandishments in one way or another: these are the "newborn bourgeois elements" specified by Chairman Hua in 1978.

Old habits are hard to break, and most objective observers, Chinese and foreign, feel that it will be a long time before there will be substantial changes, a criminal code notwithstanding. After all, China has long had eloquent constitutions guaranteeing freedom of speech and religion, neither of which exists. To allow people to openly express their political thoughts strikes at the roots of Communism, and so as old heresies are forgiven, new ones fill up the dungeons. It is not properly understood in the West that Communism is a secular religion, that to question the dictatorship of the proletariat is as unforgivable as questioning the doctrine of papal infallibility or transubstantiation in the Roman Catholic Church. In the West, the Church no longer has the temporal power to enforce its doctrines, but when it did its actions were not unlike those of the Party.

Thanks to an accident of timing, I had a unique chance to get some direct insight into thought reform and detention in China. Shortly after the Chinese troops returned home at the end of March 1979 from the short but bloody border war with Vietnam, the Chinese Government decided to begin a new propaganda strategy. To this end, the Foreign Ministry invited a number of foreign correspondents in Peking to travel to the Guangxi Autonomous Region bordering Vietnam to inspect prisoner-of-war camps. Some of us were chary of the invitation and fretted about being drawn into the propaganda war; but the opportunity to travel to an important military district usually forbidden to outsiders was too tempting to pass up.

In retrospect, I have to doff a cynical cap in salute to the cleverness of the authorities. The trip was so tempting that we all left Peking at precisely the same moment that the government made its first major crackdown against political activists throughout the country.

On the evening before the journalists boarded a train for the long ride to Guangxi, I was driving a Chinese friend, who had visited me for a few hours, back to his neighborhood. This had been a standard practice for some months, and I thought nothing of it when we first set off. It was also the day I first heard about Vice-Premier Deng Xiaoping's speech attacking activists and calling for their suppression. The details of the speech were still sketchy, and I was unaware that this night would bring arrests all over the city and that the crackdown would also affect those Chinese who had established unapproved friendships with foreigners like myself.

As we drove out of the diplomatic compound, my Chinese friend and I shared a silly joke and laughed as we headed toward Chang An Avenue. It was quite late in the evening, and as usual, there was virtually no traffic on the street, save for a few bicycles and the occasional donkey or horse cart. Suddenly I noticed in the rearview mirror that we were being followed by a large Mercedes-Benz sedan without its headlights on. Although fellow journalists in Moscow often told stories of being followed by the Soviet police, this was a new experience for me in China. It was so new, in fact, that for a while I tried to persuade myself that I wasn't being followed. To satisfy myself, I speeded up, but the sedan kept pace. Then I slowed down to a crawl. The sedan slowed too.

The whole exercise would have struck me as hilarious—to tail a car when there was no other car on the road seemed the definition of stupidity—had it not been for the reaction of my Chinese friend. Instantly, he realized what was going on. I knew I was in no danger. The worst that might happen to me was expulsion, and being expelled from a Communist country is always a feather in a correspondent's cap. My friend, though, was in imminent danger, and the first thing I thought of doing was to lose the tail. That's when I discovered that a Toyota, admirable car though it may be, is no match for a high-powered Mercedes—the favorite vehicle of the Public Security Bureau.

I turned sharply off Chang An Avenue and raced up a side street. The Mercedes kept up the whole time. To my horror, I soon discovered that all the police street kiosks (stations where officers switch traffic lights by day) were manned, even though there was no traffic and the lights were not functioning. The city was lousy with police that night.

The one thing I knew I couldn't do was return my friend to his neighborhood. He would be picked up in a second and subjected to heaven knows what: an imagination is a rotten companion in such circumstances. Through a ruse, I managed to slip the vehicle, but it was an unpleasant experience, and I worried for the safety of every Chinese I knew.

Despite this fear and not fully appreciating how widespread the crackdown would be, I set off for Guangxi early the next morning, arriving eventually in the town of Baice, only a few miles from the Vietnamese border. I did not have great expectations of discovering much at the prisoner-of-war camp. I was sure conditions would be exemplary.

It was with increasing incredulity, therefore, that I toured the camp. At the introductory talk, the People's Liberation Army camp commandant gave the rundown on the number of prisoners and how well they were being treated. All the prisoners had been issued new clothing—better clothing, in fact, than could be seen on the backs of the villagers in Baice, which struck us as a relatively prosperous community. Food rations were excellent, and prisoners were encouraged to participate in games and study. What kind of study? we asked the commandant. "They study documents related to the present conflict between our two countries," he said. What kind of documents? "Vietnamese translations of the *People's Daily* and other pertinent documents."

As we continued to question the commandant and other army officials, it became clear that the Vietnamese were not only being "encouraged" to study, they had no choice. In addition, they were rigorously segregated from their colleagues—and particularly from their officers—to ensure the "correct atmosphere" for study. All prisoners had been divided up into small groups of five or six—no larger. It was only within these groups that they could have conversations, which were closely monitored by specially trained PLA personnel. All other conversation, except to Chinese guards, was forbidden.

Prisoners were encouraged to write down their thoughts on particular issues, and Chinese supervisors would then examine these thoughts each day "to help clear up misunderstandings and misinterpretations." Drawing himself up with considerable pride, the commandant announced that most of the prisoners had come to see that their own country was "the aggressor" in the current dispute and that we journalists would be able to roam freely about the camp to ascertain the truth in the matter. Indoctrinating prisoners of war and encouraging them to denounce their own country is, of course, strictly contrary to the Geneva Convention; but China has never signed the convention.

As I toured the camp, I suddenly realized that I was being given, somewhat indirectly, an extraordinary opportunity to witness thought reform in action. I went inside various dormitories and saw the POWs in their groups of six sitting around tables as Chinese army officials guided their thoughts.

Nothing looked repressive, but the strategy was clearly geared to the needs of the situation. The POWs were mostly teen-age boys, recently recruited by the Vietnamese from villages in the area. They were the simplest of peasant youths from one of the poorer parts of an impoverished nation. Kindness and generosity were what first softened them up. From their own officers they had been fed lurid stories of how the Chinese would treat them if captured. Castration seemed to be the mildest prospect. Carefully, the Chinese applied kindness, making sure that the Vietnamese officers could not get at them.

A daily routine was established that never varied. The PLA officials rarely acted as interrogators; instead, they became concerned "elder brothers" or "sisters" (there were about twenty female prisoners in the camp). Good behavior and change of attitude resulted in tangible rewards. As the goodies were passed out, the relentless message hit home.

To be fair to the Chinese, we did discover some Vietnamese who quietly maintained that they felt China was the aggressor, but I got the impression that these people were almost model holdouts, sent our way to show Chinese evenhandedness and to reinforce the central fact that the majority either had ratted on their country or, at the very least, were prepared to admit an ambivalent view.

The tranquillity and sweet reasonableness of the scene were deceptive. I asked the commandant at one point if he was fully aware of the fate to which he had consigned these young prisoners. "You know, of course, that the Communist Government in Vietnam is ruthless," I said, "and that our reports will be carried throughout the world and will be closely scrutinized by that government. When the time comes to repatriate these POWs, they will certainly be harshly dealt with for talking in this fashion. Most likely they will be shot as traitors. Does this bother your conscience?"

"We have simply presented you with the facts as they are," he said with a stern smile. "We have no control over what you will write. We have invited you here to see the facts, and what you write is your own business. Therefore, their possible fate is in your hands, not ours. In any event, we cannot be held accountable for the criminal actions of the Vietnamese Government." A masterpiece of cynicism.

Life for the average Chinese citizen, of course, is not like that of Vietnamese prisoners of war. Citizens' thoughts, though, are still monitored whenever possible for "misunderstandings and misinterpretations." Many Chinese, grown accustomed to the reality around them, would not acknowledge many of the things we in the West consider human-rights abuses. Part of the reason for this is caught up in history. Chinese governments have traditionally sought to leave a strong imprint on the people's consciousness. To survive as a nation with such a huge population has necessitated a degree of cohesiveness in society that can be traced back thousands of years to the first efforts at controlling flooding along the banks of the Yellow River, the heartland of Chinese civilization. The Chinese Communist Party is the inheritor of an ancient propensity for ordering human affairs in an extremely rigid and doctrinaire fashion.

History is a fact to be reckoned with, however, not an excuse to perpetuate iniquity. No one knew this better than Mao Tsetung, that supreme example of Chinese individualism who successfully used the results of Chinese history—peasant discontent, social cohesiveness, national and racial pride, a yearning for egality and a hatred of bureaucracy—to stage one of the mightiest revolutions of all time. History was used to bring about dramatic change and progress. Having achieved this, it was a supreme irony that he eventually fashioned a state apparatus that controlled the lives of citizens more closely and rigorously than any dynastic autocrat. The parallels and comparisons for Mao's feat are all back in Chinese history, and his achievements usually surpass all of them.

Every Chinese citizen today is a member of a work unit of some sort. This is the basic social grouping of Communist Chinese society with the exception of the family, which is a product of natural events and therefore could be said to be an unofficial grouping. Having lost the battle to displace the family, the Party has sought to co-opt its functions as much as possible. A Unit might be the school you attend, the factory where you work, your commune or a government office. The Unit's importance and control over individual activities can be easily measured by its responsibilities and functions. It is the Unit—and in practice that means the Unit leadership, however it is formed—which provides housing and employment. It is to your Unit that you must apply for permission to marry. It is the Unit which allocates your rations of clothing, of meat and oil, of shoes. It is a formal letter from your Unit which gives you permission to stay at out-of-town hotels. If you have saved enough money to buy a bicycle, you usually must apply to your Unit for permission to purchase it.

Such things would strike many Westerners as intolerable intrusions into everyday life, but most Chinese would not see it this way. The business of bicycles, for example, is typical. The state can produce only a certain number of bicycles a year. The Chinese do not consider it intolerable that people should first of all prove the need for a bicycle before getting permission to buy one. In scarcity, need rather than buying power seems to them to be a more equitable way of dispensing available products. If certain foods are hard to obtain, it is surely fairer to ration them widely than to allow hoarders to buy up all the stocks. This is part of the price of being Chinese and living in a densely populated poor country. Socialism is a demonstrably fairer system of distribution—in theory, anyway, and often in practice—than anything that existed in China previously.

The necessity to obtain permission to marry is another sore point with some Westerners who criticize the Chinese human-rights record, and yet many of these same critics—unless they were totally oblivious to the problems of overpopulation—would consider the Chinese Government irresponsible if it didn't make a major effort to curb unbridled population growth. Ethics and reality are often on a collision course in a country of one billion people, and requiring citizens to wait until they are in their mid to late twenties before they can marry and begin child rearing is neither illogical nor unduly cruel. Penalties in the form of reduced rations to couples who have more than two children ("two is good, one is better" says the propaganda) fit into the same category. It is clearly an intrusion into privacy, but a government that does not consider the welfare of the total population and the future direction of the nation could fairly be accused of criminal negligence. Many of those things thought to be human-rights abuses in China are, in reality, the products once again of necessity.

In Taiwan, where the government has totalitarian tendencies remarkably similar to those of Mainland China, it was clear that increased prosperity can eradicate the majority of those burdens the Chinese people endure which we in the affluent West would consider intolerable. One doesn't have to go very far back in our own history to find certain kinds of material conditions in everyday life that produced restraints to individual activity similar to those which exist in China today.

What is a source of contention with many Chinese, however, is the advantage taken by the Communist Party and government of all this necessity. On one level, it is simply a matter of corruption: those who control the system sometimes take advantage of it to feather their own nests and withhold what rightfully belongs to the people.

Far more sinister than simple corruption is the Communist Party's propensity to institutionalize necessity in order to consolidate its grip over everyone's life. The structure of power in China has been such that with the right sort of connections and determination, a tiny group of people can impose its will on everyone. The Gang of Four and Lin Biao were no aberrations: they were tangible proof of the possibilities under the Communist system in China. The new government tacitly admits as much when it argues that a criminal code and democracy—its criminal code and its version of democracy, of course—are needed to prevent "swindlers" like the Gang from ever "usurping" power again. But by this definition, Mao himself was a swindler, and so were Hua Guofeng and Deng Xiaoping. They all came to power and maintained it by manipulating a system whose direct connections to the masses became increasingly theoretical and arbitrary.

Backing up a rigidly hierarchical party structure is the world's largest bureaucracy with its twenty-four well-defined ranks of cadres or officials, each having distinctive perquisites, status and wages. Many who come to China never fully appreciate this point. China is one of the most class-conscious and class-ridden societies in existence today. There is no secret about this. Officially, when the Communists took over, class was turned upside down, not obliterated. In theory, the most important classes, the peasantry and proletariat, were raised to the top, while the capitalists were flung to the bottom. That's in theory. In practice, a new elite quickly formed, complete with all the usual reinforcements and appurtenances: special schools for offspring, better living conditions, power, privacy, travel opportunities and access to products and services unavailable to the masses. A cadre high up in the pecking order—say at the eighth or ninth level—can live a fine life, despite the modest way he presents himself to the people. That old fox Guo Moro, for example, the "poet laureate" of Communist China who ratted on every friend or ally he ever had whom he perceived as threatening his position, loved the perks of his official position: his state limousine, his vast mansion which once housed the family of a high Manchu official, his impressive collection of antiques, his flock of aides, his access to the best hotel rooms in the country, his scenic retreat, his ability to settle scores with any foes or potential foes.

"We were just going to a restaurant," said an official who had once seen Guo Moro in action, "and you should have seen his performance. An aide was sent ahead to ensure that everything at the restaurant was up to his standards. Limousines were ordered up to convey everyone to the building, which was only two blocks away. The police were alerted and several officers were on special guard duty. Finally, we all left and he arrived with much ceremony. The restaurant was closed to everyone else, thanks to the intervention of the aides, but when Guo Moro arrived he suddenly realized that he had left his false teeth back home, and so another aide was dispatched to fetch them."

Another official, a young man attached to the Foreign Ministry, had a run-in with a state limousine which nearly cost him his chances of good employment. The incident occurred in 1975, when he was still a university student. He was riding his bicycle home one day when suddenly the loudspeakers at a police traffic kiosk started to blare out, ordering bike movement to stop. Police officers poured out into the middle of the intersection and stopped all north–south traffic. After waiting patiently for five minutes, the young man looked everywhere but could not see anything happening. He was late and anxious to get home, so he got on his bike and tried to move surreptitiously through the crowds, which by then were growing immense. Within seconds, several police had grabbed his bike and pulled him bodily to the ground.

A few moments later, a huge black Hongqi ("Red Flag" limousine) glided past the scene. A minister was returning home from work, nothing more. Normal traffic was soon allowed to continue, but the young man was hauled off to the Public Security Bureau for close questioning. He was beside himself with rage and demanded to know by what law a citizen was forced to come to a standstill just to let an official on his way home from work drive past. In short order, he was reported to his university Unit, and since he was also a member of the Communist Youth League—a sort of feeding farm for the Party—he was reported there too.

He was lucky. He got off lightly after signing an abject apology and self-criticism, which was delivered in person to the Public Security Bureau, his Unit and his local branch of the Youth League. Had he remained obstinate, he had stood a real chance of being expelled from both university and the League, which would have ended all his chances for a good future.

The public manifestations of officials' privileges are widely hated. During the Cultural Revolution, one of the favorite pastimes during the early years was to raid the homes of officials and check out the material conditions. Although most weren't impressive by Western standards, they shocked many ordinary Chinese, who had little idea precisely how lucky one was if one had position and status in China.

The Cultural Revolution turned the cadres' lives upside down, and many of the most prominent were thrown out of office and ended up cleaning latrines or guarding gateways. Some were killed.

Mao Tsetung had always recognized that you can topple a dominating class in society, but you cannot stop another class from rushing in to fill the void. He had destroyed the old class structure in China but helped create a new class. His solution to this problem was to call for never-ending class struggle, and it was under this battle cry that the masses were so effectively mobilized to attack Mao's own minions from 1966 to 1968. What Mao did, however, was simply replace the so-called "new class" of Communist cadres, which was steadily becoming less responsive to his wishes, with a newer class of more servile officials. The army had played a leading role in putting down the chaos Mao had unleashed, and not surprisingly, the army started providing many of the newer definitions of privilege. The Communist Party itself fell into such disrepute that ambitious young people began turning to the PLA for advancement rather than the Party. As with so much of radical Maoism, romantically attractive theories led to utter chaos and tragic repercussions.

Other aberrations poured in. Under the iron broom of the Cultural Revolution, education was supposed to have become fairer and more egalitarian. Many people in the West, especially radical educators, looked on adoringly at the elimination of examinations, the humbling of autocratic teachers and the "democratization" of entrance qualifications to universities. Most Chinese will tell you these were more frauds, although some of those same Western educators are still so enamored of their theories that they refuse to believe the Chinese themselves.

There was never any widening of the university population. In all of China, only a few hundred thousand students make it into higher education. During the Cultural Revolution, one gained a university position not through intellectual achievement, but through correct class background and political or army connections.

There were plenty of abuses under the old system, but China was still able to produce some impressive results. There were many more abuses under the Cultural Revolution system, and China graduated a generation of dummies. The best-educated young people of that period were those who learned ethics and philosophy through the rigors of real life and who sometimes had parents supplementing this with formal lessons in everything from foreign languages to science.

The classic product of the Cultural Revolution's higher-education scheme was a young woman at a Peking language institute who was considered one of the most accomplished Spanish speakers in the country. When a Chinese delegation went to an international event in Mexico in 1975, she was chosen as the official translator. When she got there, however, she found she couldn't understand what Spanish-speaking people were saying, and she had to be replaced by a translator supplied by the Mexican Government. The experience humiliated her, but it was also a kind of emancipation, for she saw for the first time what a fraud her education had been.

She had spent all this time learning Spanish, and yet she could barely understand a few words when they were spoken to her. And as the woman herself pointed out on her return to China, she was "among the best."

It was perhaps in partial recognition of its own failings and bankruptcy that the newer class collapsed so easily after the Gang of Four was purged. For years, many Chinese had tried to improve their lot by faith in fundamental Maoism and had gotten nowhere. The gains of the Cultural Revolution—greater political awareness on the part of many people and the shaking up of the hierarchy—had been overwhelmingly negated by the fascist state that arose from the initial chaos and decline in people's standard of living. To the surprise of no one, the traumatized bureaucracy quickly adjusted to the new realities, and by 1969 it had become even more omnipresent than it had been before. The army, which had hitherto generally played a positive role in Chinese life, became contaminated by political power, while cadres of various stripes continued to lord it over the people in a fashion unchanged from the days of dynastic rule.

Tales of bureaucratic privilege are endless. A campaign to reform the working style of officials received state approval in 1978, and a number of outrageous offenders were arrested, with attendant and massive publicity. The official campaign against cadre privileges seemed impressive, especially as it gathered up steam during 1979.

Chinese television got into the act in a most riveting way. The Peking station set up a video camera in a shopwindow on busy Wang Fu Jing Street, directly across from the parking lot of the popular Number One Department Store. Limousines and army vehicles, regularly used to ferry the families of the elite to and from their personal shopping expeditions, were constantly in that lot. The cameras faithfully recorded the limousine on this particular day, and focused on the occupants as they scampered off to the store and later returned with all sorts of parcels and packages. "Who are these people, and what are they doing?" asked the somber announcer when the footage was aired on television later in the week. As the cameras took in the cars and their occupants the announcer went on: "The law states that these limousines are only for use on state business. Is this state business?"

The item was featured on Peking television two nights in a row. A day later, for the first time, there was no problem getting a parking spot in that lot. The only vehicles there were either taxis ferrying foreign tourists or foreign residents' cars.

I was impressed at how the word had got around until I drove home by a circuitous route and discovered eight Hongqi limousines parked on a small street two blocks away. The television item had only moved the cars a few blocks away. "If the campaign against the abuses of officials was a real campaign, then we would discover that the officials would be nervous and upset," read a poster on the Xidan Democracy Wall a month or so before this incident. "However, the officials are not upset in the least. They are so far from being nervous that they are enthusiastically supporting the campaign. The Chinese people could learn lessons from this, but it is not likely. There have been other campaigns against the abuses of officials, but still we are plagued by these locusts. This one appears to be no different."

Perhaps it was because of the kind of people who befriended me, but I rarely saw cadre abuse close up. Although many of my friends came from this class, they had all been through a terrible time in the Cultural Revolution and had undisguised contempt for those who refused to learn some of the lessons—a contempt that sometimes included their parents. One friend had access to restricted foreign films, but he always declined to go because he felt the system was so iniquitous. It was they who railed away at the mentality of many of the cadres' children, who expected privileges as a matter of course and took them without a second thought. With this special insight into their own class, they defined official corruption as the most serious problem facing China, one that undermined the last strands of integrity in the Party.

"My father joined the Party when he was a young man, before Liberation," one friend said on this subject. "He was disgusted with the Guomindang, and he really believed that the Communist Party was the only possible hope for China. I would say he joined the Party for national reasons rather than ideological reasons. In time, he became a firm believer in the ideology and always tried faithfully to carry out the Party's policy. Even when he was disgraced during the Cultural Revolution, he told us that the situation would eventually be corrected and not to lose faith in the Party.

"Today, he feels vindicated, and he does not like to hear my criticisms. I have joined the Communist Youth League to please him, but it is not anything I have any enthusiasm for. Most of the

members have no idealism. They have simply joined, either because they had no choice, like me, or to seek advancement. It is just
a question of access to power and position. They know what life is
like for most people, and they want something better. I would say
this characterizes the spirit of the Party today. There are some good
people, who have a strong conception of a better society, but they
are in a minority and find themselves compromised all the time."

The city of Qingdao (pronounced "ching-dao"), on the Shandong coast beside the East China Sea, is something of a mythical
place to a lot of Chinese. No emperors made invocations there, no
outstanding historical buildings exist, there were no significant revolutionary battles and the city is surrounded by a huge and ugly
industrial belt that embodies Blake's vision of "dark Satanic mills."
And yet when you mention Qingdao to many Chinese, their faces
light up. If they were lucky, they may have traveled there briefly
on a holiday; most likely, though, they have heard about it from
friends and relatives who themselves may have got their information at second or third hand.

Qingdao has won its way into the affections of so many Chinese
because it's the best holiday town in the country. But more than this
singular fact, Qingdao is also completely different and—in outward
appearance—completely Western. Not even Shanghai has such a
concentration of Western-style civic planning. Germans came to
Qingdao eighty years ago to reap the advantages of cheap Chinese
labor. They created the city virtually from scratch, and to make
themselves feel more at home, they tried to create a little touch of
Bavaria or Hanover in the Orient. Since Qingdao was planned and
built methodically, it is exceptionally well laid out, and maximum
advantage has been taken of the coastal setting. Pathways beside the
many beaches are charmingly landscaped, and as one rounds a cove
there is usually a long walkway pier pushing out into the ocean,
with a charming pavilion at the end.

The architecture is completely European, *circa* 1900. A massive
cathedral on a hill dominates the entire city, and it is impossible to
go anywhere in Qingdao without seeing it. The cathedral must still
be something of an embarrassment or sore point with the authorities, because it is impossible to find one postcard for sale that has
it in view: Qingdao postcards begin either to the immediate left of
the cathedral or to the immediate right.

There are more young women in skirts than anywhere else in China, and many of them have their hair done up in a far wider variety of styles. Here, pigtails are hard to find. Men sport jaunty caps of all sorts, and people seem to walk about the place with a kind of ease and carefree nonchalance that is as disarming as it is weird.

At the hotel where we stayed there was a loud buzzing in the air that sounded vaguely familiar, but I couldn't remember why. It wasn't until we got up to our room, which overlooked the public beach, that I discovered where it came from. Sea fleas! The bay was filled with those pesky, noisy little motorboats which most cottagers in Canada would like to see permanently banned. Flitting all over the place, the sea-flea fanatics had a hard time avoiding about seven large motor launches that were pulling water skiers. Water skiers? In China? In proletarian, never-forget-the-class-struggle China? Quite literally, I didn't believe what I was looking at.

The beach itself was a mind-boggling sight. Our room was sufficiently high up to take in the whole panoramic sweep of the beach and bay. It was impossible to see an open square foot of sand anywhere. Thousands of people were sunning themselves, playing volleyball or swimming in the water. The old pictures of Coney Island bathers in New York on a July 4 weekend depicted a wilderness area in comparison with this sight.

From conversations on the beach and around the town I learned that the easiest way to get a Qingdao holiday was to have a friend or relative living there. But there are many hotels and guesthouses to suit most workers' pocketbooks, and people come from hundreds of miles away. The largest contingent I met were from Shanghai, and most of the Shanghailanders were either professionals, like doctors and teachers, or students out for a rest and a lark between terms. Although a place like Qingdao is not where you would find a rustic peasant cavorting about, a few offspring of peasants go there —the lucky ones who have been accepted at various institutes of higher education. It was they who made us focus on the nature of privilege in China.

"Many people want to come to Qingdao," said one, "but it is not easy to make the arrangements even if the person has the money. For the most part the people who are here are attached to special places which have made the arrangements for them. There's a model workers' hostel, and most of the people who stay there are members of the Party. At the least, they have been given a trip to Qingdao as a reward for doing well in their work. There is a large naval establishment here, and it is considered the best posting in China. Actually the sports club that supervises all those motorboats is mostly made up of naval people. We tried to see if we could get in a boat and learn how to water-ski, but we were told that use of the boats was restricted."

Even when Chinese speak English well they will often make use of a particular Chinese word if it has a lot of force. "Restricted" is one such word. The Chinese is *neibu,* and from a certain perspective, it could well pass as the motto of New China. Travel anywhere in the country and you will stumble up against things that are *neibu.* In all the major cities, to cite the most obvious example foreign tourists can see for themselves, there are special stores and restaurants restricted to the use of foreigners. No Chinese may enter unless it is on official business. Cadres and their families all attend private screenings of special movies that are *neibu* to the masses.

Any Chinese who doesn't fit into the right category will find out that a great deal in China is *neibu.* And if something isn't *neibu,* it may well turn out to be *buxing* (pronounced "boo-shing"). *Buxing* can mean a variety of things, depending on the context. Essentially, it simply stands for "not correct," but this doesn't give you any insight into the use of the word. An old codger who looks after the gates of a school might shout *"Buxing!"* to a schoolchild and it isn't particularly serious. A policeman who comes up behind a couple walking through a public park a trifle too adoringly might also say *"Buxing,"* and while this is a stupid (and increasingly infrequent) invasion of privacy, it too is not particularly serious. But let a Chinese visit a foreigner's apartment at the wrong time and *"buxing"* takes on an altogether new context. The phrase can lead to direct police interrogation and a host of miseries.

We had gone to the local branch of the Bank of China in Qingdao to exchange some traveler's checks for Chinese money. While we were in the foreign-currency department, a middle-aged resident approached the same window where we had been doing business. Money exchange takes a while in China. As far as I could tell, there are at least six people at every branch of the Bank of China who want to personally count and re-count each cent that comes in or is grudgingly let out. The fellow had a letter with him that bore United States stamps. From the conversation that ensued it became apparent that the man had just recently established contact with an overseas relative who was beginning to send regular remittances.

This practice is very common in South China, the traditional area for emigration over the centuries. During the Cultural Revolution, overseas remittances mostly stopped because they got the Chinese relatives into deep trouble: a connection abroad was almost proof positive of evil intentions or, at the very least, lack of faith in the socialist Motherland. Before the Cultural Revolution, however, and again today, overseas remittances are encouraged by the government, which thereby gains millions of dollars annually. Chinese citizens are allowed to cash in the remittances for Chinese currency at arbitrary rates the government periodically announces. Still, these sums are a great boon to many people, and now they are also an integral part of the government's ambitious Four Modernizations program, which has necessitated the purchase of much machinery and equipment from the West.

The woman bank official was being peremptory with the man, but since this was obviously his first experience with an overseas remittance, he was winning the day by his persistent questioning of every detail connected with the transaction. At one point he said he would prefer to have the entire remittance in cash. Then he paused. "May I have some of it in American cash?" he asked, almost as an afterthought. The response was deafening.

"BUXING!"

The other tellers in the room stopped working and looked toward the man. The official turned to her colleagues and said that the man had asked for American cash. One or two of her colleagues shook their heads in amusement. No Chinese citizen save those officially approved for travel abroad would ever be able to get foreign currency. Also, in theory, there would be no way he could spend American dollars inside China. That's in theory. In practice, there is a black market in which wafers of gold and foreign currency could be handsomely traded, but the fact that the man asked for the dollars so openly was proof that he was an innocent, or if not, he was the dumbest black marketeer in the entire country.

Qingdao has a large and very cushy residential district reserved exclusively for the use of high officials. In the old days this neighborhood, with its spacious houses, broad streets and welcoming beaches, had been reserved for the exclusive use of the German industrialists who made fortunes from cheap Chinese labor. Now, I suppose, it is the gift of the masses to their proletarian leaders. All Chinese who have been to Qingdao know about this area, even if they haven't actually seen it with their own eyes. The reason they probably haven't seen it is that the neighborhood is *neibu*. Army guards patrol all the entrances, and there are signs on the approaching streets telling citizens that they must go no farther unless they are residents or are on official business. Through devious means, I managed to get inside for two hours.

The attractions of the neighborhood are considerable by Chinese standards; it was a favorite retreat of Vice-Premier Deng Xiaoping, who came there for rest breaks from time to time. The beach provides the most immediately striking contrast with the rest of Qingdao. At any time of day, the public beach is jammed with tens of thousands of people. On the two occasions I saw the cadres' beach, there were never more than eighteen serenely contented souls. There is a kind of club where staff members bring out lunches and cold drinks on trays and older officials can be seen playing bridge on the ample verandas. My presence was not appreciated, and I cleared off fast.

Walking around the streets of the area, one is reminded of the West again: the European-style houses with broad, well-manicured lawns seem like any number of older residential districts in Canada and the United States. Healthy-looking kids play tag or kick a ball around. Houses have a basketball net on the side of the garage, and teen-agers can be seen practicing their shots with the same single-minded determination as their peers in the United States. Walking out of the neighborhood and back to Qingdao proper, glimpsing the public beach in the distance, with all those bodies squashed into a few acres, is like walking out of a fantasy land. The quiet and serenity vanishes in a twinkling.

The officials' neighborhood in Qingdao was not a decadent, extravagant place. To the average middle-class North American it might even appear a little run-down and seedy. What distinguishes such places in China from the neighborhoods of the elite in capitalist countries is hypocrisy. Clearly, officials don't want the masses to see how they live. The official Party rhetoric holds that cadres must be a part of the masses, conduct themselves in a humble fashion and never forget "to serve the people." Their advantages and perquisites give the lie to this propaganda, and for all the talk of making the workers and peasants "masters of the state," it is a little difficult to see the qualitative difference between the essence of the cadres' life-style and that of the former capitalist owners of the fine houses at Qingdao.

There are no doubt some romantics in the West who think that things were different during the Cultural Revolution. They never got to Qingdao during that period. A number of cadres were indeed evicted from their fine digs and sent down to the countryside, but the homes did not remain vacant for long. Leading army personnel took them over and lived there in a style they quickly became accustomed to. Mao himself set the pattern for his own radical elite with his chain of homes and his famous private swimming pool at Zhong Nan Hai. His wife Jiang Qing aspired to rather special heights when she closed down two of the most popular parks in Peking—Bei Hai and Coal Hill—so she could ride her horse there in peace and quiet.

Not surprisingly, many Chinese detest such practices. This hatred was part of the reason Mao had such success in unleashing the chaos of the Cultural Revolution; but the privileges of an elite are hard, if not impossible, to put down. To those who aspire to joining that elite, such privileges often seem proper and fitting. There are even a few ordinary people who support the Communist Party's antiegalitarian tendencies.

One young man I met defended the system and had swallowed the hypocrisy whole. Curiously, he had no qualms in talking to a foreigner: usually those who follow the Party line tend to avoid foreigners like the plague. Our conversation took place at a time in China when Mao's record was being openly and widely reevaluated for the first time since the Hundred Flowers Campaign of 1956, so the young man's attitude was not likely to earn him a good report card.

"The cadres work for the good of the people," he said on the subject of the *neibu* neighborhood. "They have to work harder than ordinary workers, and their responsibilities are greater. Therefore, they have earned special considerations. As the material conditions of the masses improve, the contradictions will decrease. The Chinese people accept these contradictions today because they know they are a product of history and will change." I nattered on about this point for some time, arguing that Elizabeth and I knew many Chinese people who did not accept the contradictions in this light. He laughed and said these were people who did not keep the needs of the whole society in mind when they made criticisms. I supposed that he was from the official class and was defending the perks he had himself enjoyed, but he assured me his father and mother were ordinary workers.

Another thing that marked this person off from most of the Chinese of his age was his reverence for the memory of Chairman Mao.

Inevitably, history will deal with the Great Helmsman more judiciously than many of his countrymen today are prepared to do, because they have particular and specific grudges to bear. Contemplating the thought and theory of Mao is a far more rewarding task than perusing his actual handiwork.

It is impossible to live in China for very long without appreciating the enormous tasks that Mao assigned both himself and his Party. His feat of transforming China from a pathetic country to a cohesive, united nation whose territorial integrity is everywhere respected is amazing, especially in such a short space of time. He is the only leader of a Communist nation who has publicly identified the sins of the "new class" of Communist officials, while his lifelong determination to improve the lot of the Chinese peasantry makes him one of the most outstanding figures in the long history of China. As a dreamer and idealist, he was a giant. Yet he condoned much that was evil and criminal, and to his single-minded objectives he brooked little opposition, even though he made innumerable calls for criticism. His dreaming raised China high and then led the nation into chaos. In the end he bequeathed his countrymen a totalitarian regime along with frustrating visions of emancipation: the two still sit badly together. It is this bequest that governs many of the actions of Chinese people today, because every citizen, in one way or another, to a greater or a lesser extent, has to come to terms with the Communist Party.

Since they are a resourceful people, the way in which the Chinese deal with Communism is complex. There are a variety of responses, and various people at various times employ a number of them. The simplest response, and certainly a common one, is mere absorption, the acceptance of the status quo. This is a universal trait, and any distinctiveness the Chinese have brought to the business is simply caught up in the distinctiveness of China itself. A good example is how they cope with the deluge of propaganda that has been poured over them for years.

When one first goes to China, the plethora of propaganda billboards—just to cite one example easily seen by outsiders—seems numbing. Nearly everywhere you turn in the cities, there's a wretched slogan urging the masses on in some way or other. In the countryside, whole hills used to be despoiled with revolutionary dictums. Tourists who profess shock at such sights, though, have forgotten their own responses to the propaganda of a capitalist society. Almost anywhere in a North American city, it is hard to miss a billboard touting the latest products. Unless the ads are new or particularly provocative, however, we pass them by without a second thought, until we become oblivious to their very presence. Chinese are no different. Just to prove this to myself, one day I stood below a massive propaganda billboard in Shanghai for nearly an hour. Tens of thousands of people passed by on bicycle or on foot and no one so much as looked up. This may seem a trivial point, but propaganda signs have been such a feature of Chinese life under Communism that outsiders ascribe to them unusual powers. Repetition and overfamiliarity kill propaganda campaigns just as easily as does ubiquitous advertising.

Perhaps in recognition of this, the government has now begun a policy of replacing some of the propaganda posters with traffic-safety precautions and even Western-style advertising. This caused a great stir among the foreign community when these ads first appeared in Peking late in 1979. Where once Mao's quotation about never forgetting the class struggle dominated a street scene, there was now a silly advertisement promoting the qualities of "Squirrel brand paintbrushes." The change was accepted with more ease, I suspect, than "Never forget the class struggle" would be if it suddenly appeared on a billboard in Times Square. Well, that's not strictly true. Xiao Huang announced one day that "the Chinese people do not like advertising," but he was the exception. The Chinese people had got the measure of the advertisements quite well: they were a manifestation of the new Party line and thus a continuation of propaganda.

If acceptance defines the majority response of Chinese people to Communism, it does not necessarily mean acceptance lying down. Chief among the ways the masses cope with the burdens placed on them is ingenuity. Overall government control on so many aspects of life brings bureaucratic bungling and insensitive attitudes toward the needs of the people. Faced with stupidity, Chinese people usually know exactly what to do.

Toward the end of 1978, a progressive decision by the government allowed the state publishing houses to release tons of hitherto forbidden books for public purchase. The firms also started printing new translations of quite a number of Western classics. All this fare had been banned during the Cultural Revolution, a time when the nation's bookshops seemed to come straight out of *1984*—only the selected works of Chairman Mao and a few other tracts were available. Suddenly, all that changed, but with typical bungling, the distribution scheme dreamed up turned out to be a nightmare. The publishing houses would send huge cartons of books to several stores, and long lineups would result as eager purchasers waited patiently to get their hands on the precious volumes.

I went down to the East Wind Market in Peking to watch the operation a few days after the books were released. It was a remarkable scene. A citizen was permitted to purchase only two books. Ostensibly, the limit was imposed to ensure that a maximum number of people were able to get copies, a reasonable enough policy. Purchasers had to show identification, and there was a way of making sure they didn't simply rejoin the lineup to purchase another two: I was told a special mark was made on the ID to prove someone was already a purchaser. So far so good. Necessity dictated a ration system, but it seemed fair.

The problem arose from the attitude of the publishing houses. Evidently, books were regarded as so many cabbages. A citizen had the choice of buying one or two books, or indeed no books at all. What he couldn't do was choose the title of the book. You lined up, paid your money and got whatever two books were handed to you. Later, as the pressure eased off, some of the titles made it to book racks and purchasers could make individual choices, but during these first days, cartloads of books arrived and were sold on the spot. The cartons were behind a stall, and as people handed over their money, clerks reached into any available carton and handed out the "cabbages." There seemed to be only five titles for sale that day, one of which was *The Forsyte Saga* by John Galsworthy. This was a very popular item, but you couldn't ask for it specifically. One lucky person ended up with two copies of the book, and you could sense his excitement as easily as the disappointment of the woman who got stuck with two copies of Tang Dynasty poems. Galsworthy, I learned, traded better than Tang poems.

A few steps away from the lineup, hundreds of people had formed an impromptu book market to beat the system. There was nothing illegal about it as far as I could determine. Occasionally, the authorities seem to be able to recognize the fact that they have screwed something up and let the masses resolve the matter among themselves. Purchasers took their books around the milling crowd in search of someone who had a book they actually wanted. As unobtrusively as I could, I followed the man with the two Galsworthy novels. Clearly, he wanted one copy for himself, which he duly tucked away in his canvas bag. Then he went shopping. After making several inquiries, he found a woman who had a book he wanted and tried to obtain it in exchange for *The Forsyte Saga.* But she had a copy of that already. What she really wanted was another novel. The man went off again, and at first I thought he had concluded the deal with the woman; in fact, he'd gone off in search of someone who had what she wanted so that he could work a three-way deal. I lost track of him after he had made one further inquiry because there were several hundred people and the atmosphere was a bit like that on a stock-exchange floor.

One encounter I did see needed six people, and I got dizzy trying to work out the permutations of who was trying to get what from whom, depending on the variations possible with twelve books. Although the prices of the books were not uniform, they were all cheap—the most expensive was sixty cents—and the exchangers did not seem interested in recouping the few pennies' difference that some swaps entailed. The potential for chaos in such a scene was considerable, but since these people were determined to get what they wanted, confusion was kept to a minimum, and many compromised on their original choices because they could see things were getting too complicated. The bonanza book sale lasted for five days, and many people returned on other days to continue the bartering.

Responsible subversion was another response to the status quo, a tactic often practiced by people who had no particularly strong aversion to Communism, but who recognized that stupidities arose which had to be circumnavigated. On a lowly level, responsible subversion was the hallmark of a practical peasant. State directives that made no sense at all were simply ignored as discreetly as possible. Such directives might prohibit a daughter's wedding feast or raising a few animals on the side. If a commune wasn't in the front line of an ideological campaign, this sort of thing was regularly countenanced during the Cultural Revolution. In many cases it is now government policy, but for a period it could have got people into serious trouble.

One woman was a Dazhai inspector until 1978. Her job was to visit communes and see if they were properly emulating the famous model commune of Dazhai. A Party member, she nevertheless felt that many of the central government's agricultural policies were madness, and she had won the trust of her rural peers because she listened to complaints. For a long time she had little recourse and could never pass along complaints to higher authorities. However, she could and did turn a blind eye to local practices that would have had the authorities in Peking spluttering with rage.

This became such a common practice over a period of three years that she occasionally got into trouble by letting her guard slip in the presence of more ideologically zealous officials. Fortunately, she was reasonably well connected and was always able to cover up the matter at a local level. She had strong support from most commune leaders, although she admitted that if the Gang of Four hadn't been purged, these same leaders might one day have been forced to denounce her to save their own skins. Curiously, she said this without any contempt for the people who she suggested might inform on her. It was part of the game, apparently, and she was unusual only in that she was prepared to take more risks than most officials at her level, who try to cover themselves on all issues. She told me, however, that there were enough people like her to have kept agricultural productivity from total chaos during those difficult years. It is also cadres like her who account for what lingering respect still exists for the Party in the countryside.

On all levels of Chinese society, the most significant and potentially destructive response to Communism is "the back door"—the euphemism for all transactions between people that are not countenanced by the state. The back door is common to all Communist societies: it is a natural result of an overly planned economy in which consumer desires are placed well below state priorities on production. In the cities, a good example is a pair of leather shoes. Anyone can buy as many cloth shoes as he or she can afford, but will need ration coupons to buy leather shoes. Each year, a citizen can get only two of the three coupons necessary to purchase leather shoes. The back door solves this problem in a trice: a friend might be willing to forgo one coupon for coupons of another sort or for some service that is hard to obtain. This is the back door at its simplest level. Better still is to know someone who either works at a leather-shoe factory or has a back-door connection there—then one can dispense with coupons altogether. Not only that, buyers have a far better chance of getting the size and style they want than they would have with three coupons at a state store, where variety and choice are minimal.

Most Chinese don't hesitate to use the back door, because it is often necessary, and they know that the officials use it outrageously. Officials, to begin with, have access to more and better-quality goods than ordinary people. Special stores exist in Peking for cadres above a certain level. But the law of insatiable demand works the same way at the top as it does at the bottom—only the type of commodity desired changes. A cadre may have no problem getting a pair of leather shoes, but may well find it difficult to purchase a foreign tape cassette or digital wristwatch. However, with a connection at the Ministry of Foreign Trade the business is managed quite easily, especially if the official wanting the watch is from, for example, the housing department of Peking and thus can arrange to get you better accommodations.

New policies bring new potential to the back door. Now that some Chinese students can get permission to study abroad, a connection with the Ministry of Education is extremely useful. Many thoughtful Chinese despise the back door even as they use it and will tell you it is the major source of corruption in the country. The government, from time to time, cracks down on a few notorious cases, but generally it lets the back door alone because it has no choice—the entire bureaucracy is riddled with practitioners. The black market, which is not large, considering the size of China, is a further aspect of the same situation. It appears that increased contact with the outside world has increased the potential of the black market, and this too will be difficult for the government to clamp down on. It has been noted by many Chinese that a number of members of the Politburo—including Chairman Hua himself—sport expensive digital watches. At that level, of course, there is no need of the back door or the black market, but the example has been duly noted.

Such a situation naturally arouses a fair measure of cynicism and opportunism, and these are both traits that afflict the body politic of China today. In many countries this would hardly be worth noting, but in China the Communist Party claims to be the moral and ethical center of the nation, so the hypocrisies it unofficially condones every day eat away at the core of its own presumptions and official values. Once again, the ecclesiastic parallel arises: when churches espousing poverty and humility succumb to opulence and arrogance, the effect on the faithful is similar. Membership in the Party does not guarantee a trouble-free life. The Party has its own disciplinary procedures for members, above and beyond anything that exists for chastising the masses.

After the first crackdown on contacts between foreigners and Chinese, I still managed to see some people discreetly. But those friends who were Party members were particularly vulnerable to "internal" repercussions—called "Party discipline"—and continued contact with them was exceedingly dangerous. Also, many Party members had just gone through two decades of political turmoil in which ideology was turned on its head, and if they didn't want to be utterly destroyed in the process, they had to dance to new tunes at regular intervals.

These flip-flops quickened the growth of cynicism, and many Chinese, their faces contorted in disgust, will tell tales of Party members who often went to absurd lengths to get on the bandwagon of every new change in the ideological line. Even during the bad days, though, when the Party ranks were demoralized and decimated, it seems to have retained sufficient privileges and advantages to entice opportunists to join up. Now it finds itself weighed down by those who give little and take much.

One of the reasons the new government sought to rehabilitate so many of the older cadres who had been disgraced in a variety of Maoist campaigns was that they were precisely the ones who cared about the Party's image and in many cases had made constructive criticism in a genuine effort to reform bad practices. Their places had been filled by those who knew that the Party was a ticket to a better life in everything from jobs to housing, from travel opportunities to education for their children. Less than five percent of the population holds membership in the Communist Party, and thus the possibilities for abuse can be imagined from the statistics alone.

The philosophy of the opportunists was straightforward: "If you can't beat them, join them." They were all comers and survivors, people who didn't intend to be defeated by circumstances and who took every chance available to improve their positions. One cannot go very far in any profession without bumping directly into Party matters, and even if people don't actually join the Party, they must make their accommodation. Sometimes lack of Party membership means that people will become even more sycophantic to the presiding ideology, and there are no more compromised people in

China than these sad souls. They are the bane of nearly every institution in the country. Timorous to the core, they resist change of any sort unless they are sufficiently protected and spend an inordinate amount of time shoring up their positions from all possible attacks. Xiao Luo described them as the real "running dogs," despised alike by confident Party members and the general populace which tries to get by from day to day with a minimum of fuss. Just cycling along the back lanes of Peking, you can see their local representatives on the neighborhood committees: institutionalized snoops who make everyone's business their own.

"He makes it his business to be friends with everyone, and as a result, no one trusts him," said Xiao Wang, describing a supervisor at the factory where his sister works. "For example, he tries to engage his fellow workers in political conversations. We all know such types report to the local Party secretaries. But more significantly, people from the same Unit never talk serious politics together—you do that with your closest friends and usually only if they are from other Units. This fellow also has a habit of being more vocal on the correct line than even Party members, and you can count on him to talk on at great length during the political meetings. For this alone, he is appreciated: he saves the rest of us the bother of having to do the same."

The picture is not one of unrelieved opportunism. Despite institutionalized Communism's abysmal record on human-rights issues, democracy and the advancement of people's material conditions, it still hinges on a certain amount of idealism, and unless people on the outside understand this, they will never be able to come to terms with its latent and actual power. The Roman Catholic Church has produced both saints and dissenters through the years, and that is because the nature of faith draws on deep resources of remarkable people. In this regard, Communism is similar. There are some absolutely exemplary Communists in China who are revered and respected and who, in turn, arouse the zeal of idealistic young people. One could go on endlessly discussing the relative merits of the late Premier Chou Enlai and his ambivalent role during the Cultural Revolution, when he survived any number of plots against him while the colleagues of a lifetime fell by the wayside. But the fact remains that he is a revered figure in China, one whose image ultimately transcended the worst politics of Communism. He remains a model for cadres of the better sort, and the modesty and humility with which he conducted his life earned him genuine and widespread affection, something that eluded Mao all his life. Mao had to make do with fanatic adulation at one extreme and intense loathing at the other: he was never lovable.

Elizabeth once met a man who tried to explain the phenomenal outpouring of grief after Chou Enlai died in 1976. She had been looking at some photographs of people prostrate with grief at the loss of Chou, and the grief seemed extreme even for a revered public leader. Even the assassination of President John Kennedy never produced pictures quite this dramatic.

"It was not just for Chou Enlai himself that people cried," said the man, trying to explain the complexity of the grief. "Of course they thought him a good man, a kind elder uncle whom they trusted. But in a way, they were also crying for themselves. Chou Enlai seemed to be the last vestige of goodness and justice in the government. With his death, people could not see beyond the terrible people, like Jiang Qing, who would now be in total control. They were crying for the lack of justice in China, for their children who had been sent down to the countryside, for the continuing hardships of life from which there seemed no escape. His death aroused all these thoughts, and after years of repression the passing of Premier Chou seemed the last burden the people could tolerate. With him there had been some hope; without him all seemed lost. It was a terrible, terrible moment."

There are lesser Chou Enlais in China now. They are good and decent people who still believe in the promise of the Revolution and go about their affairs in the best way they see fit. In Gongxian (pronounced "gong-shian"), the local head of historical sites was a Party member. Even though he was escorting foreigners around, he felt no need to disguise the backwardness of the area or to make apologies. He explained some of the policies being tried out and acknowledged their mixed results. Several times as we walked about the Sung Dynasty ruins we came across peasants hard at work, and I saw their eyes light up at his approach. He always went directly to them and talked in a very down-to-earth, uncondescending manner—the same way he dealt with us. In a small village, when crowds became immense and sometimes uncontrollable at the sight of two foreigners, he would tell people straight out who we were and what we were doing. Nothing was made mysterious, either to us or to the people we met. He even encouraged us to have some simple conversations with the peasants.

On the other side of the coin, there are an equally small number of people who have the courage to stand up to the continuing evils of repression. They are the Luthers of Communism: they have lost faith in the Party, but they still have hopes for China. The West does not hear a great deal about them. For every Wei Jingshen in Peking, whose arrest was covered by most major newspapers in the world, there are hundreds of other people in China who have made their stand and suffered accordingly. We know little about them save that they exist—court proclamations announcing their prison sentences or executions are one way to find out about them; provincial broadcasts monitored outside China are another.

The lack of information about these people has supported the myth of Chinese docility. During the early seventies, for example, a number of foreign visitors came to China and assumed that there was no dissent whatsoever. In fact, this was a period when many people were being rounded up to be either incarcerated or exterminated. The dissent took many forms, and it was certainly not just for American-style democracy. Court proclamations have been seen by foreigners announcing the execution of "counterrevolutionaries" who started illegal Marxist-Leninist study groups. That will be surprising only to those who have never considered the subject of heresy, religious or secular.

China today pits the individual against very basic dilemmas. Most Chinese, like most people the world over, eschew direct confrontation with those dilemmas, while a few tackle them head on. We cannot pass judgment on the responses of the Chinese before we have properly considered what our own responses would be given similar circumstances. For myself, I suspected I would be a bit like the young cadre at a leading government institution who kept abreast of all the latest developments in politics, both at the top and at places like the Xidan Democracy Wall. He would never actually have put up a poster himself, although he admired those who did even if he thought them naive and foolish. He bucked the system only so far as he thought he could safely get away with it, although he longed for real reform. While he knew that the discrepancies between his relatively high standard of living and that of most Chinese people had to be narrowed if China was going to make it safely into the twenty-first century, he nevertheless had few qualms about enjoying the extras of life that came his way. He wasn't a hero or a villain. He was simply human.

19

The Four Seasons

In a country of one billion people birth and death come like the tide, leaving a residue of statistics that stagger the imagination. It always amazed me, as a Canadian, to contemplate the singular fact that the entire population of my country was easily duplicated in China in less than a year. What kind of life awaits the latest batch of millions?

The first thing one has to do to find out the answer is put the statistics to one side. The birth of a child in China is as signal an event as it is anywhere, and consideration of the millions has always clouded outsiders' views on the particular joys and sorrows, expectations and frustrations that greet the arrival of each baby in this singular nation. The fate of a Chinese child is caught up in the reality of China today, of course, and certain obvious predictions can be made based on whether it was born in the city or the countryside, whether it is male or female, whether its parents have a "good" class background and so on. But these considerations aside, all Chinese seem to adore children, and the exigencies of life are forgotten, however briefly, to celebrate the renewal of hope for the future that birth heralds. In this, the Chinese are no different from any other people.

The Communist Party can be credited, among other things, with significantly improving the standards of public health over the past thirty years, which has led to a dramatic decline in the infant mortality rate. Chinese medicine, with its combination of traditional herbal remedies and Western techniques, is inadequate in a number of ways, but today such inadequacies have mostly to do with insufficient financial resources. Where common sense, basic rules of sanitation and the recognition of simple medical principles are applied, remarkable results have been achieved. In most places in the countryside, Chinese babies come into the world in clean, if spartan, clinics or rural infirmaries. In addition to medical or paramedical help, most mothers have their own mothers close at hand to offer advice and practical assistance.

The Chinese affection for little children is one of the easily observed wonders of the place and manifests itself in a variety of ways. Drab and uniform as much adult clothing in China is, for example, children are dressed to the nines. Parents seem to put all their couturier skills and imagination into outfitting their offspring. The most wonderful sight in Peking during the stark winters is the little bundles of babies in their garish red or yellow cloaks covering even bolder spectrums of color than a rainbow. Babies are cosseted and cuddled within an inch of their lives, and not just by their mothers and doting grandmothers: the tenderness and loving-kindness many young Chinese fathers bring to baby rearing is something to behold. On the streets, in buses or at the Workers' Stadium, a clutch of fathers are always stumbling over themselves in pride and adoration of their tiny offspring.

A deformed or mentally handicapped child represents a tragedy anywhere in the world, but in China such unfortunate children bear a special burden. There are institutions for the severely mentally and physically handicapped in China, but it is safe to assume they are primitive in the extreme. Foreigners are never taken to such places, even when requests are made by special-interest groups. Only a few Chinese I met could confirm that institutions for the handicapped even existed. More ominously, none of China's several medical journals ever deals with the problem of retardation.

A young doctor whom I met in Qingdao told me that if it is apparent at birth that a child is in any way abnormal, hospitals do little to keep it alive. This is not the result of a euthanasia policy; it is simply the continuing product of tradition in a society with too many mouths to feed and few resources to care for those who cannot ultimately fend for themselves. The few exceptions to this rule are usually grotesque. Chinese scientists, for example, are fascinated by the so-called ape babies that are born from time to time. Such infants are covered with body hair from their heads to their toes and are thought to be interesting as a link to our Darwinian past. Much is made in propaganda magazines about them and their "equal opportunity to make contributions to socialism," but they are clearly regarded as freaks and maintained as such. No efforts appear to be made to remove the unwanted hair. I got the distinct impression they were required to go through life with their flowing manes to disprove religious conceptions of the origins of humanity.

If a handicapped child survives birth and possesses intelligence, life can be particularly bleak and frustrating. No matter how bright the person is, no matter how diligently he or she copes with the handicap, no matter how excellent the academic record, that child will never be admitted to a university or other institute of higher learning. With fifty million high school graduates competing for barely three hundred thousand university positions, the selection system is cruel enough for those without any handicaps, while those with physical disabilities are simply barred.

In Wuhan, a bright twenty-one-year-old man who had contracted polio in his boyhood was luckier than most. As the son of a middle-level cadre, he had a wheelchair contraption with a hand-driven bicycle chain which he could operate with amazing dexterity. Largely on his own initiative, he had taught himself English, which, tied to his natural scientific curiosity, made him just the sort of eager young person the government is seeking to encourage to further the ambitious modernization program. So far, however, he has had no success whatsoever in persuading educational authorities to get him study materials and some professional assistance to advance his self-taught education in electronic engineering. Even his father's connections have been no help, although, as he himself points out, the authorities could make terrific propaganda with him.

"Even though I am a cripple, I am working full out for the Four Modernizations," he said with a sardonic laugh. He may well pull off his plans, for he has more determination and guts than any ten of his unhandicapped peers; but it will be in spite of the system. One educational official told him he would be better off working with cane and bamboo—a career he rejects with the same anger felt by intelligent handicapped people in the West when similar propositions are made to them. He was very frank about his situation and said that he had got as far as he had thanks only to his father's superior position in society. I asked him what would happen to the child of a peasant or an ordinary worker if it was stuck with the same predicament. "Don't ask it," he said. "There is no future for such people. You can only wait for death."

As normal Chinese children grow up and prepare to enter primary school at the age of seven they gradually start their encounters with larger realities. Since nearly all mothers in China work, children are soon enrolled at day-care centers if their parents live in advanced communes or are attached to well-established institutions in the city. More than likely, though, the day-to-day rearing will be done by an older relative. There is far less day care in China than is generally believed by foreigners, who are all shown model establishments during their three-week tours of the country. Well-placed couples with better salaries might even be able to arrange a live-in *ayi,* or nanny, but this is very rare. Far more commonly, parents are forced to send their children to faraway relatives who can provide better rearing. This is always a painful business, and most mothers resent the necessity. It is a regular practice, for example, for country people with city connections to send their children there for a better education. And in outlying areas like Tibet, parents posted from the Chinese interior will have their children, whenever possible, brought up elsewhere.

It is at primary school, whether in the countryside or in town, that the Communist Party begins its major battle for the hearts and minds of the Chinese. It is impossible to talk about consistency in Chinese education, because there have been so many philosophical and ideological flip-flops in theory over the past thirty years; but in the endeavor to drive home the importance of the Party there has developed an institution approaching the unalterable. Before long, nearly every child becomes a Young Pioneer and proudly sports the red kerchief around his or her neck. Traditional Chinese precepts on conformity, buttressed by the Party's penchant for uniformity, have a seemingly powerful effect on young minds. Individual expression, generally speaking, is frowned upon. Because of this and a number of other factors, outside observers have repeatedly stressed that the Chinese take a fundamentally different approach to life than do Westerners, with their cult of individual action and responsibility.

This never seemed quite so self-evident to me. In making the argument it is first of all necessary to dismiss those many forces in Western society—from churches and community-action groups to the common desire for a better life—which bind many people together despite our much-advertised fractiousness. It is also necessary to ignore those many aspects of Chinese society which are evidence of nonconformity. The progress of the Cultural Revolution, which released the genie of anarchism, should have been proof enough; so should the massive state apparatus set up to enforce conformity. If the Chinese people were by instinct so utterly docile and enamored of uniformity, that apparatus would be redundant, and the dictatorship of the proletariat would not be the menace it is today. Ironically, outsiders often attribute traits, such as docility, to the Chinese masses that the Communists or the Guomindang Party in Taiwan would never dream of attributing to them.

In any society, the most volatile and potentially disruptive age group is between fifteen and twenty-five. A lot of insight into a country and its government can be gained through observation of the way in which the transition from childhood to early maturity is managed. It is the age of increasing sexual awareness, of growing physical and mental prowess, and of dawning ambition. It is a revolutionary age, and in a purportedly revolutionary country it is quite amazing to see how resolutely the authorities seek to defuse the obvious danger. The one exception was during the Cultural Revolution, when Mao Tsetung tried to ignite it and make it serve his own political ends, but after barely a year he too was overwhelmed by all the implications of youthful zeal and ingenuity and vigorously set out to contain them.

Because the Party has presumed to put its stamp on all aspects of life and society, young people are urged to channel their pent-up emotions and longings into safe, Party-regulated areas. Efforts are made to get the brightest young people to join the Communist Youth League, and there is constant proselytizing to work full out to achieve the goals of socialism. Not surprisingly, this works with some young people. The objectives of Communism are hitched to Chinese nationalism, and this can have a potent effect on idealistic young people who are seeking ways to work for a larger purpose than self-interest. Others, whose idealism ranges further afield into forbidden areas, are fated for tragedy.

The first major adult crunch comes toward the end of a high

school career, at least in the cities. Most young people will not go on to higher education, and many are still sent to the countryside. There is no real way of knowing how many greet this prospect with any degree of equanimity, but most resent it keenly. Eventually, some youths adjust to the force of circumstances and come to enjoy the rough transition, but the policy of sending down educated youths is such an openly acknowledged sore point that we can assume the vast majority never cease to feel bitter about their situation. Ambitious peasant youths in the countryside have a different perspective. Even under the now-discredited radical education policies that sprang from the Cultural Revolution, they hardly had a chance to go on to higher education. Indeed, they would be lucky if they got more than a total of four or five years of schooling.

The most popular way out of your native village and the incessant demands of Chinese agriculture is to be accepted into the People's Liberation Army. Like India, China has never had any need of conscription. In the three-million-strong standing army, there are at least ten applicants who aren't accepted for every one who is.

The PLA is a remarkable institution. Its responsibilities far exceed the ordinary work of soldiering and range from capital construction to propaganda. In between, the army is a major component in the stability of the country, its productive output and even its cultural life. Thanks to the chaos of the Cultural Revolution, the PLA grew in importance; during this period it was the principal tool Mao had to keep control. Previously, it had a relatively apolitical presence in China. During the sixties and seventies, however, the power and influence of the PLA expanded tremendously. While this expansion had a detrimental effect on the governing of China, it enhanced the position of army members, who began controlling many aspects of ordinary, day-to-day life. The appeal of the PLA to the millions of peasant youths who strove mightily to join its ranks is self-evident.

The army is, first and foremost, an escape from an otherwise inevitable round of rural drudgery. Like the medieval Catholic Church, it offers a tangible means of betterment and promotion when all other avenues, because of either social or economic conditions, are effectively sealed off. A peasant youth in the PLA gets to travel the country, has access to vastly superior housing and material conditions, can earn far more than he would ever dream of earning at home and thus can take far better care of his family.

There also seems to be a genuine respect for the army among many citizens which exceeds anything felt for Party members.

Part of the reason for this is that older Chinese people identify the army with the revolutionary period, when Mao's troops became the first soldiers in Chinese history to respect peasant rights and never looted or raped as they made their way from battle to battle. Mao saw his army as the most important instrument in winning the sympathy of the peasants for Communism, and his theory was proved absolutely correct. Time tarnishes many reputations, however, and the PLA has come in for its share of criticism. The increasingly arbitrary actions of the army, especially in commandeering formerly civilian institutions and prerogatives, has been a sore point for some years. As one woman in Wuhan, who viewed the army with a somewhat jaundiced eye, said, it is better than the Public Security Bureau, but the hard work of three peasants is still required to support every soldier.

In the country, job hunting as such does not exist. Those who are not chosen for the army or for the ranks of the Party proceed on in life as their parents and ancestors have done for several millennia. This accounts for the vast majority of Chinese who are tied to the land more securely than the ghost of Marley was chained to his account books. For some time to come, the situation will remain basically the same. All the talk of modernizing the country by the year 2000 is fine, but it doesn't take into account a province like Sichuan and its one hundred million people. If China were able to bring large-scale mechanization to agriculture in Sichuan in the near future, it would be a calamity of major proportions. With so many peasants and the resulting cheap labor, mechanization would make millions redundant—the economic forces being what they are —and agricultural production would probably be much more expensive. It is unwise to predict political events in China, but it is safe to assume that people yet unborn will still be plowing fields by hand in Sichuan forty years hence—fields that have been fertilized by human waste carried in pails on shoulder poles.

In the cities, though, the scramble for jobs is intense. There just aren't enough to go around—not nearly enough. China has the most overemployed population in the world. In any factory in the nation one sees proof that there are at least two people for every job. This is counterproductive and a waste of able-bodied workers, but necessity determines reality. The authorities have concluded that it is better to have overemployment, whatever the dilatory results, than people without jobs.

The enduring agony for the Chinese Government is that even with massive overemployment, rigidly controlled city populations and a large-scale birth-control program, serious unemployment continues to exist. Recent experiments to reduce factory manpower and encourage higher productivity have only aggravated the situation. Unemployment was something that was never admitted before 1979, but the seriousness of the problem can no longer be hidden. This unemployment is not simply a result of the return of young people from the countryside in such huge numbers. High school graduates often wait up to two or three years and even longer before the state is able to assign them a position. Only a tiny handful of Chinese citizens have the privilege of trying to find interesting work tied to their aptitudes and qualifications; for most people it is just a question of finding a job—any job.

With employment secured, or even before, a young person's fancy turns to matters of the heart, and on this subject alone a great deal of Western speculation has revolved. Sex in the People's Republic is neither as repressed nor as complicated as some observers have assumed. The main starting point for any consideration of the question is the straightforward reality that the Chinese people have been able to reproduce themselves without much difficulty for a very long time.

If one looks at China peripherally, sex does not appear to be a big issue. But in fact, it is the source of a considerable amount of public policy making and private decision taking. Birth control has been written into the Chinese Constitution, and while the program has had a significant success in the cities, which have twenty percent of China's population, peasants in the countryside continue to resist the reputed benefits. For many peasants, children are still directly related to security and prosperity: the more children you have, the more chances you have to make it through to old age safely. A large family brings in a lot of work points, and work points mean money and money means security. Three decades of socialism and Mao Tsetung Thought have done little to change this simple equation in the minds of millions of Chinese. In city institutions and within the Party there are retirement plans and pensions; in the countryside such privileges are few and far between.

An important aspect of the birth-control program is preventing men from marrying until they are twenty-eight and women until they are twenty-five. A whole system of restraints and rewards supports this policy, although for many young people it is very hard indeed. Foreign students at Peking University report that when springtime comes along, many of the Chinese male students bring a special ferocity to their athletic endeavors, and in their spare time they can be found lolling around with the lassitude of lovers who have nothing to focus the object of their passions on. The Communist Party tries to harness those passions, and as you might expect, there is a great deal of sublimation going on. The sublimation takes both orthodox and unusual directions. Group activities and political fervor is one way. Someone once described the whole of Communist China as a "summer camp" presided over by Camp Director Mao. It's not a bad analogy. The Party tries to assume many parental prerogatives and preaches both its definition of morality and the appropriate endeavors for young people. There are no actual laws involved, but the unwritten rules are well known; break them and suffer the consequences.

The Party is aided in keeping young people's minds off sex by the material conditions of China. In the West we have lost touch with our own recent past in this matter. Sex as a sensual business is tied up with a host of appurtenances: privacy, leisure time, a minimum of guilt and any number of material allurements. When these things were available in China to a small privileged class, the Chinese showed themselves as sensual as any race. In rural America a century ago, the hardships of life kept sex in greater perspective than would be possible today.

There is sufficient official evidence of violence in China to assure ourselves that rape and prostitution exist and that the Chinese hold no monopoly on righteousness, but it is generally true to say that sex is more successfully balanced with life than it is in the West. For all the talk of our sexual revolution in the last three decades, we nevertheless have created a small army of the walking wounded, who have been turned off sex almost entirely. For them, and for many others, the concentration on flesh in the West is a daily assault that turns them ever inward. In China, the walking wounded are at the other extreme. During the Cultural Revolution, Xiao Wang told me, there were a significant number of Red Guards who stopped sublimating altogether when their adoration of Mao evaporated and managed to act out even the most bizarre sexual fantasies.

As in other Asian countries, prohibitions between young men and women lead to intense friendships with the same sex. While this may well be a form of unconscious homosexuality, it is considered a normal thing and usually does not amount to anything. In traveling through India or Vietnam or China, one often sees men holding hands with other men and women indulging in close embraces with women. When the United States first became involved in Vietnam, the sight of local soldiers in battle dress holding hands so upset the American GIs that orders went out forbidding that practice, which was a normal part of the culture. The day after the last United States soldiers left South Vietnam, the hand holding began again. Shortly after I arrived in China, I watched a huge parade in Tienanmen Square. Incredulously, I noted that many of the sailors and soldiers passing through the Square were holding hands even while they were marching. Evil is in the eye of the beholder in all this. Homosexuality is a big taboo in China, although it certainly exists. Until 1978, if a Chinese official was asked by a foreigner about homosexuality, he usually replied that there was none. There is, but it is kept discreetly out of view.

My favorite account of a foreigner's trying to find out about homosexuality in China involves something that occurred in 1979, shortly after Sino-American relations had been normalized. A somewhat offbeat American press delegation came to China for a three-week trip, and most of the members were from California, including the precocious editor of a gay newspaper in San Francisco. On the second day of their trip, they were taken to a people's commune, and when the inevitable question period came up, the editor put up his hand.

"Can you tell me about the gay situation on your commune?" he asked.

There was some mumbling between the interpreter and the commune leader, but after a few moments they were both beaming.

"Thank you very much for your question," said the commune leader through the interpreter. "Everyone is very happy. So kind of you to ask. It is proof of the good feeling between the American and Chinese peoples."

The chumminess of young Chinese males can still make a disconcerting sight, even to veteran observers from the West who have become used to such public manifestations. On January 1, 1979, some members of the foreign community were invited to attend a special production of traditional opera at the Great Hall of the People. All of China's most important leaders were in attendance. They came in their huge Red Flag limousines, all driven by People's Liberation Army drivers. In the main foyer of the Great Hall, there was a bench fifty yards long for the drivers' use as they waited for their charges, and during a break in the show I went out there to make a telephone call. I could scarcely believe what I saw. About two hundred soldier-drivers were seated on the benches, and the vast majority of them were cuddling up to each other, some even fondling calves and thighs. Senior officers and officials came and went and took no notice. It was an extraordinary sight certainly, but as with many things in China, there was probably a lot *less* than meets the eye. In the West we have come to see such things in terms of ultimate consummation; in China, unconscious and innocent suggestion is usually as far as anything goes. Most of these men will be married and happily fathering in a few years.

Maleness, however, is a valuable commodity in China, although the Communists have inherited the old Christian missionary zeal in trying to improve the condition and status of women. Since it is still possible to see a few older women with feet crippled from the barbaric practice of foot-binding, it doesn't take much imagination to realize how far China has had to come in this regard.

In the early days of the revolutionary struggle, most of the (male) leaders of the Communist Party came close to espousing free love. People like Liu Shaoqi, Zhu De and Lin Biao—and Mao himself, for that matter—ditched wives when it suited them. When Jiang Qing, a young coquette from the Shanghai film world, first arrived in the Communist-controlled headquarters in the north, she quickly caught the Great Helmsman's fancy, and Wife Number Two had to make way for her. Old revolutionaries and old coquettes apparently forget their former predilections, and by the time Mao controlled all of China, such attitudes were frowned upon.

Building on traditional Chinese values, the Communist Party came to espouse a rigid and puritan attitude toward sex. The habits of revolutionary days became *buxing.* They were a source of contention, though, even then. In the early forties, the woman writer Ding Ling attacked the hypocrisy of the male revolutionary leadership in matters relating to women. She discovered very quickly that women's liberation was to be defined by Mao, not by women, and she paid a heavy price for her rebellion on this and other disputatious points. After a brief reprieve, she was attacked again in the mid-fifties and suffered imprisonment and exile. It was only in 1979 that she was "rehabilitated."

Women, said Mao once, hold up "half of heaven." Sometimes in China it seems as if they get stuck with three-quarters of the job. Theoretically, all professions and work positions are open to them, and many liberation-conscious Western women have assumed that their Chinese sisters have approached near equality. A simple perusal of those who wield real power puts the lie to this. There are only a handful of women on the Central Committee, and most of them are there because their husbands have rank. The Chinese Communist Party is a bit like the Salvation Army in this regard: revolutionary wives rise along with revolutionary husbands; they also fall into disgrace when their husbands fall. On a more lowly level, women seem to get more of the burdens of liberation than the spoils. In any work team, they will usually have the inferior positions. One notable exception is street cleaning in cities, which is left entirely in women's hands (except that they are usually assigned to their streets by men). Immediately after Liberation, there were dramatic changes in the status of women, but since the mid-fifties their position has remained static, like so many other initially promising developments in New China's earliest years.

The Party cannot be blamed entirely for this state of affairs. There is still an awesome backlog of what Chinese call "feudal attitudes" in the matter. Even though most Chinese women work at full-time jobs, they are usually expected to manage the housework and shopping. There are a few couples who have worked these things out equitably, and in such relationships the wife will say her husband is not feudal. This is the exception, however. Just as in the West, male prerogatives in politics, business and leisure are so well entrenched in China that it is very difficult for intelligent or industrious women to make any real headway. An additional problem is that the Party frowns on independent proselytizing. Women's liberation as it has developed recently in the West would be considered by the authorities in exactly the same light as the Xidan democracy movement—*buxing*. Women would be told that they were putting their own interests ahead of the nation's; and in such matters it is always wise to remember who is the final authority as to what exactly constitutes the nation's interests.

Much is made of the fact that "the Chinese people" put community and national concerns ahead of individual and personal interests. Many no doubt do. There are people in the West who are capable of such things too. Yet the presiding concerns of the nation and community are always exclusively identified by the authorities, a trait of authoritarian Chinese governments that goes back well beyond the Communists. The recent policy change to allow "local conditions to dictate local needs" in certain economic areas is proof that previous definitions of national and community needs did not reflect what either the nation or the community actually needed or wanted.

There are conflicting views on the relationships between men and women in China. Many arranged marriages still occur in the countryside, although they are supposed to be illegal, while "feudal traditions" of large dowries and elaborate wedding feasts are regularly denounced in the official press. Elsewhere, marriages based on love have a reasonable chance of occurring, although there are certain considerations peculiar to China. A bad class background can still be the ruin of an engagement. One's background is closely scrutinized, and if you do not choose carefully where you bestow your affections, you could be asking for a lot of trouble. Marrying someone whose family had a bourgeois history can still affect your chances for getting a good job and endanger the future security of your children.

The new government appears to be making an effort to diminish the corrosive effects of thirty years of institutionalized class struggle, but it still permeates relationships, and the damage that has already been done will take years to correct. It would be a foolish person who did not at least consider the distinct possibility of renewed class struggle if the current Party line changes.

Things have a way of seeming to become very firmly fixed in China in a short time, thanks to the deluge of one-sided propaganda that greets each new ideological direction and the total dearth of formal opposition. If someone writing about China in 1974 had said that class struggle would soon be put to one side, that private plots would make a comeback and that China would invade Vietnam, he or she would have been classified as a raving lunatic, despite the fact that there were clues to hinge each prediction on if you explored Party history and traditional regional rivalries. Today it is considered heresy to even suggest that there might be another shift someday toward radical Maoism. The death of Mao is supposed to be the principal hedge against this; but if the current government's policies fail to improve the lot of ordinary Chinese and backfire in other areas, the resulting explosion will be frightening. Politically sensitive Chinese know this to be true even if they dismiss any thought of another Cultural Revolution as "too disgusting to even talk about."

If the matter of a bad class background is not an issue with a couple wanting to get married, it certainly will be with their respective Units—the powerful, official social grouping in China to whom they must apply for permission. If the other prospective partner is a Party member or has shown an interest in joining, the marriage will not be approved. Normally, people with Party aspirations wouldn't allow themselves to have any affectionate dealings with a person whose class background is questionable. But it does happen from time to time. A cadre with the Ministry of Foreign Trade told me that he had tried to marry a woman whose grandfather had been a landlord in the old days, and he didn't hear the end of it for over a year. The matter was taken out of his hands when the woman was reassigned to another city. He told me the story matter-of-factly and showed no remorse or bitterness over the incident. He was now married, presumably to someone with a good class background, and they had one daughter.

It's easy to pass judgment on something like this, but I usually tried to think of parallels from my own society. When I told this to one Chinese friend, he scoffed at my attempt to understand and said, "If he had joined the Party he should have known better than to pursue the relationship. Party people deserve all the miseries they have created for themselves. I don't have any sympathy for him, only for the girl. The Party is always talking about the feudal customs of peasants in marriage. What is more feudal than its own attitude?"

Sympathy, in any event, is rather redundant. If the Unit doesn't give permission for a marriage, it can't take place. Even if the actual civil ceremony were somehow managed, it is one's Unit that provides accommodation for young couples, and without a place to live together a marriage doesn't have much logic to it. Actually, some couples do get permission to marry, but because of acute housing shortages in the city they may have to wait for many months or even years before accommodation can be obtained. This is particularly true for those who make the mistake of marrying someone from another city. Not only does the accommodation have to be arranged and approved; one of the partners has to apply to his or her (usually her) Unit for permission to move to another city and then find another Unit to provide work as well. Still, if the Units are agreeable, a solution will eventually be found, and Chinese people are conditioned to accept frustrations like this, which continue after marriage. One of our Chinese friends who has been married for eleven years has been able to spend only six of them with his wife, owing to innumerable special assignments away from home and the rigors of the Cultural Revolution, when families were repeatedly split up by stints of work in the countryside.

Although divorce occurs in China, it is neither easy to obtain nor, in the woman's case, easy to recover from. The positive aspect of this is that neighbors and work colleagues are often brought into the domestic squabbles to try to resolve them. Couples are urged to reconcile, even though they are having profound difficulties, and only after this rather laborious procedure can they go to a court and try to have the marriage dissolved. The court itself will usually try to patch things up too, and the couple may be required to live together for another stretch to satisfy the authorities. No statistics are available on how many bad marriages in China are saved in this fashion, but relatively few divorces are granted. Often couples who have grown apart simply stay together to avoid all the fuss and bother. If a divorce is approved, all sorts of problems arise, from child custody to arrangements with your Unit for new accommodation. One couple I knew of in Peking had been given an official divorce in 1977 but were still living together in 1979 because separate housing was simply unavailable. A divorced woman will find herself marked as "spoiled goods." It is highly unlikely that she will ever marry again, and her social horizons will become considerably narrowed. Her former husband will experience far less hardship.

Even when most conditions favor a marriage it can be tough to pull off because of the housing shortage in all of China's cities. In Peking, the government built a series of new apartment buildings below Tienanmen Square. Each of the buildings was about fourteen stories high, and all the apartments had been accounted for by various institutes in the city. One of the buildings was promised to the New China News Agency. Love had blossomed between some of the agency's co-workers, which is the best possible event in China because they are all members of the same Unit and the bureaucratic encumbrances are correspondingly less. Since 1976 they have been told to be patient because the new apartment building would soon be ready.

The building was completed in late 1978, but by April 1980 no one had been able to move in. The construction work had been so shoddy that the precast sewerage and plumbing pipes had disintegrated and the buildings were next to useless. The authorities had enlisted the help of German building experts, who came to Peking, examined the disaster area and told the Chinese that the cheapest and wisest thing to do was tear them all down. That is unlikely to happen—the loss of face would be too catastrophic—and some solution will no doubt be found. In the meantime, though, the eager couples at the New China News Agency remain unmarried, and the prospects for early nuptials don't look good.

Chinese housing, old or new, is fairly primitive by our standards, but most Chinese people do not complain. They are grateful for a roof over their heads and the chance to keep the family together. There are very few institutions for older people in the country, and grandparents are a traditional and enduring fixture in the Chinese family. This is one of the genuinely attractive aspects of Chinese society. Older people are generally highly respected and are also a much-appreciated help around the home, doing all sorts of domestic chores, from baby-sitting to marketing. There are problems, though. Several posters went up on the Xidan Wall complaining of the cramped conditions in Chinese residences, where three generations were sometimes forced to live in the same room.

Space is at a premium throughout China, but no more so than in the cities. One of the reasons parks are so popular is that there is breathing space. At night, in good weather, much of the population repairs to the street for gossip or card games. There are few nooks in Chinese homes for quiet little naps or a bit of private reading, and the forced proximity of family members, on top of the close proximity of politics, has necessitated a special Chinese etiquette that could serve as a model to a world coming to terms with overcrowding.

When death comes, it is handled discreetly but with dignity. Even for those Chinese who still hold religious beliefs there will be no religious ceremony as such unless it is done on the sly in the countryside. Whenever possible, the state disposes of corpses by cremation, which is preceded by a civil memorial service to which friends and colleagues are invited. China is officially an atheist country. Token toleration of religion returned after the Cultural Revolution, but the toleration has severe limits. Nevertheless, death, like birth, is a signal event, and Chinese people appear to have retained considerable reverence for it. The Party has sought to co-opt the annual Qing Ming Festival honoring the dead, but traveling through the countryside during this period (early April) you will see considerable evidence that the traditional faith of generations of Chinese still endures.

At Qing Ming time, graves all over the countryside will be festooned with paper wreathes honoring the dead. Many Chinese people still feel it incumbent upon them to account to their ancestors for their deeds. Party hypocrisy is rife in this area too. Although the Communists frown upon religious services, ancestor worship and the burial of bodies in the ground, their own ceremonies are parodies of all three things. There are special *neibu* cemeteries, like Babaoshan in Peking, for the Party faithful that would be the envy of Western undertakers. In Nanking, I visited a cemetery for local "revolutionary martyrs" in which all the uncremated bodies were deposited into elaborate aboveground cement vaults, although peasants are deemed feudal if they do the same thing in simple earthen graves in a field. Memorial services for departed Party Pooh-Bahs can ascend to maudlin heights of pseudoreligiosity.

The nonsense surrounding the mausoleum for Chairman Mao brought the whole message home. The bodily sanctification of Communist leaders in China, Vietnam and the Soviet Union in their see-through coffins is a particularly ghoulish embellishment and deeply repugnant to a number of Chinese people, including those who consider Mao a great figure. Chou Enlai, sharp to the end, left strict instructions to have his body cremated and his ashes scattered around his Motherland. The symbolism of this compared with the repellent cadaver in Tienanmen Square has been noted with considerable sarcasm by a number of Chinese.

Chou Enlai and his widow, Deng Yingchao, had a relationship that is a kind of model to many Chinese people. They were never able to have children, and because of this many ordinary Chinese have succumbed to the romantic conceit that *they* are their children. That is a common and very heartfelt statement. Chou's kindly demeanor was beloved by Chinese women, who often have a difficult time with their men.

One friend speculated that the first time a Chinese woman had a really open and fully loving relationship with a male was when she produced a son. Husbands and fathers, she suggested, were usually authoritarian and selfish, and Chinese society still supports these tendencies. Chou and Deng seemed to have a very equal and honorable relationship, one that survived the test of time and politics. The widespread affection felt for them appears to have crossed all barriers of politics, upheavals and betrayals. This may or may not be a true picture of their relationship, but it hardly matters. It was what the Chinese people thought the relationship was like, and in thinking so, they give expression to their own ideals and hopes. The contradiction whereby people distrust and even loathe the Party and yet love and revere one of its leaders is just that—a contradiction. Contradictions are woven into the fabric of life in China. Some of them have been arbitrarily imposed; others arose naturally from history or the force of circumstances. What often strikes us as strange or inscrutable in the Chinese way of doing things usually has an interior logic, which it is wise to scrutinize.

20

The Chinese Way

Along the Pilgrim's Way, that joyous mountain climb at Tai Shan which so many Chinese have aspired to make throughout the ages, there are a number of small grottoes wherein lesser Daoist deities are alleged to reside. Except for the faithful who will furtively leave incense sticks and small offerings of flowers and food, the grottoes are primarily of historical interest. One or two have been attractively refurbished by the authorities following the iconoclasm and vandalism of the Cultural Revolution. A nonbeliever may dismiss the mystical marvels attributed to the grottoes as so much nonsense, but unless the heart is entirely hardened, one cannot fail to find them refreshing and curious way stations. In the heat of the climb, the cool enclosures offer respite, and some of the remaining carvings and old proverbs chiseled into the rock still have the power to provide a chuckle or a contemplative thought. After looking at three of these grottoes on the lower reaches, I couldn't find any more for a considerable length of time as I continued my ascent. Then one appeared and I made my way eagerly in—too eagerly. Within seconds, I recoiled with nausea and disgust. This grotto had become more than a way station. It was filled with human excreta. I staggered out to warn my wife not to make the same mistake.

The repulsive side by side with the sublime! This is the ultimate contradiction in China, and it is not possible to ignore it out of either politeness or embarrassment. Ubiquitous "honey carts" are a fixture of every neighborhood as they pick up daily offerings from the hundreds of thousands of public latrines in China. The valuable commodity is transported to commune farms and deposited in vast cesspools to await service as fertilizer. The smell of excrement is often in the air, and it is no more pleasant for Chinese to inhale than it is for outsiders—they are simply more used to it.

Just to the west of the Xidan Democracy Wall there is a further wall which was used for posters during the most hectic months when space at Xidan was at a premium. This adjunct to the *vox populi* was directly beside a particularly foul-smelling latrine, and sometimes you would see dozens of people reading a poster while holding handkerchiefs over their noses and mouths.

One poster writer, with a rather perverse sense of humor, decided to take advantage of this drawback. At one point in his attack on the privileges of high bureaucrats, which was prominently posted directly beside the latrine entrance, he wrote: "Breathe deeply, comrades. That is the smell of the Chinese people. It is an honest smell that does not pretend to be other than it is. It is the sweetest of smells compared with the stench from the pleasure palace of Wang Dongxing!" (Wang was a vice-premier and former bodyguard of Chairman Mao's. Although he was instrumental in abetting the purge of the Gang of Four, he was too closely associated with the Gang's policies and the opportunism of the Cultural Revolution to escape ultimate reckoning. For several months, common gossip and wall posters focused on his multimillion-dollar home in Zhong Nan Hai. Ordinary people in Peking seemed to know even the exorbitant cost of individual doors in the house. He was eventually demoted in early 1980.)

Since chemical fertilizers are still scarce and expensive in China, and also because sewerage facilities continue to be primitive, the use of human excrement as fertilizer will continue to be a basic, and everpresent, fact of life. Once again, in necessity, the Chinese make do and have even turned the collection of night soil into a kind of virtue. This does not mean the Chinese are a race of coprophiliacs; their generally fastidious concern for cleanliness is proof against that. One will often hear southern Chinese complain of the filthy habits of northerners, that they take a bath or a shower only three

or four times a year, but that is not so. Consciousness of the importance of personal hygiene has increased tremendously throughout
China in the past thirty years, although the enthusiastic spitters of
Peking have not yet understood the connection between tuberculo-
sis and their earthy habit.

A Chinese home may have an earthen floor, but it will usually be
spotless. Again, because of necessity, nothing that can be reused is
wasted, and Chinese garbage provides the leanest pickings of any
on earth. One of the hardest things for each new batch of Chinese
students studying in the West to accept is our conspicuous waste.
To them it seems almost criminal what we throw out without a
second thought, and anyone traveling through China, Vietnam or
India would be forced to agree. Western propensities in this regard
are well known in Peking. There is a special team of garbage
women who service the diplomatic apartments. Their sole task is to
retrieve anything that might possibly be recycled.

In illustrating Chinese contradictions, however, excrement and
garbage go only so far. They are among those many things which
Chinese people take for granted. However, I did notice that no one
passed up the chance to use decent indoor, flushable plumbing
when it was available.

It is another sort of contradiction altogether to talk about speedy
modernization in a land where so many people are still required to
be beasts of burden, but without aspirations there are never advances. This is the way of the world, and equivalent contradictions
are known in all countries. Was it not equally absurd for the United
States to think about putting a man on the moon when the ghettoes
of New York lay festering and poverty continued to afflict Ap-
palachia? What is fascinating about China is the way people manage
to endure conditions while trying to rise above them. History and
circumstance have imposed a remarkable degree of stoicism on the
Chinese. Stoicism is a response to uncontrollable events, and despite all the Communist propaganda about the people being their
own masters, the tenacity of Chinese stoicism is a blunt reminder
that the Chinese are not yet masters of their destiny and do not
expect to be for some time.

The poem "Tolerance" posted at Xidan shows that some people
rebel against this traditional trait and ascribe to it many of the
miseries the Chinese have allowed themselves to endure. For an
average citizen, though, who does not consider persecution and

prison a kind of salvation and who works patiently for a better life, stoicism seems the best response. Bad times and evil rulers will pass; lie low and try to survive; when the good times come, enjoy them to the fullest, for they too will pass. This philosophy is the bane of groups as diverse as the democracy activists and the Communist Party, which are themselves the products of contradictions, and which are trying, in their various ways, to break the fatalism underlying this cycle.

It is supposed to be inappropriate and nonsensical to imagine that Western philosophical concepts of government can be grafted onto the Chinese experience. This, I have been told, is the conceit of the egotistical West. Against such strictures, the singular fact that the philosophy of a German—Karl Marx—took root in Russia and holds sway today in China sits rather uncomfortably. So does the fact that so many Western youths found inspiration in the perceived struggle of the Cultural Revolution. Of course, Chinese Communism is a distinctive Chinese fabric into which have been woven some of Mao's homespun homilies and traditional Confucian values.

The Western, romantic conception of what the Cultural Revolution was all about went through a similar transformation. You will never find the Communist Party making the mistake of dismissing the influence of Western thought on Chinese minds. Wherever possible, Western ideas are either co-opted or censored by the Party before they are made available to the masses. Older Party members whose minds hadn't become totally ossified may well have thought they were hearing echoes of their own youth in the shouts for democracy at Xidan. They too shouted such things during the May 4 Movement, which started in 1919 and led, among other things, to the founding of the Chinese Communist Party. They too were once part of a "tiny minority" struggling for major changes in a predominantly peasant society in which most citizens stoically accepted fate and tried to lie low until troubled times passed.

The principal difference between that time and the present is that the Communist Party is a strong ruler with an effective grip on the livelihood of the population. To many Chinese and most foreigners from the West, that grip seems too often oppressive, but there are contradictions within the Party itself which could ameliorate some of the burden of the masses. These are contradictions that have emerged in every line struggle the Party has had because the theories of ideologues usually get distorted by the nature—both good and evil—of the human condition. A sterling example is the Communist Party attack on religion.

As Mao's Eighth Route Army crisscrossed the north in the thirties and forties, it confiscated the land of the most rapacious landlords and distributed it among the peasants. "It is not your old gods who gave you this land," soldier-propagandists would lecture the peasants, "but Chairman Mao and the Eighth Route Army." Understandably, this had a powerful effect. Efforts at far-reaching land reform had always been stymied in China, and now it was a fact.

The Chinese always took a very pragmatic attitude toward their deities, which can still be easily observed in Taiwan. If a god does a good job, delivers on prayers and is associated with happy times, it will be honored and worshiped. Come a disaster or some other tragedy for which all invocations and supplications for divine intervention have been uttered in vain, that same god would be cast out without remorse. Such were the terms of the ancient Mandate of Heaven by which emperors ruled and dynasties fell. Legitimacy in government was based on the ability to obtain power and hold on to it. This couldn't be done if the majority of citizens were in open revolt. It was a very practical theory, which did not exclude adherence to whatever laws prevailed or whatever spiritual concerns seemed important.

Making inroads against "feudal" Daoist deities was easy enough on one level for the Communists because their system of organizations and rewards was seen and experienced to be better than what had existed. A secular Mandate of Heaven descended on the Party. More transcendent religions, like Buddhism and Christianity, as well as the lingering influence of nationalistic Confucianism, proved more troublesome for the Party to deal with.

In certain intriguing areas, the Communists were heirs to the Christian-missionary social-action tradition. The history of missionary influence in China is ambivalent: some clerics were certainly there as adjuncts to imperialism; many others, though, got caught up in reform for reform's sake. Emancipation of the mind from "feudal fetters," higher education, a better deal for the peasants, improving the lot of women—missionaries were fighting for all these things before the Communists emerged as a major force. Even when they were required to leave China after 1949, some

Western missionaries felt the Communists were simply taking over where they had been forced to leave off.

The sympathetic missionaries were impressed by the ethical roots of Chinese Communism, and admired Maoism for its antimaterialism, its egalitarianism and its concentration on raising the people's consciousness. In fact, Communism has a staunchly materialist base, which is today being reasserted, and China remains a stubbornly class-institutionalized country. Also, it was soon apparent that consciousness raising too often meant simply subscribing to one ideology. Nevertheless, the radical Maoist line, which was pushed to the forefront with such a vengeance during the Cultural Revolution, seemed a kind of vindication to the old missionaries, while the ideological wrangles were not very different from the denominational and theological disputes that were a familiar part of their own lives.

There is something to be garnered from this strange conjunction of Chinese Communism and old missionary endeavor. Although the Communists proved to be ruthless in supressing all religious manifestations except token expressions, which were tolerated in order to show that there was "freedom of religion" as stipulated in the Constitution (although even this was abandoned during the Cultural Revolution), they engendered a degree of spirituality in the Chinese that is quite remarkable.

So much of the promise of Communism in China has had to be accepted on faith. As a recipe for salvation, it is drummed into children's ears almost from the moment they start talking. The absurd proportions this practice assumed during the Cultural Revolution indicated not a deviation, but rather an extension of cultism not dissimilar to that which has flourished in the bosom of more orthodox Christian denominations in the West. Confessing one's sins and failures to a picture of Chairman Mao while holding the *Quotations from Chairman Mao Tsetung* next to the heart, as millions did for a time in the late sixties, may make Chinese shake their heads in self-amazement today, but it was an indication of the extent to which faith can still be aroused in the Chinese. Having been told that such actions would improve their lot, Chinese responded with precisely the same amount of fervor as many Middle Americans do to old-time Bible Belt revivals. The new line which prevails in the Party today casts scorn on such things, but it too has its precisely defined areas which must be accepted on faith: from the presiding role of the Communist Party to the latest explication of the dictatorship of the proletariat. Many Chinese, if they don't accept such things on faith, nevertheless prefer to leave such matters unchallenged. In this they are really no different from the majority of Europeans and North Americans who, up to recent times, more or less accepted the moral value system enunciated by various churches.

Part of the enduring potency of the Communist Party, however, which is distinct but not separate from its sheer dictatorship, is that it does have this ethical base even if its various members don't always live up to it. The Communists did end opium and other drug trafficking, they did define precisely the nature of exploitation involved in everything from prostitution to graft and they do preach the importance of "serving the people" and self-abnegation. These things are touted in precisely the same way as the Christian Church promotes clean living, humility and brotherly love, and while hypocrisies abound, the ideal still has the power to appeal. A great deal of the cynicism and criticism about the Party and its record are put forward with the aim not of destroying the institution but of reforming and changing it.

Many outsiders, even those who have lived in China, shake their heads at the improbability of anything approaching genuine democracy being established there. It's the numbers that seem so staggering: how can you have open, fully participatory democracy with a billion people? This seems as much of a barrier as the heritage of autocracy from the feudal past and the totalitarian instincts of the Communist Party. Curiously, these are contradictions more apparent on the outside than on the inside. To begin with, the Communists have shown such a genius for organization, right down to the neighborhood level, that democratic management is now probably as feasible as totalitarian control. China is not so much a country of a billion people as a collection of thousands of constituent organizations. Indeed, a form of quasi-democracy already exists on some levels and is being given cautious encouragement. It is what the Party likes to call "socialist democracy."

If one looks closely at China today, it can be seen that every Unit and larger organization also has its constituent leaders who have to be chosen in some way or other. Moreover, they preside over regular political meetings which are now as familiar to the Chinese as the sun and the moon. There is procedure and form and a measure of accountability. Even during the chaos of the Cultural Revolution, when so many of the controlling Party and non-Party structures—from the most basic working Unit right up to the central government ministries—became the focal point for factional struggle and intrigue, their essential significance never waned. Indeed, many Chinese learned the hard way about the importance of gaining ascendancy in various organizations in order to protect themselves. Such a system, while ripe for totalitarian manipulation, is also ripe for democracy. When the government of Hua Guofeng and Deng Xiaoping announced that elections would take place, with more candidates than offices, for some of the positions on lower levels, like factory and brigade leaders, it was not a difficult feat to pull off. Just about everything from anarchy to fascism has been tried in China except democracy. Essentially, everything else has failed to a lesser or greater extent and left a residue of bitterness and disappointment. Democracy is an idea whose time has come, and that is why the government is making such an effort to push its own version of "socialist democracy."

Even in a one-party state, there is no lack of wildly different approaches to government and problem solving. The differences between radical Maoists and the current pragmatists are far greater than anything that separated Barry Goldwater and Lyndon Johnson, or Richard Nixon and Hubert Humphrey. What is lacking under Chinese Communism is a safe and legitimate way to voice real opposition. The greater degree of criticism permitted today may lead to something tangible in this direction, but for the moment it is mostly window dressing. The authorities continue to define the permissible parameters of debate, and while these are considerably wider than what their predecessors allowed, there are still severe restrictions. Whenever reigning authorities are the sole judges of what is acceptable criticism, then that criticism can never be more than a mere placebo.

The symptoms remain. After thirty years of Communism, the Chinese people are still restive. The change of government and improved conditions have assuaged and diverted some of this restiveness, but it is only a temporary respite. If the new policies fail to deliver on the broad expectations of the workers and peasants, then the Chinese Government is headed for real trouble. Stoicism and restiveness are contradictions, and yet they too exist together in China. The way one may take precedence over the other depends on prevailing conditions. Outsiders have often been mystified at the wild, seemingly sudden shifts in China's direction. Most of this surprise has arisen from our inability to examine closely the circumstances, atmosphere and events leading up to the shift. Also, the Chinese are stuck with a system that has so far effectively prohibited gradualism in politics, so that when change comes there is a backlog of grievances to be settled, and a host of often conflicting aspirations to be achieved. As the world has seen, the resulting eruptions are loud.

The purging of the Gang of Four and the dismantling of radical Maoism were managed as easily as they were because that line had become thoroughly discredited. Despite its superiority in arms, men and foreign allies, the old Guomindang regime collapsed because it too had become thoroughly discredited. Chairman Mao's personal political ambitions notwithstanding, he had for most of his life a genius for anticipating the people's discontent, and during the Cultural Revolution he was able to turn it on his enemies. All of these events should be seen in context. In the case of the Guomindang, people had had their fill of corruption, poverty, ineptitude and national humiliation. With the Cultural Revolution, people were fed up with bureaucratic autocracy, poverty and the arrogant new class of Communist officials. As for the Gang of Four, people had again had their fill of increasingly senseless political campaigns, ruthless police methods, abysmal productivity and poverty.

In looking for the seeds for a similar shift in the future, one doesn't have to search very deeply. Poverty endures as always. So do bureaucratic arrogance and corruption. The egalitarian instincts of Chinese people, firmly rooted in a history that has seen peasants turned into emperors and nobles returned to the peasantry, will be a troublesome force to reckon with as the modernization program accentuates the gulf between the privileged and the masses, between the rural peasantry and the urban elite. If the Chinese people have the facility, born of necessity, to absorb contradictions, it is only a predominant trait, not a consistent one.

Like Mao, Vice-Premier Deng Xiaoping has a good feel for the masses. All of the current shifts in Communist ideology and policy bear his distinctive hallmark, and as a survivor of so many cataclysmic events in modern Chinese history, he has a lively overview of Chinese frustrations. He has sought to take the sting out of class struggle, to inject material incentives into the economy, to give peasants a greater say in their day-to-day work and to dissipate the Party's penchant for purges and counterpurges. As a victim of lawlessness and arbitrary actions, he is trying to establish a degree of justice that will give China "stability and unity" as well as leaving the Communist Party—and his line—in control.

In Chinese politics, Deng is an amazing figure and has a wide following because he has tried to deliver on some of the promises of Communism. But his miracles can go only so far. Moreover, he is a product of the same system he has tried to buck for so long. Already, his plans for bringing in capital investment from abroad and building up the productive base at home have run into serious setbacks. Inherited problems like housing and unemployment are getting worse. The modest increase in salaries of most of China's crucially important factory work force has not come close to meeting expectations. Financial incentives have been more disruptive than helpful. Mass political campaigns and other ideological circus tricks diverting the people's attention from their plight won't work anymore, and there is a certain desperation in the Party's plea for patience, stability and faith. It is in this context that all the theorizing on democracy has become so compelling. By involving the Chinese people in the nation's problems in a way that goes well beyond even the popular and successful mass reconstruction campaign of the early fifties, the Party can dissipate some of the resentment that would otherwise logically be focused on itself. Whether the Communist Party of China is capable of successfully abdicating some of its comprehensive control over people while still maintaining its preeminent role will be one of the major questions of the eighties.

The Party's attitude toward the Chinese population today is purely schizophrenic. The people are constantly buffeted by positive and negative initiatives. One day, "speaking out boldly" and "mind emancipation" are being pushed; the next day, Party solidarity and the glories of the dictatorship of the proletariat are all-important. Without a regularly revised and popularly based mandate, the Party is uncertain about the mood and thinking of the people. The Xidan poster wall and its equivalents in most of China's major cities were one useful bellwether, as well as being a safety valve for pent-up frustrations. But the leadership was ambivalent about such things right from the beginning. Vice-Premier Deng described Xidan as "a good thing" at the same time as he warned that some of the posters there were "against the interests of stability and unity." The ambivalence was no doubt a reflection of the various uses made by the authorities of the democracy movement, from cementing American goodwill for the normalization process to smoking out the bravest opponents of the status quo. Such ambivalence was both cynical and naive.

There are undoubtedly high Party strategists who, like Mao in the Hundred Flowers Campaign, live under the illusion that all criticism will be "correct," that people will somehow know how to restrain their logic. Every hint of liberalization in any Communist country, however, has ultimately shown that no such "restraint" can exist. With the exception of Hungary and Czechoslovakia, every Communist party that encouraged such changes lost its nerve and took refuge in autocracy. In Hungary and Czechoslovakia, of course, the Soviet Union had to impose the retrenchment, since the local parties showed themselves unwilling or unable to do so. At the moment, no one knows if there is a compromise possible between democracy and Communism because no Communist government has ever had the courage to find out. China is the most fascinating country to speculate about in this regard because Soviet troops are unlikely to march in to suppress whatever is going on.

On another level entirely, the people's attitude toward the Communist Party also approaches schizophrenia. For one thing, the Party is having a bad time trying to restore faith in its ultimate ability to bring salvation to the Chinese people. This is something quite apart from day-to-day reality and is part of the spiritual dimension of the Party's relationship with the people. In the Cultural Revolution, people abandoned reason and tried pure faith in Maoism to improve their lot. It didn't work; in fact, their standard of living was lowered. Ever practical, many Chinese started searching around for an alternative spiritual dimension.

Some have examined the relative success of Western democracies and placed their faith there. Others have discovered the great twentieth-century religion of science and can rouse themselve to great fervor when discussing how the scientific approach and modern technology will cure all the nation's ills. Most intriguing of all, there is something that can only be described as a religious revival occurring in China, and this is a direct affront to Communism. It may be, as Marx said, that religion is "the opiate of the masses," but after all the downers dispensed by the Communists for so long, some of the masses feel a need for their own choice of an upper.

It is impossible to say how widespread this is, and I must admit to a disposition that searched out things metaphysical. Despite this disposition, I had come to China with the firm conviction that religion had been obliterated. What I found, first of all, was a remarkable curiosity on this subject. Even among those Chinese who reject religion out of hand as sheer nonsense, there is a keen desire to try to understand how people accustomed to "advanced materialism" and "scientific reality" could still be intrigued by spiritual matters.

I never brought up the question of religion with our friends. My own faith, such as it is, is not built on a sturdy foundation, and when I was asked to explain certain Christian denominational beliefs I felt distinctly uneasy. Try explaining how wine turns into blood to someone who has never heard the theory of transubstantiation before; or the idea that God is divided into three equal parts and how Jesus, one of those parts, sits "on the right hand" of God the Father, another of those parts, and you get some quick insight into why missionaries offered bowls of rice along with their message, just to ensure the conversion. Such antics aside, I discovered that Chinese people who had been through the Cultural Revolution could relate religious mysticism to their own experience. After the Jonestown mass suicide in Guyana, the questioning got hot, and I offered no significant explanations apart from noting the phenomenon of crazy California cults. One friend described the tragedy as "a Christian cultural revolution."

There are growing signs of genuine religious faith that transcends mere curiosity. The rise of religion has been openly acknowledged in Party newspapers, and it is blamed on the Gang of Four, who "encouraged superstition and mystified Mao Tsetung Thought." In places where established religion had been strong before the Communists took over, like Fujien and Guangdong provinces, or the national minority areas like Tibet and Sinjiang, religion was only driven underground, and it is resurfacing stronger and more potent than it has been in years. Daoism, Buddhism, Islam and Christianity are all represented in this religious resurgence. Daoism, the faith of the peasants, seemed to the Communists to be the easiest of the religions to co-opt because it is such an adjustable, accommodating faith. It can incorporate Christ as easily as the Green Dragon. Whatever works is good and is part of the correct order of things. Whatever doesn't work is bad.

What the Party neglected to realize is that this co-opting business works both ways. It may have come as something of a rude shock to Mao (if he ever found out) that some peasants tried to appease his photographed image with incense and offerings of fruit and flowers. Tibet is perhaps a special place where religion is still intertwined with race and nationalism, but in places as far afield as Canton and Sian, Shanghai and Chengdu, Nanning and Tianjin, people want answers to questions on religion. If the Communist Party is appalled at this, and its official pronouncements attacking religion show it to be, then it has no one and nothing to blame but itself. It would take a millennium for missionaries to get so many people into the frame of mind the Chinese are in today.

The Party is not without alternative resources in making inroads into Chinese sensitivities and shoring up its position. This is part of the ambivalent attitude the Chinese have toward Communism, which, on the one hand is as familiar to them as Catholicism is to Italians, and on the other is so distinctively Chinese that it is closely tied to the crucial question of nationalism. Familiarity does indeed breed contempt, and this familiarity has seriously eroded the Party's spiritual appeal to the Chinese. Its nationalist stance, however, is as pure as it has always been, and on this fact alone is hinged much of the Party's legitimacy to the Chinese.

The idea of China, the ancient Motherland for which so much has been endured for so long, transcends most things and accounts for much of the forbearance with which the Communist Party has been received. Whatever its sins, it was the force that united China and made it a nation to be reckoned with after a long period of foreign domination. This is not abstraction, but a living and powerful reality.

Lao Fei, a friend in Peking who was ten years old in 1949, has little positive to say in behalf of either the Party or Chairman Mao. Trained as an agronomist in the fifties, he was making real contributions to Chinese agriculture when the Cultural Revolution turned everything upside down. Like Galileo three centuries before, he lived to hear himself deny observable scientific truths to satisfy the orthodoxy of the day. He did it to protect his family and himself, and would do it again if necessary. If he's not a hero, he's not a coward either. During the early seventies, he took it upon himself to try to teach a small group of interested younger people some of the things he knew to be true. Had he been caught, he could have got into serious trouble.

Lao Fei is also someone who is fascinated with Western manners, habits and traditions. He professes to see in the Western respect for individual initiative the main reason for our material advantages. He longs for an increasingly open and freer Chinese society, and for more contact with foreigners. But you don't have to scratch Lao Fei very far before you find a one-hundred-percent, bona fide Chinese.

"Our family lived in the Drum Tower district," he said one day, talking of his youth in Peking. "Although we were of the educated class, my father had died young and we were quite poor. My mother welcomed the arrival of the Communists, and so did most other people. Even if we didn't understand all the politics, we knew that they were Chinese and wanted to make China strong. The Guomindang had lost all the respect of the Chinese people in this regard. I have a very vivid memory of something that happened in my neighborhood when I was eight or nine. This was before Liberation. Behind the Drum Tower is the smaller but higher Bell Tower, and there is a good view of the city from the top. One day, some Americans came to the Bell Tower and climbed all the way up. They were part of some official delegation, I think. In any event, when they got to the top a bunch of us kids were down below waiting to catch sight of them again. Suddenly, the Americans started throwing down coins, and all the children ran around crazily to get them. I have never forgotten that. It made a very profound impression on me."

It's impressions like this that work in the Party's favor, and since no other force in the country is allowed to wrap itself in such nationalistic garb, it's little wonder that the Party has become the principal beneficiary of Chinese patriotism, the strongest binding force in the country. It is also the source of some less-than-attractive traits in the Chinese, which the Party has never hesitated to reinforce.

All the interest in the West and the "outside world" one encounters has to be placed against the general lack of interest in anything outside of the Chinese experience which many other Chinese feel. It is amazing to go through a Chinese museum and not see any evidence that other civilizations existed, except perhaps for a few comparative references on how advanced the Chinese were in various crafts and professions as compared with other cultures. The civilizations of Egypt, of Greece, of Rome; the Renaissance and the Reformation; the Industrial Revolution in Britain and the technological revolution in the United States—these things can be learned only by those with special access to restricted book stacks in libraries, and even then one has to be careful with what is done with such knowledge. It is not the ignorance of the outside world of so many ordinary Chinese that is deplorable; it is the control and manipulation of that ignorance. I doubt very much if most Westerners know that much about Chinese history and culture, or are much concerned about their ignorance. But there is access to information should anyone ever want it, access that is unavailable to most Chinese.

Other unattractive traits are part and parcel of Chinese distinctiveness. The cohesion of society is not nearly as complete as it appears on the outside, but in a crunch many Chinese invoke the will of the majority to solve tricky problems, which means that personal responsibility is minimized. Much is made of "Chinese conformity." It is encouraged by the Party and seems monolithic from the outside. It is also a convenient veil hiding controversy and remarkable diversity, and when it suits their purposes, officials and ordinary people will flee individual culpability for the safe territory of "the masses" or "the Chinese people" or some other sacrosanct manifestation of conformity. And except for the most self-righteous or brainwashed, they know exactly what they are doing.

For example, in 1977 the Chinese Government was going all out to encourage its scientists "to scale the heights" in research. To this end the government sponsored a national science conference. The foreign press corps was invited to meet some of the leading scientists in the country at a special press conference. There I learned that China was going to acquire a proton accelerator, a highly sophisticated piece of equipment for use in rarefied fields of nuclear research. Even for a major North American university it is very expensive equipment, costing tens of millions of dollars. During the Cultural Revolution, one of the few areas left free of political struggle was nuclear science and related defense research. Although the explosion of China's first nuclear device and the launching of its first satellite were attributed to the power of Mao Tsetung Thought, they were nothing of the sort. Uninterrupted research and massive financial support put China into the nuclear and space age, and officials knew this even if politics required them to keep quiet on the subject.

One journalist quizzed a nuclear physicist from the Academy of Science on the spending of so much money in such a specialized field of nuclear research when there was so much to be done on more basic levels. There were appropriate answers to the effect that "we cannot afford to be left behind" and "Chinese science must be allowed to aspire." The problem was then put from a different angle. What responsibility did Chinese scientists and technologists feel toward the vast majority of Chinese for whom their scientific efforts will mean little and which could produce chronic dislocation and loss of livelihood? What coordination was there between scientific and social goals?

"That's not a problem," said the physicist. "Our colleagues at the Academy of Social Sciences will certainly be attending to this." Pressed further with specific instances in which technological advances had harmed people's livelihood, in both other Third World countries and the affluent West, the scientist decided to cut the subject dead: "The Chinese people will resolve this contradiction." That was that.

Many of the mindless stupidities and frustrations with which the bureaucracy afflicts ordinary Chinese are products of conservatism, which the Revolution has done nothing to displace. Attached to this are an often awesome subservience to established practice and an understandable reluctance to take a stand. Because foreigners are generally treated extremely courteously in China, they don't get to see a lot of the less attractive side of the Chinese. However, if you push hard enough at officials and people who would rather not have anything to do with you, it is possible to stir the sleeping tigers all about. At various times in China, I encountered arrogance (army officers in Tibet), rudeness (an elevator operator in Shanghai), stupidity (most of the staff of a hotel in Chongqing), deceit (officials lying about the reasons for a delayed flight), unscrupulousness (innumerable police officers), cruelty (a grandmother beating the living daylights out of her tiny charge on the streets of Canton), obsequiousness (the senior official at Peking's International Club), sycophancy (leading personnel of the steel factory in Wuhan when in the presence of Peking officials), favoritism and nepotism (housing conditions for some of my better-connected acquaintances), corruption ("gift" giving in Canton between foreign businessmen and trade-fair officials: digital watches and tape cassettes are a matter of course, with a few Mercedes-Benzes thrown in on a special "sharing" arrangement) and male chauvinism (everywhere).

Such sins, of course, are not unique, but they are important to recognize in coming to terms with the Chinese because they establish their ordinariness and membership in the human race. Too many outsiders look upon the Chinese as a breed apart and have even persuaded some Chinese to do the same. In seeing their flaws clearly, one can accept their distinctiveness and appreciate their unique contributions to the world in a spirit of equality and genuine affection. The myth of the inscrutable Chinese who is brighter and more devious than we becomes as unacceptable as the myth of the docile automaton.

No account of the Chinese is valid without an attempt to explain their genius for survival against fearsome odds and their facility at meeting the vicissitudes of life with humor, a healthy understanding of reality and unbounded grace. In China, life often cuts to the quick. Issues are very basic, and necessity narrows choices to a degree we would probably consider intolerable. And yet with what spirit and hope do the Chinese still confront life! The Cultural Revolution and its vicious aftermath wounded them badly—psychologically, physically, morally and politically. Some of the wounds will take generations to heal; and there is no absolute assurance they won't have to go through something like it again. It was a world George Orwell warned of in *Animal Farm* and *1984*, and yet the Chinese people survived. Some of them even survived gloriously. In this politically corrosive and increasingly fanatical world, no one could have felt more privileged than I to discover this singular fact.

Epilogue

Voices in
the Multitude

By the end of September 1979, Elizabeth and I had packed up all
our belongings and were preparing to leave China. I had been
given the opportunity to stay on longer, but had decided against it.
My decision had had to be made in the prolonged wake of the first
crackdown. Having been welcomed so enthusiastically and openly
into the wider life of China and the Chinese, I found it intolerable
that the barriers should now come crashing down. It was not possible to go back to the old ways. Concepts of the masses had been
dissolved into real friendships with real people, unaided by government and unhampered by cultural and historical differences. Suddenly, foreigners who had tried to reach out beyond the ghetto
were being told, in effect, that the old order was to prevail and the
new directions were *buxing.* Sadness and anger came often to me
then, and I tried to get around these moods by traveling as much
as possible and remembering what I knew to be true. Within a few
months, freshly posted diplomats and journalists moved to Peking,
and the number of foreign witnesses to the phenomenon of Xidan,
and all it represented, diminished. Before long I heard the new
people talking about the docility of the Chinese and the practical
impossibility of bringing democracy to a billion people. Such talk
was also intolerable.

By September, though, I began to wonder if our departure was not a mistake. The political atmosphere was heating up. The Xidan Democracy Wall started to become lively again. Even the *Peking Daily,* the redneck mouthpiece of the municipal authorities, printed provocative commentators' essays on such subjects as "In a true socialist country, there can be no prisoners of conscience." It seemed as if the government were coming to its senses and had realized that the activists were not a threat but lively indicators of the interest young Chinese took in the direction of their country; that contacts between Chinese and foreigners might cause some problems but were a necessary factor in dismantling paranoia and institutionalized repression; that a freer exchange of ideas and theories could lead to precisely the atmosphere of creativity and innovation the authorities professed to want. The straws in the wind gave reason for optimism.

Literally hours before we left, a fascinating confrontation occurred at the Peking Art Gallery. Young artists had set up an unofficial exhibition along the outer railings of the gallery. The Public Security Bureau, in typical style, deemed this a politically insupportable act and sought to impound the paintings, some of which depicted the sorrow of China during the Cultural Revolution with eloquence and style. In days past, that would have been the end of the business. Instead, this time, the gallery officials found some residue of courage and defended the artists, going so far as to take the paintings into the building and protect them.

By the time I got wind of the story, a curious encounter was taking place at the gallery. Police officials were running about like chickens with their heads off trying to wage a two-pronged battle: first with the gallery officials to get possession of the offending paintings, and secondly with the artists themselves, who were outside by the gates giving a play-by-play commentary to foreign journalists and any interested Chinese on the events that had so far ensued. The PSB was having no luck in seizing the paintings, but to frustrate the artists' testimony it had unleashed its vociferous gang of young thugs who do "auxiliary" work for the PSB from time to time. (I knew the gang well from previous encounters at the Xidan Wall and during the demonstrations by the poor peasant petitioners.) As the artists were calmly explaining the situation at the gallery, the thugs would push and shove at those who were trying to listen, and shout things like *"Duo xiao qian? Duo xiao qian?"* ("How much money? How much money?"). The police loved to spread rumors that Chinese who spoke to foreigners did it for cash and thereby sold out their country.

Encouraged by the support of the gallery, the artists went as a delegation to both the Ministry of Culture and the Chief Procurator's Office and, again surprisingly, won their support. In the end, a compromise was reached and the paintings were shown in the gallery proper. The compromise was an important achievement and very encouraging. The PSB is accustomed to ride roughshod not only over the people, but also over government institutions, which have a tradition of shying away from a confrontation of this sort. Here was proof that independent action and decisions were being taken on several levels, and this was something new.

Elizabeth and I walked for the last time along the Xidan Democracy Wall. It was a bright, sunny day, and we ran across two foreign friends who were also making the rounds of new posters. The several thousand Chinese who were there were in good spirits, and our mood was also happy, although heavy with nostalgia. This was not a pretty part of Peking, but I loved every square inch and had seen it in four seasons. It was a harbinger of hope for all that time, despite whatever setbacks had to be endured. A place of dreams and noble aspirations, the Xidan Democracy Wall drew from its very plainness and ordinariness a special mystique. I walked past the place where I had given the report on Deng Xiaoping's interview and where I had placed my own *dazibao* about the stupid ring. A vain conceit passed quickly through my mind: I had, however peripherally, passed through here before; I had been caught up with Chinese people and Chinese things. It was a good feeling.

Off in the distance, I spotted something strange on the southwest corner of the Xidan and Chang An intersection. There seemed to be some tables set up right on the sidewalk, with people sitting beside them. This was a new sight in my old neck of the woods. On closer inspection, it turned out to be an outdoor restaurant—the first I had seen in Peking. Responding to the problems of unemployed people, the municipal authorities had agreed to allow neighborhood committees to come up with their own solutions. A group of unemployed youths in the area had organized, with the help of a loan from the local committee, a sidewalk café. It was a cooperative venture in which members could keep a share of their profits, and I could scarcely credit what I was soon sitting down to enjoy.

A street that had seemed, like so many streets in Peking, dead to anything but routine coming and going was now alive. Groups of Chinese stopped to quaff an ale or two, and the service by the co-op members was energetic and efficient to a degree I had never previously experienced in China. They were actually hustling to bring the drinks and snacks to the tables. It had just opened, and perhaps the ebullient mood wouldn't last, but on our final day in China it was quite a discovery. In the distance I could see the poster wall, and the physical conjunction of these two spots made me wonder how anyone could doubt the genius, industry and courage of the Chinese if they are given even half a chance—if they give *themselves* half a chance.

I was under no illusions about the glories of capitalism, and now I had a better understanding of some of the inequalities of the system I would be returning to. Rampant individualism was tearing many Western nations apart, and the disadvantaged suffered accordingly. But the Chinese had a perspective from the other side: they knew the inequalities that arose from too tightly enforced cohesion and from central socialist planning, which prohibited individual initiative and endeavor. A fantasy of my childhood, of digging a hole through the center of the earth and ending up in China, where everything would be upside down, came back once again. Elizabeth and I were struck with the same thought. We did not want to leave this place and these people. But go we had to, and go we did, although it was through a haze of tears. My proudest moment came at the airport. Some of my closest Chinese friends somehow managed to sneak out to say good-bye. There were more Chinese than foreigners, and it was traumatic in the extreme.

Even the Speculator turned up. He is a friend whose entrepreneurial skills rather frightened me from time to time, and who never ceased to amaze me with his ability to appear in the most untoward places. I nicknamed him the Speculator because he was always up to something, always had some deal going on somewhere. At the same time he was busy pursuing a medical education, he also seemed to be running a vast lending library of Western books and magazines. He had chosen me personally to assist in the great task of improving his English.

On those occasions when I thought I was too busy for yet another weird lesson on English grammar in the darker reaches of the

Forbidden City or some grove of trees in the Temple of Heaven Park, he would be sure to remind me of the selfless way my compatriot Dr. Norman Bethune had served the Chinese people during the revolutionary wars. "All the Chinese people revere the memory of Comrade Bethune," he would say to me when I tried to beg off from a particular meeting. "Do you understand my meaning?" I understood only too well, for I was the fool who had taught the Speculator the meaning of the word "revere."

In the midst of the farewell festivities at the Peking airport, I excused myself to go to the men's room for a moment. As I stood before a large porcelain urinal, I heard a distinct *"Ssst"* in my left ear. Startled, I turned around, and there was the Speculator, smiling as he stood in front of the neighboring urinal.

"I've come to say good-bye to you, my true friend Fu Ruizhe."

I was delighted to see him, and the setting in the men's room seemed entirely appropriate. The week before, I had told him the time of my departure, but I hadn't expected to see him or any of the other Chinese, because the airport was a considerable distance from the center of Peking.

"Come and join us in the restaurant," I said. "There are other friends. Come and have some tea."

The Speculator looked around the room to reassure himself no one else was about. "You have no other Chinese friends but me. All those other Chinese you are with are from the police. I am your only friend."

With that, he pulled a package out of his canvas satchel and handed it to me. "I will not forget you," he said. His eyes were welling up a little, which would have got me going too if he hadn't started to speak again. "You must not forget me. We are friends. Good-bye."

And off he went. I put the package in my coat pocket and remembered it only an hour later, when we were already flying on our way to Canton, en route to Hong Kong and home. He had given me a notebook with a red plastic cover. Inside, on the flyleaf, was a drawing on silk of a mythical Chinese maiden contemplating a butterfly, and written on the first page was this:

Good friend: True friendship lasts forever! I wish you happiness! I wish Mai Kailan [Elizabeth] happiness! You are a true friend from the land of Comrade Bethune! Best regards, Your friend.

That was the Speculator for you. Bethune right to the bitter end. How I miss him.

Before the end of 1979, the Chinese authorities tried Wei Jingshen on charges of counterrevolution and treason. He was sentenced to fifteen years' imprisonment. Lesser charges sent Fu Yuehua, the leader of the poor peasant petitioners, to prison for three years. The Xidan Democracy Wall was officially declared an outrage to the Chinese people. Those who placed posters there, said the *People's Daily,* argued for counterrevolution under the guise of "ultrademocracy." The Wall was damaging the stability and unity of China and made "the Chinese people lose face."

On our last day in China, I had blithely pondered the promise of China and the potential of the Chinese Communist Party. Both seemed worthy of hope. We left China knowing that whatever setbacks might occur, there were many Chinese people determined to make China a better place, a more democratic place, a more extraordinary place. They were seeking Chinese solutions for Chinese problems, although they did not disdain to look beyond the borders of the Middle Kingdom for possible answers.

The sentencing of Wei and Fu was sheer institutional vindictiveness. Neither of them had advocated violence, and both of them had made considerable sacrifices for ideals they thought were patriotic. The state never debated the issues they brought forward. It responded in the classical way: repression. Both trials made a mockery of China's reputed new rule of law.

Even before he was formally found guilty of anything, Wei was being referred to in the official press as "a counterrevolutionary." A few weeks later, Vice-Premier Deng Xiaoping defended the fifteen-year sentence handed out to Wei. Speaking to a delegation from the *Encyclopaedia Britannica,* Deng reportedly said, "We needed to make an example of him."

Fu Yuehua's ordeal had to be twice postponed because even in a show trial, the authorities couldn't make the charges against her sound realistic. Finally, abandoning all pretense at fairness and justice, they mounted a mock trial, and the sentence that had been awaiting her all along was pronounced.

The fate of Ren Wanding, the head of the Chinese Human Rights Alliance, is still unknown. He has simply disappeared. Throughout China during this period, other activists were sentenced to long prison terms along with common thieves, murderers and rapists, or like Ren were removed without benefit of trial.

It hardly needs to be said, except that it should be, that Wei and Fu and all the others did not make the Chinese people "lose face." They became the conscience of China. Countering tradition and one of the most all-enshrouding regimes the world has known, they spoke their minds. If they spoke for no one, they would not have presented a threat of any sort. Fifteen years, however, speaks eloquently about what the Chinese Communist Party fears most—the judgment of the people.

Things could have been worse. A few years earlier, a death sentence would have been mandatory. Wei Jingshen won the real victory. He forced a seemingly benign new regime to show its true colors. The only "face" that was lost in the tragic encounter was that belonging to all the Party officials who hope the sentencing will be an end to the business. In China, there is no wilderness in which prophets can find themselves and come to terms with the reality around them. There is only the multitude. Despite the din, there has never been a time in China's history when it was not possible to stand a bit aside and listen to some of the voices crying above that multitude. Once, one of those voices belonged to Mao Tsetung himself. Thanks in part to his own legacy, and also in spite of it, you can hear his truest and best successors today.

The closing of the Xidan Democracy Wall ended the chapter of China that I walked into, but such a diverse, complicated and surprising country cannot be concluded so neatly as a book. It would be handy to surmise that the old totalitarianism was reasserting itself after a short period of necessary adjustment, but the fact that foreigners cannot hear the ferment inside China does not mean the ferment has ceased to exist. Although Wei Jingshen and his peers are victims of rank injustice, there has been no significant indication that the Communist Party wants to go through another convulsive mass political or rectification campaign.

The policy today might best be described as one of chopping off only some of the blooms before they come to full flower. Clearly, the Party and the government are serious about trying to modernize the country, and even if their definitions of free speech and democracy remain travesties, they are lesser travesties than those which prevailed for over a decade. The spirit of Xidan is down, but not out. To dismiss Xidan is to dismiss the potential of the Chinese people to rise above their lot, and by logical extension, the potential of all people to do likewise.

Herein lies the most profound lesson we in the West can learn from the Chinese, for they present to us a mirror image of ourselves. Different conditions have given them a different history, but our shared *human* condition means that we are inextricably bound together in the common lot. It is not a case of their totalitarianism versus our democracy, for example, or our traditions of individualism versus their propensity for conformity. That kind of thinking leads nowhere. If we hold out a hope for the democratic emancipation of the Chinese people, then we must accept the totalitarian instinct lurking in all of us. We cannot dismiss that instinct because of the superiority of our institutions. If we do, we will never be able to account for our own yearnings after "strong leadership" and "a more cohesive society." Nor will we be able to account for the tyrannies of our own system, in which such things as selfishness and pornography often seem more revered and protected than the idea of the common good. The germ of totalitarianism lies within the Western soul as surely as the aspiration for freedom lies within the Chinese soul. Living among the Chinese, you do not see them cringing daily from fear of their fate or their masters: they go about life as we would do, faced with the same circumstances. It is from looking deeply into ourselves, first and foremost, that we will best be able to understand what it is like to be Chinese. All the rest, however strange or confusing, is merely context.

A friend in Peking sent me the translation of a letter to the remaining activists attached to the unofficial newspapers and magazines that were so much a hallmark of Xidan. It is addressed to "all editorial staff of the people's publications":

Dear Comrades:
   Here we are into the year 1980, but have we started off on the right foot? Are we worthy of the days which have just ended, worthy of the cause for which we are striving, worthy of those relentless warriors of the April 5 Movement? Is our conscience clear?
   To be sure, we have begun a battle. In the course of the past year, we have faced the misunderstandings of ignorance and the ordeal of malicious slander. We have suffered attacks on the front, on our flanks and from the rear. Still, taking the broad look, not only did we launch

an undertaking, but it has succeeded. Our magazines were born at Democracy Wall. In no time, they spread to the four corners of our republic. Within the short span of twelve months, our magazines and newspapers appeared all the way in the far north and to the far south, as did comrades to publish them.

However, since last October [1979] we have been experiencing severe difficulties. We look this situation in the face. Some of our comrades have been arrested and imprisoned. Some of our publications have had to cease operations while others have been seized. Moreover, we are witness to a spreading phenomenon: in Changsha, the open distribution and circulation of our magazines is forbidden; in Tianjin, in Wuhan and in Canton the same prohibition is in effect.

This is a very grave problem. A ban on the open publishing and distribution of our magazines means that we may smother to death. Enthusiasm for publishing has suffered a setback. Circulation has fallen dramatically and the impact and sphere of influence of our publications has dwindled. In addition, there are financial difficulties.

Our publications are therefore facing a most serious challenge. Why is this? Is it because of their illegality? Or is it because of "public disturbances" promoted by a "handful of persons with concealed interests"? Of course not. It is the straightforward question of a fight to the death between the new and the old, of the frenzied reprisals and repression of malicious forces against new things.

The development of any new thing must go through this process. But the new will without question triumph over the old and must take its place. Continuing success and the nature of ultimate victory will depend on the soundness of our attitude and our publishing methods. We have never imagined that the law would be sufficient to check malevolent forces! We have never thought that we would succeed by mere luck. How ought we then to proceed? In our view, the following is necessary:

First, we must put aside all illusions and prepare ourselves for combat. Our ancestors persevered through thousands of years in learning how to cross the gap between walking on all fours and walking on two legs. Over several dozen years in which hundreds and millions of our citizens were affected, we have worked arduously to achieve the rapid transformation of our country—the "sick man of Asia"—into a force to be listened to and reckoned with. If our publications are to survive, we must be prepared for an unrelenting struggle that may take two, three, five, or perhaps as many as ten years.

But moral preparation is not enough. We must know how to fight the battle. . . .

The manifesto goes on to detail what positive steps editors and writers can take. If the state issues a new law stating that all such publications should be officially registered, then register them, it says. Articles in the Chinese Constitution are cited, along with pertinent references to the few existing laws on publications, to provide the correct legal context. At all times, urges the manifesto, the country's existing and expanding legal system must be invoked. If the laws are changed or arbitrarily dismissed by malevolent forces, then that is a hypocrisy exposed and a battle won. A national magazine is suggested, but whether this suggestion is taken up or not, all activists are urged to work together in a common cause, a variation on Chairman Mao's "united front." In a manner I had seen time and again during my stay in China, the strategy of the Communist Party is invoked to taunt the Party's own totalitarian propensities:

> What we must do now is act in a united front to achieve freedom of publishing and to keep our publications alive. Guerrilla tactics by individuals acting on their own will only lead to the failure of our publications, one by one. The importance of this lesson should be uppermost. We must not wait until all our sticks are broken one by one before we seek to preserve them by holding them in a bundle. Malevolent forces will thus be required to act against all and because of this they will fall.
>
> Comrades, let us put away and have done with our anxieties and hesitations. . . . Let us firmly bind our publications to the interests and needs of the masses in order to win their lively support. The people, that unfailing wellspring, must be the anvil on which our will shall be forged. . . . No one shall smite our revolutionary cause. . . . For the dignity of the Constitution of the People's Republic of China and for civil rights, let us unite ourselves in a struggle of solidarity.

There is in all this a naiveté of almost sublime proportions. A few weeks after I received the letter, the government arbitrarily changed the Constitution and removed the so-called four great freedoms: "to speak out freely, air views fully, hold great debates and write *dazibao.*" There are those observers who considered this turn of events a monstrous calumny, a guarantee turned into a gag.

For myself, I succumbed to positive-thinking cynicism: those free-doms never really existed, except when it suited the Party's pur-poses, and removing them from the Constitution makes it a margin-ally more honest document. Perhaps the authorities will try to honor what is left. A naiveté that places such faith in "the dignity of the Constitution," however, is a hard thing to fight, and with forces working from within the government, the bureaucracy and even the Party itself, it is far too soon to dismiss the possibility of an end to totalitarianism in China.

A final straw in the wind was the news that my musical friend, Huang Anlun, has received permission to attend the University of Toronto as a "special student." I shall now be able to repay some of the kindness and love I received from him and his family in China. Communist authorities throughout the world have not been in the habit of allowing their brightest citizens the right to travel and study abroad. China is now permitting it. In this alone, there is a measure of courage and hope.

As for me, I am home in Canada and more or less happily so. It took more of an adjustment to walk back into the normality of my former life than it ever did to adapt to China. Still, I have done it, although like many foreigners who went to China and have known the Chinese, a part of me feels in permanent exile. It's an ache that just won't go away.